The International Relations of the European Union

We work with leading authors to develop the strongest
educational materials in law, bringing cutting-edge thinking
and best learning practice to a global market.

Under a range of well-known imprints, including Longman,
we craft high quality print and electronic publications which
help readers to understand and apply their content,
whether studying or at work.

To find out more about the complete range of our
publishing, please visit us on the World Wide Web at:
www.pearsoned.co.uk

The International Relations of the European Union

By Steve Marsh and Hans Mackenstein

PEARSON
Longman

Harlow, England • London • New York • Boston • San Francisco • Toronto
Sydney • Tokyo • Singapore • Hong Kong • Seoul • Taipei • New Delhi
Cape Town • Madrid • Mexico City • Amsterdam • Munich • Paris • Milan

Pearson Education Limited
Edinburgh Gate
Harlow
Essex CM20 2JE
England

and Associated Companies throughout the world

Visit us on the World Wide Web at:
www.pearsoned.co.uk

First published 2005

© Stephen Marsh and Hans Mackenstein 2005

ISBN-10: 0-582-47293-8
ISBN-13: 978-0-582-47293-8

British Library Cataloguing-in-Publication Data
A catalogue record for this book is available from the British Library

Library of Congress Cataloging-in-Publication Data
Marsh, Steve, 1967–
    The international relations of the European Union / by Steve Marsh and Hans
Mackenstein.
        p. cm.
    Includes bibliographical references and index.
    ISBN 0-582-47293-8 (alk. paper)
    1. European Union—Foreign relations. 2. National security—European Union
countries. 3. International relations. 4. International economic relations.
I. Mackenstein, Hans, 1961– II. Title.

JZ1570.M37 2005
341.3′094—dc22

                                                                2004044706

10 9 8 7 6 5 4 3
09 08 07 06

Typeset in 10/12pt Sabon by 35
Printed in Malaysia
The publisher's policy is to use paper manufactured from sustainable forests.

In memory of my father – Hans Mackenstein
To Nuria, my compass in turbulent times – Steve Marsh

Contents

Acknowledgements

This book was born of our frustration with what we felt to be a gap in the literature on the international relations of the European Union. For a number of years since, this book has also been our frustration. Deciding what to leave out was harder than writing about what we chose to include, and in the process undoubtedly contributed handsomely to the coffers of Anglo-German telecommunications companies. Frustration was incurred too as a consequence of the awkward habit of the EU and of contemporary international relations of evolving just as the ink dried on the manuscript. Eventually a line had to be drawn in early December 2003 and for this we will be forever grateful to our publishers!

Along the way we have incurred numerous personal and professional debts. We are grateful to the officials of the North Atlantic Treaty Organisation, Western European Union, European Commission and the Council of the European Union who spared us their time and indulged our questions to provide us with essential background and insights. Our thanks also go to the referees of the book, and to colleagues who have read chapters, for their guidance and constructive comments. It is also important to register our gratitude for the research funding afforded by the School of European Studies at Cardiff University and to Morten Fuglevand at Pearson, who stood by us through our ill health and/or personal loss. A special mention from us both goes to Dr Lorenzo-Dus for her painstaking proof-reading and suggestions for textual refinement.

Finally our deepest thanks must go to our respective family and friends. They have maintained our sanity, reminded us at key moments that there is more to life than academia, and sustained us in so many ways. They have also underwritten the costs of this book through enduring our moods and sacrificing precious time with us as we each retreated into our thoughts and studies. Herein Hans Mackenstein would like to express his special thanks to Peter and Steve Marsh to Nuria. Thank you, both.

Abbreviations

ACP	African, Caribbean and Pacific group of countries
APLMs	anti-personnel land mines
ARF	ASEAN Regional Forum
ASEAN	Association of South-East Asian Nations
ASEM	Asia–Europe Meeting
Benelux	Belgium, Netherlands, Luxemburg
BOP	balance of payments
BSE	bovine spongiform encephalopathy ('mad cow disease')
BTO	Brussels Treaty Organisation
CAN	Andean Community
CAP	Common Agricultural Policy
CARDS	European Community Assistance for Reconstruction, Development and Stabilisation programme
Caricom	Caribbean Community and Common Market
CCP	Common Commercial Policy
CD	Conference on Disarmament
CEE6	Bulgaria, Czech Republic, Hungary, Poland, Romania, Slovakia
CEECs	Central and Eastern European countries
CEMAC	Central African Economic and Monetary Union
CESDP	Common European Security and Defence Policy
CET	common external tariff
CFA franc	Franc de la Communauté Francaise d'Afrique (for WAEMU)
CFSP	Common Foreign and Security Policy
CIA	Central Intelligence Agency
CIS	Commonwealth of Independent States
CJTF	Combined Joint Task Force
CNN	Cable News Network
COMECON	Council for Mutual Economic Assistance
COPS	Political and Security Committee
CSCE	Conference on Security and Co-operation in Europe
CTBT	Comprehensive Test Ban Treaty

DPRK	Democratic People's Republic of Korea (North Korea)
DSB	Dispute Settlement Body (of WTO)
EADS	European Aeronautic Defence and Space Company
EBRD	European Bank for Reconstruction and Development
EC	European Community
ECs	European Communities
ECAP	European Capabilities Action Plan
ECB	European Central Bank
ECHO	European Community Humanitarian Office
ECJ	European Court of Justice
ECMM	European Community Monitoring Mission
ECOWAS	Economic Community of Western African States
ECRE	European Council on Refugees and Exiles
ECSC	European Coal and Steel Community
ECT	Treaty establishing the European Community
EDC	European Defence Community
EDF	European Development Fund
EEA	European Economic Area
EEC	European Economic Community
EECT	Treaty establishing the European Economic Community
EECT(1957)	Treaty establishing the European Economic Community (original version)
EFTA	European Free Trade Association
EIB	European Investment Bank
EMS	European Monetary System
EMU	economic and monetary union
EP	European Parliament
EPAs	economic partnership agreements
EPC	European Political Co-operation
ERM	exchange rate mechanism (of the EMS)
ERP	European Recovery Programme (Marshall Plan)
ESDI	European Security and Defence Identity
EU	European Union
EUPM	European Police Mission (in Bosnia and Herzegovina)
Euratom	European Atomic Energy Community
EURRF	EU Rapid Reaction Force
FATF	Financial Action Task Force
FDI	foreign direct investment
FRG	Federal Republic of Germany
FSCs	foreign sales corporations
FTA	free trade area
FTAA	Free Trade Area of the Americas
FYROM	Former Yugoslav Republic of Macedonia
GATT	General Agreement on Tariffs and Trade
GDP	gross domestic product

GDR	German Democratic Republic
GM	genetically modified
GMOs	genetically modified organisms
GMP	Global Mediterranean Policy
GNI	gross national income
GNP	gross national product
GPS	Global Positioning System
GSP	Generalised System of Preferences
IAEA	International Atomic Energy Authority
IBRD	International Bank for Reconstruction and Development
ICBMs	intercontinental ballistic missiles
ICC	International Criminal Court
IF	Investment Facility
IFOR	Implementation Force
IGC	intergovernmental conference
IMF	International Monetary Fund
IPE	international political economy
IR	international relations
ITO	International Trade Organisation
JAP	EU–US Joint Action Plan
JHA	Co-operation in Justice and Home Affairs
KEDO	Korean Peninsular Energy Development Organisation
LAC	Latin America and the Caribbean
MAD	mutual assured destruction
Mercosur	Mercado de Sur (Common Market of the Southern Cone of Latin America)
MNCs	multinational corporations
MNEPR	Multilateral Nuclear Environmental Programme in Russia
MRA	Mutual Recognition Agreement
NAFTA	North American Free Trade Agreement
NATO	North Atlantic Treaty Organisation
NCPI	New Commercial Policy Instrument
NEI	(US) Northern European Initiative
NGOs	non-governmental organisations
NMD	National Missile Defence
NMP	New Mediterranean Policy
NPT	Treaty on the Non-proliferation of Nuclear Weapons
NSC–68	National Security Council Resolution 68
NTA	New Transatlantic Agenda
NTBs	non-tariff barriers
NTM	New Transatlantic Marketplace
OCCAR	Joint Armaments Co-operation Structure
OCTs	overseas countries and territories
ODA	Overseas Development Aid
OECD	Organisation for Economic Co-operation and Development

OEEC	Organisation for European Economic Co-operation
OPEC	Organisation of Petroleum Exporting Countries
OSCE	Organisation for Security and Co-operation in Europe
PCA	Partnership and Co-operation Agreement
PFP	Partnership for Peace
PHARE	Pologne et Hongrie: Actions pour la Reconversion Économique (Programme of technical and financial assistance to the CEECs)
PPEWU	Policy Planning and Early Warning Unit
PRC	People's Republic of China
QMV	qualified majority voting
R&D	research and development
SALT	Strategic Arms Limitation Talks
SAP	Stabilisation and Association Process
SAR	Special Administrative Region
SEA	Single European Act
SEM	Single European Market
SFOR	Stabilisation Force
STABEX	System for the Stabilisation of Export Earnings from Products
SYSMIN	System for the Stabilisation of Export Earnings from Minerals
TACIS	Technical Assistance to the Commonwealth of Independent States Programme
TEP	Transatlantic Economic Partnership
TEU	Treaty on European Union (Maastricht Treaty)
TNCs	transnational corporations
UK	United Kingdom of Great Britain and Northern Ireland
UN	United Nations
UNCTAD	United Nations Conference on Trade and Development
UNCHR	United Nations Commission on Human Rights
UNPROFOR	United Nations Protection Force
US	United States of America
USSR	Union of Soviet Socialist Republics
USTR	US Trade Representative
WAEMU	West African Economic and Monetary Union
WEU	Western European Union
WMD	weapons of mass destruction
WTO	World Trade Organisation
WW1	World War One
WW2	World War Two

Preface

As a union of 25 states with over 450 million people producing a quarter of the world's Gross National Product (GNP) the European Union is a global actor: it should be ready to share in the responsibility for global security.

Javier Solana, 20 June 2003[1]

In making this statement Javier Solana, the European Union's (EU) High Representative for Common Foreign and Security Policy (CFSP), was anticipating the scheduled EU macro-enlargement of 2004 and advancing a case for an EU global security strategy ahead of the potentially momentous internal reforms being developed by the European Convention. Particularly interesting were the equation of economic size with global actorness, the apparent moral obligation upon the EU to accept global security responsibilities and the implicit differentiation between the EU's activities in international economics and in international security. Set against the background of EU disarray over pre-emptive US-led military intervention in Iraq, the statement also begged timely questions about whether the EU of today has laid to rest long-standing caricatures of its being 'an economic giant but a political dwarf'.

That these issues are salient and recurring is reflected in their comprising a core element of this book, the origins of which pre-date Solana's plea by over six years. It is the product of our different research foci and of our joint frustration. When we first met and discussed our interests in international political economy (IPE) and international relations (IR) it reinforced how entwined they were and struck us how potentially instructive it would be to combine them in a study of the EU's external relations. Considerations of international systems and actors, the exercise of power and influence and the interplay between global, regional, national and sub-national factors have long transcended the staple diet of the traditional realist school of IR. The EU in particular, as a *sui generis* entity, defies categorisation, and an understanding of its international relations requires a combination of approaches. The three-pillar structure adopted in the 1993 Treaty on European Union (TEU) embodies the divisions traditionally drawn between the 'low' politics of economics and the 'high' politics of foreign and security policy. Yet these divisions resulted not from considered action in response to the evolving nature of international relations but from a political expediency foisted upon the EU by the need to satisfy minimally the interests of then twelve member states, each with their different external policy cultures and concerns. Constant efforts ever since to develop co-ordination across the European Communities (ECs), CFSP and Justice and Home Affairs pillars bear testament to this. They also demonstrate the merging of politics, economics and security and an expanding intermestic agenda as the foreign and the domestic realms blur.

Our first aim, therefore, was to contribute to enhancing contemporary understanding of the EU's international relations through a combined IPE/IR approach. Our second aim followed from our frustration incurred when teaching about, and supervising on, the EU's international relations. There was little published material that directly examined the IR *and* IPE dimensions of EU international relations. Nor was there much that concentrated on what the EU actually did and what happened. With one or two notable exceptions, the emphasis was on conceptualising the EU as an international actor, analysing its institutions, or studying its policy-making procedures. Alternatively, there was a number of books being published on the EU's CFSP, interesting in itself but too narrowly focused either to reflect our interests or to meet our purposes. We thus resolved consciously to eschew theoretical, institutional and policy-making discussion in favour of an empirically orientated research agenda: what has the EU actually done in its international relations, what happened and what does this tell us about the EU as an international actor?

From this two-fold ambition came difficult methodological choices. Foremost of these were what to include and what to exclude? This is always contentious. To cover too little would defeat our aims but to cover too much might do likewise by forcing a superficiality of analysis. Similarly, there was the choice between writing integrated chapters that combined explicitly our IPE/IR approaches or broadly 'paired chapters' that allowed for greater analytical depth and for the reader to develop a more detailed conjoint picture. Ultimately we opted for the latter in the hope, too, that this would make the book more accessible to non-specialist readers and, although the paired chapters are meant to be read in tandem, enable them also to be read meaningfully in isolation. These methodological reasons, rather than necessarily considerations of relative significance, explain why some aspects of EU international relations have been omitted from discussion. A further logical consequence was that we each took responsibility for those chapters closest to our interests. Chapters One, Three, Four, Six and Eight were consequently written by Steve Marsh, Chapters Two, Five, Seven and Nine by Hans Mackenstein, and the Conclusion was written jointly to pull together the different approaches and key themes.

The structure and presentation of the book flow directly from our aims and methodological choices. Although its predominant focus is on the post-Cold War period, the first two chapters are dedicated to the historical evolution of the EU's international relations in the conviction that this context is essential to understanding the significance and difficulties of its multifaceted contemporary external relations.

Chapter Three is dedicated to providing an overview of post-Cold War ECs/EU competencies, key external relations policies and instruments and the Union's presence in the wider world. Chapters Four and Five examine the post-Cold War EU–US relationship in its security and economic aspects respectively. Chapters Six and Seven investigate the EU's external relations with its immediate neighbours. The former examines its security relationships with the countries of Central and South-Eastern Europe and its place within the evolving European security architecture. The latter focuses on EU economic ties within the 'Euro-Med Agreement', with Central and Eastern European countries and with European Free Trade Association members. Chapters Eight and Nine examine the EU's international relations in a global context. Chapter Eight addresses three key themes developed in Solana's global EU security vision within a Eurasian context – the Union's security relationship with Russia, the prospects for strategic partnership with China and the issue of failed states, which is considered in the context of North Korea. Chapter Nine then assesses the EU's economic relationships with the African, Caribbean and Pacific countries, Latin America, and the Far East, principally Japan but also China and the Association of South-East Asian Nations. The Conclusion draws together the book's principal findings and arguments in order to assess the EU's strengths and weaknesses in its external relations, to take issue with some popular misconceptions about EU capabilities and to highlight some of the issues likely to affect its future course as a global economic and security actor.

Finally, and to avoid confusion later, a note on terminology. First, as far as possible we have tried to minimise academic jargon and have provided a comprehensive list of abbreviations to guide the reader through the unavoidable multiplicity of acronyms. Second, we believe that an appreciation of the EU in international relations requires an understanding of foreign policy far more expansive than simply CFSP. The terms foreign policy and external relations policies are thus used interchangeably in recognition of the importance for the EU in its international relations of not just pillar two instruments but also those drawn from pillars one and even three. Third, and perhaps most potentially confusing, is that the EU is a moving target and one of the many problems posed therein is that how it is referred to has changed repeatedly. In 1965 the Merger Treaty, which came into force in 1967, led to the European Coal and Steel Community, European Economic Community (EEC) and the European Atomic Energy Community becoming known collectively as the European Communities. Over time this became commonly referred to as simply the European Community (EC) until November 1993 when the entry into force of the TEU created the EU, complete with its three pillars.[2] We have consequently sought to use the term EC(s) when talking of events before 1993 and EU afterwards, except where questions of competence require a distinction to be drawn. However, as the reader will discover, it is not always easy to maintain this practice, especially as events and anticipatory politics often spanned the EC/EU transition.

Notes

1 Solana, J. (2003) 'A Secure Europe in a Better World', SO138/03, 20 June 2003.
2 Confusingly, the TEU renamed the EEC as the European Community (EC).

CHAPTER 1

The European Community and international security:
from World War Two to post-Cold War

In November 1993 a European Union (EU) Common Foreign and Security Policy (CFSP) came into force. In December 1998 an Anglo-French summit meeting at St Malo laid foundations for the development of an EU Rapid Reaction Force (EURRF). In December 2002 the Union decided at the Copenhagen Summit to admit a further ten countries to full membership, the majority of which were formerly communist Central and East European countries (CEECs). These are but three of the dramatic changes that the EU has undergone in its evolution as an international security actor since the end of the Cold War. Yet to assess how and why these changes were made, and to appreciate fully their significance, it is just as necessary to understand the past as it is the present.

This chapter places the development of integration and of the European Community (EC) as a security actor in the context of international systemic change. It examines how the legacies of World War Two (WW2) and post-war international events helped first to catalyse integration and then to mould the EC's subsequent development as an international security actor within a bipolar system where the security environment was dominated by Cold War concerns. It then explains how a fine blend of purposive action, serendipity and changes in the international system help account for the EC's rise as an influential international security actor and how the transatlantic relationship served as a sensitive barometer of the Community's growing role and impact. Finally, it outlines how the collapse of the Cold War suddenly recast the security assumptions of four decades' standing and introduces some of the enormous changes and challenges with which the EC was newly confronted.

Post-war Europe – no place for integration?

Winning the peace has throughout history often proved to be as difficult as winning the war, if not more so. This fact was amply demonstrated by the onset of WW2 just two decades after the conclusion of World War One (WW1), the so-called war to end all wars. It was a fact, too, not lost on those in power during WW2. The failure of collective security under the League of Nations, the United States' (US) retreat to isolationism, the weaknesses of the Versailles peace settlement, ideological rivalry, historical enmities – such as those between France and Germany – and a severe economic recession that produced conditions ripe for political extremism: these were but some of the factors identified as contributing to Europe's descent once more into war in 1939.

Allied leaders thus planned for a post-war order that would combat such factors and provide instead for a new international system and lasting peace. This planning was driven predominantly by the US and Britain and was modified by the Union of Soviet Socialist Republics (USSR) as best as it could. The envisaged post-war order was still to be based on independent sovereign states and its design reflected a calculated blend of old-style realist power politics, collective security idealism and neo-liberal institutionalism. Collective security, based on the notion of all for one and one for all, was to be provided through the creation of the United Nations (UN). The installation, though, of Britain, China, France, the US and the USSR as the veto-wielding permanent members of the UN Security Council demonstrated the tempering realism of great power politics. It also marked an implicit recognition of traditional spheres of influence in which each great power bore particular responsibility and in which its legitimate security concerns would be recognised.

In addition, the US sought to install itself at the helm of a new international monetary regime that would prevent a recurrence of destructive inter-war parochialism and drives for self-sufficiency by promoting economic reconstruction and multilateral free trade. The foundation for this was laid in 1944 in the form of the Bretton Woods system. The dollar replaced sterling as the world's dominant currency. Currency convertibility and fixed but adjustable exchange rates were established and the twin institutions of the International Monetary Fund (IMF) and the International Bank for Reconstruction and Development (IBRD) were created to facilitate system stability, capital flows and balanced economic growth. This was augmented three years later when the General Agreement on Tariffs and Trade (GATT) helped to compensate for the failure of a proposed International Trade Organisation (ITO).[1]

Despite the wartime calls of Resistance movements and encouraging rhetoric from political leaders such as British Prime Minister Winston Churchill, the principal architects of the proposed post-war order perceived no need for states to move beyond co-operative arrangements and consequently envisaged no specific place for European integration. However, their post-war 'grand design' depended upon maintaining workable relations between, in particular, the US, Britain and the USSR. This was possible between the former two on account both of their so-called 'special relationship',[2] which was based around common values, shared experiences and unprecedented co-operation during the war, and of US leverage over Britain due to the latter's accelerated wartime decline and dependence on American economic aid.[3] The same was not true of the USSR. It only joined the Allied cause in a Faustian pact in 1941 once the 1939 Nazi–Soviet Pact proved chimerical and its subsequent co-operation was laden with distrust. For example, as the USSR endured massive casualties on the eastern front, Stalin and the Soviet Politburo feared that the West would either conclude a separate peace with Germany or leave the Red Army to engage the bulk of Hitler's *Wehrmacht* by delaying D-Day. Also, although provision was made for state-controlled economies in the Bretton Woods agreement, the promotion of neo-liberal institutions and international capitalism was anathema to the communist system, and ideological differences subsumed to combating the Axis powers progressively returned to the fore as attention shifted to the spoils of war. Indeed, there was recurrent mutual suspicion about post-war intentions, and Soviet insecurity was exacerbated by successful US development of the atomic bomb, the American monopoly over which offset the USSR's superior conventional forces in Europe.

By the end of 1945 key post-war questions remained unanswered, despite the Yalta and Potsdam conferences. Inter-Allied relations were deteriorating rapidly, a trend exacerbated by the breaking of the wartime Roosevelt–Churchill–Stalin triumvirate owing to the death of the US President and Churchill's general election defeat. Germany's fate was foremost of the outstanding issues. Traditional problems posed by its *Mittellage*[4] were exacerbated by its potentially pivotal role in economic reconstruction, widespread fear of German revanchism and the developing East–West distrust that made any solution to temporary quadripartite Allied occupation of Germany a vital security concern.

Meantime the West and the USSR engaged in a series of actions that each, rightly or wrongly, interpreted as 'unfriendly'. From Moscow's perspective history, ideology and security demands arising from the USSR's geo-strategic position underscored the need to strip German assets and to establish buffer zones that could serve as defensive barriers against future German revanchism or against the West in general. It was thus logical and justifiable to re-incorporate the Baltic states, which protected maritime access to the central Russian plain and land access to Leningrad, to secure communist control over Romania, Bulgaria and Hungary – all of which had been willing German wartime accomplices – and to establish a Polish state that would be responsive to Soviet concerns, not least because Poland had been the launch-pad for three invasions of Russia within the preceding thirty years.[5] It was equally reasonable to regard with concern the exclusion of Soviet forces from the occupation of Japan, Western demands for national self-determination within Soviet-controlled Europe and, particularly, the apparent reneging on commitments made at Potsdam when in September 1946 US Secretary of State Byrnes aired plans for

German rehabilitation and self-government, at least within Anglo-American zones of occupation.

Conversely, history, ideology and *realpolitik* seemingly justified Western suspicion of Soviet expansionism, particularly following Stalin's call for Soviet rearmament in 1946 and his refusal to withdraw forces from Iran that same year. Likewise, Western criticism of Soviet tactics in Poland appeared well-founded in view of agreements reached at Yalta and the fact that Britain and France had nominally gone to war to protect Polish independence against the Third Reich's quest for *lebensraum*. In addition, salutary lessons drawn from inter-war appeasement of Nazi Germany, value clashes between liberal democracy and totalitarian regimes and the inherent conflict between capitalism and communism underpinned predictions contained in George Kennan's famous 1946 Long Telegram of inevitable Soviet expansionism and his consequent call for resolute Western containment of this threat.[6]

Europe, indeed the world, was slipping into the Cold War. Although its precise origins remain a source of debate,[7] the Cold War brought about an international order very different from that envisaged by Allied wartime planners. Moreover, Europe became the first major test of wills as East–West suspicion deepened, reciprocal threat perception heightened and the US acknowledged its interdependence with continental Europe. In 1947 the US Central Intelligence Agency (CIA) concluded that the principal threat to American national security was economic collapse in Western Europe and the consequent accession to power of communist elements.[8] Europe had experienced a general post-war political shift to the left. Communists were in coalition governments between 1945 and 1947 in France and Italy and national Communist Party membership in these countries exceeded 1 million and 1.7 million respectively in 1946. Worse still, American officials who visited Europe – such as Under-Secretary of State for Economic Affairs William Clayton – found that economic distress was far more serious than anticipated, that political and social collapse was probable and that this could benefit only communism. The response of the US Truman administration, containment policy, was to shape the Western world's security for over four decades. It was also to open the door for the development of European integration.

Integration's Cold War stimulus

The US emerged from WW2 in an unrivalled position. It held a monopoly over the atomic bomb, led the world in conventional weapon technology, had almost doubled its gross national product (GNP), possessed the vast majority of the world's financial reserves and had access to enormous domestic and overseas sources of vital raw materials, such as oil. Nevertheless, it needed a revitalised Europe to provide effective Cold War allies in the containment of communism and healthy markets to help prevent severe economic depression.

In consequence, the Truman administration decided to extend security guarantees, provide aid for economic rehabilitation and, crucially, rethink American wartime planning and projected international commitments.

Considerations of hard security began to dominate the international agenda. The US had little to fear in 1947 from the USSR's military threat, but West European nations were much less secure. Hence, in March 1948 Britain, France and the Benelux countries concluded a mutual defence agreement by setting up the Brussels Treaty Organisation (BTO). This, however, was targeted at least in part against a future German threat and, with Germany occupied, France and Italy devastated and Britain in financial crisis, could do little should the 2.9 million men that the USSR still had under arms be ordered to march across continental Europe. Under considerable pressure from European countries and from a perceived mounting communist threat, the Truman administration reluctantly sought to allay European fears and to combat communist pressure on countries elsewhere, such as Greece and Turkey. In 1947 President Truman made a revolutionary pledge, in what became known as the Truman Doctrine, of a US peacetime commitment to Europe and to help nations to resist aggression from internal and external sources. More concretely, in April 1949 the US agreed the North Atlantic Treaty Organisation (NATO), an intergovernmental military alliance that provided for mutual defence and that dominated West Europe's hard security arrangements throughout the Cold War.

Still, though, events seemingly moved against the West. A US recession badly exacerbated the economic difficulties of Western Europe, China was lost to communism and in September 1949 a Soviet atomic test broke the US monopoly over the atom bomb, hitherto the shield behind which risks involved in containment policy could be undertaken in relative security. The Truman administration responded again, this time with a strategy that changed the face of the Cold War and the nature of containment. Formally developed in National Security Council Resolution 68 (NSC-68), the US globalised and militarised its containment strategy.[9] Kennan's original conception of containment was stripped of its flexibility and a grossly simplified perspective of international relations developed. Viewed through the lens of containment strategy, the international system was bipolar in configuration, being composed of two antipathetic ideological blocs. The US and the USSR were each hegemonic within their respective bloc and international relations were reduced to a 'zero-sum game' whereby any gain for communism was perceived as a loss to the West and vice versa. Also, NSC-68's prescriptions meant that loss of the atomic bomb monopoly had to be compensated for by the search for even more powerful weapons of mass destruction (WMD) and a massive accretion of conventional military power.

None of this, however, was possible if economic devastation led Western Europe either to succumb to communism or to be incapable of undertaking the required massive rearmament programmes. The US thus had to stimulate West European economic reconstruction and co-operation if communism were to be combated, transatlantic recession prevented/mitigated and the necessary weaponry and wealth generated to enable declining West European states to contribute effectively to European military defence and to maintain their overseas commitments. This conclusion was tremendously important for European integration because it persuaded the Truman administration to sacrifice America's drive for multilateral free trade upon the Cold War altar and instead to countenance and encourage regional integration, which it had hitherto considered an obstacle to its trade objectives.

Put simply, the new international situation meant that the potential benefits of integration to the US now outweighed the downside risks. First, integration provided an opportunity to remake 'the Old World in the likeness of the New'[10] – strength and prosperity could be returned to Europe by applying to it the American model of interstate trade and a single market. Second, integration could be a vehicle for political reconstruction and psychological reconciliation. The collective European memory had somehow to be quickly overridden such that nations that had been on opposing sides during WW2 would co-operate in order to combat together a new threat. Third, Europe's potential economic powerhouse, Germany, had to be rehabilitated. Co-operation, deepening interdependence and, in particular, supranational controls offered a potential means to overcome slowly the wartime legacy of acute distrust and recrimination.[11]

In 1947 the US backed its conviction in transatlantic interdependence and its new-found enthusiasm for European integration with the announcement of the European Recovery Programme (ERP), alternatively and more popularly known as the Marshall Plan.[12] Some $17 billion of economic aid spread over five years was tied to participating countries devising a common recovery programme as a prelude to European unity. Contemporaneously Britain and the US forced the issue of Germany's future. In May 1946 General Lucius Clay suspended German reparation shipments from the American zone of occupation. In January 1947 Britain and the US merged their zones and subsequently a new currency, the deutschmark, was introduced.

These measures were cumulatively highly provocative to the USSR and precipitated the first major Cold War crisis. The Soviets blockaded western sectors of Berlin and the West countered with a prolonged airlift from June 1948 to May 1949.[13] Also, although Marshall Aid was offered Europe-wide, it was correctly anticipated that the USSR would regard the plan as an attempt to lure Soviet satellites into the Western camp and, consequently, find unacceptable its conditions and its inherent capitalist contagion of command economies. In response the USSR consolidated its hold over Eastern Europe, establishing the Council for Mutual Economic Assistance (COMECON) in 1949 and shifting from coalition tactics to a process of Stalinisation, most notably in the February 1948 communist coup in Czechoslovakia. In effect, the Marshall Plan, the closely entwined Anglo-American-led drive to rehabilitate Germany and the subsequent resolution of the Berlin crisis combined to imbue the reconstruction of the Federal Republic of Germany (FRG) with an inexorable momentum, as well as both to stimulate integration and to ensure that it would be delimited to the western parts of a divided Europe.

Integration, security and second order action

By 1951 the Cold War had reconfigured the post-war international system into a bipolar arrangement and had impacted profoundly on European security and integration. Containment strategy, though it would undergo various permutations, was established as the dominant consideration in US-led Western security and would remain so for the next forty years. NATO was installed as the unrivalled defence institution and hard security considerations of military defence consistently headed the agenda. Although integration had been geographically delimited to Western Europe, it had nonetheless secured a new-found place in the post-war international order, not least because international events meant US conversion to support of regional integration and an imperative to rehabilitate West Germany.

However, this overlay of Cold War strictures should obscure neither that West Europe's second order powers retained scope for independent manoeuvre nor that the unique geo-political cocoon of superpower rivalry that encased Europe actually facilitated the development both of integration and of its influence in international relations.[14] The former is well demonstrated by the inability of the US to fashion integration decisively. The era of Marshall Aid represented possibly the pinnacle of US economic and political ascendancy over Western Europe during the Cold War. Yet the integration that resulted directly from the terms of Marshall Aid was minimal, to the point that the ERP has been argued to represent a dismal failure in the breaking down of national frontiers.[15] The Organisation for European Economic Co-operation (OEEC), the institution ultimately set up to administer Marshall Aid, was inter-governmental in nature and, comprising eighteen historically, politically, economically and geo-strategically diverse countries, ill-suited to act as an instrument of integration.

Europe's first major post-war integrative project, that of the Jean Monnet-inspired European Coal and Steel Community (ECSC), was devised and shaped by European countries, albeit with US approval and support. The security considerations of pooling Franco-German coal and steel resources under a high authority, together with those of any other nation that wished to participate, were obvious. Coal and steel were key materials for war and their sharing under supranational control marked a critical juncture in Franco-West German reconciliation and a potential enhancement, through the common market, of Western Europe's rearmament programme. Equally clear was that an ECSC membership of just France, FRG, Italy and the Benelux countries revealed the ability of Europe's capitals to choose whether or not to become involved in integration. Neither the Scandinavian countries, which had demonstrated previously in the Congress of Europe and the Council of Europe grave reservations about supranationalism, nor America's closest ally, Britain, could be persuaded to partake of the ECSC. In fact, the need to rehabilitate Germany as a consequence of changes in the international system and of relations therein had a much greater bearing on European integration than did Marshall Aid *per se*.[16] The centrality to post-war French modernisation plans of a punitive policy toward Germany was overcome primarily by Anglo-American policy making FRG recovery a *fait accompli*. Thereafter the question became how best to control German rehabilitation rather than how to prevent it?

The ECSC had provided an initial and partial answer to this question. However, the issue was quickly rejoined as the diversion of forces from Europe to fight along the free world's perimeter fence, such as in the Korean War, exposed a dangerous shortfall in military manpower along the East–West frontier in Europe. The only latent potential capacity lay in West Germany, and on 12 September 1950 US Secretary of State Dean Acheson accordingly dropped the so-called 'bomb at the Waldorf': West Germany had to be rearmed to the tune of ten divisions within NATO. The consequent scenario was of a newly sovereign FRG regaining military as well as economic power, something that was bound to generate deep consternation regardless of Germany's Cold War division. France in particular was deeply opposed to rearming the FRG. At the same time it was poorly placed to resist pressure, especially from the US, owing to a combination of Cold War exigencies and its need of Marshall Aid and of American support for its faltering military position in Indochina. As a result France made another reluctant proposal for supranational integration in the form of the Pleven Plan. The idea was to create a European Defence Community (EDC) and an associated European Political Community, which evolved from Article 38 of the EDC Treaty signed on 27 May 1952. All German units were to be placed within a supranationally controlled European army and there was to be a centralised procurement system. If the FRG had to be rearmed, then French planners were determined that it should have neither control over its own troops nor parity with France, which would commit only a percentage of its forces to the EDC.

The security initiative failed this time. Britain, West Europe's strongest military power, wanted no part of the EDC. It feared being drained by too close an association with a militarily weak Europe, reviled the EDC's supranational characteristics and, in Churchill's words, saw the idea of a European army as nothing better than 'a sludgy amalgam'.[17] Even in France Gaullist-led opposition to sharing sovereignty over national defence meant that the EDC ultimately failed to secure ratification from the National Assembly. German forces were subsequently incorporated into NATO in May 1955 via British-sponsored membership for Italy and the FRG of an expanded BTO, which took the form of the Western European Union (WEU). Nevertheless, that the EDC got as far as it did was testament to the attraction, for some countries at least, of integration as a vehicle for controlling and harnessing German recovery, for promoting reconciliation and for countering the threat of communism.[18]

When the 1957 Treaty of Rome created the European Economic Community (EEC) and the European Atomic Energy Community (Euratom), it was perhaps self-evident that it also marked the point at which the Communities would begin to exert international influence. Half of the EEC's founding members were colonial powers and they immediately brought their overseas ties into the Community, something institutionalised in 1963 in the EC's first development agreement, the Yaoundé Convention, which linked member states and seventeen associated states and Madagascar. Also, under Article 238 of the Treaty of Rome the Community was charged with responsibility for the creation of association agreements with third countries, which involved a raft of special measures and reciprocal rights and obligations. Furthermore, some EC internal objectives had largely non-purposive but nevertheless significant repercussions for the Community's external presence. For example, transatlantic relations quickly reflected the impact of the EC's discriminatory Common Agricultural Policy (CAP) and the effects of the Common External Tariff (CET), which was necessitated by the objective of a common market. Indeed, the Dillon Round demonstrated that the Community's growing economic power meant that the US could no longer dominate GATT and in 1962 EC–US relations degenerated into the first serious trade dispute, the so-called chicken war.[19]

Although the primary emphasis of the Treaty of Rome was on internal economic integration, not least because of the ECSC-demonstrated merits of a functional approach, there were actually numerous international security considerations implicit within the Treaty. Predictably little was said about hard security, an issue widely seen as the purview of NATO and as one that, in the wake of the EDC débâcle, was so sensitive that military equipment was excluded from common market provisions. Even so, defence was not a sphere of activity that was ruled out of Community competence and expansion into it was potentially provided for under Article 235's remit of future Community action in areas not anticipated when the Treaty was signed.[20] Nor, despite Western Europe's reliance on the US nuclear umbrella in particular, was the Cold War a period devoid of ideas for hard security alternatives to NATO. For example, the 1961 French Fouchet proposals championed, albeit unsuccessfully, a political union of EC members to cover defence and foreign affairs. Similarly in the early 1980s, as European fears heightened about US President Reagan's aggressive Soviet policy and transatlantic differences deepened over issues such as the deployment in Western Europe of Cruise and Pershing II missiles, France led a campaign to resurrect the WEU as a basis for an alternative European defence identity. Furthermore, there was no shortage of different national defence responses to the Cold War. French President Charles de Gaulle famously withdrew France from NATO's integrated military command in 1966. Austria regained its status as a sovereign, democratic and capitalist state only when the USSR leader, Nikita Khrushchev, withdrew the Red Army in May 1955 in return for an Austrian promise of Cold War neutrality that prevented it joining either NATO or the EC. Sweden also adopted a stance of armed neutrality, and, within NATO, Norway and Denmark disassociated themselves from the Alliance's nuclear strategy.

The Treaty of Rome was also silent on issues of foreign and security policy. Again, though, opportunity was provided, even expectation created, for development into these areas. For instance, the Treaty's preamble noted members' commitment to strengthen the safeguards of peace and liberty, and Article 224 stated that '[m]ember states shall consult one another for the purpose of enacting in common the necessary provisions to prevent the functioning of the Common Market from being affected by measures which a Member State may be called upon to take in case of serious internal disturbances affecting public order, in case of war or serious international tension constituting a threat of war or in order to carry out undertakings into which it has entered for the purpose of maintaining peace and international security'.[21] Moreover, in many respects the EC itself constituted a security community. It created a zone of unprecedented peace and stability in Western Europe based on mutual dependence where resort to violence became almost unthinkable and where repeated game-plays and transactions built confidence and helped develop behavioural norms. EC membership also implied sufficient sharing of values and interests to promote foreign and security policy co-operation, especially as the Cold War helped to homogenise members' geo-strategic interests and principal threat perceptions.[22]

It is thus unsurprising that efforts at the 1969 Hague Summit to re-launch integration in the wake of the debilitating Empty Chair crisis of 1965–66, when de Gaulle withdrew French representation from the Council of Ministers in a battle over Community competence and institutional powers, included a call for foreign policy co-ordination. Indeed, the interdependence of members' foreign and security concerns was highlighted by contemporaneous events. Fears grew of a resurgent and possibly neutralist FRG, not least because of Chancellor Brandt's development of *Ostpolitik* as a central tenet of West German policy and the dominance within the EC of the deutschmark and the German economy, which was starkly revealed by the forced devaluation of the franc in 1969. Also, US preoccupation with Vietnam and the beginnings of *détente*, which marked a temporary thawing of East–West relations, questioned the permanency of American security guarantees and raised suspicions that, without concerted action, Europe might find its future negotiated away by the two superpowers. And then there was the pressing question of what to do about Britain. De Gaulle had twice blocked its EC entry in 1963 and 1967 for reasons that included its Atlanticism. Nevertheless Britain still wished to join, and whilst its traditional opposition to supranationalism made it a potentially 'awkward partner', its membership might also afford the Community greater influence *vis-à-vis* Washington, offset French intransigence and help to counterbalance the FRG's weight within the Community.[23]

The EC's need of closer co-operation was reflected in the decision taken at the 1972 Paris Summit to institutionalise summitry in the form of the European Council. Initially designed to deal mainly with internal matters, it quickly became used as a forum for discussing and pronouncing upon foreign and security policy matters, such as French-inspired calls for a conference on European disarmament as a spill-over from the Conference on Security and Co-operation in Europe (CSCE). In addition the Davignon report, a product of the Hague

Summit, recommended in May 1970 that the rotating presidency of the Community preside over biannual meetings of foreign ministers and more frequent meetings between their senior officials. Adopted in the Luxemburg report of 1970 and refined in the 1973 Copenhagen report, the result was European Political Co-operation (EPC), a process designed to secure greater intergovernmental foreign and security policy co-ordination and the precursor of today's CFSP. The bulk of business was conducted by a Political Committee, composed of the European Commission and political directors in foreign ministries, and was facilitated by the establishment of Coreu, a secure telegraphic network that encouraged the swift pooling of information and intelligence.

EPC's setting outside Community structures and its restriction to political and economic dimensions of security demonstrated the continued unwillingness of member states to move beyond intergovernmentalism in these sensitive areas of activity. The consequent need for consensus meant also that EPC was largely reactive rather than proactive in nature and that policies generally reflected the lowest common denominator of the member states. Decision-making thus became increasingly problematic as the Community enlarged to twelve members by the end of the Cold War. Moreover, EPC was often found wanting as discussions were rapidly overtaken by unfolding events – such as the Soviet invasion of Afghanistan in December 1979 and the declaration of martial law in Poland in 1981.

Nevertheless, EPC reflected and encouraged common EC security concerns and responses, promoted the Community's international profile and to a limited extent challenged NATO supremacy by providing an alternative forum for multilateral European security consultation. Indeed, EPC revealed the Community's growing willingness to assert itself collectively *vis-à-vis* US policies, such as its declaration in June 1980 against US Middle Eastern policy and in favour of a Palestinian homeland and of Palestinian participation in Arab–Israeli peace talks. Furthermore, although repeated co-operation within EPC demonstrated institutional shortcomings and problems created by dividing dimensions of security into EC, EPC and exclusively national competencies, it also built mutual confidence which could then be translated into sufficient political will to address these difficulties.

In 1987 Article 30 of the Single European Act (SEA) finally gave EPC a symbolically important treaty base, codified a series of incremental adjustments made over the previous decade and set about strengthening co-operation within EPC and between EPC and the EC. For example, member states undertook to 'endeavour jointly to formulate and implement a European Foreign Policy', which included prior consultation with, and consideration of the views of, fellow member states in deciding policy, and a permanent secretariat was established in Brussels to assist the presidency. Even more significantly, Article 30 noted members' belief that closer co-operation would 'contribute in an essential way to the development of a European identity in External Policy matters' and attempted to instil EC foreign and security action with internal and external coherency. The Commission was fully associated with EPC and, together with the presidency, was charged with responsibility for ensuring consistency in the actions of EPC and EC external policies. Also members undertook to seek common positions within EPC and to present these in international institutions and conferences. Furthermore, members were encouraged to organise political dialogue wherever appropriate with third countries and regional groupings and to work with the Commission in intensifying, through mutual assistance and information, co-operation between their representatives accredited to third countries and to international organisations.[24]

Systemic change and the augmentation of the EC in international security

The EC's role and capabilities in international security did not grow solely as a consequence of internal policy development and purposive action. They developed also as a consequence of external opportunities and expectations. This can be seen in regard to the changing focus and nature of the Cold War. It can be seen, too, in systemic changes that encouraged new calculations of power and security, that loosened the bonds of the post-war transatlantic relationship and that recognised the increasing importance of non-state actors.

The EC's international presence and its importance as a security actor grew as a consequence of the focus of the Cold War shifting from Europe and as 'soft' tools of statecraft received increasing attention following the initial dominance of the military dimensions of East–West conflict. By the 1960s an enduring *status quo* had developed in Europe. NATO and the 1955 Warsaw Pact had consolidated beyond realistic challenge the informal division of Europe drawn by Marshall Aid, albeit with the possible exception of Yugoslavia. Despite lofty US rhetoric about 'roll-back', no one seriously believed that anything could, or should, be done when the Soviets intervened in Hungary in 1956 and in Czechoslovakia in 1968. Even the contentious issue of Berlin, where the West feared that the Soviets would woo the FRG into neutrality in return for reunification, had been *de facto* resolved when Khrushchev ordered the Berlin Wall built in August 1961.[25]

The new imperative was to fight for the hearts and minds of the developing world. Here the Cold War was often seen as an irrelevance next to considerations such as poverty, famine and national self-determination. Also a combination of revolutionary nationalism and the era of decolonisation seemingly threatened a symbiotic relationship between national liberation and communist expansion. True, this fight for the developing world was often conducted through military instruments, which included base agreements and the provision of arms, military intelligence and counter-insurgency training to proxy states and intra-state factions. Nonetheless, such instruments were accompanied frequently by a range of soft security measures, primarily in the form of economic aid and trading ties, and these were just as much the purview of the EC and its member states as they were of the US.[26] Moreover, EC member states' colonial legacies meant that the Community was endowed with a rich vein of established connections with the developing world that the US did not possess.

Herein the EC's external profile and security influence again developed significantly. For instance, the EC's growing economic weight conferred upon it significant powers of economic and financial sanction. Having decided, often within EPC and in line with UN resolutions, to impose sanctions, these could be effected through either national parliaments under Article 224 of the Treaty of Rome or the EC, as a part of trade policy, under Article 113. Such sanctions were applied during the Cold War on a number of occasions, targets including Rhodesia, Iran, Argentina and the USSR.

More positively, as a major influence in the global economy and as a non-state and non-military actor, the EC was able to develop positions that were seen to be distinct from the US. This helped it to develop relationships with neutral and non-aligned nations such as the Nordic countries. Also, because of its economic weight and its member states' traditional global ties, the EC drew numerous nations from across different continents into its orbit and locked them there through a variety of agreements. Indeed, by 1975 it was linked to over 40 per cent of the entire UN membership through association, co-operation or trade agreements[27] and its influence continued to expand rapidly thereafter – such as through the 1983 agreement with the Latin American Andean Community countries of Bolivia, Colombia, Ecuador, Peru and Venezuela.

Significant, too, was that the EC was less ideologically driven than the US – which until 1972, for example, absurdly insisted that Taiwan was China and that the world's most populous country did not officially exist.[28] This allowed the EC to maintain important links with socialist regimes such as Angola and Ethiopia, and even with communist countries such as Tito's Yugoslavia. Furthermore, the EC was politically more acceptable to developing countries than were either the US or Europe's stigmatised and declining imperial powers. As such it served as a mechanism through which its member states sought to control the decolonisation process and to re-bind former dependencies to the West through preferential trade and aid agreements. The EC thus developed a web of bilateral agreements with former colonial countries, such as with India in 1973. In the wake of British accession that same year, the Community also concluded the world-renowned multilateral Lomé Conventions with African, Caribbean and Pacific group countries (ACP). Comprising a combination of non-reciprocal trade concessions, development aid and innovative mechanisms such as STABEX and SYSMIN[29] to protect developing countries' vulnerable export income against market fluctuation, the first of these was concluded in 1975 with forty-six countries. Three further successive conventions were successfully developed with a rapidly expanding membership before finally being replaced in June 2000 by the Cotonou Agreement, a new twenty-year partnership arrangement with seventy-seven ACP states that together represented more than 650 million people.

The EC's role in international security also became increasingly prominent as a consequence of calculations of power being revised in response to technological development and changes in the international system such as deepening economic interdependence, the growing number and importance of non-state actors and the evolution of *détente*. This can be demonstrated in four respects. First technological advances, especially the development of mutual assured destruction (MAD), signalled the end of the drive for Cold War victory through military preponderance. MAD stabilised East–West nuclear relations through mutual vulnerability and the consequent promotion of common interest in preserving system stability – something underscored starkly by the 1962 Cuban missile crisis and partially reflected in the conclusion of the Limited Nuclear Test Ban Treaty in 1963. It also induced a qualitative change in the nature of the Cold War that shifted the emphasis in East–West conflict from military to economic power and potentially broadened the security agenda beyond narrow military issues to include, for example, economic and development factors.[30] This, of course, played to the principal strength of the EC.[31]

Second, by the 1970s the traditional Westphalian state-based international system was being challenged by the emergence of what Keohane and Nye called complex interdependence, in which power became more multidimensional and was dispersed across states, multinational corporations (MNCs), non-governmental organisations (NGOs) and international regulatory regimes.[32] The EC epitomised this growth of powerful non-state actors within a developing 'mixed actor system'[33] and its primarily economic presence again promised to enhance its external security role as WMD and thickening webs of interdependence combined to emphasise the exercise of economic influence within international relations. The latter was particularly well illustrated by American impotence in the highly asymmetric Vietnam War and by the 1973 energy crisis where the Organisation of Petroleum Exporting Countries (OPEC) used oil as a political weapon during the Yom Kippur War.[34]

Third, bipolarity began to break down in the late 1960s/early 1970s as the two superpowers laboured under the enormous burden of maintaining hegemonic leadership and as other centres of power, especially economic centres, developed. Most significant for the EC was the relative decline of the US. Successive American administrations battled balance of payments (BOP) difficulties exacerbated by swollen military budgets, fought a losing campaign in Vietnam and sought forlornly to combat waning confidence in the dollar – something most spectacularly demonstrated in the collapse of the Bretton Woods system in 1971. Concomitantly, American leadership faltered amid transatlantic wrangles, such as over Vietnam and divergent reactions to the 1973 oil crisis, and as the so-called 'imperial presidency' drew to a close in the face of a Vietnam-inspired end to US bipartisan foreign policy consensus and a consequent congressional reassertion.[35] The product was two-fold. Western Europe's regional security agenda slowly began to differentiate itself from that of the US, and the EC found greater scope for, and confidence in, external action.

Fourth, all of these changes induced important shifts in international behaviour that again afforded the EC new opportunities to exert external influence. Foremost of these adjustments was the development of *détente*, due not least to the Nixon administration's recognition of American overcommitment and the rise of communist China, the EC and an economically booming Japan as alternative centres of power within a newly bipolycentric system. Defined by US National Security Assistant Henry Kissinger as the evolution of 'habits of mutual restraint, coexistence, and, ultimately, co-operation',[36] *détente* was symbolised by the conclusion in May 1972 of the Strategic Arms Limitation Talks (SALT) I to limit anti-ballistic missiles and to establish interim agreements to limit offensive strategic missiles. Within this the EC secured a hitherto rare opportunity to assert itself directly in East–West dialogue through the CSCE in 1973. In addition, *détente* – and the reasons underlying its introduction – served to loosen Cold War bonds between the US and Western Europe irrevocably. Technological development, notably inter-continental ballistic missiles, reduced US need of Western Europe as a secure frontline base and, together with MAD, raised European doubts about US nuclear guarantees. The consequent diminished need to maintain tight, cohesive alliances also combined with relative US decline to make American administrations increasingly reluctant to absorb the costs of hegemonic leadership. This led in turn to a more fractious transatlantic security relationship over issues such as offset payments for the stationing of US troops in Europe. Conversely, the EC's rapidly growing size and economic weight gave it the confidence to challenge US leadership and encouraged its member states to pursue policies against American wishes that would have been inconceivable just two decades earlier – such as the FRG's *Ostpolitik*, which by 1973 had brought about treaties between West Germany and Poland, Hungary and the USSR.

The EC and the transatlantic security community in the 1980s

By the 1980s the EC had become a major player in international security. Its most obvious success was in securing Western Europe as a zone of peace and stability. By 1987 the Community had enlarged from six to twelve members and, with the Mediterranean enlargements of the 1980s, had helped consolidate new democracies in Greece, Spain and Portugal. Equally, however, its multiple economic and humanitarian agreements and initiatives had reached out to, and bound to the West, countries as diverse as the European Free Trade Association (EFTA), Lomé and Andean groupings. Moreover, it had steadily complemented its *de facto* international presence as the world's largest trading bloc with an expanding external policy agenda and institutional developments designed to make it a credible and capable international security actor.

Placing the EC within the 1980s transatlantic security community reveals interesting aspects of its development as an international security actor. The most obvious is the shift in the nature of the transatlantic relationship itself. Within thirty years the EC had gone from economic and security supplicant to, at least in some aspects, full and genuine partner. Consider that Europe in the immediate post-war years has been characterised variously as having experienced US hegemony, 'voluntaristic empire', or American 'empire by integration'.[37] By the 1980s landmark books appeared charting and predicting the further decline of American power amid high US interest rates, an overvalued dollar, an annual trade deficit that topped $200 billion in 1985 and a national debt of $1.8 trillion.[38]

More revealing, however, is the variegated nature of the transatlantic security relationship.[39] Unlike the US or even its own member states, the EC's entire development as a security actor was the product of a unique international system that both encouraged integration and then spared and denied it responsibility for hard security issues. Admittedly, the 1980s witnessed sharp transatlantic exchanges about Cruise and Pershing II missiles, about Ronald Reagan's Strategic Defence Initiative (better known as 'Star Wars') and about French-led moves to resurrect the WEU as confidence waned in some European countries about American security guarantees. Nevertheless, American leadership in hard security was never under serious challenge. The USSR provided a focusing clear and present danger, and despite the deterrent of independent British and French nuclear capabilities, Western Europe remained heavily dependent on the US nuclear umbrella. Moreover, the EC's isolation from hard security considerations remained underpinned by the extreme sensitivity of key member states, especially Britain, to any hint of establishing supranational control over armed forces.

Matters were significantly different in the economic and political dimensions of security, the 1980s transatlantic relationship experiencing in these areas an unpredictable combination of close collaboration, competition and conflict. Factors that help account for this include the EC becoming the world's largest trading bloc, the development of EPC and the failure of President Reagan to instil into the so-called Second Cold War the American commitment and leadership that characterised the first. On Argentina's invasion of the Falkland Islands (*Las Islas Malvinas*) on 2 April 1982, America and the EC eventually co-ordinated sufficiently to exert combined pressure on Buenos Aires to withdraw, albeit not without its prior engagement with British military forces. Both condemned Argentina's act of aggression, the EC imposed economic sanctions with surprising speed under Article 113 of the Treaty of Rome and, after an initial ambivalence that infuriated Britain, the US followed suit by suspending arms sales and credit guarantees by the Export-Import Bank and the Commodity Credit Corporation.[40]

In contrast, on the issue of communist Cuba, America and the EC could agree in wanting reform of Castro's regime but adopted competitive approaches to achieving this. The US imposed a total economic embargo to try to force

Castro from power, whilst the EC preferred a policy of engagement and social-isation, including humanitarian aid and allowing European companies to develop trade links with Cuba. In consequence EC and US policies largely counteracted one another to the detriment of their shared security objectives.

On other issues the EC and US disagreed so strongly that they sometimes found themselves in opposing corners. For example, the US was bitterly dis-appointed by the failure of EPC in 1986 to support measures against Libya in retaliation for its alleged terrorist links, even more so when France and Spain even denied their airspace to American aircraft in launching military strikes against selected Libyan targets. Arguably more controversial still, especially given the US tendency to regard Central America as its own sphere of influence, were differences over the civil war in El Salvador and the conflict in Nicaragua between Contras and Sandinistas following the 1979 revolution. The US backed the Contras in Nicaragua and successive repressive governments in El Salvador. The EC, however, provided Nicaragua with considerable food aid and at the 1983 Stuttgart European Council called for a peaceful resolution to conflicts in Central America based on principles of respect for human rights and, poignantly, non-intervention. In September 1984 it also took part in what became known as the San José Process; the US was pointedly absent from this first meeting, which was designed to explore avenues for peaceful settlement of regional conflict.[41]

In addition to issue-specific problems within the economic and political aspects of the transatlantic security relationship, there were more generic difficulties. Negotiations over aspects of economic security in particular were sometimes bruising affairs. This was due in part to relative parity in EC–US economic weight and to the EC having legal competence in external trade. The latter provided for European positions that were often better co-ordinated than within EPC and which were also often quite inflexible on account of the nego-tiating mandate accorded by the member states to the European Commission. Difficulties were also due, however, to the fungibility of trade and economic security issues. For example, what elements of trade should be embargoed to communist countries on grounds that it would bolster their national security at the expense of the West? This had been a repeated source of dispute within NATO's Co-ordinating Committee for Export Controls and it was thus no sur-prise that it spilt over into EC–US relations.

One good example in the early 1980s of the fine line between trade and eco-nomic security is the major spat over sales of oil and gas industry equipment to the USSR and the building of a pipeline that would deliver Siberian gas supplies to Western Europe. The US opposed these on grounds that the transfer of technology and equipment to the USSR would indirectly aid its military effort and its national security. In June 1982 the Reagan administration accordingly levied sanctions against American subsidiaries and licence-holders in Western Europe involved in the pipeline project. The Europeans disagreed with US arguments and were outraged by the unilateral imposition of sanctions. The EC immediately denounced the action as illegal and took measures to compel national companies to fulfil their legally binding contracts. Even British Prime Minister Margaret Thatcher, Reagan's closest and staunchest European ally, 'continuously harangued the President and his advisers about the extraterritorial application of US sanctions'.[42]

Cold War collapse

The EC thus seemed set to continue its incremental and *ad hoc* development as an international security actor. In this capacity it would gradually exercise increasing influence whilst retaining the characteristics of a civilian power, being limited in physical extent to the western half of a divided but stable Europe, and nestling safely within the North Atlantic security community. However, suddenly and largely unexpectedly, the Soviet Union imploded and the Eastern bloc collapsed. Debate continues about the extent to which the consequent end of the Cold War did or did not transform the world order,[43] but between 1989 and 1991 the security assumptions, predominant concerns and potentially the institutions of four decades were swept away. The implications of this dramatic transformation for the EC as an international security actor were far-reaching, complex and even potentially contradictory – such as simultaneous processes of fragmentation and integration in Europe.

At the broadest level, the end of Cold War overlay accelerated the trend towards a more expansive security agenda and a re-conceptualisation both of security and of the international system. Ideas for new sources of global conflict were quickly proffered, notably Huntington's hypothesis that 'in this new world . . . [t]he great divisions among humankind and the dominating source of conflict will be cultural'.[44] What, too, would the relationship be between security and national sovereignty? How, for example, should resurgent ethno-nationalist violence be dealt with and what implications did its predominantly intra-state character hold for concepts of sovereignty and international law? Moreover, a vibrant and ongoing debate developed about what constituted a security issue in the post-Cold War era, some fearing that the 'indiscriminate broadening and widening of the concept of security will inevitably rob it of any analytical utility'.[45]

The task nevertheless remained of arriving at agreed boundaries between security and non-security issues, especially as institutions such as NATO and the EC began to use security in increasingly expansive and non-traditional ways. For example, in its 1991 New Strategic Concept NATO concluded that 'security and stability have political, economic, social, and environmental elements as well as the indispensable defence dimension. Managing the diversity of challenges facing the Alliance requires a broad approach to security'.[46] This problem had added layers of complexity resulting from ongoing developments in international relations. For a start, processes of globalisation had progressively blurred the boundaries of foreign and domestic policy. Hence

US President Clinton declared in his first inaugural speech on 20 January 1993 that '[t]here is no longer division between what is foreign and what is domestic – the world economy, the world environment, the world AIDS crisis, the world arms race – they affect us all'.[47] In addition, EC integration, such as the 1987 SEA, had had the effect of transferring traditionally domestic law and order concerns such as immigration to the international level, where they were securitised within the broader post-Cold War agenda.[48] Indeed, this reflected broader pressures to internationalise security issues as states found their unilateral capabilities waning in the face of technological development and ever-deepening interdependence.

Furthermore the end of the Cold War signified, to some scholars at least, the end of the Westphalian system, thus challenging traditional state-centric security models and raising new questions about the referent of, and conditions for, security.[49] What was it that was being secured: a state, a nation, a society, a civilisation, or something else? What constituted the principal threat: traditional state rivalries, the proliferation of WMD, ozone layer depletion, international terrorism, the erosion of societal security? And what conditions would provide for security: protection against an internal or external enemy, combating embedded socio-economic inequalities, promoting democratic governance, environmental sustainability?

In and of itself this conceptual and indeterminate broadening of security had potentially profound implications for the EC as an international security actor, increasing both its own opportunities and expectations of it. However, the end of the Cold War also raised a raft of immediate questions about European security in particular. For a start, what would become of Europe's established security institutions? The WEU, Council of Europe, CSCE, NATO and even the EC itself were all Cold War creations. Now that the Cold War was over would, or could, these institutions survive in the absence of the cohering force afforded them by the common threat of the USSR? If they did survive, how would they adapt and what would their interrelationships be? NATO in particular, as a defence alliance created specifically to combat the Soviet military threat, had seemingly lost its *raison d'être*. And in turn this raised disturbing questions about both the degree to which the US would choose to remain embroiled in European security and its willingness to continue to absorb the costs of providing security leadership, especially in its 'hard' aspects. In this respect history certainly provided no comfort in view of US inter-war isolationism and its rapid demobilisation in the immediate aftermath of WW2.[50]

The political and geo-strategic topography of Europe was also radically redrawn by the collapse of the Cold War. Of foremost importance in the changes was the renewed issue of Germany's future. Should it remain divided in two separate states? For some, certainly, the alternative prospect of a reunified Germany sitting at the heart of a new Europe was too much to bear.[51] It would potentially be increasingly dominant in the EC, be best placed to capitalise on new opportunities opening up to the east and be less restrained on account of Russia's unusually truncated condition. This was obviously deeply perturbing to France,[52] but among the most visceral expressions of opposition to a reunified Germany were the interview given to *The Spectator* in July 1990 by British Secretary of State for Industry Nicholas Ridley, and Margaret Thatcher's leaked discussion that same month on the 'German Question'.[53] Ultimately, however, any potential opposition was futile as the popular breaching of the Berlin Wall on 9 November 1989 combined with developments elsewhere in Eastern Europe to give reunification an unstoppable momentum. Moreover, President Bush welcomed Chancellor Kohl in 1989 as a 'partner in leadership' of a 'new world order' and never wavered from the difficult diplomatic task of facilitating Germany's reunification in 1990. The consequent questions once more revolved around how to manage Germany's *Mittellage*?

Beyond Germany lay a host of other security challenges and opportunities. The removal of Cold War overlay dissipated the imperative to cohere, for which some states, notably Yugoslavia, paid the ultimate price of dismemberment as pre-Cold War behavioural patterns and tensions re-emerged. Elsewhere a raft of newly liberated states faced economic dislocation and uncertain political futures in the general absence of traditions of liberal democracy, thus potentially contributing, too, to further regional insecurity. Then there was the question of what to do about the strategically homeless – states not traditionally in the Western camp but now no longer anchored within Russia's vastly reduced sphere of influence? Even in the old Western Europe there developed a diffusion of strategic focus and questions about the future orientations of Cold War neutrals such as Austria and Sweden. Furthermore, Cold War collapse and talk of a new world order did not mean that the EC would be spared considerations of what to do in the event of conflict – which the 1990/91 Gulf War quickly demonstrated. In fact, small-scale conflicts were actually more likely as the end of East–West balance reduced the impact of nuclear deterrence and transformed conflict scenarios from low risk but high intensity to high risk but low intensity.

All of this had, of course, further spill-over implications that reflected the wider security agenda. What should be done in the event of potentially large migratory flows as a consequence of regional instability/conflict and the attraction of the West to economic refugees? How should organised cross-border crime be tackled, particularly in the context of a post-Cold War surfeit of cheap and readily accessible weapons from the former Eastern bloc? What measures should be developed to prevent the smuggling of nuclear materials and technical knowledge to either non-nuclear states or terrorist groups? In addition how, given severe political and economic dislocation and decades of systematic neglect, was environmental degradation within the former Eastern bloc to be addressed? Particularly pressing in light of the 1986 Chernobyl disaster, which produced nuclear fallout the equivalent of ten Hiroshima bombs, were measures to assist crisis-ridden Russia decommission dangerous power-plants and its decaying strategic arsenal.

Then, of course, there were innumerable security problems that stretched beyond the redrawn borders of Europe. Some of these were new. How would remaining communist states react and how should they be dealt with? Most important within this was the future position of China, as a nuclear power and a permanent member of the UN Security Council; and how should the West deal with it, a question made pressing by the brutal and very public violation of human rights in the Tiananmen Square massacre on 4 June 1989? Many issues, however, had simply been subsumed beneath Cold War overlay and now re-emerged, sometimes with a vengeance. In the Middle East there was the ongoing Palestinian issue, rising Islamic fundamentalism and the emergence of so-called rogue states – such as Saddam Hussain's Iraq. In Africa there was widespread famine and disease and ongoing issues of apartheid in South Africa, genocide in Rwanda and Burundi, and continuing civil wars, such as in Mozambique, Chad and Liberia. Problems in Asia included the Taiwan Straits, relations with North Korea, instability in countries such as Indonesia and renewed tension between Pakistan and India, particularly over Kashmir. And in the western hemisphere civil war continued in countries such as El Salvador and Guatemala, Haiti's fragile democracy was overturned just seven months after Jean-Bertrand Aristide's election in December 1990, and the US, in accord with the 1823 Monroe Doctrine and the 1904 Roosevelt Corollary, intervened in Panama in 1989 to depose General Noriega. Additionally there was the old transatlantic chestnut of Fidel Castro's regime, there being seemingly even less reason for the US to continue its total blockade of tiny Cuba.

Conclusion

The development of the EC as an international security actor was a consequence of a complex interplay of factors including external expectation, internal reactions to external opportunities and pressures, member state national interests, and intense competition for policy competence both between EC institutions and between the institutions and the member states. The EC's influence stemmed foremost from its economic weight, which was itself accorded significantly increased importance as a consequence of deepening interdependence, recalculations of power and the development of a mixed actor system over which the Cold War held progressively less sway. Of particular importance was the zone of peace and stability that it created within Western Europe. However, the EC's extensive links with Africa, Asia, the Middle East and the western hemisphere, though primarily economic and humanitarian in nature, also performed invaluable security functions in tying developing countries to the West, especially at a time of decolonisation and suspicion about US policies. Moreover, as economic integration deepened and widened, pressure developed for greater foreign and security policy co-ordination and conditions evolved that enabled the Commission to expand EC competence into areas such as external environmental policy.

There is no doubt that by 1989 the EC had become an important international security actor, albeit that its overall influence differed from region to region and from issue to issue. A new and unexpected phase of development was then laid open by the collapse of communism in Eastern Europe. The EC faced critical new questions about where it fitted into the new international security system and whether it was sufficiently equipped to deal with the new challenges, to seize the new opportunities and to meet significantly increased expectations of it. How, for example, would the EC's relationships evolve not only with states but also with the growing number of NGOs and international regimes in areas as diverse as environmental issues and nuclear arms control? In part the answers to these questions would be decided by external expectations of the EC and willingness to recognise it as an independent international actor. They would depend, too, on the ongoing internal battle for competence in external affairs and the ability of EC institutions to develop and implement policies in the radically changed environment. Perhaps most of all, though, they would depend on the political will of EC member states, especially their willingness or otherwise to move beyond declaratory diplomacy and to address the problems posed by the artificial divide of international security functions into EC and non-EC competencies.

Notes

1 Dobson, A.P. (2002) *US Economic Statecraft for Survival 1933–1991*, London: Routledge; Gardner, R.N. (1980) *Sterling–Dollar Diplomacy in the Current Perspective*, New York: Columbia University Press; Woods, R.B. (1990) *A Changing of the Guard: Anglo-American Relations 1941–46*, Chapel Hill: University of North Carolina Press.

2 Views of the special relationship differ, with some contesting the justification of applying this appellation to Anglo-American relations. See, amongst others, Marsh, S. (2003) *Anglo-American Relations and Cold War Oil*, Basingstoke: Palgrave; Dobson, A.P. (1995) *Anglo-American Relations in the Twentieth Century: Of Friendship, Conflict and the Rise and Decline of Superpowers*, London: Routledge; Watt, D.C. (1984) *Succeeding John Bull: America in Britain's Place*, Cambridge: Cambridge University Press; Leuchtenburg, W.E. et al. (1979) *Britain and the United States: Four Views to Mark the Silver Jubilee*, London: Heinemann; Danchev, A. (1997) 'On Friendship: Anglo-America at the Fin de Siècle' *International Affairs* 73 pp. 247–59.

3 By 1945 Britain's exports were 30 per cent of the 1939 total, import prices had risen 50 per cent, and there were acute shortages of raw materials and industrial equipment. Its wartime effort had required liquidation of £1,118,000 of overseas assets, incurred it huge debts (including £2,143 million to the sterling area alone), and more than halved its gold and dollar reserves. For more details see Cairncross, A. (1985) *Years of Economic Recovery: British Economic Policy 1945–51*, London: Methuen, p. 7. British economic dependency was reflected in the acrimonious 1946

American loan. For details see Strange, S. (1971) *Sterling and British Policy: A Political Study of an International Currency in Decline*, London: Oxford University Press, chapter 8; Burnham, P. (1992) 'Re-evaluating the Washington Loan Agreement: A Revisionist View of the Limits of Postwar American Power' *Review of International Studies* 18 pp. 241–59.

4 Germany's central position in Europe has traditionally made it a source of instability, be it through weakness which has invited great power rivalry over German lands since medieval times, or through strength following the assertion of Prussian military power.

5 MccGwire, M. (1994) 'National Security and Soviet Foreign Policy' in *Origins of the Cold War*, Leffler, M.P. and Painter, D.S. (eds), London: Routledge, pp. 63–8.

6 For the text of the Long Telegram see Kennan, G. (1968) *Memoirs 1925–50*, London: Hutchinson, Appendix C, pp. 547–59.

7 Traditional interpretations emphasised a US response to a Soviet threat. Revisionists, though, pointed variously to factors such as US economic greed and America's own expansionist tradition. From the 1970s onwards a host of other explanations were advanced that have been characterised as post-revisionist, corporatist, neorealist or world systems. Further revisions are currently under way as a consequence of new material becoming available from former Soviet archives. For an insight into this interpretative debate see Feis, H. (1970) *From Trust to Terror, 1945–50*, New York: W.W. Norton; Appleman Williams, W. (1972) *The Tragedy of American Diplomacy* 2nd edn, New York: Dell Publishing; Yergin, D. (1977) *Shattered Peace: The Origins of the Cold War and the National Security State*, Boston: Houghton Mifflin; Gaddis, J.L. (1983) 'The Emerging Post-Revisionist Thesis on the Origins of the Cold War' *Diplomatic History* 7 pp. 171–90; Leffler, M.P. (1984) 'The American Conception of National Security and the Beginnings of the Cold War, 1945–48' *American Historical Review* 89 pp. 346–81; Gaddis, J.L. (1997) *We Now Know: Rethinking Cold War History*, Oxford: Clarendon Press.

8 Leffler, 'The American Conception of National Security', p. 364.

9 For an overview of containment see Dobson, A.P. and Marsh, S. (2001) *US Foreign Policy Since 1945*, London: Routledge, pp. 18–45. For a number of interpretations of NSC–68 see May, E.R. (ed.) (1993) *American Cold War Strategy: Interpreting NSC 68*, New York: Bedford Books. For details of containment see especially Leffler, M.P. (1972) *A Preponderance of Power: National Security, the Truman Administration, and the Cold War*, Stanford: Stanford University Press; Yergin, *Shattered Peace*; Gaddis, J.L. (1982) *Strategies of Containment: A Critical Appraisal of Postwar American National Security Policy*, New York: Oxford University Press.

10 Hogan, M. (1987) *The Marshall Plan: America, Britain and the Reconstruction of Western Europe, 1947–52*, Cambridge: Cambridge University Press, p. 52.

11 There are a number of good overviews of the development of general post-war European integration. These include McAllister, R. (1997) *From EC to EU: An Historical and Political Survey*, London: Routledge; Dedman, M. (1996) *The Origins and Development of the European Union 1945–95*, London: Routledge.

12 See Hogan, *The Marshall Plan*; Wexler, I. (1983) *The Marshall Plan Revisited: The European Recovery Program in Economic Perspective*, Westport, Conn.: Greenwood; Mee, C.L. (1984) *The Marshall Plan: The Launching of Pax Americana*, New York: Simon and Schuster.

13 For details of the Berlin crisis see Shlaim, A. (1983) *The United States and the Berlin Blockade, 1948–1949: A Study in Crisis Decision-Making*, London: University of California Press; Morris, E. (1983) *Blockade: Berlin and the Cold War*, London: Hamilton.

14 Overlay refers to a condition whereby local patterns of security virtually cease to exist as a consequence of great power rivalry. See Buzan, B. et al. (1990) *The European Security Order Recast*, University of Copenhagen: Pinter Publishers, pp. 15–16.

15 Milward, A. (1992) *The European Rescue of the Nation State*, Berkeley: University of California Press, p. 282.

16 For the Germany-integration link see Wurm, C. (ed.) (1995) *Western Europe and Germany: The Beginnings of European Integration 1945–1960*, Oxford: Berg.

17 *Foreign Relations of the United States* 1952–54, vol. 6, part one, Secretary for Defense (Lovett) to Supreme Allied Commander Europe (Eisenhower), 24 January 1952, pp. 859–61.

18 EDC signatories were Germany, the Benelux countries, Italy and France. The former four ratified the EDC and Italy was expected to. For the EDC see especially Fursdon, E. (1980) *The European Defence Community: A History*, London: Macmillan. For the formation and development of the WEU see Rees, G.W. (1998) *The Western European Union at the Crossroads: Between Trans-Atlantic Solidarity and European Integration*, London: Westview Press; Dockrill, S. (1991) *Britain's Policy for West German Rearmament 1950–55*, Cambridge: Cambridge University Press.

19 For the chicken war see Talbot, R.B. (1978) *The Chicken War*, Ames: Iowa State University.

20 Taylor, T. (1984) *European Defence Cooperation*, Chatham House Papers **24**, London: Routledge, p. 18.

21 http://www.eurotreaties.com/rometreaty.pdf.

22 For the early development of ideas of security communities see Deutsch, K. et al. (1957) *Political Community and the North Atlantic Area*, Princeton: Princeton University Press.

23 For early British attitudes to integration and subsequent approach to the EC/EU see George, S. (1998) *An Awkward Partner: Britain in the European Community*, Oxford: Oxford University Press; Lord, C. (1996) *Absent at the Creation: Britain and the Formation of the European Community, 1950–52*, Aldershot: Dartmouth; Young, J. (2000) *Britain and European Unity 1945–1999*, Basingstoke: Macmillan.

24 European Communities (1987) *Treaties Establishing the European Communities*, Luxembourg: Office of Official Publications. For more on the development of EPC see Nuttall, S. (1992) *European Political Co-operation*, Oxford: Clarendon Press; Regelsberger, E., Wessels, W. and de Schoutheete de Tervarent, P. (eds) (1997) *Foreign Policy of the European Union: From EPC to CFSP and Beyond*, London: Lynne Rienner Publishers.

25 Formal agreement about division was reached in September 1971 when the USSR and the West acknowledged the division of Berlin, with the Western sector linked to, but constitutionally separate from, West Germany. Ausland, J.C. (1996)

Kennedy, Khrushchev, and the Berlin–Cuba Crisis, 1961–64, Oslo: Scandanavia; Gearson, J.S. (1998) *Harold Macmillan and the Berlin Wall Crisis 1958–1962: The Limits of Interest and Force*, Basingstoke: Macmillan; Schick, J.M. (1971) *The Berlin Crisis, 1958–1962*, Philadelphia: University of Philadelphia Press.

26 Examples of initiatives developed under Kennedy include the Alliance for Progress, the Peace Corps, which by 1963 had dispatched 9,000 volunteers to over forty countries, and the Food for Peace project, which used American agricultural surpluses to aid the developing world.

27 Piening, C. (1997) *Global Europe: The European Union in World Affairs*, London: Lynne Rienner Publishers, p. 4.

28 For the change in US policy toward China see Kim, I.J. (1987) *The Strategic Triangle: China, the United States and the Soviet Union*, New York: Paragon House; Harding, H. (1992) *A Fragile Relationship: The United States and China Since 1972*, Washington D.C.: Brookings Institute.

29 STABEX: System for the Stabilisation of Export Earnings from Products. SYSMIN: System for the Stabilisation of Export Earnings from Minerals.

30 Authors are thus right to suggest that the Cold War 'narrowed and militarized thinking about security, such that security had come to be regarded predominantly as about military threats to the interests of states'. However, this characterisation is itself overly rigid because the 1960s and 1970s saw military tools of security downgraded in relative terms and the security agenda slowly expanded. Indeed, it is no coincidence that by the early 1980s academics were challenging the traditional Cold War definition of the security agenda. Clark, I. (2001) *The Post-Cold War Order: The Spoils of Peace*, Oxford: Oxford University Press, p. 198; Buzan, B. (1983) *People, States and Fear*, London: Wheatsheaf Books; Ullman, R. (1983) 'Redefining Security' *International Organization* 8 pp. 129–53.

31 For example, in 1972 Duchêne was already arguing that the EC's civilian power status did not prohibit it playing an increasingly important part in international relations. Duchêne, F. (1972) 'Europe's Role in World Peace' in *Europe Tomorrow: Sixteen Europeans Look Ahead*, Mayne, R. (ed.), London: Fontana, pp. 32–47.

32 Keohane, R.O. and Nye, J.S. (eds) (1973) *Transnational Relations and World Politics*, Cambridge, Mass.: Harvard University Press; Keohane, R.O. and Nye, J.S. (1988) 'Complex Interdependence, Transnational Relations and Realism: Alternative Perspectives on World Politics' in *The Global Agenda*, Kegley Jr., C.W. and Wittkopf, E.R. (eds), New York: Random House, 2nd edn, pp. 257–71.

33 Young, O.R. (1972) 'The Actors in World Politics' in *The Analysis of International Politics*, Rosenau, J.N., East, M.A. and Davies, V. (eds), New York: Free Press, pp. 125–44.

34 At the time the EC drew approximately 63 per cent of its energy needs from Middle Eastern oil. Dinan, D. (1999) *Ever Closer Union?*, Basingstoke: Macmillan, 2nd edn, p. 70.

35 The imperial presidency encapsulated the progressive post-WW2 concentration of power in the hands of US presidents and their inner circles, on grounds of national security, at the expense of the checks and balances on the executive traditionally ensured by Congress. See especially Schlesinger Jr., A. (1974) *The Imperial Presidency*, New York: Popular Library.

36 Kissinger, H. (1977) *American Foreign Policy*, New York: W.W. Norton, p. 305. For more about Kissinger's *realpolitik* approach and the policy of *détente* see Garthoff, R. (1994) *Détente and Confrontation: American–Soviet Relations from Nixon to Reagan*, Washington D.C.: Brookings Institute; Isaacson, W. (1992) *Kissinger: A Biography*, New York: Simon and Schuster.

37 Keohane, R.O. (1997) *After Hegemony: Cooperation and Discord in the World Political Economy*, Princeton: Princeton University Press; Lundestad, G. (1997) *Empire by Integration: The United States and European Integration 1945–1997*, Oxford: Oxford University Press.

38 Kennedy, P. (1988) *The Rise and Fall of the Great Powers*, London: Unwin Hyman; Calleo, D.P. (1987) *Beyond American Hegemony*, New York: Basic Books. Figures from Dobson and Marsh, *US Foreign Policy since 1945*, p. 125.

39 Texts published during the 1980s bear testament to the EC's relative rise in trans-atlantic relations: Rubenstein, R.L. (ed.) (1987) *The Dissolving Alliance: The United States and the Future of Europe*, New York: Paragon House; Joffe, J. (1987) *The Limited Partnership: Europe, the United States, and the Burdens of Alliance*, Cambridge, Mass.: Ballinger; Smith, M. (1984) *Western Europe and the United States: The Uncertain Alliance*, London: Allen and Unwin; Goldstein, W. (ed.) (1986) *Reagan's Leadership and the Atlantic Alliance: Views From Europe and America*, London: Pergammon-Brassey.

40 It should be noted that the EC embargo did not survive the crisis intact. For details see Edwards, G. (1984) 'Europe and the Falkland Island Crisis 1982' *Journal of Common Market Studies* 22 (4) pp. 295–313.

41 For further details see Smith, H. (1995) *European Union Foreign Policy and Central America*, Basingstoke: Macmillan.

42 Dobson, *US Economic Statecraft for Survival 1933–1991*, p. 267. For further details of the pipeline crisis see Blinken, A.J. (1987) *Ally Versus Ally: America, Europe and the Siberian Pipeline Crisis*, New York: Praeger; Thatcher, M. (1993) *The Downing Street Years*, London: Harper Collins, pp. 253–56.

43 For some, such as Waltz and Mearsheimer, the end of bipolarity meant simply a restructuring of power relationships within a continuing framework of states operating in an anarchical international system. Others disagreed. Some emphasised the relative decline of the state in the face of globalisation and the rise of new international actors such as the EU, which Ruggie describes as perhaps 'the first truly postmodern international political form'. Some even hailed the end of the Cold War as marking the 'end of history', with the triumph of cosmopolitan or universal values. Waltz, K.N. (2000) 'Structural Realism after the Cold War' *International Security* 25 (1) pp. 5–41; Waltz, K.N. (1993) 'The Emerging Structure of International Politics' *International Security* 18 (2) pp. 44–79; Mearsheimer, J. (1990) 'Back to the Future: Instability in Europe after the Cold War' *International Security* 15 (3) pp. 5–57; Ruggie, J. (1993) 'Territorality and Beyond: Problematizing Modernity in International Relations' *International Organization* 47 (1) pp. 139–74; Fukuyama, F. (1992) *The End of History and the Last Man*, London: Hamish Hamilton.

44 Huntington, S.P. (1993) 'The Clash of Civilizations' *Foreign Affairs* 72 (3) p. 12.

45 Hyde-Price, A. (2002) ' "Beware the Jabberwock!": Security Studies in the Twenty-First Century' in *Europe's New Security Challenges*, Gärtner, H., Hyde-Price, A.

and Reiter E. (eds), London: Lynne Rienner Publishers, p. 35. For different positions in the debate on post-Cold War security see, amongst others, Alder, E. and Barnett, M. (1998) 'Security Communities in Theoretical Perspective' in *Security Communities*, Alder, E. and Barnett, M. (eds), Cambridge: Cambridge University Press; Baldwin, D. (1997) 'The Concept of Security' *Review of International Studies* **23** pp. 5–26; Buzan, B. (1997) 'Security after the Cold War' *Cooperation and Conflict* **32** (1) pp. 5–28; Clarke, M. (ed.) (1995) *New Perspectives in Security*, London: Brassey's for the Centre for Defence Studies; Freedman, L. (1998) 'International Security: Changing Targets' *Foreign Policy* **110** pp. 48–63; Waever, O. et al. (1993) *Identity, Migration, and the New Security Agenda in Europe*, London: Pinter.

46 NATO, 'New Strategic Concept', http://www.nato.int/docu/comm/49-95/ c911107a.htm. For the EU see, for example, the final report of Working Group VIII – Defence: 'The concept of security is very broad, by nature indivisible, and one that goes beyond the pure military aspects covering not only the security of States but also the security of citizens'. CONV 461/02, 16 December 2002, p. 3.

47 President Clinton, first inaugural speech, 20 January 1993, http://www.australianpolitics.com/usa/clinton/speeches/inaug93.shtml.

48 For example, within SEA provisions to establish the Single European Market (SEM) the so-called four freedoms were given legal force – free movement of goods, services, capital and labour. Member states thus began to lose control at the national level over the movement of people between states.

49 Kegley, C.W. and Raymond, G.A. (2002) *Exorcising the Ghost of Westphalia: Building World Order in the New Millennium*, Upper Saddle River, N.J.: Prentice-Hall; Lyons, G.M. and Mastanduno, M. (eds) (1995) *Beyond Westphalia? State Sovereignty and International Intervention*, Baltimore: Johns Hopkins University Press.

50 In 1945 the US had 11.8 million men under arms. By 1947 it had just 1.6 million. The extent of this demobilisation even concerned American Secretary of Defence James Forrestal. Millis, W. (ed.) (1952) *The Forrestal Diaries: The Inner History of the Cold War*, London: Cassell, p. 213.

51 It should be noted that there is disagreement whether the events of 1990 should be called reunification or unification. See Roberts, G.K. (1994) 'Review Article: German Reunification' *West European Politics* **17** p. 207, note 1.

52 For analyses of how the French reviewed their security environment in 1990/91 see Gordon, P. (1993) *A Certain Idea of France: French Security Policy and the Gaullist Legacy*, Princeton: Princeton University Press, chapter 7; Yost, D. (1990/91) 'France in the New Europe' *Foreign Affairs* **69** pp. 107–28.

53 For Ridley's defence of his position see Ridley, N. (1991) *My Style of Government: The Thatcher Government*, London: Hutchinson, pp. 223–6. For the text of Thatcher's discussion see Charles Powell's leaked Chequers memorandum in James, H.J. and Stone, M. (eds) (1992) *When the Wall Came Down: Reactions to German Unification*, New York: Routledge, pp. 233–9. Thatcher also noted her desire to 'curb German power'. Thatcher, *The Downing Street Years*, p. 760.

The European Community's rise to economic might:

from regional free-trade arrangement to global economic power?

The European Economic Community had two overarching aims from the onset: to create a common market and, more generally, to move towards 'ever closer union'.[1] Owing to the particular circumstances of the time, the political ambitions for integration were pursued primarily by way of economic integration. The latest and most visible development of such economic integration has been the creation and implementation of a common currency: the euro – since 2002 legal tender in twelve of the currently fifteen EU member states.

This chapter examines the development of what is now the EU as an economic power, and places this within the context of the global economy. On the one hand, economic integration is – in practical terms – a largely inward-looking affair. On the other hand, no such development takes place in a vacuum. European economic integration has consequently been partially shaped by the outside world and has itself exerted considerable external influence. With these considerations in mind, it is useful to begin with a historical overview of how the EU evolved first and foremost as an economic entity and then proceed to assess the international framework in which it developed. Finally, the 'internal' and the 'international' are linked in order to develop a general picture from which to address in later chapters the Union's role as an international economic actor.

Economic integration – a largely internal affair?

As one of the original goals of the EU was to create a common market, it is worth establishing at the onset what this is and how it fits into the progressive development of economic integration. Economic integration theory distinguishes four stages in the movement towards full economic integration: the agreement to set up a free trade area (FTA), the move towards a customs union (CU), the establishment of a common market and the eventual creation of full economic union. Each step has certain internal and external effects. The starting point is that there are a number of individual, fully sovereign countries, none of which practise totally free trade. In the absence of free trade there must be so-called trade barriers, which traditionally took the form of tariffs but that more recently comprise also non-tariff barriers (NTBs). These range from quantitative restrictions (quotas) to measures that are perhaps not primarily implemented to hinder trade but still have such an effect, such as certain health and safety standards. In very general terms, a FTA is based on an agreement amongst at least two countries to abolish trade barriers for goods between one another but to maintain their individual trade regimes *vis-à-vis* third countries. The effects of such an arrangement are trade creation and trade diversion. The former refers to a development inside the FTA, the latter affects trading links with the rest of the world, and therewith represents an external effect.

Internally the abolition of trade barriers may result in a product being cheaper to buy in another FTA country than to produce it domestically. This way trade is created, perhaps even leading to a more sustained specialisation in the production of the respective good in the country that can produce it more advantageously. It may, however, also be the case that a product formerly bought from a country still outside the FTA has now become cheaper to purchase from a partner inside, since a relatively high tariff, for instance, has been abolished as a result of the FTA agreement. In this scenario, trade is liable to be diverted to within the FTA at the expense of a third country.

The formation of a FTA brings with it a number of economic benefits for the member countries without reducing significantly their scope for political manoeuvre. Such a step is thus usually judged to be politically uncontroversial by the participating countries, if not by those outside the FTA.[2] This political assessment changes if/when countries decide to take a further step towards deeper economic integration by creating a customs union. The main difference between a customs union and a FTA is that the former requires a common external tariff *vis-à-vis* third countries. Economically, this means another resetting of trade conditions between members and non-members, which may well sponsor political difficulties too. Within the CU the main political issue is that a common external trade policy and an agreement on how to share revenues raised from the CET are required. What the creation of a CU also means is the beginning of positive political integration, since it requires common policies and therewith fora in which respective decisions can be taken.[3]

The third theoretical step within economic integration is the creation of a common market, which is what the EEC set out to become at its inception. The term common market is largely self-explanatory. Rather than merely trading with one another, participating states decide literally to merge their national markets into one. As is the case with any national market, this requires not only goods to be exchanged without hindrance but also that capital can flow, services be offered and people be allowed to move and settle freely across national borders within the territory of the common market. To achieve all of this, mutually accepted rules and regulations have to be established for the entire market. The task at hand is to remove not only tariffs, quotas and other quite obvious obstacles to the creation of the common market, such as border and capital controls, but also all those not-so-visible NTBs that distort markets. This requires mutual recognition of, for instance, vocational and academic qualifications, product specifications, rules on state subsidies, and the like.

The effect that the creation of a common market has on third countries is that services, labour and capital are likely to be re-directed in a similar fashion to the way that trade was diverted as a result of the creation of a FTA. This means that some countries outside the common market may lose out to another member state because intra-common market deals have become easier and/or more profitable. What the creation of a common market should not lead to, at least in theory, is additional barriers being erected to make market access even more difficult for third countries. Were this to be the case, then the next and final step towards full economic integration would have been taken: the initiation of economic union. The exact distinction between a common market and economic union is not always clear. However, following Tinbergen's distinction between negative and positive integration,[4] a common market can be seen to result from the removal of all the barriers and obstacles that prevent it from fully functioning. An economic union, though, is identified by common rules and regulations, such as a common monetary policy and/or common fiscal policies, or perhaps even by the existence of shared institutions – in other words by positively pushing the integration process ahead.[5]

Similar to the effects that the CET has on countries outside a customs union, common provisions on how easily services, capital and labour can be transferred in and out of the economic union make it either an open or a protectionist entity. Whether, or rather to what extent, this matters to the rest of the world depends on the size of the economic union. If two small countries decide to create an economic union, this will naturally still have repercussions for third countries, but they can safely be said to be of minor significance. The external repercussions are obviously magnified if perhaps six, nine, twelve, or twenty-five countries combine their economies, especially if some of the member states are amongst the world's largest and/or strongest economies. In other words, the creation of an economic union can – potentially – bring with it power, might and influence on an international scale. How far this potential is realised depends on the type of economic union. Those at the weaker end of the spectrum are characterised by a comparatively loose arrangement between participating countries to agree on common rules as and when the need arises. The more powerful economic unions tend to have a totally integrated system with their own institutions, possibly their own government. And how well potential power is translated into operational influence with the rest of the world depends heavily on the ability to speak 'with one voice'.

This is exactly one of the points that this book seeks to make in respect of the EU. It is widely assumed that the Union is a powerful international economic actor. Yet the situation is more complex than this, for the Community is not as powerful an economic actor as it could be. Admittedly, its sheer size and status as the world's largest economic entity give it a strong international presence. But this is achieved without any direct action required by the EU and could, in accordance with Tinbergen's thinking, be regarded as its 'negative' role. For it to fulfil its potential as an international economic force, the EU would have to be able to shape positively the international economic environment. In other words, it would have to be a strong, i.e. highly integrated, economic union. Is this the case? A look at the actual history of European economic integration helps to answer this question.

The European Communities clearly did not follow the comparatively straight path set out by economic integration theory. The first of the three European Communities was the ECSC, established in 1952 with the principal aim of linking the FRG closer to France.[6] This was done by pooling those industries then most closely linked to warfare, namely coal, steel, iron ore, scrap metal, and putting them under the supervision of a supranational high authority. With an eventual membership of France, FRG, Italy and the Benelux countries, the ECSC effectively created a common market in the above fields of activity. This common market, however, already possessed features that theory would link to economic unions, such as positive common rules and regulations and the high authority that had a comparatively strong position. Concomitantly, since an economic union is by definition all encompassing, the talk was and is of a common market in the products falling under the mandate of the Treaty of Paris that set up the ECSC.

For six years the six original members of the ECSC thus collaborated quite intensely in certain, limited fields of the economy, whilst remaining competitors, and thus totally independent from one another, in the rest. This changed when the same countries set up the EEC and Euratom in 1958. The latter created another sectoral common market, this time in the field of atomic energy, whilst the former contained a commitment for the creation of a Common Agricultural Policy and established for all other goods a FTA with the eventual aim of creating a general common market and therewith closer political integration.[7] The CAP came into existence in 1962 and created yet another sectoral common market, which was (and largely still is) of a particular kind.

Heavily influenced by the post-WW2 experience of food shortages and production and supply problems, the EEC resolved upon a rather interventionist approach for the CAP. Prices were fixed artificially in order to achieve self-sufficiency, stable prices for consumers and stable incomes for those employed in the farming sector. This way seasonal or multi-annual price fluctuations were avoided for both producers and consumers. Prices were set high enough to entice farmers to produce their goods, yet low enough for consumers to afford respective products. The most controversial aspect of the whole construction transpired to be the guarantee by the EEC to pay farmers the same price for any quantity produced, which eventually led to enormous overcapacities, widely known as milk and wine lakes, and butter and beef mountains. Naturally, this led to protests within the EEC, mainly by consumer groups who felt that people were charged twice for the CAP since they paid higher-than-world prices for their food and had also to subsidise storage and disposal measures in their function as taxpayers. The artificial price system also had an enormous effect on countries outside the EEC. Farmers from third countries who could produce at prices below the reference price of the Community were either prevented from entering the EEC market altogether or, if allowed to sell their products, could only do so at a price artificially inflated by a so-called 'variable levy' that was designed not to fall below the reference price. An even worse potential external effect was that under the CAP export subsidies were to be paid to bridge the gap between high Community prices and low world prices for internal producers. In practical terms this meant that EEC producers could even achieve the guaranteed price for selling their products outside the Community. For some producers in non-EEC countries this had potentially devastating consequences, since world prices were kept artificially lower than they would have realistically had to be. In other words, the EEC's CAP had a market-distorting effect outside its own borders[8] and has ever since been the source of numerous international controversies for the EC/EU.

Returning to the evolution of the European Communities (ECs) towards an economic union, the next significant step was taken in 1968, when – a year ahead of schedule – the EEC turned from a general FTA into a customs union. This, of course, necessitated agreement on CETs for all kinds of products and prompted the Community to adopt a common external trade policy, which came into force in 1970 under the name of the Common Commercial Policy (CCP – see Chapter Three for more details). The late 1960s were a time of great momentum and initiative. Next to the CCP, a new system to finance the Communities was introduced[9] and ambitious plans to transform the EEC into an economic and monetary union (EMU) were commissioned. In 1970 the Werner Plan[10] set out a step-by-step approach to achieve EMU by 1980. That this was not realised at the time owed to a number of external and internal factors.

Internally, two principal factors help explain the failure of the Werner Plan. The first of these was an ideological division within the original six ECs member states over how to proceed towards EMU. Two opposing 'camps' emerged: the 'economists' and the 'monetarists'. The former were led by the FRG and the Netherlands and argued that to create EMU the right preconditions 'on the ground' had to be put in place before common policies and institutions could be implemented. This approach has also been referred to as 'crowning theory', indicating that a convergence of economic conditions throughout the ECs would have to be achieved first and that this effort would only eventually be 'crowned' by EMU, including a common currency. France led the monetarists, with Commission support, and they argued that common policies and institutions should be created immediately, thereby almost forcing the gradual convergence of economic conditions across the EC. This approach was dubbed 'locomotive theory' as it likened the effect of creating EMU to the way in which a locomotive pulls all carriages of a train simultaneously in the same direction.[11] Interestingly, these different economic philosophies both continue through to the present and in their approaches towards EMU heavily resemble Tinbergen's differentiation between negative and positive integration respectively.

The second internal reason for the failure of the Werner Plan concerned yet another outcome of the momentum for further European integration at the end of the 1960s: the decision to enlarge the Communities by up to four new member states. In the event, three of the applicant countries joined the three Communities on 1 January 1973 – Denmark, Ireland and the United Kingdom (UK).[12] Trying to integrate three new members into the general customs union and the various sectoral common markets, especially the CAP, was a huge task in itself. All three, naturally, brought with them different preconditions for membership, not only in economic terms but also in respect of their political ideas over what the ECs should do or become. Economically, Ireland in particular was much poorer, and its economy structurally less developed, than those of the other eight member states. This meant that economic convergence – the precondition for EMU as demanded by the economists – was now even more difficult to achieve. At the same time, the accession of the UK had strengthened the political influence of the economists.[13] As will be seen later, the unfavourable external environment then sealed the fate of the Werner Plan.

During the 1970s and early 1980s economic integration almost disappeared from the EEC agenda in light of internal and external problems and developments that required a readjustment of priorities at both national and supranational, i.e. Community, level. As was seen in Chapter One, the Cold War was in flux during this period as *détente* eventually gave way to Reagan's 'Second Cold War' and transatlantic differences grew. Attempts by the EEC to integrate monetary policies during the 1970s also stalled as the collapse of the Bretton Woods system in 1971 threw the international economic system into disarray. In addition, the Communities struggled to meet internal challenges. Greek accession in 1981 meant yet another poor member, which increased both economic divergence within the ECs and the need for institutional reform. Perhaps most difficult, however, was for the ECs to digest British membership. There were all sorts of difficulties over its preferential trading links with the Commonwealth and successive British leaderships demanded renegotiation of the terms upon which the UK entered the Communities in 1973. Most famous of these was Margaret Thatcher's insistence on renegotiating Britain's contributions to the Communities' budget, wherein she managed to hold the Communities to (political) ransom until she 'got her money back' at the Fontainebleau European Council meeting in 1984.[14]

The resolution of the British budgetary question opened the way for fresh initiatives at the ECs level. By the early 1980s it had become evident that economically the Communities had been falling further and further behind their main competitors, the US and Japan. A *'trade gap*, a *productivity gap*, an *employment gap*, an *investment gap* and a *technology gap'*[15] between the ECs and their two principal competitors were identified. In the search for reasons for this development, one main culprit was found: the still heavily fragmented state of the EEC economy. Whereas Japan and the US had domestic markets of around 120 million and 230 million potential consumers respectively, the Communities consisted of ten national economies (and hence markets) with 'diverse technical standards, business laws and industrial policies',[16] and with populations ranging between 61 million in the FRG and only 380,000 in Luxembourg.[17] With the disease diagnosed, the cure was – more or less – clear: the EEC had to be transformed from a general customs union into a true common market.

In 1985 the British Commissioner Lord Cockfield presented a White Paper containing roughly 300 measures through which obstacles still in the way of realising the so-called 'Single European Market' (SEM) were to be removed. These provisions formed the basis of the 1986 Single European Act – the constitutional amendment aimed at getting the single market established by the intended completion date of 31 December 1992. The established practice towards removing NTBs within the sectoral common markets was to harmonise respective standards and requirements. However, for the SEM this would have required agreement on hundreds of such common provisions, which would have been extremely time-consuming and replete with potential conflicts – both within the EEC over exactly what standards to decide on and with third countries, not least because of their fears, encouraged by the example of CAP, of a 'Fortress Europe'. Rather quickly, therefore, EEC decision-makers adopted a different way forward – the principle of 'mutual recognition'.[18] Instead of seeking common ground over issues such as academic and vocational qualifications, food or other product specifications and the like, each member of the EEC agreed to accept the standards applied in the other member states. This way the SEM process was speeded up and the fears of third countries eased – at least to an extent.

The further 'deepening' of the European integration process that the creation of the SEM represented was accompanied by another round of 'widening' in 1986, when Spain and Portugal joined the ECs. Then, in 1988 – merely a year after the SEA had come into force[19] – the European Council decided at a meeting in Hanover to task a committee headed by Commission President Jacques Delors to study once again ways in which to progress towards full EMU. One often-heard argument at the time was that a single market required a single currency and the Delors Report, published in April 1989, did contain much more detail on further monetary integration than on truly transforming the SEM into a proper economic union. Like its predecessor, it foresaw a three-step approach towards full EMU by the year 1997 at the earliest and 1999 at the latest.[20] But whilst these steps contained quite detailed requirements and actions on the monetary front, at the end of which stood the creation of a European central bank and the introduction of a common currency, the Delors Report only vaguely described the envisaged economic union as 'an unrestricted common market with a set of rules which are indispensable to its proper working'.[21] In other words, the difference between the SEM and economic union was to be a more intense economic policy co-ordination.[22]

On 1 January 1993, the official starting date of the SEM, about 95 per cent of the envisaged measures had been adopted by the EEC.[23] At the same time, however, a number of particularly sensitive market sectors had been omitted from the original SEM programme. Telecommunications, the aviation industry and energy markets are but some examples of industries that have since been tackled by the Commission. In 1995, three more countries joined what in November 1993 had become the European Union: Austria, Finland and Sweden. And on 1 January 1999, eleven of the by then fifteen member states of the EU took the ultimate step within the economic integration process by forming an economic and monetary union. Two years later, Greece joined them and together these twelve countries then introduced bank notes and coins denominated in the EU's own, common currency – the euro – thereby replacing their national currencies as legal tender. Only Denmark, Sweden and the UK remain outside this EMU arrangement which, in simple terms, imposes a common currency on a SEM that remains incomplete.

From Bretton Woods to Cancún – principal international economic developments since World War Two

The post-WW2 history of global economic relations is inextricably linked to a conference held in 1944 in a small resort in New Hampshire called Bretton Woods. There the major Allied powers, with the US and Britain assuming dominant roles,[24] decided on a new world economic order at the centre of which stood a new international monetary system called the Gold Exchange Standard or, simply, the Bretton Woods system. Due to the unsatisfactory – some would say disastrous – experiences of floating exchange rates during the inter-war period, it was widely believed that at least some of the stability provided by the pre-WW1 Gold Standard ought to be restored.

Whereas under the old system all major economies had been clearly linked to one another by fixing the prices of their currencies in terms of gold,[25] the new arrangement linked them to the US dollar – the only currency officially exchangeable into gold at a fixed price of US$35 per ounce. All other currencies were assigned par values *vis-à-vis* the US$. For example, the British pound's par value was US$2.40, the French franc's was US$0.18, and the German mark's was US$0.2732.[26] At the same time it was recognised that the various members of the Bretton Woods arrangement might encounter different pressures, caused by economic or even political developments, and that they might do so at different times, which might over a period render the original par values unrealistic. The Bretton Woods system foresaw a readjustment of par values were this to happen, which is why the Gold Exchange Standard has also been referred to as a 'semi-fixed' exchange rate system.

Politically, the establishment of the Gold Exchange Standard marked the official beginning of US dominance – at least as far as the global economic situation was concerned. This impression is re-enforced by other effects of the Bretton Woods conference: the planned establishment of three international institutions, namely an International Monetary Fund, an International Bank for Reconstruction and Development and an International Trade Organisation. The IMF and IBRD were both set up in Washington DC in December 1945. The former was designed to provide support to members of the Gold Exchange Standard in their attempts to defend their agreed par-values *vis-à-vis* the US dollar.[27] The latter, more commonly known as the World Bank, had as its main task to supply the world with development assistance. Although today the majority of this assistance goes to developing countries, the World Bank initially dealt mainly with the redevelopment of Europe.[28] So, whilst the IMF issued short-term loans to help its members fulfil their intervention requirements within the Bretton Woods exchange rate regime, the World Bank lent money long-term to assist members in their reconstruction and development efforts.

The third of the planned institutions, the ITO, had the objective of liberalising international trade. However, although it was agreed at a UN conference in 1948 to set this organisation up, too few countries eventually ratified the respective charter. This meant that the General Agreement on Tariffs and Trade, already signed in 1947 as an interim arrangement, became the only multilateral instrument governing international trade until its subsequent replacement by the World Trade Organisation (WTO).[29] GATT was guided by three basic principles. First, each member had to grant every other member most-favoured nation status, meaning that all fellow GATT members had to be accorded the same (favourable) trade conditions by a given member state as those it granted to its 'most favoured' trading partner. Second, all protection granted to a member's domestic industries was required to be, to the maximum extent possible, by way of tariffs and not through non-tariff barriers in order to increase transparency and therewith make competition fairer. Finally, each member state had to treat imported goods in the same way as those produced domestically.

These principles of non-discrimination between countries and products and of transparency and fairness in using protectionist measures provided the background to, and starting point for, the pursuit of the main aim of GATT, namely the reduction or possible elimination of tariffs and NTBs. This was to be achieved by way of large conferences, so-called 'trade rounds', of which eight were held. The first five (Geneva 1947, Annecy 1949, Torquay 1951, Geneva 1956 and Geneva 1960–62 ['Dillon Round']) aimed principally at tariff reduction. The sixth round, Geneva 1962–67, also known as the 'Kennedy Round', aimed at anti-dumping measures and reduced industrial tariffs.[30] As time went by, and the less controversial issues had already been dealt with, negotiations under the auspices of GATT became more complex and prolonged. The seventh GATT round, Geneva 1973–79 ('Tokyo Round') led to an overall reduction of tariffs to an average level of 35 per cent (5–8 per cent among developed countries) and found agreement on codes concerning the following NTBs: government procurement, customs validation, subsidies and countervailing measures, anti-dumping, standards and import licensing. The eighth and final round of negotiations, Geneva 1986–93 ('Uruguay Round') broadened the scope of GATT to include the particularly sensitive agricultural subsidies, trade in services and the issue of intellectual property rights.[31] Most significantly, however, the Uruguay Round finally brought about the establishment of a proper international trade organisation, the WTO, in 1995.[32]

This broad overview demonstrates that substantial progress had been made in liberalising international trade between the end of WW2 and the mid-1990s. However, not everything developed quite so positively elsewhere. As time went by, it became increasingly evident that the Gold Exchange Standard established at Bretton Woods in 1944 required a different kind of discipline than had the old Gold Standard – at least on the part of the US. Whereas the Gold Standard was an even and self-correcting system, the Gold Exchange Standard gave the US the role of 'leader of the pack'. With this leadership role, though, came the need for self-discipline because the system was not an automatic one yet contained all the automatisms of the old Gold Standard.

The most important requirement of the US was to keep its BOP in overall, long-term equilibrium. Were it not to adhere to this demand and, instead, run a large and continuous BOP deficit, this would mean that foreign countries would accumulate US dollars which they could exchange for gold at the guaranteed rate of US$35 per ounce at any time. And this is exactly what happened. By as early as the mid-1960s the amount of US$ liabilities had outstripped the amount of gold and it was only a matter of time before disaster struck. The day on which this happened was 15 August 1971, the day US President Nixon closed the so-called 'gold window' at the New York Federal Reserve that had been the place where foreign central banks had hitherto been exchanging their dollars for gold. As the end of the Gold Exchange Standard also marked the end of the Bretton Woods system of semi-fixed exchange rates, all major currencies began to float freely and, initially, rather erratically against one another. Despite the inherent structural problems, when it actually happened, the collapse of the Gold Exchange Standard came as a total surprise.[33]

Whilst economists world-wide intensified their academic debate over whether floating or fixed exchange rates were the 'better' arrangement, businesses were quite clear in their assessment. To them floating exchange rates meant uncertainty, and uncertainty is undesirable since it incurs costs. The governments of the Western world came under substantial pressure to agree a new deal with which to link exchange rates to one another. This was signed as early as December 1971 at the Smithsonian Institution in Washington DC. The main features of the 'Smithsonian Agreement' were a devalued US$ and slightly widened fluctuation margins before intervention to support the agreed central rate between two currencies had to take place. Under the old Bretton Woods accord the exchange rates between two currencies were only allowed to fluctuate by 0.75 per cent either way from the central rate. Now, a margin of up to 2.25 per cent in each direction was allowed. Only then were central banks obliged to intervene.[34]

The Smithsonian Agreement did not last long, for which there were a number of contributing factors. Most of the businesses affected by foreign exchange risk found the extended fluctuation margins (4.5 per cent in total) already too substantial to address their concerns sufficiently. However, probably the most serious problem perceived of the new agreement was that currencies had been pegged to one another at incorrect rates. This immediately encouraged speculators to test the system and eventually brought it down because, as soon as central bank intervention becomes the norm rather than the exception, a semi-fixed exchange rate regime becomes unsustainable. In March 1973, the world's most important currencies began to float freely on the foreign exchange markets. This situation prevails through to the present, albeit efforts to link exchange rates to one another continued in Western Europe.[35]

The early 1970s were turbulent times not only because of the monetary troubles. As a sign of protest against Israel's commencement of the Yom Kippur War, and the alleged support of the Jewish state by the West, OPEC allowed its Arab members in October 1973 to stop or considerably reduce deliveries of oil to the US and Western Europe. At the same time, the price of oil was increased substantially for all the cartel's customers. These developments caught most of the industrialised countries by surprise, not only because they were unexpected but also because they revealed starkly just how dependent on Middle Eastern oil most of the countries had become. The shortages in oil supplies resulted in a quadrupling of prices, which in turn pushed up inflation and sent the Western world into a recession the magnitude of which had not been experienced since WW2. Then, in the wake of the Iranian Revolution, another near doubling of oil prices took place in 1979, further prolonging the difficult economic situation.[36]

While the developed world was preoccupied with the primary effects of the oil shocks (i.e. initial supply shortages, price hikes and inflation), many developing countries were affected much more seriously by an indirect consequence of OPEC's pricing policy. Many of the members of the oil cartel, such as Saudi Arabia or Kuwait, became very rich very quickly and a lot of this wealth was deposited with Western banks. Banks, though, need to lend money to generate profits, and substantial loans, aimed mainly at financing big development projects, were consequently granted to developing world countries. However, several factors, all of which stemmed indirectly from the oil crises, such as rising interest rates, the global recession and low commodity prices, caused the size of developing world debt to grow fast.[37] To make matters worse, in many cases developing countries spent on consumptive measures rather than on investment, for which at least an equivalent in value would have been created.[38]

The true extent of the so-called 'debt crisis' emerged in the early 1980s when countries like Poland, Mexico, Brazil and Argentina could no longer service their debts. The unthinkable had happened: supposedly sovereign states had effectively gone bankrupt. In an effort to address the problem the IMF, which had been given new powers following the collapse of the Bretton Woods system,[39] the Bank for International Settlements, national central banks and commercial banks took concerted action and renegotiated respective loans with the affected countries. The most pressing issue was, of course, to relieve the debtor countries of the immediate need to pay. This, however, required the banks to agree to the rescheduling of debt payments by deferring them into the future and/or by stretching them over a longer period of time. Yet, the banks were only willing to do this if the debtors agreed to meet certain conditions. Such conditions, cumulatively known as 'austerity measures', included that new money received from exports or loans had to be used to repay their debts rather than for other purposes, such as investment in the country's infrastructure. This way the commercial banks, and with them the developed world, rescued their own situations and prevented default. The developing world, though, found itself in dire straits and few of those countries originally affected by the debt crisis have since managed to escape this desperate state of affairs. For many, the situation looks as grim as ever, if not worse. Most badly affected are the so-called HIPCs, heavily indebted poor countries, the majority of which are in sub-Saharan Africa.[40]

If the debt crisis had grabbed the headlines of world economic developments in the early 1980s, towards the middle of the decade attention was diverted from the plight of the poor and towards the political changes taking place in the Soviet Union and its European satellites. As early as 1981 labour unrest in Poland, which led to the imposition of martial law, gave the strongest indication since the democracy movements in the early to mid-1950s and late 1960s of popular dissatisfaction with communism in Eastern Europe.[41] There were many reasons for this, and economic factors weighed heavily. The high level of centralisation of the Soviet planned economy had proven increasingly inefficient, technology in non-military production especially lagged far behind the West and there were frequent shortages of basic agricultural and industrial products. Also, the West aggravated the USSR's economic problems through its sustained strategic economic embargo policy and, especially under the first Reagan administration, an accelerated arms race that forced the Soviet regime to divert even more scarce resources into its military at the expense of its already dissatisfied civilian population. This Soviet economic weakness was revealed clearly in its decision to withdraw in February 1989 from Afghanistan after ten years of occupation.[42]

The policies of Mikhail Gorbachev, who became Secretary-General of the Communist Party in 1985, recognised the dire Soviet economic situation and attempted a radical economic and political restructuring process known as 'perestroika'. 'Glasnost', meaning candour or openness, complemented this in an effort to relieve international and domestic pressure on the communist system. However, the combination of economic weakness and greater political tolerance, which was demonstrated by Gorbachev's non-intervention in Poland following a vote there in June 1989 in favour of a non-communist government,[43] actually encouraged the dissolution of the Soviet bloc. Worse still, essential internal reforms led to an economic downturn rather than an upswing. This was perhaps inevitable given the enormity of the task of economic transformation, but it nevertheless fuelled widespread discontent.

Set against the velvet revolutions of 1989–91[44] and a conservative coup in August 1991 that although failing to topple Gorbachev fatally wounded his political leadership, the Soviet Union officially broke up on 26 December 1991. Leaving aside the political ramifications, its collapse portended the dawn of a new international economic era. In the Russian Federation – the official successor of the Soviet Union – President Yeltsin embarked on a programme that was to turn the country into a market economy.[45] Similar steps had already been taken or were being taken in most of the other former communist states. As these countries then also gradually began to open themselves for international trade and investments, the scene was set for expanding massively the process of economic internationalisation that in the West had already gained substantial momentum through the GATT negotiation rounds. There the liberalising effects of reduced tariffs and the dismantling of NTBs, together with substantial technological progress such as cheaper and faster transportation and communication, had already allowed economic activity not only to cross national borders more easily but also to render distances between locations increasingly meaningless. Once the former Soviet bloc began to open itself to the rest of the world, then the geographical limits of economic internationalisation were removed and the foundations consequently laid to move on towards a situation that might deserve to be called economic globalisation.

Economic globalisation as a concept seemingly has as many definitions as there are books written about it[46] and is used here in terms of providing the prerequisites for a truly global division of labour. The process towards true economic globalisation consists of three main strands. First, there is participation. Only if all countries in the world are part of the international division of labour can full globalisation be realised. Prospects for this were much improved by the demise of the USSR and the subsequent economic transformation of large parts of the former Soviet empire. Second, technological progress allows for the practical realisation of global economic activity. Third, governments have to have the political will to agree to the reduction, even eradication, of all protective measures embedded in their national jurisdictions. Herein the establishment of the WTO was a big step forward. Although GATT had achieved noticeable progress in the reduction of tariffs and the dismantling of NTBs, it had a major weakness in that its rules were not, ultimately, binding. The WTO, however, has a proper institutional structure and, through its Dispute Settlement Body (DSB), a quasi-judicial system in which the organisation's rules can be contested, members 'sued', and fines (limited trade sanctions) imposed.[47] Moreover its Ministerial Conference, which meets on a minimum two-yearly basis, sets the strategic direction of the organisation, makes all final decisions on agreements within its purview[48] and in five meetings thus far (Singapore 1996, Geneva 1998, Seattle 1999, Doha 2001 and Cancún 2003) has substantially widened its agenda.[49] This now includes agriculture, services, further improved market access for non-agricultural products, trade-related aspects of intellectual property rights (TRIPS), the relationship between trade and investment, the interaction between trade and competition policy, more transparency in government procurement, and further trade facilitation.[50]

European economic integration within the international context

Setting EC economic integration against the background of major post-war political and economic developments helps reveal their interrelationship and the extent to which the European Communities have become a global economic power. It was seen in Chapter One that post-war European integration was rooted in the political U-turn by the US and Britain in favour of rehabilitating the FRG, delimited by the Cold War to Western Europe, and then shaped by the political decisions of the superpowers and of the West European countries. Economic factors, however, were also prominent. The Marshall Plan recognised and promoted transatlantic economic interdependence. The stability provided by the Bretton Woods institutions and arrangements was essential for post-war recovery and European economic integration. And the economic boom of the 1950s and early 1960s provided an economic climate that encouraged and seemingly justified the economic integration of the ECSC and the EEC. There can scarce be better testament to the ECs' economic success, buoyed further still by the German 'economic miracle', than Britain's political *volte face* and consequent application for full membership in 1961.

That integration stuttered in the late 1960s owes in part to Charles de Gaulle's stance during the Empty Chair crisis of 1965/66 and his blocking of British membership throughout the 1960s. However, that the subsequent re-launch of integration at The Hague in December 1969 also partly fell away in the 1970s owes to the international economic circumstances of the time. This was especially significant for the aspirations of the Werner Report because the sudden free floating of exchange rates stood in particular contrast to the aims of creating a monetary union.

Monetary integration actually begins with the linking of currencies by way of semi-fixed exchange rates. Initially, realignments (i.e. the readjustment of the rates at which respective currencies are pegged to one another) are needed in order to find a 'natural exchange rate' between the monies of the participating countries. However, such an exchange rate can only be sustained for as long as the economies of the countries behind the currencies perform in sync. In this respect monetary integration theory[51] supports the position of the 'economist' members of the ECs[52] in that a degree of economic conversion has to be achieved to prepare the basis for monetary integration. If and when the members of a monetary arrangement sufficiently co-ordinate their economic performances, there should be fewer and fewer realignments, eventually leading to a situation in which the exchange rates no longer change. Once this point is reached, the slight fluctuation risks that affect businesses in particular will have been removed. A number of other impediments to commercial undertakings do, however, remain. For instance, businesses still need to buy or sell currencies if they cannot pay or be paid in their own money and have to continue to 'translate' prices to enable comparability. These problems can only be solved by the introduction of a common currency – the ultimate step within a process of monetary integration.

With the Bretton Woods system gone and the Smithsonian Agreement not meeting its expectations, the EEC needed its own monetary system if it wanted to proceed towards full EMU. In March 1972, the six member states set up an arrangement that has since become known as 'the snake'.[53] The aim was to keep currencies within a range of ±2.25 per cent against one another, rather than the much wider margins that the Smithsonian arrangement allowed.[54] However, the adverse international economic environment meant that the snake began to disintegrate after the collapse of the Smithsonian Agreement in 1973 and fell apart totally as a result of the 1973–74 oil shock, which also demolished efforts to promote convergence.[55]

The oil crisis may have hit the entire industrialised world but countries felt its effects differently. At the time, the European Communities consisted of nine members, all of which were affected in different ways and to varying degrees by the crisis. Some member states already had noticeable natural resources of their own (UK, Netherlands) whilst others had next to none (Luxembourg, FRG). The demand patterns also differed according to the degree of industrialisation. As one of the most industrialised of the nine members, the FRG suffered substantially more than still comparatively agrarian members such as Ireland or even France. With the economic realities so different – even diverging – across the EEC, any attempt at further economic and monetary integration required a positive step forward. The least that would have been required was a co-ordination of economic policies. But in times of crisis countries tend to become inward-looking and in the case of the ECs each member dealt with this unique situation by itself. The consequence was that the nine drifted apart even further and cast the prospects for EMU farther into the future.

Political capital vested in integration combined with economic imperatives, however, prevented total abandonment of the integration process. Floating exchange rates meant uncertainty for businesses but managed exchange rates would reduce risk, totally fixed ones even eliminate it. This would then encourage cross-border trade within the EEC and therewith also push ahead the integration process. With these kinds of arguments Commission President Roy Jenkins proposed a successor to the failed snake.[56] Member states were initially unenthusiastic but matters changed when Jenkins managed to get the German Chancellor Helmut Schmidt and the French President Valérie Giscard d'Estaing to back the proposed new monetary arrangement. Their combined effort resulted in the establishment of the European Monetary System (EMS) in 1979.[57] Despite substantial doubt over its prospects when it was first launched, the EMS turned out to be, overall, a success. It certainly succeeded where the snake had failed in that it did provide considerable exchange rate stability within the ECs.

Realignments within the system's exchange rate mechanism (ERM) were initially quite frequent, which was expected given the need to move the economies of the participating countries back into line with one another. The political dimension of this was also clear because if exchange rates were to be kept inside their narrow ERM fluctuation bands of ±2.25 per cent,[58] member states had to co-ordinate closely their monetary and fiscal policies. This meant surrendering a considerable degree of national sovereignty in important aspects of economic policy. Some countries had also to perform significant changes in domestic economic strategy. For instance, the socialist President of the French Republic, François Mitterand, who in 1981 had succeeded the liberal Giscard d'Estaing, had initially embarked upon a considerable re-nationalisation programme. This required substantial sums of public spending and hence pushed up inflation, which in itself would not have been a problem had inflation been rising in other ERM countries too – especially the FRG, the largest of the member economies. However, whereas monetary policy was still controlled by the government in France, the independent Bundesbank performed this task in the FRG and was mandated to keep inflation low. With inflationary pressure building in France but not in the FRG, the franc came under pressure within the ERM, which threatened frequent realignments tantamount to regular devaluations of the country's money.[59] In 1983, France performed a remarkable policy reversal, responsibility for which lay with the then Minister of Finance Jacques Delors. His approach was to adopt a German-style policy of monetary stability that made the French franc as hard a currency as the deutschmark, to be aptly named the *franc fort*.[60] As this learning process continued, realignments became fewer and more infrequent, resulting in a period of not one single rearrangement of par values between 1987 and 1992.

All in all the mid to late 1980s was a time of drive and initiative within the European Communities rivalled only by the 1950s. Two more rounds of 'widening' in 1981 and 1986 brought ECs membership up to twelve and the larger and more integrated the ECs got, the more powerful they appeared internationally. Further momentum was accorded the SEM process by an upswing in the international economy and the realisation that, though much needed, monetary stability would not in itself close the perceived gap between the Communities and their main economic rivals. Moreover, a true common market, so went the argument, required a common currency, which in turn requires monetary union.

The timing of the Delors Report on EMU was propitious, for that same year the Berlin Wall came down and immediate concern, internationally as well as inside the Communities, arose about Germany's future – especially once it became clear that the German Democratic Republic (GDR) would join the FRG. Could a (re)united Germany remain part of the Western alliances, including the ECs, and, if so, would it actually want to do so? The so-called '4 + 2 talks' between the four wartime allies and the two German states decided that a fully sovereign united Germany should be able to decide for itself which way to turn. Meanwhile, the West German Chancellor, Helmut Kohl, made it known that the *de facto* enlarged FRG was not going to seek neutralism (or worse, in the eyes of its Western allies) and would remain as committed as ever to NATO and the European Communities. Crucially, Kohl chose to prove this determination by pushing for even deeper integration through parallel inter-governmental conferences (IGC) on political union and on EMU. The consequent Treaty on European Union (TEU) enshrined the objective of EMU and a single currency by 1999 at the latest and therein seemingly locked the reunified Germany into the Community structure for good.[61]

Economic integration thus appeared to be progressing well and the prospects looked good for EMU being achieved by 1997, the earliest date possible. However, member state politics and the international economy conspired in the early 1990s to slow progress once more. The three-pillar structure of the TEU reflected British-led reluctance to see a more politically integrated Europe. The delay in ratifying the TEU caused by a negative referendum result in Denmark indicated both a worrying dislocation between the European integration process and the people of the Union and a possible end of the permissive consensus. And the enormous costs and opportunities inherent in the FRG absorbing the GDR encouraged divergence rather than convergence amongst EU economies.

German reunification produced an economic boom inside the enlarged FRG, which had two main causes. The first concerned the exchange rate upon which German economic, monetary and social union[62] was founded, basically giving each Easterner one deutschmark for each two of their (rather worthless) *Ostmarks*. The second reason was the demand for Western goods by the people of the former GDR after forty years of communist rule. Thus equipped, they went on a massive shopping spree. German businesses and even politicians naturally welcomed this, especially since the demand was mainly for goods produced in the western part of Germany. However, it was a major problem for EMU ambitions because whilst Germany boomed the rest of the member states joined the UK in an economic recession of some magnitude.

In order to stimulate their economies, these member states needed a reduction in interest rates. This, however, was no longer easily done because within the ERM the deutschmark had long been the system's anchor currency, which meant that the Bundesbank indirectly set the system's monetary policy. The main problem herein was that the Bundesbank was the German central bank and therewith pursued monetary policy for Germany and not the EEC. In Germany inflation had been rising sharply as a result of the huge demand for a limited amount of goods, and so the Bundesbank increased interest rates to make money more expensive. The other central banks inside the ERM had little choice but to follow the Bundesbank's lead since the alternative would have been a mass exodus of speculative money out of their currencies and into a deutschmark that promised higher returns. The central banks of the other

ERM countries found themselves in a catch-22 situation: higher interest rates meant further economic hardship for their national economies, lower interest rates would wreck the system.

With the first Danish referendum having gone against Maastricht, and therewith the EEC's plans for EMU, and the French one looking too close to call, international speculators seized their chance. They began to sell the weakest of the currencies within the ERM first: the Swedish krona, an associated non-EEC member currency; the Italian lira, for decades known as a weak currency; and pound sterling, the one money with a less-than Euro-enthusiastic government behind it. With the benefit of hindsight, it is only too obvious that a realignment offered the best solution. It could even have been politically justified given that German reunification and its consequences could be seen as an external shock to an ERM which otherwise worked perfectly well. At the time, though, decision-makers in Brussels clearly felt that five years of monetary stability was too grand an achievement to forgo and consequently ruled out a realignment. In September 1992 the pound and the lira were forced out of the ERM, thereby temporarily saving the system. The real political test, though, occurred in August 1993 when the French franc came under pressure. This time the system was preserved only by allowing very wide fluctuation margins of ±15 per cent. This rather inelegant solution did finally fight off the international speculators but at the cost of grave damage to the reputation of the EMS.

The way was opened for EMU to be realised once a second Danish referendum approved the TEU and the treaty finally came into force in November 1993. Still, though, the road there was far from easy. The 'economist' members of the EU had successfully insisted upon a number of convergence criteria that had to be fulfilled by all who wanted to participate in monetary union. This meant that EMU would create not just any currency area, but one that had a currency as hard and stable as the deutschmark. A lot of economic and political effort, coupled with some dubious tactics and criteria fudging, subsequently allowed eleven of the by then fifteen member states to qualify for EMU by 1 January 1999. On paper, a new currency, the euro, was born. However, its real impact began to be felt after the introduction of euro notes and coins at the beginning of 2002 and there was speculation that this new money could rival the US dollar as the world's main currency. Indeed, growing international confidence in the euro is evidenced by its remarkable appreciation against the dollar at the end of 2002 and throughout 2003.[63]

Conclusion

Post-war European economic integration was first and foremost internally focused and orientated toward advancing both economic and political agendas. Its development from FTA through to EMU reflected the characteristics identified in economic theory but defied the neat progressive stages advanced therein. This is unsurprising given the ebb and flow of the integration process in response to political initiative, the implications of successive enlargements and the impact of developments in the Cold War and the international economy. That EMU was achieved by 1999, albeit with opt-outs and an incomplete SEM, was truly remarkable given the heritage of WW2.

Although the EU's becoming an international economic actor was not the driving force behind early economic integration, it was an inevitable consequence of integrating some of the world's most advanced and influential economies. Likewise, it was inevitable that successive waves of enlargement would increase the economic gravitas of the Union and enhance its international prestige as the world's largest single trading entity. This drew into the EU both foreign direct investment (FDI) and the economies of neighbouring countries, which became heavily influenced by the economic performance and policies of the Union. Moreover, the EU's economic weight helped it both to re-balance some of the traditional asymmetry in its interdependent relationship with the US and to work with the US to shape the international economic system through, in particular, GATT.

Some elements of the EU's post-war development as an international economic actor were clearly non-purposive. Its economic presence required no action and the significant and contentious international effects of the CAP were, at least initially, almost a subconscious by-product of a drive for a sectoral customs union that was shaped heavily by vested interests and particular legacies of WW2. It can also be argued that processes of economic internationalisation enhanced the external impact of the ECs' development. The Communities had simultaneously an accelerating and shaping influence on these processes and the consequences of their internal policies were felt progressively further afield as technology and transportation advances rendered distances less meaningful and economies more complexly interdependent. However, the transition from FTA to EMU required a whole range of political decisions and the creation of an apparatus to operationalise EU economic integration. One of the key developments here for the EU as an international economic actor was the decision in the transition to a customs union to create and supranationally enable the CCP. This potentially powerful mechanism for wielding international economic power was then supplemented by extensions of EC competence in other areas of external activity traditionally dominated heavily by economic instruments, such as Development Policy.

As the EU faced up to the multifaceted demands of a post-Soviet shift from economic internationalisation to globalisation, its key challenge was to complement its hitherto strong inwardly focused economic integration agenda with a more capable and robust external economic policy. To this end it needed to overhaul and enhance its global network of international economic relations. It also needed to work with the US and through multilateral fora, such as the WTO, to help numerous states transform from planned to market economic systems and to manage processes of economic globalisation. Most of all, however, it needed to translate its economic size into operational influence if it were to realise its potential as an international economic actor and be able to address the manifold economic challenges that the post-Cold War world posed.

Notes

1 See Preamble to the Treaty establishing the European Economic Community.

2 For more details on FTAs see, for example, Robson, P. (1998) *The Economics of International Integration*, 4th edn, London: Routledge, pp. 28–35.

3 Ibid., pp. 17–28.

4 'Negative integration' refers to 'measures consisting of the abolition of a number of impediments to the proper operation of an integrated area', whilst 'positive integration' concerns itself with 'the creation of new institutions and their instruments or the modification of existing instruments'. Tinbergen, J. (1965) *International Economic Integration*, 2nd rev. edn, Amsterdam: Elsevier, p. 76.

5 For a more detailed distinction between the concepts of common market and economic union, see any textbook on international economics, so for instance: Lindert, P.H. (1986) *International Economics*, 8th edn, Homewood, Ill.: Irwin, p. 174.

6 The ECSC was based on a temporary treaty that expired on 23 July 2002.

7 The original EEC Treaty also contained commitments to establish a Common Transport Policy and – in anticipation of achieving the next step of (general) economic integration – a Common Commercial Policy dealing with trade issues *vis-à-vis* third countries.

8 For a more detailed description and analysis see, for instance, Jones, R.A. (2001) *The Politics and Economics of the European Union: An Introductory Text*, 2nd edn, Cheltenham: Edward Elgar, p. 215.

9 For details see, for instance, Laffan, B. (1997) *The Finances of the European Union*, Basingstoke: Macmillan, pp. 6–8.

10 Named after its author, Pierre Werner, at the time Prime Minister and Minister of Finance in Luxembourg. For a brief summary of the plan, see Blair, A. (2002) *Saving the Pound? Britain's Road to Monetary Union*, London: Prentice Hall, p. 52.

11 On this distinction see Swann, D. (1986) *The Economics of the Common Market*, 6th edn, London: Penguin, pp. 178 ff.

12 Norway had also applied to join the ECs, but the country's population rejected membership in a 1972 referendum. For more details, see Dinan, D. (1994) *Ever Closer Union?*, Basingstoke: Macmillan, p. 81.

13 It has to be questioned, however, whether the UK seriously wanted to promote EMU the way the other 'economist' countries did, or whether its approach was not more likely to push EMU farther into the future.

14 Blair, *Saving the Pound?*, pp. 15–16.

15 Jones, *The Politics and Economics of the European Union*, p. 270.

16 Ibid.

17 Population figures calculated on the basis of information obtained from El-Agraa, A.M. (2001) *The European Union: Economics and Policies*, 6th edn, Harlow: Prentice Hall, p. 80.

18 This concept had its origin in a 1979 ruling by the European Court of Justice, the so-called 'Cassis de Dijon' case. For details, see Dinan, *Ever Closer Union?*, pp. 117–18 and 338 ff.

19 Although the SEA had been signed already in February 1986, a late referendum in Ireland in May 1987 caused the delay in the ratification process. See Blair, A. (1999) *The Longman Companion to the European Union Since 1945*, London: Longman, pp. 36–7.

20 For a detailed account of the process towards full EMU, see Dinan, D. (2000) *Encyclopedia of the European Union*, updated edn, Basingstoke: Macmillan, pp. 143–52.

21 Four elements were mentioned in this context: the establishment of the single market; the introduction of a competition policy and other measures to strengthen market mechanisms (industrial policies); the emplacement of common policies aimed at structural change and regional development; and the co-ordination of macroeconomic policy, including binding rules for budgetary policies. Committee for the Study of Economic and Monetary Union (1989) *Report on Economic and Monetary Union in the European Community*, Luxemburg: Office for Official Publications of the European Communities, p. 20.

22 Because most of the rules just mentioned had already been part of the SEA.

23 Dinan, *Encyclopedia of the European Union*, p. 420.

24 Ball, D.A. et al. (2004) *International Business: The Challenge of Global Competition*, 9th edn, Boston: McGraw-Hill, p. 183.

25 For a brief summary of how the Gold Standard used to function, see Waites, B. (ed.) (1995) *Europe and the Wider World*, London: Routledge, p. 188.

26 Ball et al., *International Business*, p. 183.

27 For more information on the IMF, see http://www.imf.org.

28 Laumanns, U. (2001) 'The World Bank Group', p. 1, www.luze.de/nmun/worldbank.pdf.

29 WTO (March 2001) *Trading into the Future*, 2nd rev. edn, p. 10, www.wto.org/english/res_e/doload_e/tif.pdf.

30 Wróblewski, S. 'History of GATT and WTO', http://knfib.zr.univ.gda.pl/History%20of%20GATT%20and %20WTO.htm.

31 Antweiler Jr., W. (1996) 'A Brief History of the General Agreement on Tariffs and Trade', http://pacific.commerce.ubc.ca/trade/GATT-rounds.html.

32 For a more detailed account of the outcome of the Uruguay Round, see 'GATT Rounds', http://www.nadir.org/nadir/initiativ/agp/free/wto/rounds.htm.

33 Ball et al., *International Business*, pp. 181 ff.

34 Dinan, *Encyclopedia of the European Union*, p. 149.

35 Ball et al., *International Business*, pp. 188–9.

36 Government of Canada (2002) 'Autumn 1973 – The OPEC Oil Crisis: Forcing Up World Oil Prices', http://canadianeconomy.gc.ca/english/economy/1973opec.html.

37 Unattributed (2000) 'The Third World Debt Crisis', http://www2.gol.com/users/ bobkeim/money/debt.html.

38 Archdiocese of St Paul and Minneapolis, Office for Social Justice, 'The International Debt Crisis', http://www.osjsom.org/debt.htm.

39 The principal new instrument at the disposal of the IMF is called 'firm surveillance' and allows the Fund to influence, even dictate, fiscal and monetary policies of its member states if certain preconditions are met. For more details, see Ball et al., *International Business*, p. 155; or http://www.imf.org.

40 Ball et al., *International Business*, pp. 221–3.

41 In 1953, workers in Eastern Germany had protested against a tightening of rules. The protest was put down by Soviet tanks. See Mann, G. (1990) *The History of Germany Since 1789*, London: Penguin, p. 852. Similar events in Hungary and Prague in 1956 and 1968 respectively were ended likewise. See Wegs, J.R. and Ladrech, R. (1996) *Europe Since 1945: A Concise History*, 4th edn, New York: St Martin's Press, p. 126.

42 'The End of Communism', *The New World Order Files*, http://user.pa.net/~drivera/ 46commieend.htm; Kegley Jr., C.W. and Wittkopf, E.R. (2001) *World Politics: Trend and Transformation*, 8th edn, Boston: Bedford/St Martin's Press, p. 535.

43 Boughton, J.M. (2001) *Silent Revolution: The International Monetary Fund 1979– 1989*, Washington: IMF, p. 60.

44 In a kind of domino effect, the communist governments in Eastern Germany, Romania, Czechoslovakia, and other countries belonging to the wider Soviet sphere of influence were either forced to make substantial concessions or deposed altogether – in the case of Romania even ending in the execution of the country's dictator, Nicolae Ceausescu, and his wife. Hirsch Jr., E.D. et al. (eds) (2002) 'Collapse of Communism', *The New Dictionary of Cultural Literacy*, 3rd edn, http://www.bartleby.com/59/10/collapseofco.html.

45 'The End of Communism'.

46 In the most general sense, globalisation can be defined as 'the process of integration of the world community into a common system either economical or social'. Archytas, H. (2002) 'The Future of Globalization', http://lautbry.tripod.com/cpce/ globalization/.

47 WTO, *Trading into the Future*, pp. 38–40.

48 United Nations Environment Programme, International Institute for Sustainable Development (2000) 'Structure of the World Trade Organization' *Environment and Trade: A Handbook*, http://www.iisd.org/trade/handbook/3_1.htm.

49 The WTO is headed by a Secretary-General (aided by a Secretariat) and the day-to-day work is done by the General Council composed of senior representatives from the member countries. The Ministerial Conference is the overall governing body and comprise member states' trade ministers. 'Ministerial Conferences on the WTO website', http://www.wto.org/english/thewto_e/minist_e/minist_e.htm.

50 For a complete overview of the issues looked after by the WTO, see http://www.wto.org.

51 The theory is also called the 'theory of optimum currency areas'. See Mundell, R.A. (1961) 'A Theory of Optimum Currency Areas' *American Economic Review* **51** pp. 657–65.

52 As mentioned earlier, mainly the FRG and the Netherlands.

53 Blair, *The Longman Companion to the European Union Since 1945*, p. 25.

54 The Smithsonian Agreement linked all its member currencies to the US dollar. But whilst each currency had a fluctuation margin against the US$ of ±2.25 per cent away from the agreed rate, this allowed fluctuations between ECs currencies of up to 9 per cent – far too broad a margin to ensure exchange rate discipline.

55 Levitt, M. and Lord, C. (2000) *The Political Economy of Monetary Union*, Basingstoke: Macmillan, p. 31.

56 Dinan, *Encyclopedia of the European Union*, p. 309.

57 Ibid., p. 207.

58 The Italian lira was allowed a range of ±6 per cent.

59 Devaluations may have certain economic advantages (they are generally expected to help exports), but politically they are undesirable since they indicate that the economy behind the currency has been under-performing in relative terms.

60 *Franc fort* is pronounced exactly the same way as the French name for the city of Frankfurt (*Francfort*), the home of the Bundesbank.

61 Levitt and Lord, *The Political Economy of Monetary Union*, p. 56.

62 The latter meant the inclusion of the Eastern German population into the Western German welfare state system.

63 European Central Bank,
    http://www.ecb.int/stats/eurofxref/eurofxref-graph-usd.html.

CHAPTER 3

The European Union and external relations

The previous two chapters have shown that the EC developed throughout the Cold War first and foremost as an economic actor, with its role in foreign and security issues being very much both secondary and circumscribed. The subsequent promised 'new world order' not only required that the EU reform to survive but also offered the EU opportunities for an enhanced role in the global economy and for its purposive development in fostering international stability and security. The prospect of enlargement further encouraged the impetus towards the deepening and widening of integration as the EU fought to maintain cohesion in the absence of a binding communist threat and amid a growing diversity of national interests. Demands for greater effectiveness meant also improving EU co-ordination, strengthening its tools for the management of external relations and developing the institutional and policy-making apparatus to translate theory into practice.

In the aftermath of the Gulf War the Belgian Foreign Minister declared the EU to be 'an economic giant, a political dwarf, and a military worm'.[1] The pressure and determination to proceed with EU reform to address this criticism is reflected in the conclusion of three treaties within the first post-Cold War decade and in the prospect of another to follow the work of the European Convention. Much has been written on these treaties from theoretical, policy-making and empirical perspectives. This chapter draws upon this work but develops a broader overview of the EU within the global system. It places the EU in a global context by outlining its international presence. It then examines issues of external competence and representation, key external relations policies and the patterns of, and instruments for, EU external relations. Finally it considers key post-Cold War reforms to EU external relations, especially the development of the CFSP.

International presence

When looking at the EU in the global system it is sometimes easy, especially during times of crisis such as recent military strikes against Iraq (2003), to become seduced by media headlines about the great power of the United States and the international weakness of the Union. The former is undoubtedly true. The latter, however, needs a much more nuanced understanding. A good starting point in developing this necessary perspective is to consider the international presence of the EU.

The Union's most obvious asset is its economic strength. Critics point to antecedents of possible decline: low or stagnant growth rates, inflexible labour markets, adverse demographic trends (especially the combined economic burden of an ageing population with relatively high welfare standards) and growing resource dependency on volatile providers, particularly in terms of energy. However, on the one hand much the same declinist predictions have long been levelled at, and confounded by, the US. On the other, the EU has an enviable and still expanding economic position. Through over fifty years of economic integration and especially the single market and single currency, it has gained comparative advantages that far exceed those derived by others from arrangements such as the North American Free Trade Agreement (NAFTA) and the Common Market of the Southern Cone of Latin America (Mercosur). These advantages, combined with the potential of developing markets to the east, also serve as a magnet for FDI. Furthermore, the EU has not yet exhausted its enlargement process. This will bring new opportunities and greater economic influence, especially within its immediate locale. For instance, the 2004 enlargement will expand the EU's consumer base to over 450 million, bring new labour and raw material resources and offer new intra and external trade and investment opportunities.

To put the EU's economic presence in perspective it is instructive to look at some of the key financial indicators. In 2001 the EU made exports of goods and commercial services worth $2,830 billion and imports of $2,744 billion, which represented a 37.6 per cent and 36.6 per cent global share respectively. By comparison, the US accounted for $987 billion of goods and commercial services exports and $1,355 billion of imports, which represented a 13.1 per cent and 17.8 per cent share of global totals by value respectively.[2] That same year five of the top ten trading nations were based in the EU, and in 2002 only Luxemburg failed to make the World Bank's top thirty-five nations in terms of gross domestic product (GDP).[3] Indeed the EU as a whole had a GDP of $8.563 billion. In percentage terms this accounted for around 26.55 per cent of global GDP, thus far exceeding Japan's share of 12.3 per cent but shy of the US share of around 32.3 per cent.[4] Furthermore, in an era in which MNCs and transnational corporations (TNCs) often exert as much economic influence as, if not more than, some states, it is interesting to look at the 'nationality' of companies and at FDI flows. In 2000 one-third of the corporations in the

Fortune 100 list of the world's largest industrial companies were European, mainly British, Dutch, French, German and Italian.[5] In 2001 FDI inflows to the EU totalled $322,954.2 million compared with $151,899.9 million to the US. In percentage terms this gave the EU 43.9 per cent of global FDI inflows. The EU can thus be said to be an established economic superpower that plays a leading role in the global economy, is a powerful force of economic attraction within its locale and exerts considerable influence further afield through over 150 trade-based relationships with states and international organisations.[6]

It is also important, however, to recognise the EU's collective presence in spheres beyond the economic. For a start, the EU has a global network of diplomatic representation. The Commission maintains in its own right over 123 delegations and offices to countries world-wide and five to international organisations.[7] Conversely, over 160 states have diplomatic missions officially accredited to the EU,[8] and Brussels in particular is a magnet for international NGOs and interest groups. The EU's diplomatic presence is furthered, too, through its use of special representatives, who are deployed especially to crisis areas such as the Great Lakes (Africa), the Middle East, the Former Yugoslav Republic of Macedonia (FYROM), Ethiopia and Afghanistan. In addition, the EU is represented through its member states. Collectively, they have a global web of national embassies and memberships of international organisations and regimes, from many of which the EC is excluded in its own right as a non-state actor. Moreover, the states are increasingly bound to the development and transmission of co-ordinated EU positions. Article 20 of the TEU specifically stipulated that '[t]he diplomatic and consular missions of the Member States and the Commission Delegations in third countries and international conferences, and their representations to international organisations, shall co-operate in ensuring that the common positions and joint actions adopted by the Council are complied with and implemented'.[9]

The diplomatic presence of the EU does not stop here. Less tangible, but still significant, are the established international relationships of the EU constituent states. For instance, there is Germany's historically strong relationship with Central Europe and Britain's 'special relationship' with America and its leading position within the Commonwealth. Consider, too, the diplomatic advantages that accrue from the colonial legacies of the EU member states. After all, few regions of the world escaped European imperialism. Spain, for example, has extensive ties with Latin America, France with Africa, and Britain with the former dominions of its empire.

Even in the much-criticised military domain, the EU has a collective presence greater than the impression often created by media reporting in particular would suggest. First, EU member states comprise a significant proportion of NATO – Europe's leading hard security actor. Currently eleven of the nineteen NATO member states are also EU members. The scheduled enlargements in 2004 of NATO and the EU will increase that proportion to nineteen of twenty-six NATO states. Second, the EU decision to develop the EURRF has led to deepening dialogue, co-operation and co-ordination with NATO. Third, in relative terms EU member states remain militarily powerful and influential in the global arms market. Britain and France are nuclear powers. Five EU member states were in the top eight suppliers of major conventional weaponry for the period 1997–2001.[10] In 2001 three of the world's top six military spenders were EU members. Furthermore, the military expenditure that year of the collective EU fifteen totalled $175 billion.[11] This is particularly interesting when put in the perspective of the military spending of regions regarded as exhibiting security tension and/or instability. In 2001 the military expenditure of the Middle East was $72.4 billion, while Asia and Oceania spent $129 billion. Africa accounted for just $12.2 billion of military expenditure.[12]

A final factor to consider in the EU's global presence is its normative influence. In and of itself, the EU's promotion of its own values 'abroad' is a practice similar to that exercised by dominant powers and empires throughout history. However, the norms that it seeks to promote are different in the sense that they reflect its post-Westphalian construction. Likewise, the means that it chooses to promote its norms are different, especially given that its traditionally civilian power status has meant the absence of military coercion. Although there is debate about exactly what constitutes the EU's normative base, core norms flow through the historical construction of the EU, manifest themselves in its hybrid polity and have their assumptive universality projected through its external relations. These include peace and reconciliation, democracy, the rule of law, respect for human rights, liberty and equality and solidarity. Furthermore, the EU is advantaged four-fold in its normative presence. First, it is simultaneously constitutive and promoter of the predominant neo-liberal international order. Second, in much the same way that US federalism helped to provide a model for European integration, so the EU provides an example for regional integration elsewhere. Third, its wealth and economic gravitas draw neighbouring states into its normative sphere of influence. Finally, the EU enjoys leading representation in most of the key international organisations and fora, either directly or through its member states. For instance, Britain and France are two of the five permanent members of the UN Security Council. Four of the G8 countries are EU members and the president of the European Commission attends G8 meetings. All EU states bar Greece are members of the Development Assistance Committee of the Organisation for Economic Co-operation and Development (OECD). And following the 2004 enlargement, the EU will have 28 per cent of the voting rights in the IBRD and 32 per cent in the IMF.[13]

External competence and representation

The key challenge for the EU has been, and remains, translating its presence into effective action. This is a difficult task even for states that have recourse to the full and integrated range of foreign policy instruments. It is doubly difficult for the EU because it has traditionally lacked military instruments and it is structured in a way that hinders the effective and co-ordinated application of foreign policy tools. This structure was formalised when the Maastricht Treaty effectively divided the activities of the EU into the three pillars, namely the EC pillar, Justice and Home Affairs (JHA) and CFSP. These pillars reflected the concerns of member states for national sovereignty and the need to reconcile then twelve sets of national interests rather than the creation of a system most conducive for the effective management of the EU's international relations.

There lie herein two interrelated problems in particular. First, there are different actors in each of the pillars and competence is divided differently between the EC institutions and the member states. The EC is the supranational pillar in which the member states have progressively pooled sovereignty and where the role of the Commission, European Parliament (EP) and the European Court of Justice (ECJ) are consequently greatest. JHA and CFSP are intergovernmental pillars, albeit that over time the latter has developed almost as a third way between the intergovernmental and communautarian methods. To complicate matters further, the Common European Security and Defence Policy (CESDP), launched at the Helsinki European Council in December 1999, is a subset of CFSP with different actors and lines of responsibility again. Furthermore, member states sometimes maintain close control over spheres of activity even after they have become communautarised. For instance, following the transfer from JHA to the EC pillar of asylum, migration, external border controls and civil law, the requirement of unanimity remains until at least 2004.

The confusion caused by different actors and competencies and artificially divided spheres of EU activity is magnified when projected in the EU's international relations. For a start, EU external activities clearly do not fit into neat pillar separations, not least because the lines between internal and external issues have become increasingly blurred. For instance, JHA issues are predominantly internally focused yet have acquired an important external dimension, especially in the context of enlargement. More importantly, external relations issues frequently require responses that are drawn from across, rather than within, the pillars. Hence, for example, a decision taken within CFSP to impose economic sanctions on a third state has to be operationalised by the Commission since sanctions fall within its competencies in the EC pillar. Similarly, external actions that spread across pillars raise questions about budget lines. This reflects the ongoing battle for competence, especially *vis-à-vis* EP attempts to increase its foreign affairs influence through its rights in non-compulsory expenditure. This caused the EU serious embarrassment on several occasions in its CFSP before a deal was reached in the Amsterdam Treaty. Even this compromise, though, means *ad hoc* budget lines and responsibility, with administrative expenditure being charged to the Community budget and the member states deciding funding for operational costs on a case-by-case basis.

The internal divisions of competencies can also make EU external representation cumbersome and lines of responsibility difficult for external actors to follow and/or respect, especially given the continual process of EU reform. Compare, for instance, trade negotiations and environmental issues. The former are relatively straightforward because they generally fall within the EC pillar. Here the Commission represents the EU in accordance with a mandate laid down by the Council of Ministers. It is also empowered to investigate and take action against unfair trade practices. For instance, in 1999 EU Trade Commissioner Sir Leon Brittan launched and won a legal case against US foreign sales corporations (FSCs) that were worth some $3.5 billion per year. The WTO ruled that FSCs acted as illegal export subsidies to American-based firms and thereby also overturned a deal in GATT in 1981 that sanctioned FSCs. The situation is less clear, however, in environmental matters. The Commission has progressively acquired competencies in external environmental issues since the ECJ established the doctrine of 'parallelism' in the 1970 European Road Transport Agreement and its subsequent ruling in favour of 'potential competence'. Nevertheless, these are far from complete and member states often seek to guard their sovereignty by controlling the acquired competencies of the Commission. The product is that in some areas, such as fisheries, the Commission has exclusive competence, whilst in others it has none. More often than not, environmental agreements entered into by the EU involve 'mixed agreements' and concurrent competence whereby EU representation is shared between the Commission and the EU presidency.[14] A good example of this in practice is the Basel Convention on Hazardous Waste. The Commission has exclusive competence in its trade dimensions, the member states competence in its science and development assistance aspects, and there is mixed competence in its environmental facets.[15]

Were this not complicated enough, the *sui generis* nature of the EU means that international organisations and fora vary in their willingness to recognise it as an actor in its own right as opposed to its constituent member states. This leads, in turn, to substantial variations in the rights of the EC in different international organisations. For example, the EC was never officially recognised under GATT rules but has full membership status in the EBRD and the WTO.[16] In the UN all EU member states enjoy full membership rights but the EC remains largely confined to the permanent observer status accorded to it in 1974. It is, however, a full member of the Food and Agriculture Organisation and has been a full participant in some UN conferences, such as the 1995 World Summit for Social Development.

The modes of EC representation also vary significantly due both to internal divisions of competence and EC rights in international fora. For instance, the Commission generally represents the member states in the WTO, the OECD and the UN Conference on Trade and Development (UNCTAD). Yet matters are complicated by the fact that the CCP has covered international negotiations and agreements relating to services and intellectual property, two areas discussed within the WTO, only since the Nice Treaty came into effect.[17] Also, most respective decisions have to be taken by unanimous agreement in the Council. During the Nice Treaty negotiations France insisted that trade in cultural, audio-visual, educational, social and human health services be regarded as areas of shared competence that therefore require agreements to be concluded by both the EC and the member states.[18] In the Organisation for Security and Co-operation in Europe (OSCE), Commission representatives form part of the EU delegation but it is the national delegation of the member state holding the EU presidency that speaks on behalf of all EU states. In the Asia–Europe Meeting (ASEM), which is an informal process of dialogue and co-operation, the fifteen EU member states and the European Commission sit alongside ten Asian countries (Brunei, China, Indonesia, Japan, South Korea, Malaysia, the Philippines, Singapore, Thailand and Vietnam). By contrast, the EU is represented by the troika in the ASEAN Regional Forum (ARF), which is an informal multilateral dialogue on regional security in Asia-Pacific.[19] As for organisations such as NATO and the Council of Europe, the EU has no official recognition as a non-state actor and is therefore represented through its member states.

EU external relations policies

Turning to EU external policies, the first thing to note is the difficulty of delimiting exactly what constitutes an 'external' and an 'internal' policy. The economic weight in particular of the EU means that whatever it does, or does not do, will have an impact beyond its collective borders. Take, for example, the single European currency. This was in many ways the natural product of the SEM project (see Chapter Two). However, it was widely perceived also as a means by which the EU might both enhance its international prestige and credibility and potentially challenge the dollar's pre-eminence as the world's leading currency. Similarly, the CAP has objectives that are clearly internally focused: to increase production; to ensure a fair standard of living for the agricultural community; to stabilise markets; to assure the availability of supplies; and to ensure reasonable prices for consumers. Yet the Community preference necessary to make this system work has been one of the most serious and enduring problems in the EU's international trade relationships and in its negotiations within GATT/WTO. The US, in particular, has complained vociferously about the international trade effects of the CAP and of privileged access to EU markets granted to ACP states. The 1999 tragi-comical banana war was symptomatic of this, whereby the US accused the EU before the WTO of discriminating in favour of bananas from its former colonial countries as opposed to cheaper Latin American brands, such as Chiquita, a company based in Cincinnati, Ohio.[20]

This said, the two traditionally most prominent external policies that are specifically allowed for in the EU's treaty base are the CCP and Development Policy. The CCP is by far the most integrated of the EU's external policies and was initiated in Article 3 of the Treaty of Rome as an integral feature of the development of a customs union. It is located firmly within the EC pillar and consists of two sub-sets: an autonomous and a contractual trade policy. The autonomous part of the CCP refers to all unilateral actions and decisions taken by the Community in this field, whilst the contractual part of the CCP deals with the direct trade and related negotiations and resulting agreements between the EC and other countries or groups of countries.

The autonomous trade policy contains all measures concerning the importing and the exporting of goods that are not specifically governed by bilateral or multilateral agreements with third parties. In other words, the EU takes all measures in the field of trade 'autonomously'. Although in one way or another all these measures aim at protecting the EU's economy, they do so in different ways. The CET and the general import and export regimes (tariffs the former and NTBs, such as import quotas or export subsidies, the latter) represent the Union's set of general rules on dealing with trade and related issues. But the autonomous trade policy also entails provisions of a more defensive nature, such as anti-dumping and countervailing duty measures, with which the Community can directly react to actions by third parties that are considered to be unfair. If dumping or unfairly subsidised imports can be proven either to threaten or to have affected already an industry, the Commission may, after having consulted the member states, impose provisional anti-dumping duties. The Council can then, by a simple majority, officially levy them. Another example in this context would be the so-called 'safeguard measures', which authorise the EC to impose quantitative restrictions 'in cases where a sudden surge of imports is found to have caused material injury to domestic producers and other adversely affected groups'.[21] Owing to the rather restrictive approach of GATT and the WTO in this field, the EC has so far not made much use of this rule.

The autonomous trade policy also allows the EC to defend its interests in third markets. If the Community finds its exports unfairly treated in other countries, it can make use of its New Commercial Policy Instrument (NCPI), which gives it the right to activate retaliatory measures to force the country in question to comply with the generally accepted rules. Since the establishment of the WTO and its Dispute Settlement Body, the NCPI can be, and has been, used to enforce respective rulings in cases of non-compliance. The autonomous trade policy is also used to promote directly political objectives. For instance, trade embargoes such as those imposed quite recently on Iraq and Serbia are provided for on the basis of Article 301 of the EC Treaty (ECT), which requires the respective initiative by the Commission to be based on a decision under the rules of the CFSP and a subsequent decision by the Council based on qualified majority voting (QMV).[22]

EC agreements with third countries and its participation in multilateral agreements are provided for through the contractual commercial policy.[23] Within the sphere of the contractual trade policy, the Commission has the right of initiative and the exclusive right of negotiation. Having said this, its negotiating room for manoeuvre is severely limited by a respective mandate provided by the Council. The Council also monitors the process throughout by sending observers and by having the Commission report regularly to its so-called '133 Committee'.[24] Ultimately the Commission makes recommendations upon which the Council then has to decide. The EC has concluded a number of quite different trade agreements with third countries. Some of these agreements cover the entire gamut of trade relations, whilst others – so-called sectoral agreements – only cover certain products or product groups such as textiles. Trade and co-operation agreements usually exceed the mere trading aspect by also including rules on co-operation in fields like industry, investments, science and technology, or the environment.[25]

Even more substantial are the Community's association agreements. These are much more than simply trade and co-operation deals as they either aim at a development objective, try to improve the democratic, legal and judicial structures of the associated countries, and/or prepare them for eventual membership of the EU.[26] Association agreements are based on different rules compared to the rest of the contractual commercial policy, indicating a different quality of partnership between the EU and the thus associated countries. Whilst CCP negotiations are generally based on Article 300 of the ECT, with the exception that the procedure foresees no role for the EP,[27] association agreements are negotiated on the basis of Article 310 of the ECT which positively requires the EP's consent. The latter in particular serves to confirm the much closer relationship between the partner countries and the EU, which can be located somewhere between mere trading arrangements and full membership of the Union. Because of this quite substantial difference from the 'normal' trade agreements signed under the rules of the contractual commercial policy, some experts talk of an Association Policy in its own right.[28]

The second external policy rooted in the Treaty of Rome is Development Policy. Unlike the CCP, this is a policy area of parallel competence in that EC and member state activities run alongside one another and on the proviso that Community initiatives should be complementary to those of the states. It was, initially at least, the direct product of the need to make arrangements to meet the concerns of the founding member states for their overseas countries and territories (OCTs). In particular, measures were put into place to offset potential discrimination against the OCTs resulting from the CET, this amid a more general commitment to promote their economic and social well-being and to develop close economic co-operation between them and the EC. Subsequently, the scope and beneficiaries of EU Development Policy expanded in line with decolonisation, EU enlargement and, more latterly, a growing political interest in the ways in which developing countries evolve.

The reasons for EU involvement in Development Policy are often listed in terms of moral obligation, historical legacy and economic imperative.[29] The moral commitment stems from a general belief in solidarity and the consequent need to help combat world poverty and hunger. The historical aspect, as previously noted, comes from the extensive ties that a number of EU countries have with developing countries on account of their colonial past. As for economic imperative, developing countries provide around 30 per cent of EU exports, source crucial raw materials and, albeit some more than others, have potential to be fast-growing future markets. However, there is a fourth and increasingly prominent reason underpinning EU engagement in development matters, namely security. In June 2003 Javier Solana explicitly linked Development Policy with the Union's contribution to promoting global security. For instance, environmental security requires the promotion of sustainable development and careful resource management. Similarly, and particularly in the wake of the September 11 terrorist attacks on the World Trade Centre, economic instability and mass poverty have been linked increasingly with human rights abuses and ongoing threats to international peace and security.

The official objectives of EU Development Policy were laid out in the Maastricht Treaty as being to foster the economic and social development of developing countries, assist their integration into the world economy and contribute to the campaign against poverty. The policy was also to contribute to the promotion of good governance, respect for human rights and the rule of law, and the development and consolidation of democracy. These objectives clearly reflect economic, political and security concerns and a desire to export EU normative values. The division of competence within EU Development Policy also clearly reflects member state sensitivity towards EU encroachment upon historical national ties. Thus the member states tend to dominate financial assistance aspects of Development Policy. The EU is more prominent in its trade dimensions and performs a co-ordinating function, especially with the creation in January 2001 of the EuropeAid Co-operation Office to implement most Commission external aid instruments funded by the Community budget and the European Development Fund (EDF). The financing of EU Development Policy further reflects national sensitivities and the consequent division of competence. The EU contribution amounts to approximately 4 per cent of the EC budget. The bulk, however, is provided by the member states outside the EU through the EDF and the European Investment Bank (EIB).

There is, of course, a third and increasingly important EU external policy that developed much later than the CCP and Development Policy, namely the CFSP. Early ventures into foreign and security policy integration, such as the European Political Community, the EDC and the Fouchet proposals (see Chapter One), all fell foul of national sovereignty considerations. Even EPC was denied a treaty base until the entry into force of the SEA in 1987. For a variety of reasons, though, it was felt necessary to upgrade EPC to CFSP in the Maastricht Treaty as the framework within which most of the EU's 'sensitive' foreign and security issues are now handled. Some saw this as the natural complement to the EMU process, whilst others emphasised the need of enhanced intergovernmental co-operation to deal with the implications of German reunification and to prevent the re-emergence of the 'German question'. The wider consequences of the collapse of the loose bipolar structure of international relations also stimulated recognition of the need for greater self-reliance, especially given the uncertain future of Cold War institutions and national commitments to European security. Furthermore, the 1990 Gulf War and the initial stages of the dissolution of the Yugoslav Federation revealed painfully the limitations of EPC and incurred for the EC a significant loss of international credibility.

It was not surprising that when the CFSP was introduced in the TEU the majority of provisions merely codified much of what had developed informally over the years within EPC. Likewise, for reasons primarily of national sovereignty, competence within CFSP was retained by the member states, the Commission simply being 'fully associated'. More interesting, however, were the declared objectives of CFSP and the aspirations contained therein. The most potentially significant departure from EPC, and one that will be returned to later, was Article J.4. This stated that CFSP 'shall include all questions related to the security of the Union, including the eventual framing of a common defence policy, which might in time lead to a common defence'. The potential hard security issues arising from this aspiration were seemingly pushed the way of the WEU, which was regarded as an 'integral part of the development of the Union'.

Less dramatic but significant nonetheless were the declared objectives of the CFSP. The policy was to safeguard the common values, fundamental interests and independence of the Union and strengthen the security of the Union and its member states in all ways. It was also to promote international co-operation, preserve peace and strengthen international security in accordance with the principles of the UN Charter and the Helsinki Final Act and the objectives of the Paris Charter. Furthermore, CFSP was to develop and consolidate democracy and the rule of law, and respect for human rights and fundamental freedoms.[30] One can certainly point to the anodyne nature of these objectives. Yet they are significant in that they reflect a broad consensus on the guiding principles of EU foreign and security policy. To the extent possible, the EU would promote a post-Cold War international order that was multipolar, rule-based and geared to the securing and maintaining of peace. And to achieve this the EU would project its own norms, develop co-operative multilateralism and international law, and pursue an inclusive international order that would provide security for current and future generations.

This is triply important in the development of CFSP and of the EU in international relations. First, consensus is a prerequisite to action as most areas of CFSP either must be, or are in practice, decided by unanimity, even allowing for the introduction of constructive abstention in the Amsterdam Treaty and enhanced co-operation in the Nice Treaty. Second, broad agreement on CFSP objectives and multilateral modes of operation facilitate co-ordination. Hence, for instance, EU member states tend to co-operate closely in the UN General Assembly, and in the Security Council Britain and France vote together at least 75 per cent of the time.[31] Third, as a *sui generis* entity, the EU does not have the foreign and security policy compass provided for states by clearly defined cultural, economic, political and social interests but is instead an ill-defined amalgam of such interests. The principles agreed in CFSP thus have an intangible but important compensatory value in steering a collective foreign and security policy course.

EU external relations: patterns and instruments

It is difficult to give any hard and fast characterisation of EU external relations for they vary enormously in type, scope and participation. They can be bilateral or multilateral, issue-specific or broad-ranging, and short-term or open-ended. They can be with state or non-state actors and can involve the EC, the member states or a combination thereof. They can also be the product of EU own initiatives or the result of collective endeavours with other international actors. For instance, the EC is a member of over sixty international organisations that have been created under an international agreement to deal with a specific issue of concern, these sometimes being referred to as 'treaty organs' to distinguish them from more general international organisations.[32] The EU also has highly developed bilateral relations with key world states, notably with the US. Indeed, Javier Solana explicitly called in June 2003 for the EU to develop 'strategic partnerships' with Russia, Japan, China, Canada and India. Furthermore, the EU has a series of multilateral relationships and a range of commitments to international agreements, such as the Comprehensive Test Ban Treaty (CTBT) and the Kyoto Protocol.

This said, EU external relations indicate a distinct preference for multilateralism and for interregional co-operation. Multilateral arrangements provide stronger mechanisms through which to spread EU norms and to promote the EU integration model as an example to other regions of how to develop prosperity and to overcome regional conflicts and instability. They are also easier to co-ordinate and manage than a multitude of bilateral relationships. Less altruistic still, framework arrangements help to protect and promote EU economic, political and security interests. They also allow the EU to extend and, in some cases, institutionalise its influence farther afield than in the past. The scope and primary motivations for these interregional arrangements vary. For instance, EFTA was originally seen as a potential rival to the EC but once this faded the European Economic Area (EEA) agreement was introduced both to prepare EFTA members for potential EU membership and facilitate EFTA–EU trade and co-operation. In contrast, ASEAN was developed initially for Cold War reasons but now serves as an EU bridge into Asia and as a forum for wide-ranging discussion. In total, the EU has developed arrangements with over twenty groups of states, which means that it enjoys interregional co-operation on a world-wide basis through which it co-ordinates variously trade, aid and political dialogue. Other examples include ASEM, the ARF, Mercosur, the Euro-Mediterranean Partnership, the Gulf Co-operation Council and the Cotonou Agreement (formerly Lomé Conventions).

Over the years EC co-operation and association agreements concluded with third countries have developed in number, nature and scope so that the EU currently has over 120 association agreements with developing countries alone. First generation trade agreements developed during the 1970s were sectorally based and could be either preferential or non-preferential. Second generation agreements subsequently added financial and technical co-operation to the basic trade relationship. From the 1990s, however, agreements tended to become much more expansive. Third generation co-operation agreements provided for additional co-operation in areas such as economic policy, environmental issues and employment generation. Most significant and influential of all co-operation and association agreements are 'mixed' association agreements. These incorporate all the issues covered by third generation agreements but also include dialogue on CFSP and JHA matters.[33] Examples of such mixed agreements include the Europe Agreements, development association agreements with the Maghreb and Mashreq states, and agreements with western Balkan countries under the Stabilisation and Association Process (SAP).

EU external relationships and agreements have come over the years to exhibit a pyramid of economic preferences that reflect geography, historical legacy and a certain degree of protectionism *vis-à-vis* both economically strong states and exporters of goods and materials regarded as 'sensitive' by EU member states. At the top of the pyramid are the remaining EFTA states, which are *de facto* members of the single market through the EEA.[34] Next are the CEECs that have signed Europe Agreements. These are designed to prepare them for full EU membership and provide for phased full access to the SEM. Then there are the developing countries, within which there is a further hierarchy of preferences. The ACP countries were traditionally at the top, with the most structured relationship, greatest preferential entry to the single market and privileged access to the EDF. Other developing countries enjoyed as a minimum the benefits under the ECs' Generalised System of Preferences (GSP), which provides for the generally tariff-free import of industrial goods and many agricultural products into the EU. Recently, however, this hierarchy has been altered in an attempt to target the poorest countries for additional help. Thus in February 2001 the EU introduced the 'Everything But Arms' arrangement that allowed duty-free access to all goods other than arms and ammunition from the forty-eight least developed countries.[35] At the bottom of the pyramid come those countries accorded most-favoured nation trading status under GATT/WTO rules and those not even granted this.

It is important to note that the EU's pyramid of economic preference neither reflects its predominant trade patterns nor necessarily conforms to its political and security priorities. In some cases there is coincidence between the two. For instance, the Europe Agreements and the Balkans SAP exhibit economic preference and reflect profound EU concern for post-Cold War security issues that either emanate from or transit through these bordering regions. The most obvious converse example is the EU's relationship with the US. The US is near the bottom in terms of EU economic preferences and is the country with which the EU has most serious trade disputes and disagreements. Yet it is also the EU's most important economic, political and security partner. For instance, the transatlantic commercial relationship is worth $2.5 trillion and there is more European investment in Texas than all the American investment in Japan.[36] Similarly China, India and Russia, singled out by Solana as key countries with which the EU should develop strategic partnerships, are treated far worse in terms of economic preference than are Iceland and Liechtenstein.

Turning to the numerous instruments of EU external relations, it is particularly interesting to contrast CCP and CFSP tools since they reflect the history of European integration and the effect of competency divisions within the Union. Not surprisingly, trade instruments are the most developed and, being subject to the Community method, the most effectively co-ordinated. The CET is the most obvious of the regulatory tools available to the EU in its management of its international trade relations. This standardises member states' protection *vis-à-vis* third countries through the application of uniform customs duties to imported products, irrespective of the member state of destination. However, with the progressive liberalisation of trade under GATT and the WTO, non-tariff barriers have become more prominent and controversial. These include 'orderly marketing' arrangements such as voluntary export restraints, quotas, and agreements such as the Multi-Fibre Agreement and commercial defence mechanisms. The latter include anti-dumping measures, used especially *vis-à-vis* Asian exporters, anti-subsidy measures and defence against trade barriers. Possible actions therein include countervailing increases in customs duties and the temporary suspension of preferential agreements. In addition, the EU has recourse to a number of indirect trade control measures. One example is the control of dual use goods, including software and technology. This is done in order to maintain effective control when exported outside the EU and in line with the international commitments of the Community and the member states on non-proliferation. The EU can also resort to cultural protectionism and trade regulation on grounds of health and safety. Hence the Commission, for example, introduced a controversial and ongoing regulatory regime requiring environmental evaluation and step-by-step approval for the dissemination of genetically modified organisms (GMOs) in the wake of unsatisfactory progress in biosafety talks from 1996, environmentalist pressure and public outcry against food scares such as BSE (bovine spongiform encephalopathy or, as more commonly known, 'mad cow disease').[37]

In contrast, CFSP does not have direct use of Community instruments and has developed a set of its own outside EC structures. It has continued the EPC practice of non-binding declaratory diplomacy, issuing common statements, declarations and *démarches*. However, it has also developed potentially stronger and legally binding instruments. Common positions and joint actions, for example, were introduced in the TEU. Decided upon by the General Affairs Council, these are mechanisms to enable better co-ordination, impose an element of discipline in the implementation stage, and raise the profile of the EU. These were supplemented in the Amsterdam Treaty by the introduction of common strategies, which are decided upon by the European Council, and serve to set overall policy guidelines and stipulate objectives, resource requirements and expected duration of actions. Most ambitious, however, was the TEU provision for the 'eventual framing of a common defence policy, which might in time lead to a common defence'. Herein the subsequent development of CESDP has potentially given the EU military teeth to back its diplomacy. It has also caused some confusion in that the 'D' in CESDP is largely redundant, member states insisting that defence remain outside the EU. This resolve was underlined by the Nice Treaty's effective separation of security and defence through its incorporation into the EU of most elements of the WEU other than its mutual defence clause.[38]

Although not instruments *per se* of EU external relations policies, it is important to note too that the EU makes extensive use of other international organisations and non-state actors both to legitimise and to deliver its policies. The most obvious legitimator is the UN, and in crisis situations, for example, the EU generally acts in support of Security Council resolutions. The EU has also used its international commitments to justify controversial policies. For instance, part of the EDF contribution to Lomé IV was tied to World Bank-imposed structural adjustment programmes. Similarly, the abolition in the Cotonou Agreement of support mechanisms such as STABEX and SYSMIN and the phasing out by 2007 of non-reciprocal trade preferences was justified primarily in terms of WTO compliance. As for the delivery of external relations policies, the EU both co-operates closely with, and exerts significant influence within and over, international organisations and NGOs. For example, EC and member states' trade-related technical assistance to developing countries is largely channelled through multilateral programmes and contributions to the WTO, the UNCTAD, the Joint Integrated Technical Assistance Programme, the International Trade Commission and the Agency for International Trade Information and Cooperation. The EU also works with NGOs and has significant leverage over them through its financing of their work and its tender process. For instance, in 1976 the EP created budget line B7 6000 'Co-financing with NGOs',[39] which is now the Commission's principal instrument for supporting EU NGOs in development co-operation programmes and projects to raise public awareness of development issues. In 2002 this was worth some €200 million, with €90 million of food aid also being made available to NGOs.[40] Moreover, EU member states also provide significant contributions to organisations such as the OSCE and the UN. In the former, they contribute over two-thirds of the budget. In the latter, they afford equipment and personnel for peacekeeping and contribute significantly to the general budget. In 2001 Britain, France, Germany, Spain and Italy collectively accounted for 28.53 per cent of the regular budget, significantly more than the 22 per cent ceiling negotiated by the US for its contribution.[41]

In reality the EU frequently co-ordinates instruments from across all three TEU pillars as it seeks to promote its international interests. It combines inducing 'carrot' measures, such as prospective membership or the provision of aid, technical assistance or privileged market access, with a range of coercive tools. For instance, it may apply diplomatic pressure on a recalcitrant third party through the issue of a *démarche*. Although only declaratory, this can carry considerable force given the economic weight of the EU, the collective influence of the member states, the normative power of the EU and its ability in coalition building. The EU can also use its power to grant or refuse diplomatic recognition and take collective morally stigmatising action, such as the withdrawal of Union ambassadors from a country. More often than not, however, the real teeth behind EU external relations policies is the threat of economic sanctions and the progressive politicisation of trade and aid through the use of conditionality.

The threat or imposition of economic sanctions has long been the EU's principal punitive weapon. Strategic embargo policy was a significant tool of economic warfare during the Cold War and economic sanctions have since variously been used to defend EU economic interests, convey disapproval and force states to change policies regarded as unacceptably contrary to EU norms and/or interests. Hence, for example, the EU imposed economic sanctions upon China in response to the communist leadership's massacre of pro-democracy protestors in Tiananmen Square on 4 June 1989. Since the TEU, the use of conditionality has also become an increasingly central feature of EU agreements with third parties. Put crudely, clauses within these agreements set out minimum EU expectations of the third party and provide for their suspension in the event of non-compliance. Thus trading preferences, aid, association and co-operation agreements and prospective EU membership have all been made conditional upon partners' respect for democracy and human rights and willingness to develop 'good governance'.[42] This conditionality works in two principal ways. First, the EU programmes and delimits aid into specific schemes designed to fulfil its objectives rather than simply allowing the target government to manage the resources as it sees fit. The effectiveness of this is underpinned by a combination of target-setting, increasingly rigorous monitoring procedures and the phased programming of aid, thereby tying successive tranches of aid to assessments of satisfactory progress. Second, the EU can impose sanctions on aid where the conditions of its granting are violated. These sanctions can take various forms. For instance, within its enlargement strategy the EU can delay the prospective entry of candidate countries. Alternatively it can suspend, reduce or re-route aid.

Two examples suffice to demonstrate how in its external relations the EU seeks to combine its international presence, external policies and instruments drawn from across the pillars. Its single most influential and effective post-Cold War instrument has been its enlargement strategy. The EU's economic presence has drawn CEECs towards it. In turn, their anxiety to achieve full membership, for economic, political and security reasons, encourages their 'appropriate' behaviour and accords the EU tremendous influence over them throughout the enlargement process. During this time the EU can insist on, monitor and assist the process of their acceptance and implementation of the entire *acquis communautaire*. In doing so, the Europe Agreements allow a combination of

CFSP measures and aid, trade and technical assistance tools. They also *de facto* allow for the export of internal EU security arrangements, notably the Schengen border regime and, as shall been seen later, a high degree of EU intrusion into CEEC internal affairs.

Geography, heated debate about the boundaries of Europe and political will all mean that enlargement strategy can apply only to a small fraction of the EU's international relationships. Elsewhere the EU has sometimes pushed its international trade, political and security objectives by capitalising upon historical legacies and third countries' economic and technical weakness or even dependency. In this context it is instructive to consider development co-operation. As the world's leading donor to, and trader with, developing countries, the Union and its member states provide some 55 per cent of all international development assistance, a full 66 per cent of all grant aid, and 55 per cent of all international humanitarian aid.[43] To put this into figures, the EU fifteen provided €29,352 billion of Overseas Development Aid (ODA) in 2001 and promised at the Monterrey International Conference on Financing for Development to increase this to 0.39 per cent of gross national income (GNI) by 2006, which represents a projected €35,113 billion of ODA.[44] It combines this dominant position with a range of instruments drawn from within and without EC competence. Development aid, for instance, has an extensive range of instruments including food aid, emergency aid, technical assistance, humanitarian aid, development finance, financial aid and debt relief. This can be broken down even further into types of financial assistance. For example, EDF instruments include grants, risk capital and loans to the private sector.

Still more important is that development co-operation sees trade, technical assistance and aid instruments tied to EU objectives including poverty reduction and its environmental, human rights and world trade agendas. Indeed, the link between Development Policy and EU foreign policy was formally established in the TEU. Article 130u declared that the former 'shall contribute to the general objective of developing and consolidating democracy and the rule of law, and to that of respecting human rights and fundamental freedoms'. Thus, for example, the Cotonou Agreement involves dialogue that covers a range of political issues that fall beyond traditional development co-operation, such as peace and security, the arms trade and migration.[45] It also places strong obligations upon ACP states to respect human rights and democracy, provide for sustainable development, fight corruption and remove trade barriers progressively and reciprocally in compliance with WTO requirements.[46]

EU external relations: post-Cold War reforms

The EU is in a process of almost constant reform and adaptation, and its external relations are no exception. The Cotonou Agreement represented a marked change to the Lomé Conventions. Some issue areas have been communautarised, such as external border controls. There is a constant battle for competence, such as within environmental policy and even within aspects of trade policy. And there is continual focus upon how to improve cross-pillar co-ordination and develop the procedural reform necessary to enhance decision-making and implementation in the context of a Union that in 2004 must accommodate twenty-five national interests.

However, few areas have – arguably – received either more attention or reform than CFSP. This owes in part to its historical under-development next to trade and Development Policy. Critically, it also reflects the significant post-Cold War increase in EU member states' willingness and enthusiasm for developing the Union's political and security dimensions. Agreement may be lacking in terms of desired end forms and the precise capabilities of the EU polity, but all member states perceive the advantages of collective action in CFSP within an international environment significantly changed from that of the Cold War. Moreover, whenever political will seems to have faltered, some international crisis has found the EU wanting and restored the impetus for development and reform.

Two areas of reform already touched upon are those of procedure and representation. In terms of representation, the single most important reform has been the introduction in the Amsterdam Treaty of the role of High Representative for CFSP. Since his appointment, Javier Solana has provided a 'face' to CFSP and aided continuity in EU policy, albeit that the effect would be still greater were it not for the practical overlap with the EU External Relations Commissioner. Procedurally, greater flexibility has been sought as a consequence of enlargement, the loss of Cold War geo-strategic discipline and the different foreign and security policy cultures of the EU member states. Thus, for example, Denmark was allowed to opt out in the TEU of prospective EU defence issues. A case-by-case opt-out was effectively provided for all states through the introduction of constructive abstention in the Amsterdam Treaty. Hereby a state is not obliged to apply a decision by the EU on the proviso that it refrains from any action that might conflict with the Union's action under that decision. This allows national interests to be respected without the need for a veto, therefore still allowing the EU to act provided that a minimum of two-thirds of the weighted Council votes are in favour. In line with a general post-Cold War trend towards coalitions of the willing, CFSP flexibility was supplemented further in the Nice Treaty with the introduction of enhanced co-operation. This applies to the implementation of a joint action or common position in circumstances where they have no military or defence implications, no member state objects or applies the so-called 'emergency brake' (a call for a unanimous decision in the European Council) and where there exists a threshold of eight member states in favour.

The most dramatic development, however, within the overall framework of CFSP has been the development of CESDP and the EURRF. EU political and security ambition was reflected in the Amsterdam Treaty's incorporation of the Petersberg tasks[47] and the creation of a Policy Planning and Early Warning Unit (PPEWU) involving a Commission representative, WEU representative, three representatives from the Council of Ministers and a national represent-ative of each member country. The real impetus, though, came from a British *volte face* on its traditional opposition to the EU developing a military capab-ility and the consequent St Malo declaration with France that the EU should have the capacity to address international crises.[48] This initiative was embraced at the June 1999 Copenhagen European Council, and NATO's Washington Summit that year agreed the so-called 'Berlin-plus' arrangements whereby the EU would have ready access to NATO's planning capabilities and other milit-ary assets. The EU's Helsinki European Council in December 1999 then set Headline Goals for the EU in 144 capability areas such that it would be able by 2003 to deploy a force of 50,000–60,000 troops within sixty days and to support it with appropriate air and naval assets. This force was to be sustain-able in the field for twelve months and to be able to conduct simultaneously one heavy mission, such as interpositionary action between belligerent forces, and one light mission, such as humanitarian action.

Since then, considerable effort has been expended in developing modalities for EU–NATO interface, building the necessary EU civilian and military infras-tructure and finding the resources and equipment necessary to meet the Helsinki Headline Goals. The Nice European Council in December 2000 authorised the creation of an EU Political and Security Committee (COPS), a Military Committee and a Military Staff. A politico-military working group and a com-mittee for civilian aspects of crisis management support these. That same year the member states pledged their contributions to meeting the Headline Goals at the Capabilities Conference. The Headline Goal Task Force subsequently identified a number of critical deficiencies in military capacity, including airlift and sea-lift capacity, air-to-ground missiles, all-weather precision-guided and GPS-guided munitions, nuclear, biological and chemical protection, theatre missile defence, logistics, and command, control, communications and intelli-gence. In November 2001 the Capabilities Improvement Conference extracted further commitment pledges from EU member states and set up a European Capabilities Action Plan (ECAP) to investigate how to address remaining deficiencies. The ECAP focused on the top 50 per cent of the forty designated shortfall areas and emphasised the need to rationalise member states' defence efforts and to increase synergy between their national and multinational projects.[49]

In December 2001 the Laeken European Council meeting controversially declared that the CESDP was already at a stage where it was capable of con-ducting some crisis management operations. Not until late 2002, however, did decisions within the EU and NATO's North Atlantic Council finally overcome sufficiently the reservations of some NATO members, notably Turkey, to allow the Berlin-plus arrangements to be operationalised on the basis of a joint EU–NATO declaration on 16 December 2002. Much remains to be done in areas such as meeting capability deficits, rationalising the plethora of actors and increasing member state co-ordination in procurement and inter-operability. Moreover, this needs to be achieved against a background of national sensitivity about foreign and security policy, cross-currents of Atlanticism and European-ism, general reticence to increase military spending and the constraints imposed on most EU states by EMU rules. Many people are justifiably cautious, if not sceptical, of when or if the EURRF will finally be fully operational.

Conclusion

This chapter has outlined the EU's place in the global system, highlighted some of the difficulties involved in distinguishing strictly between EU internal and external activities, and identified some of the key EU external instruments and policies. It has also demonstrated difficulties associated with the TEU pillar system for effective international action and the associated complicated com-petency divisions between the EC and the member states. In turn this, coupled with the constantly evolving nature of the EU, has indicated some of the difficulties both for external actors in dealing with the EU and for the EU in terms of the varying recognition accorded to it by different actors.

One of the most striking things about the EU has been its mounting post-Cold War ambition to become a more rounded and capable international actor. This owes both to international expectations of it and the increasing advantages accruing to the member states of acting collectively in an era of globalisation. Its economic power has long been recognised but it has begun to use this increasingly for political and security purposes. With CESDP and the EURRF it also seems determined upon harnessing a limited but significant military capacity to its diplomacy. Indeed, this is essential if the EU is to meet its Petersberg commitments and, provided the EURRF is developed in a way complementary to NATO, to maintain the well-being of the transatlantic relationship.

Other reasons for the EU already being an important international actor, and becoming ever more so, include that its progressive reform and adaptation is slowly allowing it to translate its international presence into purposive action. Also, the EU's *sui generis* nature confers advantages in that it offers a model to others, is generally not regarded as threatening in the traditional way that sovereign states often are, and its normative foundation is the product and development of the dominant liberal international order. Furthermore, the EU has been a particular beneficiary of changes in the nature of security and of power. The post-Cold War era in particular has seen power configured differ-ently in its different aspects. Militarily it is unipolar, economically it is multi-polar and in transnational relations beyond the control of governments it is widely dispersed.[50] Moreover, military power is of declining relative utility and the EU is not threatened by the global military hegemon, namely the US.

This said, and as will be seen in subsequent chapters, the EU faces significant challenges if it is to overcome caricatures such as that by the Belgian Foreign Minister mentioned earlier or of a tripartite division of global responsibilities whereby the US fights, the UN feeds and the EU funds. Foremost of these, despite the EU having successfully embarked on ever-increasing rounds of institutional development, is the consistency problem. This is fed by the diversity of actors and processes involved in EU external relations, varying levels of policy development, competency divisions and the TEU pillar structure, and the increasing diversity of national interests in line with the loss of Cold War-imposed geo-strategic discipline and EU enlargement. Even within development co-operation, for example, the Commission recently noted the 'patchwork of initiatives' and that 'Europe should be able to go further together . . . We still have a long way to go in terms of internalisation and implementation by the Member States of Policy Frameworks and Guidelines that have been established after a negotiation at the Community level.'[51]

There are also a number of less tangible but arguably even more significant challenges. One of these is perception. This is vital. It reflects and to an extent determines how other international actors relate to the EU. As will be seen, it also partially determines EU credibility, especially if expectation is allowed or even encouraged to outstrip capabilities. Furthermore, perception-management is important if the EU is to continue to enjoy the advantages of its post-Westphalian construction. Too great an exploitation of its economic preponderance *vis-à-vis* developing countries for its own political and security agendas could, for example, cause resentment and even encourage a neo-imperial perception. More problematic still are the interrelated factors of capabilities and political will. That the EU is more than the sum of its parts in some aspects of its external relations and less so in others is the responsibility primarily of its member states. This is something that should be borne constantly in mind as attention now moves to the examination of the EU's actual performance in post-Cold War international relations.

Notes

1 Belgian Foreign Minister, *New York Times*, 25 January 1991, cited by McCormick, J. (2002) *Understanding the European Union*, Basingstoke: Palgrave, p. 197.

2 Share of goods and commercial services in the total trade of selected regions and economies 2001, http://www.wto.org.

3 Ibid.; World Bank (July 2003) *World Development Indicators*, http://www.worldbank.org/data/databytopic.

4 World Bank (July 2003) *World Development Indicators*.

5 McCormick, *Understanding the European Union*, p. 205.

6 Smith, H. (2002) *European Union Foreign Policy: What It Is and What It Does*, London: Pluto Press, p. 20.

7 http://europa.eu.int/comm/external_relations/delegations/intro/role.htm.

8 Nugent, N. (1999) *The Government and Politics of the European Union*, Basingstoke: Macmillan, p. 462.

9 http://www.europa.eu.int/abc/treaties_en.htm.

10 France, Britain, Germany, the Netherlands and Italy. Stockholm International Peace Research Institute (SIPRI) (2002) *SIPRI Yearbook 2002*, New York, p. 376.

11 Ibid., pp. 254 and 235.

12 Ibid., pp. 266–7.

13 European Commission (2003) Staff Working Document: Follow-up to the International Conference on Financing for Development (Monterrey – 2002), SEC (2003) 569, 15 May 2003, p. 19.

14 Agreements can be regarded as 'mixed' on three counts: if the EC and one or more of the member states are parties to it; if the EC and member states share competence in it; and if certain voting or financing provisions apply. For a discussion of this see McGoldrick, D. (1997) *International Relations Law of the European Union*, London: Longman, pp. 78–88.

15 Bretherton, C. and Vogler, J. (1999) *The European Union as a Global Actor*, London: Routledge, p. 89.

16 McGoldrick, *International Relations Law of the European Union*, pp. 32–3.

17 The new provisions of Article 133 (5) ECT call for unanimous agreement following consultation of the European Parliament, on such matters which affect internal policy areas that themselves require unanimity, and on such matters for which the Community does not yet have legislative authority. Monar, J. (2002) 'Außenwirtschaftsbeziehungen' in *Europa von A bis Z*, Weidenfeld, W. and Wessels, W. (eds), Bonn: Bundeszentrale für politische Bildung, p. 83.

18 Church, C.H. and Phinnemore, D. (2002) *The Penguin Guide to the European Treaties*, London: Penguin Books, p. 321.

19 There are twenty-three members: the ten ASEAN member states (Indonesia, Philippines, Thailand, Vietnam, Malaysia, Singapore, Brunei, Burma/Myanmar, Laos and Cambodia), the twelve ASEAN dialogue partners (Australia, Canada, China, North Korea, South Korea, US, India, Japan, Mongolia, New Zealand, Russia, and the EU) and the one ASEAN observer (Papua New Guinea).

20 The EU refused to acquiesce, just as it had in the face of two previous rulings from the WTO against its banana import regime. Before the WTO could rule again, the Clinton administration, with rapturous congressional approval, invoked section 301 legislation and on 3 March imposed punitive sanctions by putting a random fifteen European products on the red list.

21 Dent, C.M. (1997) *The European Economy: The Global Context*, London: Routledge, p. 183.

22 Monar, 'Außenwirtschaftsbeziehungen', pp. 83–4.

23 MacLeod, I. et al. (1996) *The External Relations of the European Communities*, Oxford: Clarendon Press, p. 283.

24 Named after Article 133 ECT which represents the principal legal/constitutional basis of the CCP.

25 Monar, 'Außenwirtschaftsbeziehungen', pp. 84–5.

26 Algieri, F. (2002) 'Assoziierungs- und Kooperationspolitik' in *Europa von A bis Z*, Weidenfeld and Wessels (eds), p. 69.

27 By way of the so-called 'Luns-Westerterp procedure' the EP is, nevertheless, informed about contents and progress of trade negotiations. See Monar, 'Außenwirtschaftsbeziehungen', p. 85.

28 Such as, for instance, Monar or Algieri in *Europa von A bis Z*, Weidenfeld and Wessels (eds), pp. 69–72 and 85.

29 See, for example, Nugent, N. (2003) *The Government and Politics of the European Union*, 5th edn, Basingstoke: Macmillan, p. 433.

30 Treaty on European Union, http://europa.eu.int/abc/obj/treaties/en/entr2f.htm#TOPFILE.

31 Nugent, *The Government and Politics of the European Union*, p. 462; 'The EU & the European Commission at the UN', http://europa.eu.int/comm/external_relations/un/intro/index.htm.

32 McGoldrick, *International Relations Law of the European Union*, p. 33.

33 Bretherton and Vogler, *The European Union as a Global Actor*, p. 63.

34 Switzerland, an EFTA member, is not part of the EEA because a respective treaty was rejected in a referendum.

35 Holland, M. (2002) *The European Union and the Third World*, Basingstoke: Palgrave, pp. 25–32.

36 Solana, J. (2003) 'Mars and Venus Reconsidered: A New Era for Transatlantic Relations', Albert H. Gordon lecture at the Kennedy School of Government, Harvard University, http://www.useu.be/TransAtlantic/030407SolanaHarvard.htm.

37 This is another and ongoing major transatlantic dispute, with the US being the world's largest exporter of GM foods in an expanding area of trade already worth in excess of $1.5 billion per year.

38 Duke, S. (2001) 'After Nice: The Prospects for European Security and Defence', http://www.theepc.be/challenge/topdetail.asp.

39 As the name suggests, NGOs have to co-fund projects to a minimum of 25 per cent.

40 BOND, EC Budget Lines: Background Info, http://www.bond.org.uk/eu/budglines.htm.

41 'The EU & the Organisation for Security and Co-operation in Europe (OSCE)', http://europa.eu.int/comm/external_relations/osce/; Federal Republic of Germany, Auswärtiges Amt (2001) 'UN Scale of Assessments (Regular Budget) in 2001', http://www.auswaertiges-amt.de/www/en/aussenpolitik/vn/finanzen_html.

42 Smith, K.E. (1998) 'The Use of Political Conditionality in the EU's Relations with Third Countries: How Effective?' *European Foreign Affairs Review* 3 p. 253.

43 http://europa.eu.int/comm/external_relations/delegations/intro/index.htm.

44 European Commission, Staff Working Document: Follow-up to the International Conference on Financing for Development (Monterrey – 2002), pp. 4 and 7. GNI is more commonly known as GNP but is the terminology currently used by the World Bank in line with the 1993 System of National Accounts.

45 General Secretariat of the African, Caribbean and Pacific Group of States (2000) *Cotonou Agreement*, http://www.acpsec.org/gb/cotonou/accord1.htm.

46 The EU had wanted 'good governance' to be included in the Cotonou Agreement as an 'essential element' whereby its violation could lead to an EU suspension of aid. It was eventually accepted as a 'fundamental element', which meant no automatic right of suspension but that serious cases of corruption might lead to that through a consultation process. ECDPM (2001) 'Cotonou Infokit: Innovations in the Cotonou Agreement', http://www.oneworld.org/ecdpm/en/cotonou/04_gb.htm.

47 The Petersberg tasks comprise humanitarian and rescue tasks; peacekeeping tasks; and tasks of combat forces in crisis management, including peacemaking.

48 'Joint Declaration on European Defence', 3–4 December 1998, www.fco.gov.uk.

49 Duke, S. (2002) 'CESDP and the EU Response to 11 September: Identifying the Weakest Link' *European Foreign Affairs Review* 7 p. 164.

50 Nye Jr., J.S. (2002) *The Paradox of American Power*, Oxford: Oxford University Press.

51 European Commission, Staff Working Document: Follow-up to the International Conference on Financing for Development (Monterrey – 2002), p. 11.

CHAPTER 4

The post-Cold War EU–US security relationship

No single security relationship has ever been more important for the EC/EU than that with the US. It was the midwife to integration and the heartbeat of Western Cold War resistance to the Soviet threat. It is rooted in shared historical experiences, liberal democratic values and commitment to market economies and the rule of law. Ingrained habits of co-operation, dense transatlantic interdependence and the pivotal position of the EU and US in developing global governance guarantee its continuing importance. And its well-being is tended by a myriad of transatlantic connections: direct EU–US contacts, bilateral contacts between EU member states and the US, contacts within multilateral fora, the accumulative impact of transnational groups, educational and cultural exchanges, and so forth.

Yet prognoses of the relationship's post-Cold War health have ranged from the optimistic through to warnings of inevitable and even terminal decline.[1] This chapter assesses why this is the case. It begins by examining continued security interdependence and mutual political will to consolidate and institutionalise transatlantic security co-operation. It then assesses factors underpinning impressions of transatlantic drift in terms of EU and US visions of the post-Cold War order, their roles within it, and their preferred methods for developing international security. Finally it addresses two key aspects of the security relationship that have witnessed co-operation but also friction, namely the debate about burden-sharing and the development of European Security and Defence Identity (ESDI) and the September 11 terrorist attacks on the World Trade Centre and the Pentagon.

Managing the EU–US security relationship

Any investigation of EU–US security relations should recognise their interdependence, determined efforts to manage their relationship constructively and their collectively dominant position in the international system. British Prime Minister Blair once called their drawing together 'the single most urgent priority for the new international order' and warned that 'bad guys' celebrate when they do not.[2] The EU and US together are economically and militarily preponderant. They form the bedrock of global governance, having largely initiated and dominated the world's principal multilateral fora, including the UN, NATO, the G8, IMF and the WTO. They share a value-laden relationship and a belief that exporting the values therein provides the basis for developing elsewhere peace and security, an assumption rooted in democratic peace theory.[3]

The continued post-Cold War importance of the transatlantic relationship was quickly elaborated by President George H. Bush, his famous 'beef hormone and pasta' speech portraying the two sides as locked into competitive co-operation. Apprehension and opportunity underscored American interest in renegotiating the EC–US relationship. It was important to keep the EC engaged. Potential European introspection played on lingering fears from the Reagan administration of a Fortress Europe and threatened to leave the US burdened with intolerable and unsustainable international commitments. Conversely, it was important to guard against possible EC 'over-assertion' upon the world stage, fears encouraged by its increasing international influence and willingness to challenge US leadership during the 1980s. EC influence seemed destined to grow, especially with a reunified Germany at its heart, and US ability to command an informal seat at the EC table was liable to weaken with the relative downgrading of mutual defence considerations. Moreover, further EC enlargement potentially threatened to incur the US additional *de facto* security guarantees through a process over which it had no control. New EU members would be able to join the WEU, and although they might choose not, or be unable, to join NATO, they could secure indirect NATO protection on account of guarantees to EU states who were members of WEU and NATO.

The flip side of US apprehension was possible co-option of the EC in sharing the security burdens of international leadership and the construction of a new world order. Together the US, the EC and its member states were strongly placed to adapt established institutions to the post-Cold War security environment. Approximate EC–US economic parity meant that there was no reason why the US should continue to bear disproportionate burdens, especially as Europe's hard security deficiencies were unlikely to be exposed disastrously in the absence of the Soviet threat. Propitiously, too, the EC seemed poised to become a more capable partner as twin intergovernmental conferences prepared the way for EMU and potentially enhanced EC powers in security issues such as non-proliferation, disarmament, terrorism, and illegal immigration.

EC considerations broadly mirrored those of the US. The EC urgently needed continued US engagement in international security generally and in Europe especially. The end of the Cold War reduced neither EC dependence on US military muscle nor, amid pessimistic warnings of Europe's going 'back to the future', the importance of America's stabilising European presence.[4] Concomitantly, though, it did weaken the rationale for both continued US large-scale peacetime military commitments to Europe and NATO – the principal vehicle of American European influence.[5] Farther afield a US withdrawal to neo-isolationism could bequeath destabilising vacuums of power, undermine the effectiveness of multilateral organisations and increase pressure on the EU in areas such as development policy as America slashed foreign aid and non-military programmes.

The US Congress, Bush's presidential election defeat in 1992 despite successful prosecution of the Gulf War and Clinton's subsequent alleged initial neglect of foreign policy all demonstrated pressure for a rationalisation of American post-Cold War commitments. Yet the EU also faced a danger that in the emergent '"uni-multipolar" world'[6] an internationalist US would exploit its status as sole remaining superpower to fashion and dominate a new order of its own choosing. Herein it might act more unilaterally and to the detriment of EU interests. The lifting of Cold War constraints, US unilateral intervention in Panama in 1989 and continued American propensity to threaten and/or impose unilateral economic sanctions encouraged these fears.[7] An arrogant use of power by an internationalist America might be as destabilising as a withdrawal to neo-isolationism. It could undermine the principled multilateralism to which Europe was committed and provoke a backlash against American neo-imperialism.[8] It could also lead the US to cast the EU in roles that it was not prepared to accept, such as being consigned in US strategy to regional power status or as America's deputy in global security management. European Commission Vice-President Leon Brittan actually warned in September 1998 that Washington needed greater recognition 'that co-operation with the European Union does not mean simply signing up the European Union to endorse, execute, and sometimes finance, United States foreign policy'.[9]

Both sides consequently recognised their continued security interdependence and sought to manage the other's behaviour through what might be termed 'co-operative containment'. EU–US security relations needed renegotiation in line with new conditions, their solidarity needed public reaffirmation, and modalities were needed to improve consultation and reduce the risk of either side engaging in actions that might surprise or unduly antagonise the other. In 1989 the Bush administration, conscious also of the need for a gesture of continued American engagement to offset European doubts about reunifying Germany, took the initiative. Bush met Commission President Jacques Delors five times during 1989, suggested closer EC–US consultative links in May that year and accorded the EC increasing recognition as a potential full partner.[10] Hence the Commission's delegation to Washington was upgraded to full diplomatic status and the then G7 approved in July the Commission having responsibility for co-ordinating aid to Poland and Hungary. In December 1989 US Secretary of State James Baker also made a key speech in which he called for a 'New Atlanticism' and stronger EC–US institutional and consultative links, possibly in the form of a treaty.[11]

The EC responded positively and in February 1990 the Irish EC presidency and the Bush administration agreed the inauguration of biannual meetings between the US President and the Presidents of the European Council and of the Commission. Biannual meetings were also provided for between the US Secretary of State, EC Foreign Ministers and Commission Representatives. In addition, there would be biannual cabinet-level meetings between the Secretary of State and the presidency Foreign Minister/or the troika, and *ad hoc* consultations where necessary. Further encouraged by US rhetoric, such as Robert Zoellick's call for an EC–US 'alliance of values',[12] the EC subsequently endeavoured to accord these closer institutional links greater visibility and to locate them within a wider framework. In summer 1990 the Italian presidency advanced the basis for a transatlantic declaration and on 20 November 1990 the Declaration on EC–US Relations was adopted.

The Declaration stopped short of the possible treaty mooted by Baker and has been widely condemned for simply repeating 'a great deal of familiar poetry' and being 'long on rhetoric and short on substance'.[13] Nevertheless it reaffirmed the salience of shared values, the Declaration's common objectives being remarkably similar to those subsequently adopted within CFSP in the TEU. It signalled mutual political will to renegotiate progressively the EC–US relationship, something epitomised by the inclusion and subsequent exercise of an evolutionary clause.[14] It marked an encouraging public statement of transatlantic solidarity and formalised contacts between the European Parliament and Congress, which had begun in 1972 and were potentially increasingly important as both institutions secured greater external affairs influence in the Cold War's aftermath. The Declaration even raised the prospect of genuine EC–US security partnership, formally recognising 'the accelerating process by which the European Community is acquiring its own identity in economic and monetary matters, in foreign policy and in the domain of security'.[15]

Limitations of the Declaration soon became evident though. Its demonstration of transatlantic solidarity was quickly overshadowed by the Gulf War and undermined by EC–US differences prompting the collapse of the GATT Uruguay Round in December 1990. Its procedures produced at best mixed results, there being a lack of co-ordination between different bureaucratic levels of dialogue and insufficient follow-through from EC/EU–US summits. It also seemed unable to stem transatlantic drift. EC/EU relative impotence to deal with spiralling crisis in the Balkans revealed a damaging 'capabilities-expectation gap' and undermined its claim to transatlantic security partnership.[16] Meanwhile Clinton's election accelerated US strategic concern shifting from Europe to Asia and, at least initially, marked a switch from the internationalism of the Bush administration towards a more introspective and domestically orientated agenda.

In November 1992 Germany's Chancellor, Helmut Kohl, advocated a more comprehensive transatlantic structure to improve continuity between summits, deepen the level of consultation (thereby helping lock the US into Europe) and provide for greater practical collaboration. The EU–US Summit in July 1994 approved three working groups, comprising representatives of the US, the Commission and the EU presidency, to examine stabilisation of Central and Eastern Europe, CFSP and international crime, including nuclear smuggling and drugs trafficking. Despite these groups running into problems, owing not least to internal EU competency battles and uncertainty about how much information to share with the US, work continued on defining a broad framework for EU–US co-operation.

Co-ordination was increasingly necessary to combat transnational security threats, avoid duplication and possibly transfer onerous responsibilities from one party to the other. Also, a Spanish non-paper in July 1995 highlighted possible transatlantic drift in the absence of a common threat, mutual introspection, unpredictable and possible unilateral leanings of US foreign policy, and demographic changes in the US that weakened American affiliation with Europe.[17] Furthermore there evolved a timely coincidence of interest. The EU saw opportunities to recover lost ground as a security partner, raise its external global profile, build American support for the nascent ESDI and further embroil the US in Balkan security and reconstruction. The Clinton administration felt that transatlantic structures needed post-TEU adaptation, focused more on foreign policy once its domestic agenda was circumscribed by losing both the House and Senate in November 1994, and wanted the EU to take a leading role in implementing the Dayton Peace Accords and Balkan reconstruction.

The product was a New Transatlantic Agenda (NTA) and an accompanying Joint Action Plan (JAP), developed by a Senior Level Group created at the June 1995 EU–US Washington Summit and adopted at the EU–US Madrid Summit on 3 December 1995. Hailed as launching 'an era of unprecedented co-operation on a wide range of political, economic and civil society issues',[18] the NTA reflected considerable political will, especially given distractions of mid-term US elections scheduled for 1996 and the EU's IGC preparation for the Amsterdam Treaty. It built on the 1990 Declaration to improve dialogue and co-ordination and sought to upgrade interactions from consultation to collaboration. EU–US relations were placed firmly within a global framework and an evolutionary clause provided for subsequent adaptation. Improved dialogue and continuity was provided for through a Senior Level Group comprising sub-cabinet-level officials, and a NTA Task Force, comprising numerous working level officials, was charged with monitoring and co-ordinating progress in designated areas. These areas were clustered around four themes – 'Promoting peace and stability, democracy and development around the world; Responding to global challenges; Contributing to the expansion of world trade and closer economic relations; Building bridges across the Atlantic'.[19] The JAP developed numerous specific short-term and medium-term EU–US actions designed to fulfil objectives contained within the four themes.[20]

Four aspects of the NTA and JAP were particularly interesting for transatlantic security relations. First, the Clinton administration had renewed the American invitation to the EU to become a global security partner. For instance, they were to exercise joint leadership in the consolidation of democracy in Russia and Central Europe and in the reconstruction of Bosnia and Herzegovina, to promote the Middle East peace process and to develop co-operative efforts to combat transnational threats including international crime and narcotics. Second, the NTA adopted a broad conceptualisation of security that explicitly recognised links between security and economic transformation and liberalisation and that cut across the EU's pillared activities, thereby also lending momentum for further EU institutional reform. Thus the EU and US were to act jointly in preventative diplomacy, provision of humanitarian assistance and promotion of multilateral free trade. Third, the NTA effectively developed a joint transatlantic security agenda, with the JAP delineating specific measures to address this. As US Ambassador to the EU Stuart Eizenstat concluded, the NTA was 'the first time we have dealt comprehensively with the EU, not simply as a trade and economic organization, but as a partner in a whole array of foreign policy and diplomatic initiatives'.[21] Fourth, the NTA acknowledged that effective security co-operation and the achievement of security objectives rested not only in the hands of national governments and the EU but also in elements such as international regimes, NGOs, lobbyists and interest groups.[22] Similarly, recognition was given to the relationship between public opinion and sustainable security co-operation, especially given the so-called CNN factor and the blurring of the foreign and domestic realms of policy.[23] Hence the People-to-People Chapter sought to 'educate' American and European parliamentarians in order to overcome potential opposition to closer EU–US co-operation that cut across vested and/or political interests and to facilitate renewed Atlanticism in the face of demographic and generational change.[24]

Understanding transatlantic security drift

The NTA remains the principal framework for an EU–US bilateral relationship that enjoys consultations of an intensity, frequency and breadth 'unprecedented in the diplomatic relations of either partner and in the history of diplomacy writ large'.[25] It is a relationship rooted in decades of close collaboration, shared values and profound and ongoing interdependence. That it remains of paramount importance to both partners is amply demonstrated by the energy expended in its post-Cold War renegotiation and the political will vested in the institutionalisation of dialogue and co-operation. And this NTA co-operation continues to be fine-tuned. At the Gothenburg Summit in June 2001 six strategic themes were set out that apparently marked 'a new chapter in the EU–US relationship, characterised by clear and sustainable political priorities and more streamlined, political and results-orientated methods of co-operation'.[26]

Conclusions of transatlantic drift, or worse, thus seemingly strike a discordant note. Yet so often have these warnings been sounded, on both sides of the Atlantic, that they should be understood and not dismissed. After all, post-WW2 transatlantic relations developed and operated within a unique international system and its loss demanded key re-evaluations by the EU and the US of themselves and of their relationship. What form should the new world order promised by President Bush take and what roles should the EU and US perform in its creation? What security issues should be prioritised? What means should be used to secure desired ends?

Within this combination of mission, priorities and means lie many of what might broadly be called 'attitudinal factors' that have complicated post-Cold War transatlantic security relations. For the EU the whole notion of mission is problematic. It implies a relatively choate conception of what the EU is, where it is headed, and what its purpose is. Member states might agree on general issues such as the EU's importance in stabilising Central and Eastern Europe, promoting democracy and human rights, and addressing security threats from transnational crime. Yet there is frequent discord about how the EU should perform these security functions and what its priorities are, difficulties that are exacerbated by questions of legal competence, sovereignty and the post-Cold War regionalisation of member states' security concerns. There is even less clarity on bigger issues, as the Convention on the Future of the European Union demonstrates. Just how far should or can the EU federalise? Should it remain a civilian power or become a meaningful military actor too? Should its security focus remain in Europe and its contiguous areas such as the Maghreb, or should it join the US as a full partner in global security management?

It is not so much that the EU lacks vision but that it has multiple and competing visions, which inevitably poses problems for itself and for its partners. Also, different member state histories and regional security concerns tend to reduce EU security consensus in proportion to the distance an issue is away from Western Europe. One consequence has traditionally been a parochial EU security focus and the dedication of enormous energy and resources to its own internal grand design, as an integration project in the making. This is not necessarily wrong. Tying reunified Germany into deeper integration through successive treaties, embracing Austria, Sweden and Finland in the 1995 enlargement and preparing carefully for the pending substantial new eastern enlargement have been crucial strategies in stabilising post-Cold War Europe. Likewise institutional reform, initiatives such as CESDP and the evolution of clearer lines of responsibility and competence should facilitate future transatlantic dialogue, policy consistency and a sense of security partnership.

For the present, however, security co-operation with the EU remains a constantly moving and frustrating target. This is obvious in terms of shifting institutions and competencies. No sooner does the US work out who has responsibility for what aspect of EU security, and what is necessary to translate dialogue into meaningful action, than the EU engages in another internal reform. This is an increasing problem given that the Treaties of Maastricht, Amsterdam and Nice occurred within a decade whilst the three previous treaty revisions spanned over thirty years. EU security postures, too, can be notoriously unpredictable and inconsistent owing to changing memberships

and especially to the 'melting pot' of at present fifteen different national interests coupled with the impact of the EC institutions, policy linkage and domestic politics. Germany's unexpectedly strong stance in summer 2002 against
possible US military intervention in Iraq was widely attributed to Chancellor
Schröder's cynical manipulation of German anti-Americanism and pacifism to
win re-election in September that year. Likewise, President Chirac's interest in
hosting a conference of African nations in February 2003 meant that the EU
had to trade Robert Mugabe's presence in Paris for subsequent French agreement to renew economic sanctions against his repressive regime in Zimbabwe.

The EU's traditional parochialism and its multiple voices also mean a lack
of self-awareness of its global role and limited ability to articulate its interests
clearly and consistently. In turn, this tends to generate structures and political
will insufficient to translate EU economic power into political and security
influence, with worrisome implications for EU–US security relations. The US
tends to be both frustrated that the EU continues to 'punch below its weight'
in international security and critical of free-riding on American global contributions, especially in terms of hard security. Even EU Commissioner for
External Relations Chris Patten conceded in December 2002 the damaging
effects on transatlantic relations of 'the gulf between our rhetoric and the reality'.[27] Increasingly the EU needs to develop its own world-view and strategy
and the means to put it into effect as prerequisite to bridging this growing
transatlantic divide and constructing a new security partnership.[28]

This is not to say that in terms of global mission/vision the EU always
contrasts negatively with the US. The articulation and development of US
foreign policy has itself suffered increasingly in recent years from the impact of
domestic constituencies and from the multiplication of its own voices. Of the
former, US policy towards Israel and the Middle East peace process is the most
obvious and enduring example. As for the latter, there has been a diffusion of
responsibility in Washington as a consequence of the blurring of foreign and
domestic, and of security and non-security, issues. The US Congress, with its
own many voices and vested interests, has also seized a growing role in US foreign policy, testament to which is an expanding catalogue of incidences where
it has either substantially amended or even overturned the foreign policy of the
incumbent US President. In December 2000 EU Trade Commissioner Pascal
Lamy, in reference to Kissinger's 1970s barbed question of who in Europe should
he call in the event of a crisis, delighted in telling the American Enterprise
Institute that 'the phone numbers are multiplying' in Washington too.[29]

However, the US does have a clear sense of its place in the world, the
willingness/ability to articulate its interests, and the capability to act in their
defence and promotion. The end of the Cold War created uncertainty in international relations but its passing was not so traumatic as to question America's
self-perception as leader of the civilised world. As President Bill Clinton
declared in his inaugural speech on 20 January 1993, '[t]oday, as an old order
passes, the new world is more free but less stable. Communism's collapse has
called forth old animosities and new dangers. *Clearly America must continue*

to lead the world we did so much to make.[30] Imbued with political traditions of exceptionalism and manifest destiny, the US mission was to propagate its values, to be a civilising force in world affairs and to facilitate an international order broadly in reflection of its own image. Imaginative would-be substitutes for containment doctrine came and went on a regular basis amid a sustained debate about US strategic interests and what relative burden of leadership it should bear. George H. Bush's new world order was born in the 1990/91 Gulf War but passed away with Operation Restore Hope in Somalia in December 1992. Clinton's democratic enlargement, a doctrine steeped in the inevitable spread of democracy and free markets assisted by US zeal, largely failed to survive Bosnia. Presently the George W. Bush administration claims to have formulated 'a new rationale for engagement' and, in the doctrine of pre-emption, to have buried America's caricature as 'the reluctant sheriff'.[31]

Transatlantic security tensions are also explained by the Cold War's demise ending the EU–US shared threat perception and their coincidence of interests in the former maintaining a Eurocentric security focus while the latter, though prioritising European security, led the free world in global containment. There evolved a 'creeping divergence of strategic interest' that fuelled different security expectations and priorities, both in type and geography. This was reflected at the extreme in the contrast between continued EU commitment to developing African security through humanitarian, aid and trade measures and Bush's declaration during his 2000 election campaign that Africa 'does not fit into our national strategic interests'.[32] The most significant dislocation of EU and US strategic priorities, however, was the EU's continued Eurocentric preoccupations and America's progressive de-prioritisation of Europe.[33]

The EU became consumed in the 1990s by successive Balkans crises, instability in Central and Eastern Europe and the need for constructive dialogue with Russia. Although the US was sucked into the Balkans mire, its involvement was reluctant, limited and marked by renewed criticism of Europe's inability or unwillingness to burden-share adequately, even in its own backyard. US strategic concern actually shifted from Europe to the Middle East and, especially, Asia.[34] The failure of surrogate states during the Cold War to guarantee Middle Eastern security led the US to become a regional hegemon. It afterwards remained locked into Middle Eastern engagement as a consequence of its commitment to Israel, oil supplies, the legacies of the 1990/91 Gulf War and, especially, because the region hosted a number of states and terrorist organisations antipathetic to the US. As for Asia, US strategists worried particularly about WMD proliferation, the nuclear ambitions and destabilising impact of North Korea, and the related 'China question', owing not least to the Taiwan Straits and China's nuclear weapons programme.

Entwined with this gradual strategic divergence was EU–US prioritisation of different security concerns. Geography, deepening integration, processes of enlargement and traditional security parochialism all led the EU to focus foremost on 'door-step' issues. Yugoslavia's disintegration was an immediate and shocking demonstration of a new trend toward ethno-nationalist and intra-state conflict, of the problems of 'failed states', and of the radically different responses required to tackle these types of threat compared to those of the Cold War. Spill-over effects of regional conflict, such as large-scale migration and asylum claims, concentrated EU minds on developing common procedures and an external dimension to JHA issues. This was further underpinned by the combination of escalating transnational organised crime and human trafficking and by potential new national vulnerabilities to these threats owing to the EU's SEM drive for an internally borderless Europe. The EU also emphasised environmental degradation, due in part to its own embrace of sustainable development, a concept first coined by the 1987 Brundtland Commission but made pressing by its contiguity to the former Eastern bloc, where environmental concerns had been systematically neglected for decades.

The US faced few of these immediate concerns. North America was geographically remote from Europe's regional environmental concerns, faced no likelihood of ethno-nationalist conflict within its borders and had none of the EU's complications of being 'a project in the making'. On the contrary, the US had the full range of tools for maintaining internal law and order and unrivalled power to defend its interests abroad, even to the point that its global position was stronger than at any time since WW2. This owed in part to the unexpected weaknesses of rivals, notably the USSR's collapse, the economic travails of Japan and the relative failure of the EU to translate economic power into political influence. It also owed to US post-Cold War performance confounding declinist predictions. Its military might and ability to project power globally became unprecedented and its economy remained the heartbeat of international capitalism. From 1993 the US actually enjoyed an amazing 107 consecutive months of economic growth and under the Clinton administration the budget deficit was erased for the first time since 1969.[35]

In consequence America's principal security concerns derived from a combination of resentment engendered by its policies and hyperpower status and technological development that rendered sovereign borders ever less defendable and the US potentially vulnerable from afar. Admittedly, the Clinton administration in particular identified the drugs trade as a threat to US societal security and launched a sustained, if inconclusive, counter-drugs offensive. Nevertheless, US foreign policy concentrated primarily on strategic threats, as evidenced in the 2001 Quadrennial Defense Review, and global challenges to American national security. Topping the bill were the interrelated threats of WMD proliferation and rogue states. The September 11 terrorist attacks subsequently made explicit the national security linkage between WMD, rogue states and terrorist organisations. Thereafter the premier US security concern became countering what Bush called the 'perilous crossroads of radicalism and technology'[36] in a world where destructive power had been privatised and the enemy was often difficult to identify and locate.

One final and very important attitudinal factor contributing to EU–US friction is the evolution of different security discourses either side of the Atlantic. These reflect different security traditions, histories and structures, are intimately entwined with preferred approaches to managing international security and, broadly speaking, represent a clash between preferences for multilateral and unilateral action and between soft and hard tools of security. Multilateralism has become the dominant currency of public discourse in post-WW2 Europe. Multilateral institutions and a multinational mode of thought have provided Europe with an antidote to its historical national antipathy, so much so that in some countries multilateralism became a moral endeavour and the basis for a new identity, especially in West Germany. The EU itself evolved from multilateral principles and contributed to the development of a Kantian-styled sub-system regulated by laws, rules, norms and multilateral consultation and co-operation. Moreover, to act effectively in international security the EU must first build, and then maintain, consensus among its members and demonstrate its continued benefits as a vehicle to protect national interests and to institutionalise their power in the face of globalisation and their own relative decline.

The EU consequently prefers the non-combative, consensual language of security challenges and talks of collective endeavours such as promoting global governance, managing globalisation, projecting stability and developing conflict prevention. In contrast, the US tends toward more adversarial language of security threats and talks of protecting its national sovereignty and interests, interventionism, forced disarmament and, most recently, of global war upon terrorism. The US has no historical reason to fear its own nationalism and no imperative to constrain voluntarily its sovereignty within supranational structures and multilateral fora. As a post-Cold War hyperpower, with its historical national traditions intact and its power uniquely unrivalled, the US is free to pick and choose between multilateral and unilateral methods and actions. Moreover, US administrations face a more direct linkage between public opinion and overseas action, and painting the world in terms of good and evil and appealing to the defence of American values and national interests is a tried and trusted tool for generating popular support.

Of course the debate is more nuanced than this. EU states do engage in action outside multilateral frameworks and in dispute with one another. Consider French unilateral action in Rwanda and Algeria, Greek flaunting of EU policy towards Macedonia, German unilateral recognition of Croatia, and controversial British support for both renewed US military interventionism in Iraq in 2003 and for Clinton's Cruise missiles attacks against 'terrorist' sites in Afghanistan and Sudan in reprisal for the bombing of American embassies in Africa. Likewise, the inconclusive debate in the US about the UN indicates ongoing American disagreement about international organisations and the appropriate balance between multilateralism and unilateralism.[37] Furthermore, the US approach is little different from its Cold War behaviour, albeit that Congress's growing foreign policy impact and the election of George W. Bush have recently encouraged greater unilateralism.[38]

Nevertheless, the post-Cold War context is much different and mutual transatlantic annoyance has developed as the EU pushes its multilateral agenda and the US operates on a basis of 'internationalism *à la carte*',[39] picking and choosing those international laws and conventions that best suit its interests. Europeans have become more fearful and more critical of the effects of US policy. Commission spokesmen have called US unilateralist tendencies 'profoundly misguided'.[40] Likewise, Chancellor Schröder has declared an 'undeniable' danger of US unilateralism[41] and former French Foreign Minister Hubert Védrine declared that 'France cannot accept a politically unipolar world . . . nor the unilateralism of a single hyper-power'.[42] Americans, unsurprisingly, find such criticism difficult to accept. Critics of the EU detect sinister motives behind its 'almost cultlike worship of multilateralism'.[43] Perhaps jealousy of US success and power leads it to try to constrain American sovereignty? Perhaps, too, multilateralism is the European way of avoiding rightful responsibilities whilst simultaneously free-riding on American commitments to international security and sniping at American leadership? Even Europeans sensitive to American opinion have recognised the dangers inherent in such sentiment. For instance, Blair pledged in April 2002 to work 'side-by-side' America and '[n]o grandstanding, no offering implausible but impractical advice from the comfort of the touchline, no wishing away the hard choices on terrorism and WMD, or making peace in the Middle East, but working together'.[44] Also US officials have repeatedly, and with some justification, argued that America is profoundly multilateralist. It was the principal architect of many of the world's key multilateral bodies, retains a critical role within them and has often provided the leadership necessary to make them effective. Even the current Bush administration has continued US funding of numerous multilateral organisations, patched things up with the UN over outstanding American financial contributions and embraced a post-September 11 strategy that combines the so-called '"posse model"' of forming coalitions of the willing with the ' "police force" model of using standing institutions to win the peace'.[45]

Problems come, in American eyes at least, when European multilateralism seemingly elevates process above policy and subsumes purpose to the quest for consensus. Where as a consequence Americans seek to provide leadership to make multilateralism effective, they incur criticism for riding 'roughshod' over others. Where they disengage or disagree with multilateral initiatives they are accused of unilateralism. As a frustrated US representative to the Conference on Disarmament (CD) declared in February 2003: 'if multilateralism of the type we have witnessed here were to persist within the CD and spread to other multilateral institutions, we would all soon be unilateralists, or at least something other than multilateralists'.[46] Moreover, EU–US officials have exacerbated matters through hubris and mutual moralistic preaching. Americans detect in EU attitudes the merging of multilateralism 'with new forms of self-righteous moralistic nationalism'.[47] Conversely Europeans see the arrogance of American power and an irksome exceptionalism that espouses the supremacy of the American model over the European. Madeleine Albright, then US Secretary of State, epitomised this when asked to explain America's relative isolation in Operation Desert Fox against Iraq in 1998: 'it is because we are America, we are the indispensable nation, we stand tall – we see further into the future'.[48]

The rights and wrongs of this debate can be, have been and are being argued back and forth with increasing bitterness. The most important lesson for transatlantic security relations is that this argument is about more than tactics. It is about values. It is about the importance of rules and norms in managing international affairs. It is about how to enforce those rules and to inculcate the spread of norms. It is even, despite wide agreement on the importance of democracy, rights of the individual, the rule of law and so forth, about exactly what values to embed in the development of a system of global governance. For instance, although united in capitalism, there remain deep EU–US differences about the right mixture of free market and welfare state, of individual freedom and social solidarity.

The danger of transatlantic dislocation in how to develop global governance is reflected in increasing EU–US disagreements over multilateral security initiatives. The EU was alarmed by the Bush administration's abrogation of the anti-ballistic missile treaty and its revived pursuit of National Missile Defence (NMD). They disagreed, too, on the establishment of an International Criminal Court (ICC) empowered to try political leaders and military personnel charged with crimes against humanity. On 11 June 2001 the EU adopted a common position in support of it.[49] The Bush administration, though, revoked Clinton's conditional signature of the Rome Convention and has since continued to oppose the ICC – despite this aligning America with states Bush cited within his infamous 'axis of evil'.[50] Similar EU–US positions developed over the 1997 Ottawa Convention for phasing out the use of anti-personnel landmines (APLMs), the Biological and Toxin Weapon Convention, the Kyoto Protocol on global warming and the CTBT. Indeed, the US Senate rejected the latter and has since been joined in its opposition by the Bush administration, regardless of an EU *démarche* to encourage ratification in May 2001.[51] EU–US disagreement about multilateral security initiatives even spills over into, and threatens, areas of formerly agreed multilateral action. For instance, in 2002 Bush administration opposition to the ICC led it to threaten to veto the UN mission in Bosnia unless the Security Council gave US troops prior exemption from possible prosecution.[52]

Finally the danger of transatlantic dislocation carries extra weight owing to divergent trends in preferred tools of international security management. As a multilateral and hitherto non-military actor, the EU favours by choice and default soft security measures. It seeks to address unsatisfactory international behaviour and 'failing states' by exporting its own values of reconciliation and encouraging reform through constructive dialogue and economic incentive. Thus it has a policy of engagement with states such as Iran, North Korea and Cuba. It promotes regional co-operation through initiatives such as the Euro-Mediterranean Partnership. It provides large-scale development assistance, already four to five times as much as the US and with more to come in line with commitments made in March 2002 at the UN Monterrey Conference on Financing for Development.[53] It has also accepted the lion's share of the cost and responsibility for nation-building in the wake of US-led military interventions in the Balkans and Afghanistan.

The US approach is different, often emphasising its martial supremacy and military tools of security. In 2002 US defence spending exceeded that of the next fifteen leading countries combined.[54] Meanwhile Congress slashed the budget for multilateral development banks by some 40 per cent from 1995, and the so-called 150 Account, the percentage of the US federal budget devoted to international affairs excluding defence expenditure, steadily declined from 4 per cent in the 1960s to just 1 per cent in the 1990s.[55] Even when Bush promised prior to the Monterrey Conference to reverse the downward trend in the US foreign aid budget, appropriations looked meagre when set against a simultaneous proposed $48 billion hike in defence spending.[56] The US also often uses its formidable economic power to try to coerce recalcitrant states, and sometimes their trading partners, into line. For instance, during the 1990s Congress passed the Helms-Burton and D'Amato legislation with extra-territorial provisions that imposed punitive sanctions not only on Cuba, Libya and Iran but potentially also on European companies trading with these nations.[57]

The product of all this has too often been transatlantic frustration and sub-optimal security outcomes. It is all too easy for Americans to see European 'engagement' of countries such as Cuba and Iran as subterfuge for preferencing their economic interests over principled strategic choices. Conversely Europeans find it easy to blame US pro-Israeli bias for stalemate in the Middle East peace process and to detect in America's combative approach to international security causes of, rather than solutions to, instability. Also, in the realm of post-Cold War interventionism there has developed a *de facto* division of labour, the US providing the overwhelming contribution to military engagements, especially air power, and the EU, put crudely, being left to sweep up the mess.[58] This is unlikely to be a sustainable state of affairs. Past interventions have witnessed acute EU–US tension, such as the question of deploying ground troops to active combat in Kosovo. The EU is unlikely to follow the US lead blindly, as evidenced by the 2002/03 transatlantic crisis over extending the war against terrorism to military intervention in Iraq in consequence of its failure to abide by UN resolutions. Furthermore, the creeping divergence of strategic interests promises that the US will not always want to get involved in European crises any more than the EU will want always to accompany the US. It has even been suggested that US commitment to Bosnia in 1995 was the product of confusion rather than of intent due to an earlier decision that, if necessary, NATO would cover the withdrawal of the UN Protection Force (UNPROFOR).[59]

Co-operation and discord in transatlantic security management

On the one hand, then, EU–US security co-operation is deeply rooted in shared values and common interests, and considerable political determination remains to maintain and further institutionalise that co-operation. On the other, there is a range of factors that have complicated post-Cold War EU–US co-operation. It is therefore instructive to examine two interrelated aspects of EU–US security interaction in practice: burden-sharing and institutional reform, and the war against terrorism.

An enduring feature of EU–US security relations has been the interlinked debate about burden-sharing, institutional development and EU contributions to military-related activities. The White House has consistently accorded ESDI/CESDP qualified support, welcoming potential greater European contributions to aspects of hard security but remaining reluctant to share leadership and suspicious of possible dislocation between NATO and CESDP. The EU has repeatedly declared its intent to burden-share and has made significant institutional development towards a limited hard security capacity. Its best efforts, however, have been compromised by the constraints of other EU policies, notably EMU, and member state reluctance either to devote necessary resources to military expenditure or to abandon national champions in key aspects of the defence market.

In principle, post-Cold War developments portended a mutually beneficial sharing of burdens and a flexibility of response potentially capable of offsetting the gradual divergence of EU–US strategic interest. In terms of combined defence expenditure and arms production there is no single power, even combination of powers, capable of challenging EU–US supremacy. In 2001 the EU and US accounted for 56.8 per cent of total global defence spending. The US, UK and France together dominated global arms deliveries with a 69 per cent share of the market.[60] Moreover, defence material supply improvements were made. For example, on the European side the Joint Armaments Co-operation Structure (OCCAR) encouraged common procurement practices. New ventures were undertaken, such as the formation in 2001 of the MBDA Missiles company that brought together the missile interests of BAE Systems, the European Aeronautic Defence and Space Company (EADS) and Finmeccanica of Italy. The European defence industry underwent rapid consolidation to a point where two giant conglomerates, BAE Systems and EADS, dominate many aspects.[61] And there developed strong potential for transatlantic defence industry co-operation and consolidation, especially given surplus capacity and considerations of economies of scale, inter-operability and dual use technology flows. Indeed, BAE Systems introduced many of the safeguards required by Congress for possible transatlantic mergers when it acquired Tracor.

EU initiatives also augured well for transatlantic burden-sharing and institutional synergy, most notably the Amsterdam Treaty's inclusion of Petersberg responsibilities and the ambitious geographic scope of the subsequent EURRF. With an operational radius of 4,000 km from Brussels, potential EURRF deployment incorporates north-west Africa, the Middle East (including much of Iraq, Palestine, Israel and even parts of Iran), Central and Eastern Europe (including the Balkans), western Russia and the Caucasus (including Georgia, Chechnya, Armenia and Azerbaijan).[62] The Helsinki Headline Goals then set the benchmark for securing EU military contributions, which have subsequently been monitored and for which further measures have been recommended. Also substantive progress has been made in developing modalities for institutional synergy between the EURRF and NATO and for the potential involvement of non-NATO, non-EU nations in EURRF actions. Furthermore, determined and repeated efforts have been made to assuage American concerns about the EURRF potentially rivalling NATO or undermining its effectiveness through the diversion or duplication of resources. Article 17 of the Nice Treaty respects member state defence commitments to NATO and declares EU commitment to compatibility between NATO and CESDP.[63] National leaders, especially British, have repeatedly emphasised, too, that the EURRF complements NATO and would only seek to act where NATO as a whole chooses not to.[64]

All of this has been made possible by EU member states undertaking significant reforms of security and defence policy, prompted especially by the end of the Cold War and consequent fears of US downsizing of its European security commitment. Herein Britain and Germany have been particularly important as the leading EU Atlanticist and economic power respectively. The genesis of the EURRF resides in the Anglo-French rapprochement at St Malo where British acceptance of CESDP as being conceptually compatible with NATO constituted something of a 'revolution in military affairs'.[65] After all, Britain had hitherto opposed consistently the absorption of the WEU into the EU as inconsistent with maintaining a strong NATO alliance. Margaret Thatcher's condemnation of Blair's commitment to the EURRF as 'an act of monumental folly' taken 'to satisfy political vanity'[66] summed up the clash between new and old British thinking. As for Germany, its leaders repeatedly acknowledged the need to make commitments more commensurate with German economic weight[67] and slowly reconceptualised its civilian power status. Incremental increases in German international military commitments began in 1991 with the deployment of minesweepers to the Persian Gulf and accelerated once the Federal Constitutional Court ruled in July 1994 that there was no legal prohibition on German military involvement in all manner of crisis and peace enforcement scenarios. Participation in the 1999 Kosovo War in particular, though carefully justified by Schröder in terms of humanitarian intervention,[68] was of great symbolic importance given a strong historically driven desire to avoid deployments in areas occupied by the *Wehrmacht* during WW2.[69]

The EU and US thus had/have built strong foundations for a complementary and flexible post-Cold War partnership in military-related operations. Yet this potential remains largely unrealised and the US continues to doubt both the long-term compatibility of the EURRF and NATO and European willingness to match institutional development with capability improvement. The so-called Dobbins Démarche[70] of February 1991 stated the George H. Bush administration's opposition to WEU development outside NATO, which Commission President Delors reformulated in terms of three US demands in the development of a European defence capability. There should be 'no internal bloc, continued globality of the Allied response, no weakening of command structures'.[71] Eight years later, Clinton's Secretary of State Madeleine Albright virtually repeated this, warning against the so-called 'three Ds' of de-linking, duplication and discrimination.[72] And the current Bush administration has reiterated the message, Secretary of Defence Rumsfeld cautioning in February 2001 that '[a]ctions that could reduce NATO's effectiveness by confusing duplication or by perturbing the transatlantic link would not be positive' and risked injecting instability into an enormously important alliance.[73] Moreover, the impact of European re-assurances about EURRF–NATO compatibility has been undermined by severe transatlantic difference over Iraq and by the different security dispositions of EU member states. France has been particularly problematic in this respect, Hubert Védrine speaking repeatedly of an autonomous European defence pillar and French Chief of Defence Staff General Jean-Pierre Kelche reportedly declaring in March 2001 both that the European defence project would remain independent of NATO and that the latter would not be given right of first refusal in a crisis situation.[74]

The US has just as consistently urged Europe to spend more, and more wisely, on defence. Europe is not being asked to match American defence spending. Nor is transatlantic partnership necessarily compromised by EU concentration on Petersberg tasks while the US ploughs ahead with full spectrum dominance, defined in Joint Vision 2020, the Pentagon's principal conceptual planning document, as 'the ability of US forces, operating unilaterally or in combination with multinational and interagency partners, to defeat any adversary and to control any situation across the full range of military operations'.[75] Nevertheless, collective EU–US military dominance conceals striking imbalances within their relationship. In 2001 the EU combined spent just 47.3 per cent of what America did alone on defence, or in terms of GDP an average 1.75 per cent compared to 3.2 per cent.[76] This imbalance constitutes part of a long-standing post-Cold War trend as EU member states sought to deliver a peace dividend, absorb increasing costs of maintaining the European social model and, predominantly, became fiscally constrained by EMU convergence criteria and the Stability and Growth Pact. Its impact is further exacerbated by low spend within the EU not corresponding to country size or economic wealth. Germany has been a particular target of American criticism, US Secretary of Defence William Cohen declaring in December 1999 that German policy had a 'profound and lasting impact' on the capabilities of itself and of NATO as a whole.[77] Between 1975 and 1979 Germany spent 3.4 per cent of its GDP on defence. In 1995 this had declined to 1.7 per cent, by 2001 to 1.5 per cent, and further reductions are planned in line with Schröder's commitment to a balanced budget by 2006, Finance Minister Hans Eichel's austerity programme, and high levels of German taxation and public debt.[78]

As for quality of defence spending, the US has begun cancelling old-style systems, such as the Crusader heavy artillery programme in May 2002, but Europe generally, and Germany particularly,[79] has been slow to re-orientate force structures and procurement to systems capable of addressing post-Cold War conditions and asymmetric threats. The impact of EU national defence spending is further limited owing to duplication, entrenched inefficiencies and, in countries such as Greece and Germany, expensive conscription policies.[80] The real military capability of EU member states is estimated to be approximately 10 per cent of America's.[81] Europe's consequent problems were reflected in the difficulty European NATO members had to muster from nearly 2 million military personnel just 40,000 troops for Kosovo and to maintain thereafter 50,000 peacekeepers in the wider Balkans.[82] They are reflected, too, in growing divisions within EU national capabilities and between the EU and the US. In the critical area of research and development (R&D) Anglo-French spending of £29 billion is more than double the collective spending of all other EU members. This is still far below the US, which spends three times as much on R&D of new weapons as the rest of NATO combined.[83] Even by its own standards, the EU has failed to translate targets into reality. Its Capability Improvement Conference in November 2001 found that only five of fifty-five previously identified major deficiencies had been resolved, and crucial collaborative military procurement programmes, such as the €18 billion A400M air transport project, have been repeatedly plagued by funding crises.[84]

It is thus with justification that some American commentators greeted with derision the EU's declaration of the EURRF as operational at its Laeken Summit in December 2001.[85] Many observers actually estimate that it will be at least 2012 before the EU will be capable of fulfilling the Petersberg tasks.[86] However, US equivocation about CESDP and apparent double standards feed transatlantic recrimination. First, US initiatives within NATO have sometimes been as much about controlling as facilitating CESDP. Most recently, in November 2002, the Bush administration potentially arrested the momentum behind the EURRF by pushing through at NATO's Prague Summit the creation of a 20,000-man Rapid Response Force capable of going 'any time, anywhere, at very short notice'.[87] The Clinton administration was generally more supportive, embracing the idea of an ESDI and announcing in 1993 the Combined Joint Task Force (CJTF) initiative,[88] which NATO endorsed in its 1999 Alliance Strategic Concept as serving to reinforce the transatlantic relationship. Nevertheless, with its central premise of separable but not separate forces, the CJTF clearly sought to head off an autonomous European military capability and to allow the US to burden-share without surrendering leadership – not least because Europe would effectively have to borrow key US assets in a military intervention.

Second, US preferential relationships, particularly with Britain, potentially constrain CESDP and European defence development. EU members with Atlanticist security orientations are naturally sensitive to Washington's line on the EURRF and NATO primacy. The Anglo-American relationship has particular impact in defence-related issues and British companies have long benefited from preferential access to US technology. This impacts on the willingness of British defence companies to collaborate in multinational European projects for fear of losing privileged access to American R&D and markets. BAE, for instance, sells more to the US Defence Department than to the British Ministry of Defence. It also leads the British government to a fine balancing act between Anglo-American and Anglo-European defence collaboration. Hence the Blair government committed Britain to the A400M project but also joined the US in January 2001 in co-operating on the Joint Strike Fighter aircraft and working towards a joint defence export controls regime, thus reinforcing the special relationship. Furthermore, American initiatives with which some EU members disagree, notably NMD and renewed military intervention against Iraq, potentially threaten CESDP by disrupting the Anglo-French rapprochement underpinning the EURRF and by weakening Britain's ability to perform its self-designated transatlantic bridging function.[89]

Third, the US has repeatedly criticised a growing transatlantic technology gap but has been inconsistent in its efforts to mitigate this. Its argument, supported by the European Commission,[90] that the European defence industry should be included in SEM regulations sits awkwardly with its own subsidies of the American defence industry. For instance, the Clinton administration gave direct assistance of $16.5 billion to assist post-Cold War reconfiguration, including $1.3 billion within the Technology Reinvestment Programme designed to promote dual use technologies.[91] Similar inconsistency marks US efforts to facilitate transatlantic technology exchange. On 24 May 2000 Madeleine Albright announced the Defense Trade Security Initiative aimed at improving US technology and arms transfers to America's closest allies. Yet the US defence market remains a 'fortress' owing to various levels of protection from FDI, joint ventures, and exports to third parties.[92] Protectionist measures include the Buy American Act, the Arms Export Control Act, the International Traffic in Arms Regulations and the Committee on Foreign Investment in the United States. This has also helped shape post-Cold War consolidation within, rather than between, the US and EU defence industries, again potentially encouraging trade restrictions and technology and compatibility gaps. Furthermore, US interests simultaneously warned of possible discrimination against American military producers in European markets as a consequence of EURRF-promoted improvements in European arms procurement co-ordination[93] and manoeuvred for potential hostile take-overs of vulnerable European companies, which risks the latter becoming subsidiaries and further widening the technology gap.[94]

Turning to EU–US security relations and the September 11 terrorist attacks, these evidenced a similar mixture of co-operation, disagreement and lost opportunity. Initial transatlantic solidarity was impressive. NATO invoked Article V for the first time in its history, EU flags flew at half-mast in Brussels and 14 September was declared a day of mourning across Europe. An extraordinary European Council on 21 September pledged total support for the American people. The EU General Affairs Council subsequently affirmed 'full solidarity with the US' and invoked a value-based transatlantic relationship in its castigation of the September 11 atrocities as 'an assault on our open, democratic, tolerant and multicultural societies'.[95] National leaders and EU commissioners repeatedly underscored the incontrovertible message of European sympathy and support for America and its people.[96]

Evidence of prospective enhanced EU–US co-operation came quickly. On 20 September the EU and US issued a joint ministerial statement pledging efforts to 'work in partnership' on a 'world-wide' scale to combat terrorism.[97] Areas targeted within this effort included aviation and other transport security, police and judicial co-operation, export controls and non-proliferation, financial sanctions, border controls and exchange of electronic data. The following day the European Council agreed an Action Plan comprising seventy-nine measures to help combat terrorism, many under the auspices of JHA. Amongst the most important initiatives were commitment to the introduction of a common EU-wide arrest warrant no later than January 2004, regulations relating to enhanced interagency co-operation, a common definition of terrorist acts and groups, and a framework decision on freezing terrorist assets. In December 2001 the EU adopted a common position, a framework regulation and an implementing decision that further augmented its legal and administrative ability to combat terrorism. For instance, the EU listed individuals, groups and entities agreed to be terrorists or terrorist-related and committed itself to freezing financial assets.[98] Six months later the Seville European Council resolved to integrate border protection further, including measures to combat illegal immigration and cross-border crime, to move towards a common asylum policy and for national border forces to conduct joint operations at EU borders by the end of 2002.

The EU complemented measures to augment its counter-terrorist capabilities with steps to facilitate direct transatlantic co-operation and co-ordination. In December 2001 the European Council adopted the decision to create Eurojust, to which the US has already provided a liaison magistrate. Efforts were also made to boost Europol, including a call for better information pooling by member states and the creation of a dedicated anti-terrorism group authorised to collaborate directly with the US. On 6 December 2001 Europol duly concluded a co-operation agreement with the US to share best practice and strategic information in criminal matters. Liaison officers began to be accredited, dialogue improved and intelligence sharing was promoted. Information was exchanged on travel documents and migration issues to boost border security.[99]

The EU also worked in tandem with the US through established bilateral channels, notably the NTA, and in multilateral fora. Commission proposals for common EU procedures for employee identification, access to airport areas, passenger control and luggage inspection emerged in conjunction with EU–US work on aviation security and joint pressure in February 2002 for the establishment and implementation of an International Civil Aviation Organisation security audit programme. In line with UN Resolution 1373 the EU and US developed measures to fight funding of terrorist organisations, such as their successful joint championship in October 2001 of the Financial Action Task Force (FATF) against money laundering specifically embracing terrorist activity within its remit.[100] And in the wake of military intervention in Afghanistan, the EU and US were prominent collaborators at the UN-backed Bonn Conference.

As of 25 September 2002, the US had disbursed $350 million of humanitarian and reconstruction assistance to Afghanistan, and the EU $432 million.[101]

Furthermore, the EU and its member states brought substantial collective and national assets to bear in the construction of an American-led coalition against terrorism and in encouraging a holistic approach that addressed the sources as well as the symptoms of radical discontent. The Commission's comprehensive strategy included 'the undemocratic behaviour of governments, as well as an unacceptable divide between the rich and the poor; environmental degradation, and crime, corruption, drugs and health issues'.[102] Within this, it pushed for a reinvigoration of the Middle East peace process with a view to creating a Palestinian state and guaranteeing Israel's territorial integrity within recognised borders. It stressed, too, the importance of legitimising action against terrorism and the integration of all countries into a fair world system of security, development and prosperity.

Herein EC and national officials co-operated with the US in steering retaliatory action through the aegis of the UN and in intensive diplomatic efforts to assuage Islamic fears of a potential 'clash of civilisations'. CFSP leaders in various combinations engaged in extensive shuttle diplomacy to key countries in the Middle East, Central and South Asia, Turkey, Russia and the Mediterranean. For instance, the troika format of External Relations Commissioner Patten, High Representative for CFSP Javier Solana, Belgian Minister of Foreign Affairs Louis Michel (holding the EU presidency) and Spanish Minister of Foreign Affairs Josep Piqué (incoming EU presidency) undertook a ten-day tour of principal Islamic capitals. The message was of engagement, of the need to curtail the activities of terrorists, and of reassurance that the response to September 11 would not be targeted against Islam. Of EU national leaders British Prime Minister Blair was particularly prominent in recruiting support for the coalition against terror and in maintaining its ephemeral basis, so much so that the *Sunday Herald* crowned him, rather than Bush, as 'King of the Coalition'.[103] For instance, Blair appeared on al-Jazeera television to rebut Osama bin Laden's claim that the West was mounting a war on Islam and first laid out the alleged evidence tying bin Laden and the al-Qa'ida organisation to the September 11 attacks.

Process and policy injected renewed impetus into the transatlantic security partnership and delivered tangible results. American officials characterised EU–US co-operation against terrorism as ' "extremely" good'[104] and were impressed by the unusual speed and decisiveness of cross-pillar EU action. As US Principal Deputy Assistant Secretary of State for European and Eurasian Affairs Charles P. Ries commented, '[f]or old EU hands, the European Union's response was breathtaking in its speed and ambition'.[105] Europe froze terrorist assets worth some $35 million within six months of September 11.[106] European authorities arrested over 300 people with suspected links to al-Qa'ida between September 2001 and July 2002 and the EU and US progressively harmonised their lists of illegal terrorist organisations. Leading EU member states were also at the forefront of NATO's positive response to the US request for its support on 4 October 2001. NATO assistance eventually included enhanced intelligence sharing, blanket overflight rights for US and Allied aircraft, access to ports and airfields within NATO territory, deployment of the Standing Naval Force Mediterranean to the eastern Mediterranean, and Operation Eagle Assist that freed American assets for action in Afghanistan by redeploying NATO AWACS aircraft to patrol US skies.[107]

The EU response to September 11 was thus encouraging for the transatlantic security relationship and conformed to the wider pattern of its 'co-operative containment' of the US. For all the progress made, however, there remained serious difficulties. As might be expected, structural problems continued to frustrate. Within JHA the rotating presidency led to inconsistency and decisions were slowed by the need for unanimity – such as Italy's initial hold-out against the common arrest warrant. Negotiations were complicated, too, by the fragmented JHA working structure that incorporates four principal levels and composes numerous EC and national officials. American officials criticised, for example, the EU's cumbersome clearing-house process for submitting and considering terrorist names for designation.

EU problems were more pronounced in CFSP. September 11 induced a limited renationalisation of member states' foreign and security policy, which Washington encouraged by predominantly circumventing the CFSP apparatus and instead dealing direct with national capitals. Numerous EU divisions quickly developed. First, the 'Big Three' of Britain, France and Germany seemingly sought a much-resented *directoire*. This was epitomised by their highly publicised mini-summit preceding the Ghent European Council on 19 October 2001 and by the gate-crashing of a similar attempt on 5 November by Aznar, Berlusconi, Solana, Kok and Verhofstadt. Second, probable military action in Afghanistan refocused attention on the weaknesses of CESDP and on broad groupings of EU countries as 'pacifist', 'neutralist' and 'militarist'.[108] Third, the response to September 11 re-opened 'Atlanticist' and 'Europeanist' divisions previously subsumed within the St Malo process. Blair's leadership style in particular indicated a reversion to 'a brand of unconditional Atlanticism which many in Europe (and even in Britain) had assumed to be anachronistic after Kosovo, the missile controversy and the Bush administration's generalised penchant for unilateralism'.[109]

EU–US value differences hindered transatlantic security co-operation too. On 12 October 2001 the US Congress approved the Patriot Act, which conferred upon the government significant enhanced powers, including the right to intercept e-mail, tap telephones and investigate bank accounts. This exacerbated existing differences between the EU and US over data protection and privacy rights and impacted negatively on the exchange of information potentially important in combating terrorism. Also, on 13 November 2001 a US presidential directive established military courts to deal with suspected terrorists with provision for the President to decide who was tried and, without jury, to order sentences up to and including the death penalty. This further contributed to European reluctance to share information with the US and to facilitate extradition proceedings, especially in light of established transatlantic differences over the death penalty. A major disagreement developed, too, over US treatment of al-Qa'ida prisoners, who were detained without trial in Cuba at Camp X-Ray in Guantanamo Bay and denied prisoner of war rights by being designated 'unlawful combatants'. The Commission and European governments protested against their treatment and the then UN Commissioner for Human Rights, Mary Robinson, brusquely reminded the US that 'there are international legal obligations that should be respected'.[110]

Perhaps most worrisome for future transatlantic security co-operation was that September 11 reactions reflected and heightened long-standing EU–US differences. Symptomatic of this was American annoyance at the EU's reluctance to designate the social and religious arms of Hamas and Hezbollah as terrorist entities, a difference traceable to EU Palestinian sympathies, policies of engagement rather than confrontation and determination to resurrect the Middle East peace process. More damaging still were widespread European fears that the Bush administration would act unilaterally and react disproportionately to the terrorist attacks. Hubert Védrine quickly cautioned against falling into 'the monstrous trap' set by terrorists of pitting the West against Islam,[111] and the EU troika warned that disproportionate action risked further destabilisation and jeopardised public support. The troika also specifically declared that '[o]ur message to the United States is that only a multilateral approach can reinforce their security, can guarantee ours'.[112] Indeed, so fast were European pledges of post-September 11 solidarity followed by frantic diplomatic manoeuvring that qualified this rhetorical support that as early as 22 September 2001 some American commentators considered only the Anglo-American alliance to have stood firm.[113]

European manoeuvring reflected simultaneous unease about Bush administration policy towards Afghanistan and hopes of engaging it in multilateralism. The real issue, though, was what would come after Afghanistan, there being a clear UN mandate for action against the al-Qa'ida network and the repressive Taliban regime.[114] Three developments were particularly problematic for EU–US and intra-European security relations. First, the Bush administration evolved a doctrine of pre-emptive self-defence and *de facto* reconceptualised sovereignty as potentially contingent upon factors such as not supporting terrorism.[115] This made likely further, potentially destabilising US intervention in the internal affairs of states unspecified and posed critical questions about international law, itself the bedrock of EU governance and multilateralism. Humanitarian intervention in Kosovo had pushed the boundaries of international legal respect for sovereign borders, but it remained contentious that sovereignty might be effectively further qualified not by the UN but by US national security policy.[116] Second, the Bush administration claimed an expansive mandate for military action by conflating combating WMD proliferation with its war on terrorism. Even before September 11 the US had a list of seven countries it regarded as sponsors of terrorism – Cuba, Libya, North Korea, Iran, Iraq, Sudan and Syria – and at least twenty-five countries that either possessed or were trying to develop or acquire WMD and/or the capability to deliver them. Third, September 11 reinforced fears of US readiness where necessary to act outside multilateral fora and to override the opinions of coalition partners. For instance, the US chose not to use NATO as a command framework for Operation Enduring Freedom in Afghanistan, instead conducting a largely unilateral war assisted by anti-Taliban militia groups and select contributions from close allies, notably British special forces. According to US Secretary of Defence Donald Rumsfeld, coalitions of the willing were important but wars could not be fought by committee: '[t]he mission must determine the coalition, and the coalition must not determine the mission. If it does, the mission will be dumbed down to the lowest common denominator, and we can't afford that.'[117]

All of these problems have become manifest in the ongoing Iraq crisis, the most serious transatlantic security rift in the post-Cold War era, perhaps even in a generation.[118] Post-Afghanistan the Bush administration quickly locked Saddam Hussein's Iraq in its sights as the next target in its conflated mission against international terrorism and WMD. On 12 September 2002 Bush spoke to the UN General Assembly and put American Iraq policy firmly in a multilateral context. The Security Council subsequently approved Resolution 1441 unanimously on 8 November for the reintroduction of weapons inspectors and possible enforcement if Iraq were found to be in breach of its UN obligations. The EU, however, rapidly divided on questions of how much time weapons inspectors should be allowed, what would constitute an Iraqi breach of their UN obligations, and, in the event that this occurred, whether a further UN mandate were necessary for enforcement action.

In the ensuing crisis Britain and Spain stood firmly by the US. The Bush administration, perhaps partially in recognition of Blair's attempts to bridge the transatlantic divide and the domestic political risks both he and José María Aznar were taking, allowed some time for a possible second UN resolution despite its insistence that this was not necessary. This transatlantic solidarity was in stark contrast to the positions taken, for instance, by Germany and France. Schröder pledged in September 2002 that Germany would not commit forces against Iraq even if given UN Security Council authorisation to do so.[119] France was less deterministic but insisted that considerably more time should be given to weapons inspectors and that a second UN Security Council resolution be obtained. In March 2003 the Bush administration's patience ran out amid transatlantic deadlock and the seeming impossibility of securing a further Security Council resolution. With British armed support, the US intervened militarily in Iraq to topple Saddam Hussein's regime. The action was successful in this respect, and at the time of writing it looks possible that an increased UN role in 'winning the peace' in Iraq might be negotiated sufficient to patch over deep transatlantic divisions. Nevertheless the crisis strained badly EU–US relations and reaffirmed the impressions of American unilateralism and of EU inability to forge a common position in times of crisis. As Poul Nielson, Commissioner for Development and Humanitarian Aid, conceded before the

European Parliament on 12 February 2003, 'the EU looks weaker and more divided than ever' and this owes to far more than 'some minor institutional inadequacies in the architecture of the EU'.[120]

Conclusion

The EU's security relationship with the US remains quantitatively and qualitatively its most important. Both sides have sought to work together in multilateral fora and to institutionalise their co-operation, first through the Transatlantic Declaration and then the NTA. Post-Cold War events have reaffirmed the binding power of shared values and EU–US capacity for co-ordinated action and combined global influence. EU claims to genuine security partnership have been boosted by the expansion of the security agenda and deepening and widening integration. Indeed, the September 11 atrocities have been cited as 'transform[ing] the transatlantic partnership into a virtual partnership of equals, attesting to the increased credibility of the EU'.[121]

Yet, in 2003, many commentators portray transatlantic relations at their lowest ebb since the Cold War, possibly since WW2.[122] Severe divisions over Iraq dominate the headlines but problems run deeper. Foremost are key attitudinal differences, rooted in different historical experiences and contemporary capabilities, which guide EU and US approaches to international security management. Consequent transatlantic tensions have often been most acute over military interventionism and burden-sharing. Here the EU most fears US unilateralism and its own relative impotence. Conversely, the US repeatedly criticises EU failure to translate CESDP rhetoric into a NATO-compatible reality, too often sees its multilateralism as a pretext for obstruction or free-riding, and underplays its soft security contributions.

Does this justify predictions of pending transatlantic divorce? Not really, for there is too much that binds the EU and US together, both within their security relationship and beyond. Nevertheless, their post-Cold War security relationship remains in a process of renegotiation, and in the struggle to contain each other co-operatively the *sui generis* EU is often proving a poor match for the US hyperpower. Where sovereignty has been pooled the EU has been better able to counter American security-related action with which it disagreed, notably extra-territorial sanctions. However, the predominantly intergovernmental JHA and CFSP pillars have frustrated the US and been unable to provide the co-ordinated EU action necessary to curb American unilateralism. Moreover, EU failure to invest sufficiently in defence expenditure has fostered a transatlantic technology gap, especially in integrated C_4I (Command and Control, Communications, Computers and Intelligence) systems, that not only costs the EU credibility in American eyes but that also potentially so undermines inter-operability that US unilateralism may not only be encouraged but eventually become unavoidable.[123] As NATO Secretary General Lord Robertson warned in January 2002, Europe 'remains a military pygmy' and '[u]nless the Europeans do better militarily in NATO and the EU, their influence in the Euro-Atlantic area and more widely will remain limited'.[124]

Notes

1 J.S. Nye Jr. has talked of 'episodic bickering, as opposed to divorce', S.M. Walt of 'drift' and W. Pfaff of 'eventual but nonetheless inevitable end to the alliance'. In contrast, A.J. Blinken has argued that 'The "crisis" in U.S.–European relations is largely a myth manufactured by elites – politicians, intellectuals, and the media – whose views clash with those of the people they purport to represent'. Nye Jr., J.S. (2000) 'The US and Europe: Continental Drift?' *International Affairs* 76 (1) p. 59; Walt, S.M. (1998/99) 'The Ties That Fray: Why America and Europe are Drifting Apart' *The National Interest* 54 pp. 3–11; Pfaff, W. (2000) 'The US Campaign is Skirting Key Foreign Policy Issues' *International Herald Tribune*, 15 January 2000; Blinken, A.J. (2001) 'The False Crisis Over the Atlantic' *Foreign Affairs* 80 (3) pp. 35–48. See also Newhouse, J. (1997) *Europe Adrift*, New York: Pantheon; Gordon, P.H. (1996) 'Recasting the Atlantic Alliance' *Survival* 38 (1) pp. 32–57; Lieber, R.J. (2000) 'No Transatlantic Divorce in the Offing' *Orbis* 44 (4), pp. 571–84.

2 Speech by Prime Minister Blair at the Lord Mayor's Banquet, 22 November 1999, www.fco.gov; transcript of Bush–Blair press conference at Halton House, 19 July 2001, www.fco.gov.

3 For a forceful exposition of democratic peace theory in the context of US foreign policy see Christopher, W. (1995) 'America's Leadership: America's Opportunity' *Foreign Policy* 98 p. 8.

4 Mearsheimer, J. (1990) 'Back to the Future: Instability in Europe after the Cold War' *International Security* 15 (3), pp. 5–57.

5 For examples of the debate about NATO and its future see Solomon, G.B. (1998) *The NATO Enlargement Debate, 1990–97: Blessings of Liberty*, Westport, Conn.: Praeger; Carpenter, T.G. (ed.) (1995) *The Future of NATO*, London and Portland, Oreg.: Frank Cass & Co.; Papacosma, S.V. and Heiss, M.A. (eds) (1995) *NATO in the Post-Cold War Era: Does it Have a Future?*, New York: St Martin's Press; (1994) 'The Future of NATO' Special Edition of the *Journal of Strategic Studies* 17 (4); Sloan, S.R. (1995) 'US Perspectives on NATO's Future' *International Affairs* 71 (2) pp. 217–32; McCalla, R.B. (1996) 'NATO's Persistence After the Cold War' *International Organization* 50 (3) pp. 445–75.

6 Huntington, S.P. (1991) 'America's Changing Strategic Interests' *Survival* 33 (1) p. 6. For discussion of post-Cold War unipolarity see Mastanduno, M. (1997) 'Preserving the Unipolar Moment: Realist Theories and US Grand Strategy After the Cold War' *International Security* 21 pp. 44–98; Krauthammer, C. (1990/91) 'The Unipolar Moment' *Foreign Affairs* 70 pp. 23–33; Wohlforth, W. (1999) 'The Stability of a Unipolar World' *International Security* 24 pp. 5–41.

7 Since 1993 the US has either imposed or threatened unilateral economic sanctions sixty times on thirty-five nations that comprise 40 per cent of the world's population. Maynes, C.W. (1999) 'US Unilateralism and its Dangers' *Review of International Studies* 25 (3) p. 517.

8 Berger, S. (2000) 'A Foreign Policy for a Global Age' *Foreign Affairs* 79 (6) pp. 22–39; Joffe, J. (Summer 2001) 'Who's Afraid of Mr Big?' *The National Interest*, http://www.nationalinterest.org/.

9 Brittan, L. (1998) 'Europe and the United States: New Challenges, New Opportunities', speech given to the Foreign Policy Association, New York, September 1998, http://www.eurunion.org/news/speeches/1998/1998index.htm.

10 Tarnoff, P. (1990) 'America's New Special Relationships' *Foreign Affairs* 69 (3) pp. 67–80.

11 Baker, J. (1989) 'A New Europe, A New Atlanticism: Architecture for a New Era', Berlin Press Club, 12 December 1989, US Department of State, Current Polity, no. 1233 (December 1989).

12 Zoellick, R. (1990) 'The New Europe in a New Age: Insular, Itinerant or International? Prospects for an Alliance of Values', US State Department Dispatch, 24 September 1990.

13 Gardner, A.L. (1999) *A New Era in US–EU Relations: The Clinton Administration and the New Transatlantic Agenda*, Aldershot: Ashgate, p. 10; Dinan, D. (1999) *Ever Closer Union?*, Basingstoke: Macmillan, p. 537.

14 For example, in 1991 it was agreed to institutionalise consultations in certain third country capitals between US ambassadors and troika heads of mission.

15 Declaration on US–EC Relations, http://www.useu.be/TransAtlantic/transdec.html.

16 The oft-used expression 'capability-expectation gap' was first conceptualised by Hill, C. (1993) 'The Capability-Expectation Gap, or Conceptualizing Europe' *Journal of Common Market Studies* 31 (3) pp. 305–28. See also Hill, C. (1998) 'Closing the Capability-Expectations Gap?' in *A Common Foreign and Security Policy for Europe? Competing Visions of the CFSP*, Petersen, J. and Sjursen, H. (eds), London: Routledge, pp. 18–38.

17 Frellesen, T. (2001) 'Processes and Procedures in EU–US Foreign Policy Cooperation: From the Transatlantic Declaration to the New Transatlantic Agenda' in *Ever Closer Partnership: Policy-making in EU–US Relations*, Philippart, E. and Winand, P. (eds), New York and Oxford: Peter Lang, p. 332.

18 Chris Patten, cited in 'The New Transatlantic Agenda', http://europa.eu.int/comm/external-relations/us/new-transatlantic, May 2001.

19 'Transatlantic Relations – The EU–US Partnership', http://www.useu.be/TransAtlantic/Index.html.

20 For the JAP see 'Joint EU–US Action Plan', http://europa.eu.int/comm/external-relations/us/action-plan.

21 Ambassador Eizenstat, cited in Frellesen, 'Processes and Procedures in EU–US Foreign Policy Cooperation', p. 333.

22 For the role of NGOs in EU external relations see, for instance, Mackie, J. (2001) 'Bringing Civil Society into Foreign and Security Policy', European Policy

Centre, 28 February 2001, http://www.theepc.be/challenge/topdetail.asp?SEC=documents&S.

23 The CNN effect encapsulates the idea that a press endowed with real-time communications technology and liberated by the post-Cold War dissolution of bipartisan foreign policy consensus is partially able to drive US and EU responses to world events. Although the debate about the power of media in the post-Cold War real-time world remains inconclusive, it has undoubtedly complicated foreign policy making. For an interesting discussion of this, and a guide to further reading, see Robinson, P. (1999) 'The CNN Effect: Can the News Media Drive Foreign Policy?' *Review of International Studies* **25** (2) pp. 301–9.

24 This educational aspect of the NTA was strengthened in 1998 by the Transatlantic Donors Dialogue and Transatlantic Information Exchange Service to facilitate people-to-people projects and by the European Commission's programme of EU Centres in the US, designed to promote American interest in, and provide information about, European integration.

25 Ginsberg, R.H. (2001) 'EU–US Relations after Amsterdam: "Finishing Europe"' in *Ever Closer Partnership*, Philippart and Winand (eds), p. 353.

26 Patten, C. (2001) 'Devotion or Divorce?: The Future of Transatlantic Relations' *European Foreign Affairs Review* **6** p. 288.

27 Patten, C. (2002) 'EU–US: The Indispensable Partnership', 3 December 2002, http://europa.eu.int/comm/external_relations/news/patten/sp_wdr.

28 Kohnstamm, M. (2003) 'The Europe We Need', 13 February 2003, http://www.theepc.be/europe; Heisbourg, F. (2000) 'Europe's Strategic Ambitions: The Limits of Ambiguity' *Survival* **42** (2) pp. 5–15; Lindley-French, J. (2002) 'In the Shade of Locarno? Why European Defence is Failing' *International Affairs* **78** (4) pp. 789–811; Ludlow, P. (2001) 'Wanted: A Global Partner' *Washington Quarterly* **24** (3) p. 171.

29 Speech by EU Trade Commissioner Pascal Lamy to the American Enterprise Institute, 18 December 2000, http://www.eurunion.org/news/speeches/2000/2000index.htm.

30 Author's italics. President Clinton, W. (1993) first inaugural speech, http://www.americanpolitics.info/clinton/speeches/inaug93.shtml.

31 Haass, R.N. (2002) 'US Engagement based on Cooperation, Consultation', http://www.useu.be/BackForth/june2602HaassEngagement.html.

32 Cited in Everts, S. (2001) 'Unilateral America, Lightweight Europe?', Center for European Reform, Working Paper, p. 15.

33 Walker, M. (2000) 'Variable Geography: America's Mental Maps of a Greater Europe' *International Affairs* **76** (3) pp. 459–74.

34 A survey published in winter 1999 of US Conservative expert opinion ranked East Asia as America's number one regional priority both today (35.4 per cent) and 2010 (48.8 per cent). Noonan, M.P. (1999) 'Conservative Opinions on U.S. Foreign Policy' *Orbis* **3** (4) pp. 628 and 632.

35 Cox, M. (2002) 'American Power Before and After 11 September: Dizzy With Success?' *International Affairs* **78** (2) p. 266.

36 Cited by Haass, 'US Engagement based on Cooperation, Consultation'.

37 For instance, in September 2000 Clinton declared to the UN General Assembly that 'those in my country who believe that we can do without the UN or impose our will upon it, misread history and misunderstand the future'. Just months previously US Senator Jesse Helms assured in the same building that 'a United Nations that insists upon trying to impose a utopian vision upon America and the world will collapse under its own weight'. The US was also heavy-handed in its prevention of Boutros Boutros-Ghali from having a second term as UN Secretary-General. Quotes from (November/December 2000) 'Start the Millennium Without U.S.' *Foreign Policy*, p.82.

38 For the impact of Congress see Calleo, D.P. (2001) 'Imperial America and its Republican Constitution' in *The New Transatlantic Agenda: Facing the Challenges of Global Goverance*, Gardner, H. and Stefanova, R. (eds), Aldershot: Ashgate, pp. 7–16; Pfaff, W. (1997) 'US Ambitions Outstrip Its Domestic Appetite' *International Herald Tribune*, 10 July 1997; Everts, 'Unilateral America, Lightweight Europe?', p. 7; Auerswald, D.P. (2001) 'The President, Congress and American Missile Defence Policy' *Defence Studies* 1 (2) pp. 57–82.

39 Spiro, P.J. (2000) 'The New Sovereigntists: American Exceptionalism and Its False Prophets' *Foreign Affairs* 79 (6) pp. 9–15.

40 Patten, C. (2002) 'Jaw-Jaw, not War-War', http://news.ft.com/ft/gx.cgi/ftc?pagename=View&c=Article&cid=FT33CZ00PXC&live=true.

41 Cited in Whitney, C.R. (1999) 'NATO at 50: With Nations at Odds, Is it a Misalliance?' *New York Times*, 15 February 1999, p. 7.

42 Cited in Blinken, 'The False Crisis Over the Atlantic', p. 41.

43 Mitchell, D.J. (2002) 'European Cult of Multilateralism', http://www.washtimes.com/commentary/20021107.

44 Waugh, P. and Brown, C. (2002) 'Hawkish Blair Tries to Calm the Doubters' *The Independent*, 8 April 2002, p. 4.

45 Tisdall, S. (2002) 'Bush Struggles with "Foreign Policy Stuff"' *The Guardian*, 26 April 2002, http://www.guardian.co.uk; Haass, 'US Engagement based on Cooperation, Consultation'. Surveys also show, even after September 11, a clear majority in American public opinion in favour of multilateralism. 'American Public Opinion and Foreign Policy' *Chicago Council on Foreign Relations*, http://www.worldviews.org/detailreports/usreport/html.

46 Rademaker (2003) 'The Commitment of the United States to Effective Multilateralism', statement to the Conference on Disarmament in Geneva, http://www.useu.be/BackForth/Feb1303RademakerMultilateralism.html.

47 Kissinger, H.A. (2002) 'NATO's Uncertain Future in a Troubled Alliance', http://www.expandnato.org/uncertain.html.

48 Albright cited by Maynes, 'US Unilateralism and its Dangers', p. 517.

49 Second Report from the Foreign Affairs Committee (2002) *'British–US Relations'*, *Response of the Secretary of State for Foreign and Commonwealth Affairs*, February 2002, London: HMSO, introduction, p. 6. For the text of the EU common position see 'European Council common position on the International Criminal Court', EC Official Journal, www.globalpolicy.org.

50 At the time of writing, those states opposed to the ICC are the US, China, Israel, Qatar, Libya, Iraq and Sudan. For more on the ICC see Schabas, W. (2001) *The International Criminal Court*, Cambridge: Cambridge University Press.

51 Second Report from the Foreign Affairs Committee, '*British–US relations*', p. 5.

52 O'Sullivan, J. (2002) 'They Don't Get the U.S.' *National Review Online*, http://www.nationalreview.com; Weller, M. (2002) 'Undoing the Global Constitution: UN Security Council Action on the International Criminal Court' *International Affairs* **78** (4) pp. 705–9.

53 The EU agreed to increase the proportion of its national income going to development assistance from an average of 0.32 per cent to 0.39 per cent, generating an extra $20 billion between 2002 and 2006 and an extra $7 billion a year thereafter. Brown, G. (2002) 'The UK and the United States: Realising Churchill's Vision of Interdependence', speech made by the Chancellor of the Exchequer to the British American Business Inc, New York, 19 April 2002, www.britanusa.com.

54 Koch, A. (2002) 'Resistance Builds to US Muscle' *Jane's Defence Weekly* **37** (6) p. 19.

55 Gardner, R. (2000) 'The One Percent Solution: Shirking the Cost of World Leadership' *Foreign Affairs* **79** (4) pp. 2–11. A bipartisan report on the State Department in 2001 warned that reliance on military solutions was liable to increase unless more funding were provided for other tools of diplomacy. Nye Jr., J.S. (2002) 'The American National Interest and Global Public Goods' *International Affairs* **78** (2) p. 240.

56 Previously standing at just 0.11 per cent of GDP and at one-third of the level of Europe, Bush promised to provide the foreign aid budget with an additional $1.6 billion in fiscal 2004, $3.3 billion in 2005 and $5 billion in 2006. Cornwell, R. (2002) 'Monterrey Aid Pledges Fail to Hit UN Target' *The Independent*, 22 March 2002, p. 21.

57 In October 2001 the UN General Assembly passed for the tenth consecutive year a vote by 167 to 3 for the end of the US embargo on Cuba. Dissenting countries were the US, Israel, and the Marshall Islands. Du Boff, R. (2001) 'Rogue Nation', http://www.nonviolence.org. For more on EU–US sanctions conflict see Falke, A. (2000) 'The EU–US Conflict Over Sanctions Policy: Confronting the Hegemon' *European Foreign Affairs Review* **5** pp. 139–63.

58 Interestingly this is exactly the sort of bargain that some members of the US Senate seemingly advocated during the Kosovo crisis: ' "we're contributing military muscle [the EU] should contribute the lion's share of the money" for post-war reconstruction'. Senator Gordon Smith, Chair of the Senate Subcommittee on European Affairs, cited by Peterson, J. (2001) 'Shaping, Not Making – The Impact of the American Congress on US–EU Relations' in *Ever Closer Partnership*, Philippart and Winand (eds), pp. 178–9.

59 Bass, W. (1998) 'The Triage of Dayton' *Foreign Affairs* **77** (5) p. 99.

60 Figures from International Institute for Strategic Studies (2002) *The Military Balance 2002–03*, London: Oxford University Press, pp. 332–7 and 341.

61 For further information see 'A Survey of the Defence Industry' *The Economist*, 20 July 2002, p. 6; Guay, T. and Callum, R. (2002) 'The Transformation and Future Prospects of Europe's Defence Industry' *International Affairs* **78** (4) pp. 757–76.

62 Clarke, M. and Cornish, P. (2002) 'The European Defence Project and the Prague Summit' *International Affairs* **78** (4) p. 784.

63 http://europa.eu.int/eur-lex/pri/en/oj/dat/2001.

64 Prime Minister Blair (1999) speech at the Lord Mayor's Banquet, www.fco.gov; Foreign Secretary Straw, J. (2001) speech at the Royal United Services Institute, www.fco.gov.

65 Howorth, J. (2000) 'Britain, France and the European Defence Initiative' *Survival* **42** (2) p. 33.

66 Thatcher cited by Harris, R. (2001) 'Blair's "Ethical" Policy' *The National Interest* **63** p. 34.

67 For examples see Genscher cited by Gordon, P. (1994) 'The Normalization of German Foreign Policy' *Orbis* **38** (2) p. 229; Kohl, H. (1996) speech given to 33rd Conference on Security: 'Security for a United Europe', 3 February 1996; speech by Rühe V. (1995) 'Bundeswehr und Europäische Sicherheit', 23 October 1995; Vernet, D. (1999) 'Kluge Ausschöpfung begrenzter Souveränität: Die Europa-Politik der rot-grünen Koalition' *Internationale Politik* **54** p. 16.

68 Schröder, G. (1999) 'Germany's Foreign Policy Responsibilities in the World', speech at the German Society for Foreign Policy (DGAP) Berlin, 2 September 1999, reprinted in *Internationale Politik* **10** p. 68.

69 Becker, J.J. (1998) 'Asserting EU Cohesion: Common Foreign and Security Policy and the Relaunch of Europe' *European Security* **7** p. 22; Krautscheid, A. (1997) 'Contemporary German Security Policy: A View from Bonn' Discussion Papers in German Studies IGS97/8, p. 20; Van Ham, P. (1999) 'Europe's Precarious Centre: Franco-German Cooperation and the CFSP' *European Security* **8** (4) p. 12; Cole, A. (2001) *Franco-German Relations*, London: Pearson, p. 125. Other German commitments include that in May 1992 when a medical unit of 150 doctors and nurses served in Cambodia as part of the UN Transitional Authority; in 1993–94 1,700 soldiers participated in the ill-fated UNOSOM II mission in Somalia; in February 1995 the potential need to extract UNPROFOR from Bosnia secured Bonn's reluctant agreement to participate in the rescue, and German Tornados flew combat missions in Operation Deliberate Force; and involvement in the Balkans deepened in the wake of the Dayton Accords, with substantial German contributions being made to the Implementation Force (IFOR) and the Stabilisation Force (SFOR).

70 James Dobbins was US Deputy Assistant Secretary of State for European Affairs.

71 Delors, J. (1991) 'European Integration and Security' *Survival* **33** (2) p. 108.

72 Albright, M. (1999) 'The Right Balance will Secure NATO's Future' *Financial Times*, 7 December 1999. For contrasting views about the motives behind strengthening CFSP and the CESDP and their complementarity or otherwise with NATO see Bolton, J. (2000) 'The End of NATO' *World Today* **56** (6) pp. 12–14; Kupchan, C.A. (2000) 'In Defence of European Defence: An American Perspective' *Survival* **42** (2) pp. 16–32.

73 Rumsfeld, D.H. (2001) remarks by US Secretary of Defence at Munich Conference on European Security Policy, http://www.defenselink.mil/speeches/2001/s20010203-secdef.html.

74 Tisdall, S. (2001) 'Conflict Looms Over Rapid Reaction Force' *The Guardian*, http://www.guardian.co.uk/elsewhere/journalist/story.

75 US Department of Defense, *Joint Vision 2020*, p. 8, http://www.dtic.mil/jointvision/jvpub2.htm.

76 Figures derived from International Institute for Strategic Studies, *The Military Balance 2002–03*, pp. 332–7.

77 Cited in Van Ham, P. (2000) 'Europe's Common Defense Policy: Implications for the Trans-Atlantic Alliance' *Security Dialogue* 31 (2) p. 223.

78 Foster, E. (2000) 'The Minster's Salvation? German Military Reform' *RUSI Newsbrief* 20 (6) pp. 55–57; (Spring 1999) *NATO Review*, p. 32; International Institute for Strategic Studies, *The Military Balance 2002–03*, p. 332; Meiers, F.J. (2001) 'The Reform of the Bundeswehr: Adaptation or Fundamental Renewal?' *European Security* 10 (2) p. 14.

79 Bertram, C. (2000) 'Reforming Germany's Army', p. 1, http://www.projectsyndicate.cz/dcs/columns/Bertram2000July.asp.html.

80 For further analysis see Alexander, M. and Garden, T. (2001) 'The Arithmetic of Defence Policy' *International Affairs* 77 (3) pp. 509–29.

81 European Commission (2003) 'European Defence – Industrial and Market Issues', COM (2003) 113 final, 11 March 2003, p. 5.

82 Gordon, P. (2000) 'Their Own Army?' *Foreign Affairs* 79 (4) p. 14; Robertson, Lord G. (2002) speech in London, http://www.nato.int/docu/speech/s020124a.htm.

83 Figure from Lansford, T. (2001) 'Security and Marketshare: Bridging the Transatlantic Divide in the Defence Industry' *European Security* 10 (1) pp. 3, 6.

84 Italy quit the project and Germany has sought to retract on its original commitment. See, for instance, Gow, D. (2002) 'Britain's Costs Rise as Germans Cut Plane Order' *The Guardian*, http://www.guardian.co.uk/Archive.

85 See, for example, Steyn, M. (2002) 'Put Up or Shut Up: Europe Spends Zip on Defence and Sneers at America's "Warmongering"' *The Spectator*, 5 October 2002.

86 International Institute for Strategic Studies (2001) *The Military Balance 2001–2002*, Oxford: Oxford University Press, p. 291; Duke, S. (2002) 'CESDP and the EU Response to 11 September: Identifying the Weakest Link' *European Foreign Affairs Review* 7 p. 167.

87 Donald Rumsfeld cited by Norton-Taylor, R. (2002) 'The US Will Be Legislator, Judge and Executioner' *The Guardian*, http://www.guardian.co.uk/comment/story,0,3604,842185,00.html.

88 Bensahel, N. (1999) 'Separable But Not Separate Forces: NATO's Development of the Combined Joint Task Force' *European Security* 8 (2) pp. 52–72; Sloan, S.R. (1995) 'NATO and the United States' in *NATO in the Post-Cold War Era*, Papacosma and Heiss (eds); Barry, C. (1996) 'NATO's Combined Joint Task Force in Theory and Practice' *Survival* 38 (1) pp. 81–97.

89 Britain has long claimed this foreign policy role and the US has long held Britain's role in Europe to be a strength rather than a weakness of the Anglo-American relationship, being, in the words of former Ambassador Seitz, 'indisputably complicating' but 'indispensable' to the relationship. Seitz cited from a speech in April

1994, Renwick, Sir R. (1996) *Fighting With Allies*, New York: Times Books, p. 400; Major, J. (1999) *John Major: The Autobiography*, London: Harper Collins, p. 578; Dumbrell, J. (2001) *A Special Relationship: Anglo-American Relations in the Cold War and After*, Basingstoke: Macmillan.

90 See, for example, European Commission (1997) *Implementing European Union Strategy on Defence-Related Industries*, COM (97) 583 final. On 11 March 2003 the Commission also adopted a communication on the development of a European defence equipment market. European Commission (2003) 'European Defence – Industrial and Market Issues', COM (2003) 113 final, 11 March 2003.

91 Lansford, T. (2001) 'Security and Marketshare: Bridging the Transatlantic Divide in the Defence Industry' *European Security* **10** (1) p. 9.

92 Moens, A. in collaboration with Domisiewicz, R. (2001) 'European and North American Trends in Defence Industry: Problems and Prospects of a Cross-Atlantic Defence Market', International Security Research and Outreach Programme, p. 7.

93 Eyal, J. (2000) 'Britain's European Defence Debate: Cliché after Cliché' *RUSI Newsbrief* **20** (12) p. 127; Van Ham, 'Europe's Common Defense Policy', p. 215.

94 Moens, 'European and North American Trends in Defence Industry', p. 12.

95 EU General Affairs Council (2001) Statement, http://www.usinfo.gov/topical/ pol/terror/01101214.htm.

96 For example, Schröder declared the attacks 'a declaration of war on the free world', Patten promised that '[w]e stand four-square with our American colleagues and friends' and Blair pledged that '[w]e stand shoulder to shoulder with our American friends in this hour of tragedy'. Cited in, respectively, 'Solid, For How Long?' *The Economist* **360** (8240) 22 September 2001, p. 37; 'Old Friends, Best Friends' *The Economist* **360** (8239) 15 September 2001; 'We're With You, Sort Of' *The Economist* **360** (8240) 22 September 2001, p. 29.

97 http://www.europa.eu.int/comm/external_relations/us/news/ minist_20_09_01.htm; http://www.eurunion.org/news/press/2001/2001067.htm.

98 'The European Union Adopts Comprehensive Anti-Terror Measures', Council Common Position of 27 December 2001 on the application of specific measures to combat terrorism, *Official Journal of the European Communities*, 28 December 2001, pp. 93–96, http://www.ict.org.il/spotlight/det.cfm.

99 'Highlights of EU–US Cooperation, July 2001–June 2002', http://www.europa.eu.int/comm/external_relations/us/news/highlights.

100 For activities of FATF: http://www.1.oecd.org/fatf/index.htm.

101 Marsden, P. (2003) 'Afghanistan: The Reconstruction Process' *International Affairs* **79** (1) p. 93.

102 European Commission (2001) 'Overview of EU Action in Response to the Events of 11 September and Assessment of their Likely Economic Impact', Brussels, 17 October 2001, DOC/01/15, http://www.europa.eu.int/rapid/start/cgi/ guesten.ksh?p_action.gettxt=gt&doc=DOC/01/15|0|RAPID&lg=EN.

103 Settle, M. (2001) 'King of the Coalition: Blair – The Mission' *Sunday Herald*, 7 October 2001. For more on Anglo-American relations and September 11 see Marsh, S. (2003) 'September 11 and Anglo-American Relations: Reaffirming the Special Relationship' *Journal of Transatlantic Studies* **1** pp. 56–75.

104 US Deputy Treasury Secretary Kenneth Dam cited by Zwaniecki, A. (2002) 'US–EU Partnership Must Adjust to New Era', http://www.useu.be/Terrorism/EUResponse/Dec0302HaassDamUS.

105 Ries, Charles P. (2001) remarks of US Principal Deputy Assistant Secretary of State for European and Eurasian Affairs to the Southern Center for International Studies annual seminar on Europe, www.usembassy.org.uk/europe.

106 Alden, E. (2002) 'Europe Freezes Terrorist Assets Worth $35 million' *Financial Times*, 8 April 2002, p. 3.

107 Bennett, C. (Winter 2001/02) 'Aiding America' *NATO Review* **49** pp. 6–7; Clarke, M. and Cornish, P. (2002) 'The European Defence Project and the Prague Summit' *International Affairs* **78** (4) p. 782; US State Department (2002) 'Fact Sheet: NATO Coalition Contributes to Global War on Terrorism'.

108 Duke, S. (2002) 'CESDP and the EU Response to 11 September: Identifying the Weakest Link' *European Foreign Affairs Review* **7** pp. 153–69.

109 Howorth, J. (Winter 2002) 'CESDP After 11 September: From Short-Term Confusion to Long-Term Cohesion?' *EUSA Review* **15** (1) p. 1.

110 'Afghan Prisoners: A Transatlantic Rift' *The Economist* **362** (8256) 19 January 2002, p. 42.

111 Védrine cited in 'Good for the (French) President' *The Economist* **360** (8240) 22 September 2001, p. 38.

112 (2001) 'The European Union and the September 11th Crisis', Working Paper Series **1** (1) University of Miami, http://www.miami.edu/EUCenter/911workingpaper.pdf.

113 Steyn, M. (2001) 'Very Well, Then, Alone' *The Spectator*, 22 September 2001.

114 For discussion of the legality of intervention in Afghanistan see Greenwood, C. (2002) 'International Law and the "War Against Terrorism"' *International Affairs* **78** (2) pp. 301–17.

115 According to Assistant Secretary of State Haass, 'what you are seeing in this administration is the emergence of a new principle or body of ideas . . . about what you might call the limits of sovereignty. Sovereignty entails obligations. One is not to massacre your own people. Another is not to support terrorism in any way. If a government fails to meet these obligations, then it forfeits some of the advantages of sovereignty, including the right to be left alone inside your own territory.' Kaldor, M. (2003) 'American Power: From "Compellance" to Cosmopolitanism?' *International Affairs* **79** (1) p. 12.

116 For an introduction to legal dimensions of the Kosovo campaign see Guicherd, C. (1999) 'International Law and the War in Kosovo' *Survival* **41** (2) pp. 19–34.

117 Rumsfeld, Donald (2002) remarks at National Defence University Washington D.C., http://www.defenselink.mil/speeches/2002/s20020131-secdef.html.

118 For instance, the House of Lords Select Committee on the European Union concluded in July 2003 that 'The European Union's relations with the United States are at their lowest ebb for at least a generation'. House of Lords Select Committee on the European Union (2003) 'A Fractured Partnership? Relations Between the European Union and the United States of America', House of Lords, Session 2002–03, 30th Report, 1 July 2003, HL Paper 134, London: HMSO, p. 5.

119 Schuller, F.C. and Grant, T.D. (2003) 'Executive Diplomacy: Multilateralism, Unilateralism and Managing American Power' *International Affairs* **79** (1) p. 48.

120 Nielson, Poul (2003) 'Statement on Iraq to the European Parliament', http://www.europa.eu.int/rapid/start/cgi/guesten.

121 Dubois, D. (2002) 'The Attacks of 11 September: EU–US Cooperation Against Terrorism in the Field of Justice and Home Affairs' *European Foreign Affairs Review* 7 p. 325.

122 Golino, L.R. (2002) 'Time to Thank Europe for its Help on Terrorism' *Global Beat Syndicate*, http://www.atlanticcomunity.org/Golino%20July%202002%20art; Garton Ash, T. (2003) 'Anti-Europeanism in America' *New York Review of Books*, http://www.nybooks.com/articles/16059.

123 Schuller and Grant, 'Executive Diplomacy: Multilateralism, Unilateralism and Managing American Power', p. 40; Gordon, 'Their Own Army?', p. 17; Falke, 'The EU–US Conflict Over Sanctions Policy', p. 141; Yost, D.S. (Winter 2000) 'The NATO Capabilities Gap and the European Union' *Survival* **42** pp. 97–128.

124 Robertson, Lord G. (2002) speech in London, 24 January 2002, http://www.nato.int/docu/speech/s020124a.htm.

CHAPTER 5

Friends or foes?:

the EU–US economic relationship

As seen in the first two chapters, the US had a strong political and economic interest in Europe after WW2. Apart from binding the Western European countries into its own sphere of influence and having them as allies against the common threat perceived to emanate from the Soviet bloc, the US also needed prosperous markets for its own goods if it were to avoid a repeat of the inter-war recession. Marshall Aid was consequently designed partially to promote US economic interests in international free trade through pushing the Euro-peans into accepting trade liberalisation under the GATT. Likewise, its encour-agement of Western European integration was geared to developing a large and successful European market that would be a strong trading partner for US businesses.[1]

The formal economic relationship between what is now the EU and the US began with the creation of the ECSC in 1952 and intensified with the intro-duction of the CAP in 1962 and the creation of the EEC's general customs union in 1968. The transfer of responsibility for trade policy to the ECs level in 1970, in the form of the CCP, marked a significant shift in the relationship whereby the Communities, rather than the individual member states, became the trading partner of, and therewith trade negotiator with, the US. A further marked evolution in the EC/EU–US trade relationship developed with the creation of the WTO in 1995. Thereafter they had to conduct their trade exchanges in accordance with the rules of a 'higher authority' and submit their disagreements to the legally binding judgement of the WTO Dispute Settlement Body.

Over time the ECs–US economic relationship became intense and pro-foundly interdependent. However, as the two entered the post-Cold War era speculation increased about a downturn in the relative balance between their economic co-operation and confrontation. This was encouraged by suggestions of geo-strategic drift slowly pulling the partners apart (see Chapter Four) and by an increasing number of bitter transatlantic trade disputes. It was also encouraged by a combination of the ECs' transition from economic supplicant to equal partner/rival and growing US concern during the 1980s of relative American economic decline. Thus, as the EC/EU became a more self-confident and assertive international economic actor, the US became concerned, for a time at least, about both the possibilities of a 'Fortress Europe' and how to preserve American economic leadership.

With this in mind, this chapter assesses the post-Cold War EU–US economic relationship and asks what is the nature of this relationship in terms of trade, investment and other commercial activities? On the one hand, it is the most voluminous in the world, the EU–US partnership is instrumental in shaping processes of economic globalisation, and the combination of the US, EU and the latter's member states dominates the leading international financial institutions. At the same time, their economic relationship has undergone radical changes, especially in terms of the relative strengths of the two economic superpowers, and the number of post-Cold War trade disputes has increased dramatically. How, then, should the EU–US economic relationship be characterised? Are they economic partners, rivals, or does their relationship stand in a different category from any other?

The most substantial economic partnership in the world

It is difficult to overstate the significance to the EU and US, indeed to the world, of their economic relationship. It is by far the most important bilateral economic relationship for both parties in terms of trade and FDI. The respective figures speak for themselves.[2] In 2002 the US was the EU's largest trading partner in goods, providing almost 18 per cent of all EU imports and accounting for nearly 24 per cent of all EU merchandise exports. The next largest exporter to the EU was China with 8.3 per cent of the total and the second largest export market for EU goods was Switzerland with 7.1 per cent of all EU merchandise sold abroad.[3] The American situation in 2002 was somewhat more variegated. The EU was America's second most important export market taking nearly 22 per cent of its external merchandise trade and being exceeded only by Canada, immediate neighbour of the US and partner within NAFTA, which had a market share of almost 24 per cent.[4] However, the EU was the US's premier source of merchandise imports with a market share of 21 per cent – considerably ahead of Canada with just over 16 per cent and of China's 12.5 per cent.[5]

The importance of this bilateral economic relationship is also reflected in the trade in services, which accounted in 2001 for some 36 per cent of total EU–US trade.[6] Herein the US is again by far the EU's most important external trading partner with a 43 per cent market share in 2001. To put this into context, the EU's second most important partner in this field was Switzerland with a share of just under 13 per cent.[7] US trade in services is more diverse. The US imported over 27.5 per cent of its services from Canada in 2001 compared to around

11 per cent from the EU and just over 10 per cent from Mexico. Canada was also the most important market for services exported from the US with a 19 per cent market share in 2001. Japan, Mexico and the EU occupied the following ranks with percentages of 14.7, 14.1 and 14 respectively.[8]

Trade figures, though, merely reflect cross-border flows of goods and services. They consequently represent only a partial measure of the extent of the EU–US economic relationship, not least because they ignore the fact that enterprises often sell their goods and services abroad through their foreign affiliates rather than export them from their home market. A more accurate picture of the EU–US commercial relationship thus has to consider other linkages too, such as capital flows – especially FDI.[9] Herein the EU and the US have by far the world's most important bilateral relationship. In 2001, 49 per cent of all FDI that left the EU went to the US and 69 per cent of all FDI coming into the EU originated there. Unlike the situation with some aspects of trade, the EU is definitely also the most important FDI partner of the US: 46 per cent of all US FDI went to the EU and the US received 54 per cent of all its FDI from the Union in 2001. This close relationship is underpinned even further by the FDI stocks that EU and US investors have accumulated in the respective other entity. By 2001, 62 per cent of all FDI investment inside the EU originated from the US, whilst 50 per cent of all EU FDI so far has been made in the US. From the American perspective, 61 per cent of all FDI made there has its origins in the EU, whilst 46 per cent of all FDI that had left the country by 2001 had gone to the EU.[10]

This unrivalled volume of bilateral trade and FDI owes in part to factors beyond direct EU–US management of their economic relationship. Businesses have developed mutual confidence over time in the other partner's stability, general commitment to trade liberalisation and value in terms of risk-adjusted returns, albeit that American criticism of 'continental corporatism' reflects disagreement about the merits of Europe's social democratic model *vis-à-vis* the free market model. Developments within each partner have also stimulated increased transatlantic trade and investment and influenced the decisions of MNCs and TNCs as to where to locate operations. For instance, the size of the EU market, the expectation of further enlargement and the comparative advantages of the single market programme have all attracted rather than deterred US inward investment into the Union.[11] Indeed, from 1995 to 2001 there was a seven-fold increase in American investment in Europe.[12] Considerations of the SEM have also been of major influence in, for example, Britain both surpassing China in 1999 to become the largest single destination for US FDI and being the base for 5,600 American companies in the European single market.[13]

Nevertheless, the calculations of commercial enterprises have always run side-by-side with careful transatlantic political oversight and in the immediate post-Cold War era the EU and US were persuaded by both positive and negative concerns to underpin the world's most important economic relationship with further solid structural foundations. On the one hand, both partners were aware of their complex economic interdependence and relative economic parity, which provided opportunities for further intensification of their bilateral economic relationship and called for structures either to forestall or to manage inevitable differences as their competition and interaction increased.[14] On the other hand, the EU and US were each anxious to 'contain' the other in defence of their economic interests. Successive American administrations were anxious to protect US economic interests and to keep the EU open to international trade. This owed not least to predictions of US relative decline, the expensive economic legacies of Reagan's Second Cold War and fears that the SEM project would lead to an introverted and protectionist Fortress Europe. Conversely, the EU was concerned to retain its attractiveness to American businesses and FDI at a time when new, potentially high-reward commercial opportunities appeared to be developing elsewhere, especially in the Asian 'tiger states'. The EU was also wary of increased US unilateralist tendencies and the aggressive promotion of American economic interests. For instance, the Clinton administration created the National Economic Council and encouraged a National Export Strategy and the Big Emerging Markets Program in order to promote exports, and it used US trade representatives (USTR) to attack reprobate trade partners and to exact so-called voluntary export restraint agreements. It also used GATT and the WTO to negotiate favourable reductions in NTBs whilst simultaneously taking unilateral action through Section 301 legislation in the 1988 Omnibus Trade and Competitiveness Act to counter what it deemed to be unacceptable trade practices by other countries.

Not surprisingly, therefore, the 1990 Transatlantic Declaration and the 1995 New Transatlantic Agenda and its accompanying Joint Action Plan all included declarations on economic co-operation between the two entities. The JAP in particular contained quite detailed aims and objectives. Under the headline 'Contributing to the Expansion of World Trade and Closer Economic Relations', the two partners, among a number of other things, agreed to set up 'a New Transatlantic Marketplace by progressively reducing or eliminating barriers that hinder the flow of goods, services and capital' between themselves.[15] Although not quite the basis for a common market between the two entities, the creation of a new transatlantic marketplace (NTM) did point in such a direction. It was also enormously ambitious, for, as has been seen in respect of the EU's own development, reducing barriers to facilitate the exchange of not only goods but also services and capital is no simple task. Indeed, the EU's common market in services is still incomplete more than a decade after the SEM was officially declared established.

It is thus particularly revealing of EU–US determination to nurture and promote their bilateral economic relationship that they decided at a summit in London in May 1998 to launch the Transatlantic Economic Partnership (TEP).[16] This initiative was undoubtedly motivated by slow progress in the development of the NTM and by numerous continuing barriers to trade and investment.[17] The TEP also demonstrated, however, mutual determination to re-ignite the economic relationship, which was reflected in its containing far more detailed provisions than did the NTM on how to proceed, including explicit target dates. Since then the TEP has admittedly progressed less quickly than hoped. In its Report on United States Barriers to Trade and Investment 2002, the European Commission stated that '[d]espite the significant co-operative efforts undertaken, a considerable number of impediments, ranging from more traditional tariff and non-tariff barriers, to differences in the legal and regulatory systems still need to be tackled'.[18] Still, though, there remains political and economic impetus sufficient to push ahead with the TEP, including a transatlantic marketplace. As American Under-Secretary of Commerce for International Trade Grant Aldonas was quoted as having said in April 2003, '[i]f there was ever a time when we really needed to . . . try and remove . . . obstacles to trade between the United States and Europe now is the time'.[19]

Clearly, then, the EU–US economic relationship is of vital importance to each partner. However, its significance is scarcely less to the wider international economy. The EU and US have by far the largest economies in the world and collectively their economic weight is awesome. A few figures help to substantiate this claim. The EU and the US are clearly the dominant players insofar as international trade in merchandise and services is concerned. Combined they secured 47 per cent of world merchandise trade and 45 per cent of world trade in services in 2002.[20] Their importance in terms of investment is even more striking. In the financial year 2000 they accounted for 54 per cent of total world inflows and 67 per cent of total world outflows of FDI.[21] Moreover, America in particular has been the driving force of the recent global economic upturn. For instance, since 1995 60 per cent of the cumulative growth in world output has come from the US, with the EU accounting for approximately a further 10 per cent.

It is also important to consider EU–US institutionalised economic power and their roles in shaping international trade and investment. Their collective influence within the leading international financial institutions is unrivalled. For example, within the G8 they constitute five of the eight member states and have added influence through the European Commission, which is present on behalf of the EU. Within the IMF the EU countries and the US enjoy a combined voting weight of 46.95 per cent,[22] and their position in the World Bank is not far behind, accounting for 41.99 per cent of votes.[23] They also each have banks that are used to advance their economic and foreign policy objectives, namely the US Export-Import Bank and the EU's European Investment Bank. One consequence of all of this is that the EU and US heavily influence the terms, conditions and amounts of, for instance, rescue packages such as that organised for Russia in the wake of its economic collapse in 1998.

Just as significantly, as the world's two largest and most technologically advanced economies, the EU and US share common problems and significantly shape the development of the global economy. For instance, both parties are pursuing what has been dubbed 'competitive liberalisation', meaning the contemporaneous pursuit of bilateral, regional and global free trade agreements. As will be seen in later chapters, the EU has developed a global web of preferential trading relationships of a variety of types and involving varying numbers of associated partners. Indeed, this is an area in which the EU has traditionally led America. USTR Robert Zoellick observed before the subcommittee on trade of the US House of Representatives in May 2001 that globally there were 130 free trade agreements. The US was party to just two of these, one with Canada and Mexico forming NAFTA and another with Israel. In contrast, the EU had free trade or special customs agreements with twenty-seven countries, twenty of which the Union had completed within the previous ten years, and another fifteen were then being negotiated.[24] Since then, the US has concluded a FTA with Chile (actually a month before the EU could finalise a similar treaty[25]), one with Singapore,[26] and is in the process of pursuing bilateral deals with Bolivia, Columbia, Ecuador, Panama and Peru, five countries in southern Africa, Australia and Morocco. It has also promised to begin negotiations with the Dominican Republic and Bahrain. In the meantime, US negotiations for a FTA with Central America are almost complete and in November 2003 the next step was agreed in Miami in the development of a Free Trade Area of the Americas (FTAA). Due to come into effect by 2005, the FTAA will cover thirty-four countries with a population of 800 million people, stretch from Alaska to Patagonia and have an output of $13–14 trillion per annum. This should also continue the post-Cold War expansion of North American exports to Latin America[27] and bring the US into greater contact with the EU, which already has established relationships with the Caribbean Community and Common Market (Caricom), the Central American countries, the Andean Community (CAN) and the countries of Mercosur (see Chapter Nine).

Concomitantly, the EU and US are key players in the quest for global free trade and are keen to shape this in line with their specific interests and concerns, many of which they share. For instance, the two were instrumental in launching the Doha Round of WTO trade talks, which the World Bank estimates could raise global income by $500 billion by 2015, of which 60 per cent would go to poor countries and help pull 144 million people out of poverty.[28] Within this context, the EU also determinedly set part of the agenda at the WTO meeting in Cancún in September 2003 by pushing the so-called 'Singapore issues' in an attempt to negotiate global rules in competition, government procurement, transparency and trade facilitation. Moreover, the EU and US share unemployment concerns in manufacturing (2.7 million job losses in the US alone over the past three years) as well as in the white-collar sector as competition increases and companies outsource or even relocate factories abroad to where costs are cheaper. Interestingly, despite their frequent disagreements over agriculture, the EU and US are also joined by their use of agricultural protectionism. The EU has consistently found the CAP difficult to reform and adjustments are becoming simultaneously both more pressing in view of imminent enlargement and more politically difficult given an appreciating euro and the consequent relative decline in the international competitiveness of its agricultural exports. The US is likewise a major subsidiser of American agriculture. For example, it heavily protects its citrus producers and is simultaneously the world's biggest cotton exporter and biggest subsidiser of producers – to the tune of over $3 billion per annum. The EU and US also face major challenges upon the expiry of the Multifibre Arrangement at the end of 2004, which has for decades allowed governments to determine trade patterns in textile markets and upon which their domestic producers and preferential trading partners in the developing world often rely.

Just how great a shared challenge agricultural protectionism is to the EU and US was demonstrated by the collapse of the WTO meeting in Cancún in September 2003. There the EU and US presented a moderate programme for freeing farm trade that fell far short of previous promises on, for example, removing farm subsidies. This was strongly opposed as inadequate by a new so-called G21 bloc of developing countries, led by India, Brazil and China – a powerful voice given that the G21 represent half the world's population and two-thirds of its farmers.[29] The EU and US consequently face a potential stream of WTO appeals from the G21 and others about their agricultural protectionism. This is particularly likely given the imminent expiry of the so-called 'peace clause' at the end of 2003, which is an agreement negotiated during the Uruguay Round not to appeal over the dumping of farm products on condition that each country honoured its farm trade commitments.

Trade wars and other conflicts between the EU and US

That the EU–US economic relationship is far from problem-free is demonstrated by their difficulties in reducing the obstacles to a more integrated transatlantic economic area. However, slow progress in realising the TEP is far less problematic, not to mention 'newsworthy', than the increasing number of cases where fierce EU–US economic competition has degenerated into trade wars. The actual transatlantic economic relationship between the US and the ECs as a supranational body officially began in 1970 with the commencement of the CCP.[30] The US, though, is not linked to the EU by way of a contractual agreement under the auspices of the CCP and is thus subject to the 'normal' external trade regime of the autonomous part of this policy. This means that the US does not enjoy treatment more favourable than any of the EU's other trading partners and that the bilateral relationship is based on respective unilateral provisions, potentially restricted only by the agreements entered into by both under GATT and later the WTO.[31]

Despite these organisations being mandated to avoid trade disputes, over time a number of conflicts between the ECs and the US have occurred. Initially there were only a few such disputes: just three during the entire 1960s and 1970s.[32] The pace quickened noticeably, though, during the 1980s when fourteen cases were fought out, only to accelerate even further following the establishment of the WTO. Between January 1995 and July 2003 there were fifty-five cases involving trade disputes between the EU or one or several of its member states on the one hand, and the US on the other.[33] This trend can be explained in part by the ever-growing and increasingly complex economic ties that have evolved between the ECs and the US. Naturally, the more they deal with one another, the more potential scope for conflict there is. However, although this certainly explains the higher incidence of complaints during the 1980s, it does not fully account for the leap in trade disputes since 1995. One must therefore consider also the impact of the improved mechanisms of the WTO over the rules of GATT – in particular the introduction of a true, institutionalised appeals mechanism in the form of the organisation's DSB. Before 1995, members of GATT had no chance to appeal if and when another signatory to a given deal failed to adhere to its own promises. The DSB of the WTO changed this by providing not only a forum before which disputes could be debated but also procedures that enabled a judgement and the possibility of sanctions in cases of non-compliance.

The latter aspect especially is also responsible for another pattern in trade conflicts between the ECs and the US – the question of who complained about whom. Of the three conflicts in the 1960s, the ECs initiated the first and the US the remainder. During the 1980s, twelve of the fourteen conflicts were initiated by the US, only two by the ECs.[34] Since 1995, however, the EU or one of its member states has complained in twenty-six cases about the US, whilst the US, either on its own or in conjunction with other complainants, has taken action twenty-nine times against the EU or one of its members.[35] This clearly indicates the EU's growing confidence to use the WTO against the US. Moreover, this willingness is underpinned by changes in the general geo-political situation. Security dependence on the US during the Cold War naturally made Western Europe hesitant to confront the US. This is reflected in the fact that the Europeans initiated only three of the seventeen trade disputes before 1990. The US, on its part, addressed the relationship during this period from a position of strength and the knowledge that the relative dependency of its European partners meant that trade disagreements could be pursued without fear of too bad a deterioration in overall transatlantic political relationships. The winding down of the Cold War, however, changed the geo-strategic balance and afforded the Europeans an opportunity to emancipate themselves – at least to a degree – from the old hegemon.[36] The quasi-judicial system of the WTO then played its part, giving the Communities the confidence and mechanisms to challenge actively the US over those trade issues about which they disagreed. The 26 (EU vs. US) to 29 (US vs. EU) ratio of post–1995 trade disputes both reflects this post-Cold War emancipation of the EU from the US and is a much more realistic representation of their contemporary relationship in which the two entities enjoy relative economic parity.

A further interesting aspect of trade disputes between the ECs and the US concerns the issues over which the two have argued. Twenty-three of the seventy-two conflicts have been about agricultural products, and within this the US has been the complainant on eighteen occasions. This rather unbalanced picture should not come as a surprise. The US, and others, would understandably like to break into the potentially very lucrative EU market. Obstructing this objective is the Communities' protectionist CAP. High import barriers, such as tariffs and quotas, aim at keeping prices within the EU stable at a substantially higher-than-world-price level, direct subsidies give farmers a further comparative advantage, and export subsidies compensate them for the differences between EU and world market prices.[37] This is primarily why widely publicised agricultural 'trade wars' have come about. As a major exporter of agricultural products the US has consistently pressed for improved access to the EU market. Meanwhile, the Union has sought to balance its commitment to liberalising international trade against the specific objectives of its CAP and its preferential trade agreements with other producers, some of which are entwined with its Development Policy programmes.

The most notorious recent example of this was the so-called 'banana war'. The EU produces only around 20 per cent of its banana consumption itself. The rest is imported, either from former colonies of some of the Union's member states in Africa and the Caribbean (so-called 'ACP bananas') or from Latin America (so-called 'dollar bananas'). The problem was that the EU's provisions on trade in bananas since the 'completion' of the SEM in 1993 quite openly discriminated between home-grown bananas, those imported from the associated ACP countries and those originating from Latin America. Home production was supported by way of subsidisation and compensation payments if and when prices fell below a certain threshold level. The ACP countries were guaranteed tariff-free access to the Union of, more or less, their entire export crop of bananas. Although the import quota for 'dollar bananas' was more than double that of the ACP countries, they were subject to a tariff of initially €100 per tonne, reduced in 1994 to €75 per tonne. Given that they could produce bananas at a much lower cost than, for instance, the ACP producers, the loss in potential trade in bananas with the EU was significant.[38] In 1996 the US, together with Honduras, Guatemala, Ecuador and Mexico, duly complained about elements of the European banana regime that they believed to discriminate unfairly against their interests. Honduras, Guatemala and Ecuador judged that they had insufficient access to the European market, and the US championed its TNCs, one of which, Chiquita Brands International, was especially keen to increase its access to the European market.[39]

The DSB of the WTO ruled in 1997 that part of the EU's import regime for bananas did indeed breach the organisation's rules. Yet this was not the end of the issue. Some EU member states were little concerned about the need to reform the offending provisions of the EU banana regime. Germany, for example, had been unhappy with the single banana regime from the onset and prior to its coming into force in 1993 was the only EU member state that imposed no trade restrictions on bananas.[40] However, many of the other EU members found it difficult to accept reforms. Spain, Greece, Portugal and France had domestic producers to consider, and Britain and France also had their former colonies in mind. Opponents of substantial change to the EU's banana regime had a majority in the Council and the changes that came into force in January

1999 were consequently largely cosmetic. Within twenty-five days the US and a number of Latin American countries went back to the WTO to complain once more about the EU's banana regime. The Clinton administration also invoked Section 301 legislation and imposed punitive sanctions by putting a random selection of fifteen European products on the red list. By April the DSB had formally awarded America damages,[41] which meant that the US was legally allowed to initiate 'compensatory retaliation' through the imposition of heavy tariffs on luxury goods imported from Europe equivalent to an annual cost of $191.4m (€215.2m).[42]

The 'banana war' finally ended when Chiquita Brands indicated its satisfaction with new provisions that came into force in July 2001.[43] Much more intractable have been EU–US confrontations over hormone-treated beef and GMOs, which are nominally agricultural disputes but which also reveal the fungible nature of trade issues and those of environment and health and safety. In 1988 the then EEC prohibited the use of a number of hormones[44] previously used for growth promotion in farm animals. Since this was justified on grounds of scientific tests having found such meat to be unsafe for human consumption, the ban was to apply to member states as well as to respective imports from third countries. What the Europeans regarded as a matter of public health and food safety, the Americans saw as a cleverly disguised form of protectionism. The US and Canada consequently contested the prohibition, and in 1997 the WTO ruled that the EU measure was not in line with the Agreement on the Application of Sanitary and Phytosanitary Measures.[45] In 1998 the WTO's Appellate Body ruled against a consequent EU appeal on grounds that the ban had not been based on adequate scientific evidence and therefore violated international trade rules.

Called upon to provide sufficient evidence to substantiate its claims,[46] the EU subsequently commissioned a number of studies that apparently show that at least one of the banned hormones causes cancer. The US, however, maintained that hormone-treated beef had legally been on sale in its domestic market and that its own research had found no evidence indicating that such meat could pose a health threat. The two were thus deadlocked, with the EU continuing to enforce its ban on meat treated with the other hormones and arguing that just because they had not been proven to be dangerous they should not be considered safe automatically.[47] Matters were mitigated slightly in April 1999 when the EU threatened to ban imports of American hormone-free beef too after scientists found traces of the banned substances in between 12 and 20 per cent of beef samples from US abattoirs labelled as not having been treated in this way. Forced onto the defensive by this surprise discovery, the US voluntarily imposed a ban on hormone-free beef whilst reviewing its own monitoring measures.[48] However, the dispute is far from resolved and EU–US differences are much more complex than was the case in the banana war. Whilst the US accuses the Europeans of protectionism, the EU maintains that it is not motivated by protecting its beef industry but by concern for the health and safety of its citizens.

This fungibility of issues is repeated in EU–US differences over GMOs and so-called 'Frankenstein foods', a transatlantic trade dispute that has been brewing since the start in 1996 of biosafety talks. The European Commission, in response to environmentalist pressure and public outcry against food scares such as BSE, introduced a regulatory regime that required environmental evaluation and step-by-step approval for the dissemination of GMOs. The US, the world's largest exporter of GM foods, has repeatedly accused the Commission of back-door protectionism and of operating an approval system that is non-transparent, unpredictable, overly politicised and unscientific. Exchanges sank to a new low in February 1999 when EU–US differences stalled efforts at the Cartagena Conference in Columbia to establish rules for the handling and transport of GMOs, GM crops and other biotechnology products. Then, prior to the WTO Summit in Seattle, the US, Canada and Japan proposed a biotechnology Working Group within the WTO. This move was widely interpreted as an effort to apply WTO rules to the conflict over GM trade and to out-manoeuvre the opposition that they had encountered in the negotiations for a Biosafety Protocol at Cartagena. A diplomatic furore subsequently broke out in Europe when at Seattle the EU Trade Commissioner, Pascal Lamy, seemingly unilaterally developed a new approach that supported the US idea. Lamy's actions not only sensitised the competence issue regarding the Commission's mandate, but also spawned a serious political row as he seemed to sacrifice all too easily the EU's environmental goals. There is thus little indication that this dispute will fade away. On the contrary, EU–US arguments over GMOs and GM foods, an expanding field of trade already worth $1.5 billion per year, could well dwarf their differences over bananas and hormone-treated beef.

However, conflicts over GMOs, hormone-treated beef and bananas should not be allowed to give an erroneous impression of a protectionist EU and of a US that is an unadulterated free trader. The single most contested product in terms of trade issues between the EU and the US is steel, which accounts for ten of the seventy-two trade rows between the two. Here the tables are turned as far as complainants and accused are concerned, with the Europeans initiating four-fifths of all EU–US cases on steel before GATT and the WTO. The first such dispute was in 1969 and the latest commenced in March 2002 when the US imposed three-year 'safeguard' tariffs of up to 30 per cent on steel imports. The Bush administration claimed that these were consonant with WTO rules, as they were temporary measures designed to ease the painful restructuring of the American domestic steel industry. Others, however, interpreted the move as a combination of unfair protectionism and domestic politics, particularly given growing concern within Congress about the costs of free trade, the power of the US steel lobby and the importance to the Republicans of steel-producing states in light of the then upcoming mid-term elections and subsequently the next presidential election. Indeed, then US Treasury Secretary Paul O'Neill made off-the-record criticisms of the tariffs and USTR Robert Zoellick once conceded that they were a sop to America's so-called 'rust-belt'. Of the four key states in question, in the last election Bush took West Virginia, Ohio and

Indiana. Pennsylvania has since been the target of a Republican charm offensive and polls in autumn 2003 suggested that the steel tariffs remained very popular there with 70 per cent approval ratings.[49]

None of this, of course, deterred the EU and seven other countries from appealing against the legality of the US tariffs to the WTO. Even Bush's closest European ally, British Prime Minister Blair, publicly denounced the US action as 'unacceptable, unjustified and wrong',[50] and the EU quickly set about preparing a \$2.2 billion list of compensatory tariffs. Moreover, these were politically targeted so as to maximise the Bush administration's discomfort. For instance, they were to include Harley Davidson motorcycle exports from Wisconsin, steel exports from Pennsylvania and West Virginia, textile and apparel exports from North and South Carolina and orange juice from Florida, the state governed by Jeb Bush and the location of the dramatic electoral recount which finally allowed his brother George W. Bush into the White House. In November 2003, the WTO ruled in favour of the EU and Trade Commissioner Pascal Lamy quickly warned that tariff 'retaliation is a racing certainty' if the US did not remove its safeguard tariffs by mid-December 2003.[51]

On 4 December, the US backed down[52] – but not necessarily because of either the EU or the WTO. Rather, the steel tariffs have had negative consequences for other key American industries, such as the car industry. Moreover, a propitious rise in world steel prices and demand, especially from China, meant that it was easier for the Bush administration to drop the tariffs because the relatively inefficient US steel industry will be better able to compete in an inflated market.[53] However, this round of EU–US confrontation over steel is unlikely to be the last. There are striking similarities between the difficulties that the EU has in reforming its CAP and those that US administrations have persistently encountered with the American steel industry. Furthermore, the rise in world steel prices may well defer necessary restructuring of the US steel industry, and once prices drop again, as they almost certainly will once China fully develops its steel-exporting potential, the cycle of protectionism and recrimination is liable to resume once more.

There are numerous other trade issues over which the EU and the US have clashed in recent years. For instance, the US cried foul over the European Commission's decision to allow production of the Airbus A380 to be supported by government loans. This effectively condoned state subsidisation and therein gave the European conglomerate a competitive advantage over its American rivals.[54] Likewise, the US is deeply suspicious about the protectionist overtones of proposed EU regulations on chemicals that require manufacturers to provide extensive details of health and environmental effects of their products. Conversely, in 2002 the European Commission complained about 'illegal' tariffs imposed by the US Department of Commerce on European producers of low enriched uranium. In June 2003 it instigated WTO action against the US for its 'zeroing practice', an accounting procedure for calculating penalties for dumping goods on a market at below cost-price. The Commission argues that this discriminates against EU exporters in trade worth several hundreds of millions of dollars per annum. And there is an ongoing row about foreign sales corporations. Partially in retaliation for the banana war, then EU Trade Commissioner Sir Leon Brittan launched a WTO case against FSCs on the grounds that they provided US companies with illegal tax concessions worth some $3.5–4 billion per year and therewith conferred upon them a substantial advantage in international trade *vis-à-vis* European competitors. This action was particularly contentious as FSCs had previously been sanctioned in a deal concluded within GATT in 1981. Nevertheless, just months after the débâcle of its Seattle Summit, where trade negotiations collapsed amid a cacophony of protest, rubber bullets and tear-gas, the WTO upheld the Commission's complaint. It also authorised the EU to impose some $4 billion of countervailing tariffs, which the EU is increasingly likely to levy should Congress spin-out interminably the rewriting of the offending sections of the US tax code.

In addition to issue-specific trade clashes, EU–US trade relations have been, and continue to be, riven by problems stemming from their mutual application of extraterritorial measures. This has taken several forms. The first is the extraterritorial application of their respective anti-trust policies, called competition policy within the EU. In the past, the ECs/EU often complained when US attempts to enforce its anti-trust laws outside its territory impinged upon businesses based inside the Communities. However in recent years, and particularly since the 1990 Merger Regulation,[55] the EU has also been increasingly assertive in its scrutiny of, and intervention in, mergers and acquisitions in other countries – something that has generated predictable angry reactions within the US. According to the provisions of EU competition policy, a merger of companies requires the approval of the European Commission, the Union's anti-trust authority, if the following conditions are met: a combined global turnover of all companies involved of more than €5 billion, and an EU-wide turnover of more than €250 million by at least two of the companies involved.[56] Since these conditions are not applied exclusively to EU-based companies, a number of purely American mergers fulfilling these criteria have required the approval of the Brussels-based institution.

The objective behind the EU's competition policy is, naturally, very much the same as that behind US anti-trust legislation, namely to avoid the building of oligopolies or, worse, monopolies, and hence to maintain plurality and a high level of competition in their respective domestic markets. Therefore, when the European Commission approved in 1997 the take-over of the American aircraft manufacturer McDonnell Douglas Corp. by its domestic rival Boeing Co., it only did so on the condition that Boeing cancelled its exclusive supplier agreements with American, Continental and Delta airlines. The idea behind this was that because the global aircraft market was already an oligopolistic one, in other words a market with comparatively few suppliers, the merger without such conditions would have given the new combined company too strong a position in this global market. Some American commentators quickly complained that the EU was now engaged upon actions that it had bemoaned when taken by the US authorities. Others suspected more cynical motivations. They feared that the Commission was using competition policy to boost European producers because the cancellation of the exclusive supplier agreements by Boeing gave Airbus, the company's European rival, at least the opportunity to vie for additional sales.[57]

Another example of the EU applying its competition policy extraterritorially was the merger of American Online and Time Warner. Here the Commission made its approval of the deal conditional upon the two companies severing all ties with the German media group Bertelsmann. Even more controversial have been instances where the Commission has actually blocked the mergers of two US-based companies. The first time this happened was in June 2000, when the institution refused to approve the take-over of the US's third-largest telecommunications company Sprint by its rival WorldCom.[58] The Commission encountered even heavier criticism over its decision to block a proposed take-over by General Electric of Honeywell in 2001.[59] In these and other cases, the Americans often suspected that the Commission interpreted 'market domination' in a rather generous way, taking into consideration not only the number of suppliers or their market shares, but also their quality or the sophistication of their products. With EU production in the so-called future industries still lagging somewhat behind that of the US, it was feared that EU competition policy could be used to prevent American companies from dominating markets through their technological leadership.[60]

A different case in which extraterritorial measures have aroused strong EU–US disagreement is the application of extraterritorial sanctions within foreign policy strategy. Herein the EC/EU has been the principal complainant, which is perhaps not surprising given the relatively recent and still incomplete development of CFSP. In Chapter One it was noted how damaging to EC–US relations was the Reagan administration's unilateral imposition of sanctions against American subsidiaries and licence-holders in Western Europe that were involved in the Siberian pipeline project. This, however, is far from an isolated instance. Such US policies have continued in the post-Cold War era, something that owes not least to domestic political pressures and an increasingly assertive Congress. Consider, for example, the Helms-Burton Act and the Iran–Libya Sanctions Act. Both of these were passed in 1996, which was a year of presidential and congressional elections, and sought to promote US foreign policy objectives *vis-à-vis* undermining Castro's communist regime in Cuba and deterring Iran and Libya from supporting terrorism, acquiring WMD and undermining the Middle East peace process. The problem for EU–US economic relations was that Helms-Burton legislation contained clauses that provided for the extraterritorial application to EU companies and individuals of the US economic isolation of Cuba. Similarly, the Iran–Libya Sanctions Act contained extraterritorial provisions designed both to increase Iran's economic isolation and to guard against American companies being disadvantaged on account of their government's legislation *vis-à-vis* their competitors from Europe and elsewhere. Specifically the Act empowered the US President to impose two countermeasures, drawn from a substantial list, upon any foreign company that invested more than $40 million annually in either the Iranian or Libyan energy sectors.

These US actions were wholly unacceptable to the EU because of their unilateral nature, extensive extraterritorial implications and because they went against both the economic interests of EU member states and the Union's preference for policies of engagement rather than of isolation/confrontation. Pursuant to Section 301 of the EC Treaty, a joint action was established within CFSP that provided for the EU to pass its first-ever blocking statute. This effectively neutralised the extraterritorial US measures by prohibiting any EU subject from participating in, or abiding by, the judgements of US courts and by providing for them to secure through the European courts compensation from the US for any damages incurred as a consequence of the relevant US legislation. In addition, the EU appealed against the extraterritoriality of the US legislation to the DSB of the WTO. Even though the EU case before the WTO was far from watertight given that it concerned investment rather than trade, it was sufficient to force a compromise. In April 1997 the EU agreed to suspend its WTO action and the US agreed to suspend continuously Helms-Burton provisions that enabled private law suits. In 1998 a more comprehensive deal was reached that, whilst not ending the dispute, provided for a negotiated stand-off. Waivers were secured for the EU and EU companies under both Acts, the US promised greater self-restraint on future extraterritorial legislation in an agreement on Transatlantic Partnership on Political Co-operation, and the EU and US agreed greater commonality in dealing with investments vested in illegally expropriated property.[61]

It is a measure of EU–US economic interdependence and mutual political will to nurture their bilateral relationship that each has continually sought to develop understandings that mitigate tensions and facilitate trade. For example, they have concluded mutual recognition agreements (MRAs) that currently cover electromagnetic emission, telecommunications equipment, pharmaceutical manufacturing practices and off-road vehicle emissions.[62] Likewise, increased transatlantic friction over extraterritoriality prompted the creation in June 2000 of a Working Group comprising the European Commission and the US Justice Department, which is responsible for American anti-trust policy.[63] However, it is also important to recognise that EU–US friction is not confined to their trade relationship. Consider, for instance, monetary issues and, in particular, the dollar–euro exchange rate and how this has been managed, or not managed, over time.

The US was for some time rather sceptical about, if not positively ignorant of, the seriousness of EU intent to establish EMU complete with a common currency.[64] It was certainly the case that EMU was driven primarily by calculations of internal benefits to the EU, stemming especially from irrevocably fixed exchange rates and the surrender of national currencies to a common currency. This removed exchange rate risk, eradicated the need to pay for currency exchange transactions and made prices comparable and therewith transparent across the entire eurozone. Yet that the euro, as the common currency of the world's largest economic bloc, also had the potential to rival the dominant role hitherto occupied by the US dollar as the global reserve currency has never been denied by people writing on, or speaking for, the EU. For some this was even an additional reason to adopt the euro, for it would reflect the Union's economic and (to an extent) political standing and increase its international profile. Others feared that a strong euro portended transatlantic friction owing to US sensitivity for the dollar's status as the dominant reserve currency.[65]

The euro was launched on 1 January 1999 at an exchange rate to the US dollar of €1 = $1.17 and took an almost immediate dive.[66] With only two brief and rather unspectacular recoveries, this trend continued for almost two years until the exchange rate bottomed-out at €1 = $0.84 on 24 November 2000.[67] This unexpected and quite severe depreciation tempered the early fears and aspirations of those who saw the euro as a rival to the dollar as the world's most used and important currency.[68] It also inspired accusations, often directly addressed at the European Central Bank (ECB), that the euro was not the strong and stable currency that the ECB and the Union had promised. In fairness, such promises had usually referred to the purchasing power of the currency inside the eurozone and hence to the ECB's principal mandate to maintain low inflation. As far as the external value of the euro was concerned, this was not the ECB's responsibility.[69] It is indicative of the pressure that the ECB nevertheless came under to justify the situation that its first president, Wim Duisenberg, was forced to defend the currency's declining value as reflecting 'predominantly the strength of the dollar rather than the weakness of the euro'.[70]

Whilst the steady depreciation of the euro against the dollar was criticised from within the EU because it meant that the currency was not playing the international role it should have done,[71] criticism from beyond the Union centred around quite different issues. The ever-weakening currency made eurozone exports steadily cheaper on the world's markets traditionally dominated by the US dollar. American exporters in particular faced the inverse situation. The continuous appreciation of the dollar against the euro made their exports comparatively more expensive and meant that they had increasing difficulty in selling to the eurozone. As early as 1999, the first complaints were heard about the EU not doing enough to help the euro recover. Alan Greenspan, the Governor of the Federal Reserve, the central bank of the US, even feared that this could lead to renewed calls for protective measures as Americans were 'losing faith in free trade'.[72]

The EU consequently attracted increasing criticism, especially from the US, for not doing enough to support the value of the euro *vis-à-vis* the dollar. This was understandable from the perspective of US businesses and of the US administration, not least because the euro's decline against the dollar stimulated an EU export boom and contributed to a record US trade deficit. How, though, could a 'correction' in the exchange rate be achieved? And who could, or would, be able to do it? The ECB's principal objective was to maintain internal price stability with a secondary consideration of generally supporting the economic policies of the EU, as formulated by the Union's Council of Economics and Finance Ministers (Ecofin). The Bank could have made the euro more attractive by raising interest rates. However, these are first and foremost tools to fight inflation, and already this was low with economic activity weakening within the eurozone. In fact, the ECB was under pressure to cut interest rates to stimulate economic activity and could consequently do little to influence the exchange rate other than to discourage further depreciation of the euro by maintaining interest rates slightly higher than otherwise necessary. The other alternative was for the EU and/or its member states to undertake structural reforms of, most prominently, over-generous welfare systems in countries such as Germany, France and Italy. Although such steps would have gradually made the euro more attractive, structural economic reforms of such magnitude are politically very difficult, of a long-term nature, and hence would have taken some time to make their respective effects felt on the exchange rate. Besides, the urgency of reforms was somewhat disguised because the low value of the euro worked as a huge export promotion programme for the Union and consequently hid the true scale of the structural discrepancy between it and the US.[73]

It is important to understand that these EU–US differences over the euro–dollar exchange rate and the problems of adjustment are not simply the product of the euro being a new currency but are actually embedded in very different economic philosophies. The eurozone has emphasised maintaining low inflation and the objective of steady growth in order to avoid 'boom and bust' cycles. In consequence, it operates under self-imposed criteria that have encouraged tight macroeconomic control and even fiscal tightening. For instance, recently the ECB has only slowly cut short-term interest rates by 2.75 per cent in a bid to stimulate growth whilst keeping inflation below its mandated 2 per cent average across the eurozone. Also, whereas the US is seemingly unperturbed by its approaching a 6 per cent budget deficit, the maximum such deficit allowed in the eurozone is 3 per cent. Already in 2003 Germany, France and Portugal have all breached this ceiling agreed under the Stability and Growth Pact and face consequent action by the European Commission. In contrast, the US is in a strong Keynesian phase in which it has prioritised economic growth and employment through a macroeconomic and fiscal loosening designed to re-ignite the American economy. For instance, the US Federal Reserve has slashed short-term interest rates by 5.5 per cent and a surge in government spending since the Bush administration assumed office has transformed the federal budget from a 2 per cent surplus in 2000 to a 4 per cent deficit in 2003. The US has also been critical of the eurozone's corporate capitalism, fiscal restraint and failure to liberalise its labour markets, which reflects transatlantic differences over economic philosophy and the appropriate balance between individualism and social solidarity. The IMF has similarly both criticised Europe's welfare burden and inflexible labour markets as contributing to the eurozone's weak economic performance and suggested that a liberalisation of Europe's employment and product markets to the American model would result in a 10 per cent increase in the region's output. Interestingly Britain, which is not bound by Stability and

Growth Pact criteria, has cautiously followed the US trend towards fiscal and macroeconomic loosening and in recent times has generally outperformed the big three eurozone economies of France, Germany and Italy.

Since late 2000 there has been a dramatic reversal of fortune and the euro–dollar exchange rate at the end of 2003 is the complete opposite of what it was. The first recovery of the value of the euro against the US dollar took place in early 2001 when the first signs of a slowing US economy were discerned.[74] The euro subsequently weakened again until the events of 11 September 2001 once more reversed this trend. The real slide of the US dollar against the euro, however, began in early 2002, and as it became increasingly evident that the invasion of Iraq had been and would for some time remain a costly undertaking, the dollar reached an all time low of just under €1 = $1.25 on 29 December 2003.[75] Not surprisingly, the tables have turned as far as complaints about the consequences of this new situation are concerned. Now it is the Europeans who are complaining that the weakness of the dollar is hurting their exports,[76] and it is the Americans who stand accused of positively talking their currency down.[77]

However, the significance of EU–US arguments over the euro–dollar exchange rate does not stop here. Rather, it is inextricably bound up in the wider global economy. As aforementioned, the recent global economic upturn has relied heavily on US economic performance, which has in turn relied upon America spending beyond its means. There is a fierce debate about for how long this is sustainable and what will happen once the US either chooses or is forced to reduce its deficit. Closing the deficit is difficult because the US economy is growing faster than others are and American imports far outstrip exports. For instance, in 2002 US imports totalled $1.4 trillion compared to exports of $974 billion. The method of adjustment, rather like in the mid-1980s, is consequently liable to be a substantial depreciation of the dollar. Just how great a depreciation may be required is reflected in economists' predictions that a trade-weighted dollar depreciation of between 20 and 50 per cent will be needed in order to bring the US current account deficit down to around 3–3.5 per cent of GDP.[78]

The IMF has underscored that this is not merely a hypothetical possibility. It warned in its World Economic Outlook in September 2003 that despite the post-2001 depreciation of the dollar 'the possibility of a rapid realignment of the major currencies carries a significant risk for the global economy'.[79] These risks for the EU and the wider international economy are potentially profound. Even if the dreaded dollar crash and financial meltdown could be avoided, the euro might still be driven upwards of two dollars. Already it has borne the brunt of dollar depreciation – since early 2002 the dollar has dropped 20 per cent against the euro compared to 8 per cent on average against its trading partners. This owes both to the added sensitivity to exchange rate fluctuation of currencies that float rather than those that are pegged and to the active intervention of Asian governments to prevent their currencies from appreciating. A further rapid appreciation of the euro could extinguish the eurozone's fragile economic recovery. For example, economists at Citigroup have estimated that every 5 per cent rise in the euro's trade-weighted value *vis-à-vis* the dollar reduces GDP in the eurozone by up to 0.5 per cent the following year.[80] Furthermore, exchange rate volatility across the G3 currency areas (eurozone, US and Japan) can have significant ripple effects. For instance, dollar–euro volatility has been found to impinge negatively on employment and domestic investment in Argentina and Brazil. Developing countries are especially vulnerable. This is because of their less-developed financial markets and structural inflexibility on account both of limited ability to borrow their own currency and the fact that even post-Bretton Woods 50–75 per cent of countries continue *de facto* to peg their exchange rates to industrial country currencies. Studies have suggested that consequences of exchange rate volatility across the G3 currency areas can include volatility and uncertainty in a developing country's real effective exchange rate, expensive re-orientations of trade as a consequence of shifts in relative competitiveness and greater negative welfare effects than in advanced economies.[81] It has even been argued that G3 exchange rate volatility and misalignments, especially the strength of the dollar, coupled with inflexible exchange rate regimes, played a significant part in the build-up to the spectacular Asia and Argentine economic crises.[82]

Conclusion

This chapter began by asking whether the EU and US are economic partners, rivals, or whether their relationship stands in a different category from any other? Quantitatively there is no comparable relationship. The EU and US are indisputably each other's most significant bilateral economic partner. Over $36 billion per day of trade and investment flows across the Atlantic.[83] As for the qualitative dimension, the EU and US both have trade and investment relationships far more preferential with other states than they enjoy with each other. However, the bilateral web of government contacts that each maintains with the other, and the importance accorded to them, has no comparator. Moreover, this is mirrored in the myriad of transatlantic business connections that have been built up over time, a fact of particular significance given the relative decline of government control over a globalising economy in which in excess of $1 trillion of foreign exchange crosses borders every day.

The bilateral EU–US economic relationship is actually quite remarkable and has justifiably been called 'a global partnership different from any other in history'.[84] Consider the transition in the relationship from a position of post-WW2 US hegemony and European suppliance to one of post-Cold War economic parity. Both sides have consequently had to make continual adjustments to the relative rise of EC/EU economic power in terms of institutional arrangements, shifting EC/EU competencies and expectations of one another's ability/willingness to assume economic leadership and the responsibilities therein. The impact of specific geo-strategic factors on the economic relationship can also be seen in the EU's growing economic assertiveness since the collapse of the Cold War liberated it of acute security dependence on the US. This assertiveness has also been encouraged by evolutions in the collective management of economic globalisation and internal EU developments. Of the former the creation of the WTO has been pivotal, for it has given the EU a quasi-judicial forum through which to seek redress over trade disagreements. As for the latter, the completion of EMU and the creation of the euro have potentially placed the EU well to challenge the currency leadership role of the US dollar.

In this respect the EU and US might well be called rivals. Certainly transatlantic friction has increased over trade, investment and even relative currency values and underpinning economic philosophies. Bananas, GMOs, FSCs, steel tariffs and arguments over agricultural protectionism all indicate an increasingly strained economic relationship. Similarly, differences over the use of economic measures in the pursuit of foreign policy objectives, particularly extraterritorial measures, have been problematic and may become more so as the EU develops its CFSP. Enhanced Commission powers, notably the 1990 Merger Regulation, have also led to friction as the EU asserts itself economically in ways that the US has hitherto been able to do without too significant a challenge.

However, the term 'rival' has too negative a connotation to reflect truly the situation that exists between the two economic superpowers. For a start, competition is a positive, constructive concept from which both sides benefit, and looking beyond tabloid headlines reveals that 98 per cent of a two-way trade and investment relationship worth a staggering US$2 trillion is conducted without dispute.[85] It also ignores the fact that the EU and US have much in common, something that is reflected in their determined pursuit of the NTA and TEP. For all their periodic acrimony over this or that issue, both share the concerns of post-modern industrial societies, the challenges of economic globalisation and the need to adjust to the rise of other centres of economic power, especially China. Ironically, they also have shared interests in simultaneously promoting trade liberalisation whilst having to defend themselves against charges of hypocrisy on account of their own protectionism – which the collapse of the WTO meeting in Cancún publicly demonstrated in respect of agricultural subsidies.

It is perhaps not surprising, therefore, that USTR Robert Zoellick has claimed that economic links rather than security alliances have become the glue of the post-Cold War EU–US relationship.[86] He might also have added that this intense and complex bilateral economic relationship has profound implications also for the wider international community and the globalising economy. Collectively the EU and US are economically preponderant in terms as diverse as technological development, wealth and institutionalised economic influence. This means that they, above all others, purposively and non-purposively set the tone for the international economy. And with such power comes great responsibility. For instance, their exchange rate (in)stability has significant repercussions for economies across the world, as do the balances between both their relative growth rates and between their import–export ratios. Their macroeconomic co-operation or otherwise, along with that of other major economies, will also help determine the seriousness of the economic repercussions of the eventual adjustment of the US deficit. Furthermore, as the EU and US both pursue competitive liberalisation, their relative priorities within this, coupled with their relationship within the WTO, will affect substantially the future fragmentation or unification of the global trading system.

Notes

1 For a more detailed analysis of the post-WW2 period in EC–US economic relations, see Geiger, T. (1996) 'Embracing Good Neighbourliness: Multilateralism, *Pax Americana* and European Integration, 1945–58' in *Regional Trade Blocs, Multilateralism and the GATT*, Geiger, T. and Kennedy, D. (eds), London: Pinter, pp. 56–78.

2 Information from the EU was obtained from the europa-website at www.europa.eu.int, with most data being provided by Eurostat, the Union's statistical office. Data from the US was also obtained from www.ita.doc.gov/td/industry/otea/usfth/tabcon.html.

3 The percentages were calculated on the basis of information obtained from the EU-website at http://europa.eu.int/comm/trade/issues/bilateral/data.htm.

4 Mexico came third with 14 per cent.

5 Figures calculated from US Aggregate Foreign Trade Data, www.ita.doc.gov/td/industry/otea/usfth/tabcon.html.

6 European Commission (2003) 'EU–US Bilateral Economic Relations' *European Union Factsheet*, p. 1, http://europa.eu.int/comm/external_relations/us/sum06_03/eco.pdf.

7 Data taken from http://europa.eu.int/comm/trade/issues/bilateral/data.htm.

8 Figures calculated from data from US Aggregate Foreign Trade Data, www.ita.doc.gov/td/industry/otea/usfth/tabcon.html.

9 'EU–US Bilateral Economic Relations', p. 1.

10 Ibid., pp. 1 and 2.

11 Aristotelous, K. and Fountas, S. (1996) 'An Empirical Analysis of Inward Foreign Direct Investment Flows in the EU with Emphasis on the Market Enlargement Hypothesis' *Journal of Common Market Studies* 34 (4) pp. 571–83; Gorg, H. and Ruane, F. (1999) 'US Investment in EU Member Countries: The Internal Market and Sectoral Specialization' *Journal of Common Market Studies* 37 (2) pp. 333–48.

12 Blinken, A.J. (2001) 'The False Crisis Over the Atlantic' *Foreign Affairs* 80 (3) p. 46.

13 Baroness Scotland of Asthal QC (2003) speech to the House of Lords, 2 May 2001, http://www.fco.gov.

14 For predictions of serious commercial challenges to the US from Europe see, for example, Thurow, L. (1992) *Head to Head: The Coming Economic Battle Among Japan, Europe and America*, New York: Norrow.

15 European Commission, *Joint EU–US Action Plan*, http://europa.eu.int/comm/external_relations/us/action_plan/index.htm.

16 European Commission (2001) 'The Transatlantic Economic Partnership' *Economic Relations*, http://europa.eu.int/comm/external_relations/us/action_plan/3_trade_economy_release.htm.

17 Ibid. On the part of the EU, assessments of the situation are being made in the annual *Report on United States Barriers to Trade and Investment*, the latest of which was published in November 2002 by the European Commission in Brussels.

18 European Commission (November 2002) *Report on United States Barriers to Trade and Investment*, p. 3.

19 United States Mission to the European Union (2003) 'Commerce's Aldonas: Shoring up the U.S.–EU Trade, Economic Relationship,' http://www.useu.be/Categories/Trade/Apr2803AldonasUSEURelationship.html.

20 Excluding intra-EU trade.

21 'EU–US Bilateral Economic Relations', p. 1.

22 http://www.imf.org/external/np/sec/member/members.htm.

23 http://www.worldbank.org.

24 Zoellick contended that this US inaction damaged the country's businesses, workers and farmers, because they found themselves excluded from the numerous preferential trade and investment agreements negotiated by the country's trading partners. He gave a concrete example: 'while U.S. exports to Chile face an eight per cent tariff, the Canada–Chile trade agreement will free Canadian imports of this duty. As a result, U.S. wheat and potato farmers are now losing market share in Chile to Canadian exports.' Zoellick, R.B. (2001) 'Prepared Statement of Robert B. Zoellick U.S. Trade Representative before the Subcommittee on Trade, Committee on Ways & Means of the U.S. House of Representatives', p. 3, www.ustr.gov/speech-test/zoellick/zoellick_3.pdf.

25 Echaleco, H. (2003) 'Chile Ratifies Free Trade Agreement With the EU' *Pravda.Ru*, http://english.pravda.ru/main/2003/01/15/42069.html.

26 Gomez, B. (2003) 'Chile, Singapore Free Trade Pacts a Priority, Says Gen. Grassley' *Washington File*, http://usinfo.state.gov/regional/ar/trade/03012702.htm.

27 US merchandise exports to Latin America grew 137 per cent from 1990 to 2000 compared to 99 per cent with the world. Service exports to Latin America grew by 96 per cent over the same period compared to 86 per cent growth to the world. Office of the US Trade Representative (2003) 'Free Trade Area of the Americas', http://www.ustr.gov/regions/whemisphere/ftaa.shtml.

28 Economist (2003) 'The WTO Under Fire' *The Economist* **368** (8342) 20 September 2003, p. 29.

29 G21: Argentina, Bolivia, Brazil, Chile, China, Columbia, Costa Rica, Cuba, Ecuador, Egypt, Guatemala, India, Indonesia, Mexico, Pakistan, Paraguay, Peru, Philippines, South Africa, Thailand and Venezuela.

30 Bierling, S. (2002) 'Die Europäische Union und die USA' in *Europa-Handbuch*, Weidenfeld, W. (ed.), Bonn: Bundeszentrale für politische Bildung, p. 649.

31 'For legal reasons, the European Union is known officially as the European Communities in WTO business. The EU is a WTO member in its own right as are each of its 15 member States – making 16 WTO members altogether. While the member States co-ordinate their position in Brussels and Geneva, the European Commission alone speaks for the EU and its members at almost all WTO meetings and in almost all WTO affairs.' Source: http://www.wto.org/english/thewto_e/countries_e/european_union_or_communities_popup.htm.

32 Prior to 1970 conflicts had been fought out between the Communities' member states and the American administration, even though the ECs as a supranational body had been a full participant in GATT since the year 1960. See Sapir, A. (2002) 'Old and New Issues in EC–US Trade Disputes', unpublished paper.

33 For information on the trade disputes under GATT, see Featherstone, K. and Ginsberg, R.H. (1996) *The United States and the European Union in the 1990s: Partners in Transition*, Basingstoke: Macmillan, pp. 168–9. Information on the conflicts under the auspices of the WTO at www.wto.org/english/tratop_e/dispu_e/dispu_satus_e.htm.

34 Featherstone and Ginsberg, *The United States and the European Union in the 1990s*, pp. 168–9.

35 www.wto.org/english/tratop_e/dispu_e/dispu_satus_e.htm.

36 There is a big debate over whether the US achieved the status of full hegemon *vis-à-vis* Western Europe. A number of authors seem to think so. See, for instance, Featherstone and Ginsberg, *The United States and the European Union in the 1990s*, pp. 168–9; Kegley Jr., C.W. and Wittkopf, E.R. (2001) *World Politics: Trend and Transformation*, 8th edn, Boston: Bedford/St Martin's, pp. 251–61; Frieden, J.A. and Lake, D.A. (1995) *International Political Economy: Perspectives on Global Power and Wealth*, 3rd edn, London: Routledge, pp. 340–2.

37 For more details, see Jones, R.A. (2001) *The Politics and Economics of the European Union*, 2nd edn, Cheltenham: Edward Elgar, p. 215.

38 For a much more detailed account of the situation, see Unattributed (2002) *Bananadrama 1: The EU Banana Regime*, http://www.bananalink.org.uk/trade_war/trade_war_main1.htm.

39 Unattributed (2002) 'Trade Wars: 1993 to 2001' *Bananadrama 2: Challenges to the EU Banana Regime*,
http://www.bananalink.org.uk/trade_war/trade_war_main2.htm#chal.

40 See Unattributed 'Banana GATT Case (BANANA)', http://www.american.edu/TED/banana.htm.

41 Elliott, L. (1999) 'US Triumph in Banana War', http://www.guardian.co.uk/banana/Story/0,2763,206264,00.html.

42 Unattributed (2001) 'EU and US End Banana War', http://news.bbc.co.uk/1/hi/business/1271969.stm.

43 According to Stephan Bieling, Trent Lott, the leader of the Republican majority in the American Senate, had given Chiquita a *de facto* veto power in the process of

finding a compromise with the EU. See Bierling, 'Die Europäische Union und die USA', p. 650; 'July 2001 Reforms' *Bananadrama 2: Challenges to the EU Banana Regime.*

44 These were oestradiol 17β, testosterone, progesterone, zeranol, trenbolone acetate and melengestrol acetate (MGA).

http://europa.eu.int/comm/food/fs/him/him_index_en.html.

45 Ibid.

46 Unattributed (2000) 'EU–US Beef Dispute Update' *ICTSD Bridges Weekly Trade New Digest*, 21 March 2000, http://www.ictsd.org/html/weekly/story8.21-03-00.htm.

47 Unattributed (1999) 'Cancer Scare Over US Beef', http://news.bbc.co.uk/1/hi/business/the_economy/334874.stm.

48 'EU–US Beef Dispute Update'.

49 Economist (2003) 'Hard Choices' *The Economist* **369** (8350) 15 November 2003, p. 55.

50 Unattributed (2002) 'The Steel Trap' *Wall Street Journal Europe*, 22 March 2002, p. 6.

51 Lamy cited in BBC News (2003) 'EU to Hit Back in US Steel Row', 4 November 2003, http://newsvote.bbc.co.uk; Fuchs, R.A. 'Dancing Around the Steel' *europaspiegel*, http://www.fu-berlin.de/eurosi/english/steel_09_03.html.

52 Cable News Network (2003) 'Bush Administration Lifts Steel Tariffs', http://www.cnn.com/2003/ALLPOLITICS/12/04/elec04.prez.bush.steel/.

53 See also Economist.com (2003) 'Scrapped', http://www.economist.co.uk/agenda/displaystory.cfm?story_id=2261621&CFID=19092570&CFTOKEN=25f638f-59f 64d42-0724-455e-be5c-62ddf83edf5d.

54 Bierling, 'Die Europäische Union und die USA', p. 650.

55 Council Regulation 4064/89, see Friedrich, H.B. (2002) 'Wettbewerbspolitik' in *Europa von A bis Z*, Weidenfeld, W. and Wessels, W. (eds), Bonn: Bundeszentrale für politische Bildung, p. 359.

56 Bierling, 'Die Europäische Union und die USA', p. 651.

57 Ball, D.A. et al. (2004) *International Business: The Challenge of Global Competition*, 9th edn, New York: McGraw Hill/Irwin, p. 376.

58 Bierling, 'Die Europäische Union und die USA', p. 651.

59 Ball et al., *International Business*, p. 376; European Commission (2001) 'EU Commission Prohibits GE's Acquisition of Honeywell' *News Release* **52** (1) http://www.eurunion.org/news/press/2001/2001052.htm.

60 Bierling, 'Die Europäische Union und die USA', p. 651.

61 Falke, A. (2000) 'The EU–US Conflict Over Sanctions Policy: Confronting the Hegemon' *European Foreign Affairs Review* **5** p. 160.

62 Ries, C. (2002) 'The U.S.–EU Trade Relationship: Partners and Competitors', http://www.state.gov/p/eur/rls/rm/2002/15491pf.htm.

63 Bierling, 'Die Europäische Union und die USA', p. 651.

64 See Ball et al., *International Business*; Bierling, 'Die Europäische Union und die USA', p. 652.

65 Feldstein, M. (1997) 'EMU and International Conflict' *Foreign Affairs* **76** (6), pp. 60–73.

66 Cecchetti, S.G. (2000) 'Who Should Care about the Euro-Dollar Exchange Rate Anyway?' *Occasional Essay on Current Policy Issues* **8**, http://people.brandeis.edu/~cecchett/pdf/cpi8.pdf.

67 Andrews, E.L. (2003) 'Strong Dollar, Weak Dollar: Anyone Have a Scorecard?' *New York Times*, http://www.globalpolicy.org/socecon/crisis/2003/0924strongweakdollar.htm.

68 See, for instance, World Economic Forum (2001) 'Euro Rising, Dollar Falling', http://www.weforum.org/site/knowledgenavigator.nsf/Content/Euro%20Rising,%20Dollar%20Falling_2001?open&country_id.

69 On the position of the ECB, see ibid.; or Wittrock, O., 'Das neue Dreieck' *europa-digital*, http://www.europa-digital.de/text/aktuell/dossier/euro/dreieck.shtml.

70 Barnard, B. (June 1999) 'Euro, Dollar, Yen: What Role Will Europe's Single Currency Play in World Markets?' *EUROPE Magazine* **387**, p. 8, http://www.eurunion.org/magazine/9906/euro.htm.

71 See, for instance, Cecchetti, 'Who Should Care about the Euro-Dollar Exchange Rate Anyway?'.

72 Barnard, 'Euro, Dollar, Yen', p. 8.

73 There are indications that respective reforms are beginning to happen, notably German Chancellor Schröder's 'Agenda 2010' programme of economic reforms that is designed to reduce labour costs and increase economic flexibility.

74 Bierling, 'Die Europäische Union und die USA', p. 652.

75 'Euro Foreign Exchange Reference Rates: US Dollar', http://www.ecb.de/stats/eurofxref/eurofxref-graph-usd.html.

76 Andrews, 'Strong Dollar, Weak Dollar'.

77 Lefebvre, A. (2003) 'US–Europe Tensions Grow as Washington Talks Down the Dollar' *World Socialist Web Site*, http://www.wsws.org/articles/2003/jun2003/doll-j04_prn.shtml.

78 Economist (2003) 'Shrink-Proof: Why America's Deficit is Hard to Turn Around' *The Economist* **368** (8342) 20 September 2003, p. 16.

79 IMF (September 2003) 'World Economic Outlook', Chapter II, p. 92.

80 Economist (2003) 'A Hitch to Recovery' *The Economist* **369** (8350) 15 November 2003, p. 44.

81 IMF (September 2003) 'World Economic Outlook', Chapter II, pp. 94–5.

82 Ibid., pp. 97 and 103.

83 Blinken, 'The False Crisis Over the Atlantic', p. 46.

84 Schnabel, R. (2002) 'U.S.–EU Relations: Drift or Common Destiny?', http://www.state.gov/p/eur/rls/rm/2002/14755pf.htm.

85 Ries, 'The U.S.–EU Trade Relationship'; Burghardt, G. (2001) 'Prospects for EU–US Trade Relations', paper held at Duke University, http://www.eurunion.org/news/speeches/2001/010215gb.htm.

86 Economist (2002) 'Bob Zoellick's Grand Strategy' *The Economist* **362** (8262) 2 March 2002, p. 57.

CHAPTER 6

The EU and security in Central and South-Eastern Europe

Europe was the most logical region for the EU to develop its credentials as a leading post-Cold War security actor. Yet the region constituted a security environment more challenging than many first imagined. The East–West ideological divide was replaced with new divisions such as differentiated memberships of key security institutions, grave differences in economic development and environmental security and a new psychology of insecurity prevalent especially in the geo-strategically homeless of Central and Eastern Europe. The removal of Cold War overlay gave rise to a number of vulnerable new independent states and to a potential security vacuum, unleashed secessionist conflicts and required more 'peace' operations on European soil than in any other region of the world.[1] It also facilitated East–West transnational crime and encouraged migratory pressures. Borders became more vulnerable, wealth inequalities provided push and pull incentives, drug trafficking from the Golden Crescent through the Balkans blossomed and new criminal opportunities were afforded such as human trafficking and the smuggling of firearms and nuclear materials.[2]

This chapter assesses three aspects of the EU's response to these security challenges in its 'own backyard'. The first section examines its efforts to stabilise Central and Eastern Europe through, principally, the enlargement process. This has seen co-ordinated cross-pillar activity, a prioritisation of JHA issues as external policy towards candidate states became progressively 'domesticised', and a difficult balance struck between maintaining EU internal security and exporting security to CEECs. The second section examines the EU's role in South-Eastern Europe and explores its very mixed record in handling security challenges posed by the disintegration of Yugoslavia and consequent Balkan instability. The final section places EU aspirations to a leading role in European security in the wider context of an evolving post-Cold War security architecture and of the different security preferences of its leading member states.

The EU and Central and Eastern Europe

The European Commission hailed the 1989 revolutions in Central and Eastern Europe as 'probably the most significant event in global terms of the past 45 years' and as 'a challenge and an opportunity' for the EC.[3] That the region would subsequently become the principal focus of EU external relations was self-evident. This was confirmed in June 1992 when the Lisbon European Council developed three criteria for determining EU foreign policy priorities: geographical proximity; overwhelming interest in the political and economic stability of a region or state; and the existence of a potential threat to the Union's security interests.[4] It was equally certain that other international actors would expect the EC to exert leadership in stabilising its own backyard, something quickly demonstrated by the G7's delegation to the Commission in July 1989 of responsibility for co-ordinating G24 financial assistance to Central and Eastern Europe. After all, the US was concerned principally with Russia. Moreover, the EC had developed relations with COMECON long before the end of the Cold War,[5] especially once a joint declaration on 25 June 1988 finally established mutual EC–COMECON recognition and encouraged the conclusion of a number of first-generation trade and co-operation agreements.[6]

The strength of the EU position in exporting security to Central and Eastern Europe stemmed foremost from its pronounced normative power *vis-à-vis* the region. Throughout the Cold War the ideational impact of the democracies' co-operative successes acted as a magnet that drew Eastern Europe and the Soviet Union towards Western political values.[7] In its aftermath the EU seemingly symbolised Eastern bloc aspirations for prosperity, liberal democratic values, security and tolerance. Its post-Westphalian system of governance provided for a security community of great appeal to the newly strategically homeless in which diversity and solidarity were successfully combined. The EU also provided a model of how history could apparently be overcome through reconciliation and co-operative reconstruction, something of particular salience given Central and Eastern Europe's fragmentation, instability and history of ethnic and nationalist rivalries. Indeed, the European Commission was quick to emphasise the EC's function as a capitalist 'role model' for CEECs.[8] The EU's normative appeal was further enhanced by a prevalent psychology of insecurity in Central and Eastern Europe.[9] Embracement of Western norms appeared synonymous with inclusion in Western security structures, constituted a powerful rejection of the communist era and afforded some comfort *vis-à-vis* fears of Russian *revanchism* to the east.

In this respect the EU's normative attainments were arguably more immediately influential with newly independent CEECs than its empirical dimensions.[10] Nevertheless, this had practical implications that included inflated CEEC expectations of EU capabilities and a widespread aspiration to join the Union. By June 1996 no less than ten CEECs had formally applied for full membership.[11] This clearly posed the EU problems. The Union was preoccupied with the Maastricht process, the next wave of enlargement was already focused on four relatively wealthy European Free Trade Association countries – Austria, Finland, Sweden and Norway – and incorporation of relatively backward CEECs would pose an unprecedented challenge. In fact Commission President Delors, amid fears of pan-Europeanism causing a 'melting away' of the EU, was sceptical about the prospects of CEECs securing full membership within twenty years.[12] The danger herein was that failure to embrace them might foster disillusion and instability, undermine the process of democratisation and compromise EU ability to combat security threats such as organised crime, illegal immigration and terrorism.[13]

The flip side of CEEC aspirations and expectations was that the EU secured disproportionate influence over their development. EU member states quickly capitalised on this to protect their security interests, especially in insulating themselves against mass migration, illegal immigration and trans-border crime. For instance, the Budapest Process was initiated in October 1991 to bring together EU member states, Austria, Switzerland and thirteen CEECs in an effort to harmonise restrictive migration policies. In 1994 EU member states concluded with CEECs a common Declaration for Co-operating in the Fight Against Organised Crime, which was subsequently strengthened in 1998 in the EU's enhanced pre-accession strategy as a Pre-accession Pact on Organised Crime. Furthermore, a variety of bilateral and multilateral initiatives sought to bolster CEEC capabilities in combating criminal activity. For example, the Central European Police Academy was set up originally as an Austro-Hungarian initiative but was later joined by Germany, Poland, Switzerland, Slovakia, Slovenia and the Czech Republic.[14]

At the EU level, though, the prospect of enlargement was undoubtedly the single most important tool for promoting Central and East European security. This had, and still has, a hugely significant psychological dimension. First, it held out the opportunity to erase Cold War legacies of division and the West's 'abandonment' of Eastern Europe after WW2. The EU was consequently anxious to avoid an exclusionary dynamic that could impact negatively upon security and stability, something reflected in the Commission's determination to avoid distinctions between Central Europe and Eastern Europe and in its consequent expansive definition of CEECs.[15] Second, as the UN observed, the EU could 'exert a major influence on the expectational environment in all the transition economies' through leaving no doubt as to either side's commitment to the ultimate objective of membership and setting out a clear path to securing this.[16]

Enlargement was, and is, also an enormously influential practical aspect of the EU's external relations and a principal vehicle for the dissemination and inculcation of its operational and theoretical norms. CEEC anxiety for links with, and ultimately membership of, the EU has enabled its *de facto* intervention in their domestic and foreign policies in ways that seemingly set aside traditional principles of non-interference in the internal affairs of sovereign states.[17] The Europe Agreements, which the EU began to conclude with CEECs from 1991, encapsulated how the EU would use its economic leverage and control over enlargement aspirations to develop its security interests in Central and Eastern Europe. The preamble to the Agreements recognised the ambition of the associated countries to secure full Union membership and, although primarily of an economic nature,[18] developed inclusivity through institutionalising links between CEECs and the EU security community. That the Europe Agreements were not merely economic in motivation was reflected too in their scope, strong normative dimension and emphasis on anticipatory socialisation. They constituted a new generation of 'mixed' agreements in that they went beyond trade to include political dialogue – essentially a reference to foreign and security policy. They also contained stipulations regarding cultural co-operation and respect for democratic principles and human and minority rights. Sanctions in the event of non-compliance were provided for through emergency clauses allowing suspension of the agreements.

In June 1993 the EU formally laid out the so-called Copenhagen criteria which applicant states would have to meet before achieving full membership. Some of these again carried strong security overtones. Would-be acceding states had to be able to assume the obligations of the entire *acquis communautaire* and possess stable institutions that guaranteed democracy, the rule of law, human rights, and respect for and protection of minorities.[19] Moreover, policy towards CEECs became progressively 'domesticised' once the principle of eastern enlargement was formally accepted. JHA rather than CFSP considerations came to the fore, especially given that enlargement would transfer to CEECs the burden of external border control and responsibility for dealing with front-line illegal immigration and asylum issues.[20] For instance, the EU began incorporating readmission clauses into agreements with CEECs that established commitments to readmit stateless persons or persons of another jurisdiction who entered the EU illegally from the country in question, or vice versa.[21] Likewise, JHA security concerns were undoubtedly a motivating factor in the Amsterdam Treaty's incorporation of the Schengen *acquis* and the transfer of immigration and asylum policy into EC competence. Thereafter the CEECs also had to meet the demands *in toto* of the 3,000 pages of the Schengen *acquis* prior to EU membership.[22]

The EU's concern for European security was further demonstrated in its timing of, and preparation for, enlargement. The December 1995 Madrid Summit maintained an inclusive dynamic for CEECs by committing the EU to negotiate *en masse* with potential accession countries six months after the IGC preparing for the Amsterdam Treaty. In *Agenda 2000* the Commission subsequently assessed the progress of CEECs and recommended in June 1997 that accession negotiations begin in 1998 with the Czech Republic, Estonia, Hungary, Poland and Slovenia.[23] Placement of Slovenia and Estonia in the fast-track grouping reflected geo-political concern to reinforce inclusivity by adding a northern and southern dimension to enlargement. It also represented a strategic move. It might assuage the disappointment of some CEEC and EU member states with NATO's decision that year to limit its first post-Cold War enlargement to Poland, Hungary and the Czech Republic.[24] Also, Slovenia's inclusion tentatively extended the EU's security community to the Balkans, and security spill-over from Estonia potentially boosted Baltic stability by accelerating transformation processes in Latvia and Lithuania. Furthermore, the EU took steps to alleviate as best as possible the fallout from its planned phased approach to enlargement. From 30 March 1998 all ten potential CEEC members were accorded reinforced pre-accession strategies in the form of accession partnerships. Within this, PHARE aid was made conditional upon how well the applicant country implemented its accession partnership agreement, including security commitments such as democratisation and provisions for nuclear safety.[25] In addition, the European Conference was initiated from 12 March 1998 as a multilateral forum involving all ten CEEC candidate countries for the discussion of issues of common interest, including foreign and security policy, justice and home affairs, and regional co-operation.[26]

The EU's approach to stabilising Central and Eastern Europe, principally through a progressive and structured strategy towards enlargement, has undoubtedly paid dividends in a number of security-related areas.[27] At a macro-level the EU's insistence that candidate countries adopt the *acquis communautaire* in full has laid the basis for an extension of its security community eastwards and encouraged commitment to regional dialogue and multilateralism. For instance, enhanced dialogue as part of the structured relationship with CEECs has encouraged both their alignment with a number of CFSP statements and common positions and popular support for CFSP and CESDP.[28] The *acquis* also means that CEECs have to implement the international conventions and commitments that the EU has made and accepted over the years, such as effective application of the 1951 Geneva Convention, the Europol convention and relevant UN and Council of Europe conventions relating to drugs. It has also helped processes of democratisation. For instance, the Commission's recommendation in 1997 that Slovakia not be considered for membership on grounds that Prime Minister Vladimir Meciar's regime lacked sufficient democracy and respect for human rights stimulated sufficient reform that the country was later readmitted to the accession process.[29]

Enlargement leverage has enabled the EU to promote security in a number of more specific facets too. It has facilitated the improved treatment of minorities by CEECs, such as Russian minorities in Latvia and Estonia, and thereby lessened both internal and external tensions.[30] It has also enabled schemes such as the PHARE Horizontal Programme on JHA and the Odysseus programme to help transfer EU standards and practices to candidate countries. Furthermore, the 'Holy Grail' of EU membership has provided a crucial impetus for promoting environmental security. The EU has been at the heart of the 'Environment for Europe' process, with the Commission developing an Environmental Action Plan for Central and Eastern Europe in conjunction with the World Bank and OECD. It has also included environmental requirements from the Europe Agreements onwards. Given the associated costs and that Western assistance has tended to reflect donor rather than recipient priorities, it is difficult to imagine that CEECs would have diverted scarce resources to meeting Western priorities without the perceived link between stronger environmental security and protection and EU accession.[31]

Not surprisingly EU policies towards Central and Eastern Europe have been cited both as proof of its ability to construct a common, coherent external policy and as constituting, through 'democracy by convergence', perhaps the most decisive international dimension of democratisation.[32] Nevertheless, EU stabilisation of Central and Eastern Europe has had limitations. For a start, the EU has had to perform a very delicate and difficult balancing act. Enlargement is a 'consumable power resource' that is lost once granted,[33] which means that, in principle at least, it has been in EU interests to stretch out the pre-accession process, for it is during this period that its influence over candidate states is greatest.[34] This theoretically provides time for essential EU internal reforms and to ensure that candidate countries are sufficiently developed and prepared such that the Union will not, through enlarging, either import insecurity from its erstwhile neighbours or grind to a halt under the weight of its additional members. However, an overly-long preparatory period for CEECs might foster resentment and instability. Likewise, the phased approach to enlargement set out in *Agenda 2000* threatened to draw new lines of inclusion and exclusion across Europe. Indeed, Lithuanian Prime Minister Vagnorius and the Romanian Foreign Ministry both warned after their countries were consigned to the 'second wave' that phased enlargement would create 'artificial and discriminatory frontiers' and potentially damage transition processes.[35]

Whether the EU has struck a satisfactory balance between these competing forces is open to debate. Certainly its decision to include eight CEECs in its scheduled enlargement for 1 May 2004 is more inclusive than the Commission's original approach in 1997.[36] Yet doubts remain as to whether the acceding states and the EU are actually ready. For instance, will the acceding states be able to cope with the demands of longer EU external borders? After all, these traverse a region of greater security challenge and potentially stretch from the northern twin town of Narva-Ivangorod on the Estonian–Russian border, along the borders of Belarus, Ukraine, Romania and through South-Eastern Europe.[37] Similarly, can the EU's existing security infrastructure cope? Already the Danish EU presidency confirmed in 2002 that the Schengen Information System will be unable to cater for the envisaged 2004 enlargement and that its replacement, Schengen Information System II, will not be ready until 2005 at the earliest.[38]

EU reactions to concerns for societal security have also raised contentious issues. Many CEECs are home to expanding illegal drugs manufacturing and/or transit routes from other drug-producing areas, such as the Central Asian republics of the Commonwealth of Independent States (CIS) which have recently become major producers of opiates and cannabis.[39] More politically charged still are issues of immigration and asylum where a careful balance needs to be struck between the right of communities to their own customs and the right of society to cohesion. The dual prospect of East–West migration from acceding CEECs and greater illegal immigration through more porous CEEC-maintained external borders has caused widespread concern. This was demonstrated in 2002 by the massive vote for French National Front leader Jean-Marie Le Pen, the popularity of Dutch politician Pim Fortuyn and the tightening of immigration laws by normally tolerant Denmark. Even Germany, traditionally a post-WW2 liberal in regards to asylum and immigration, led calls for strengthened border measures and a seven-year transitionary restriction on free movement from acceding CEECs.[40] Moreover, after the September 11 attacks on the Twin Towers, there has been a tendency to link anti-terrorism with stricter asylum and immigration controls. As Luc Vandamme of the General Secretariat of the Council of Ministers warned, in November 2001, '[o]ur risk perception however may currently lead us to put somewhat more emphasis on security, building high walls around that so-called fortress Europe'.[41]

Spurred by domestic public opinion, September 11 and CEECs' place in illegal immigration, human trafficking and the drugs trade, the EU has emphasised the restrictive dimensions of border control in particular, and has effectively securitised its immigration and asylum policy.[42] One consequence, particularly when coupled with the disproportionate influence accorded to the EU by its economic power and control over enlargement, has been the danger of its being seen as 'neo-imperial'. Insistence on complete adherence to the *acquis* has constituted a largely one-sided 'export' of governance whereby the EU has effectively expanded the JHA security regime beyond its borders.[43] Double standards further aggravate this problem. For example, existing EU members such as Britain and Ireland have maintained their opt-outs of the Schengen *acquis*. Also, acceding countries in 2004 are expected to adopt 'hard' Schengen borders without benefiting immediately from free movement within the EU, something that also poses the problem of differentiated rights within the EU's Amsterdam Treaty commitment to an area of freedom, security and justice.

Particularly contentious is that the extension eastwards of the JHA security regime has both seemingly exported to the poorer CEECs some of the costs of providing security and paid insufficient attention to the geo-political consequences of the process. On the former count, aid for JHA adjustments was initially rather limited[44] and readmission clauses have been seen as transferring the burden of immigration and asylum to CEECs, effectively making them EU repositories for rejected asylum seekers, expelled illegal immigrants and would-be economic migrants unable to enter the Union.[45] Also, CEECs will bear upon accession both the burden of maintaining the integrity of EU borders and the immediate brunt of security challenges such as illegal immigration, trans-border crime and human trafficking. Compensatory objectives such as a European Corps of Border Guards still seem some way off and human rights organisations in particular have voiced concern about the 'unbalanced, inhumane, and internally contradictory' nature of EU policies.[46] For instance, following the June 2002 Seville European Council, the European Council on Refugees and Exiles (ECRE) warned that the concept developed there of evaluating EU relationships with third countries according to their willingness to manage migratory flows portended the shifting of responsibility to often less developed countries and the imposition of a disproportionate burden on transit countries.[47]

As for the geo-political consequences of JHA regime expansion, its practical effects, especially the insistence on strict prior implementation by applicant states of all EU restrictive border provisions, appears to belie EU rhetorical aspirations to maintaining a certain degree of openness to prospective post-enlargement neighbouring states.[48] First, the EU has demonstrated heightened enthusiasm for readmission agreements. The Seville European Council Summit decided that future EU association or co-operation agreements should contain a mandatory readmission agreement and that failure by a signatory to uphold its commitment might lead to retaliatory measures or positions. Subsequently, in what may be interpreted as an attempt to insulate prospective new EU borders, the General Affairs Council resolved in November 2002 that the EU should intensify relations with Russia, Ukraine, Albania, Turkey, Yugoslavia, Tunisia and Morocco with a view to concluding readmission treaties.[49] Second, one of the major post-Cold War achievements of Central and Eastern Europe has been the development of rights of freedom of movement and flourishing informal cross-border trade, and this has also been a stabilising factor.[50] However, the strict application of the Schengen border regime in general, and visa policy in particular, threatens to affect and reinforce directly the growing socio-economic and psychological gap between the two parts of Europe.[51] For example, the obligations of the EU *acquis* take precedence over extant CEEC border agreements and draw new divisions between those set for membership in 2004 and those left behind. The potential instability caused by this, although mitigable, should not be understated, especially given the impact on minorities accustomed to moving across borders for family and economic reasons. Consider, for example, Belarussians in Poland, Hungarians in the Ukraine, Yugoslavia and Romania, and the Slovak minority in Romania.

Finally, there are important questions about the transparency of EU security measures and their compatibility with extant arrangements in Central and Eastern Europe. One of the pressing issues with regards to transparency is how the EU compiles its discriminatory visa regime. According to one analyst, the criteria 'leaves room for manoeuvre that leads to a quasi total discretion to the European Union (or more precisely the Schengen countries), mixing political and legal considerations, facts, expectations and acts of encouragement'.[52] As for the compatibility of EU measures with extant arrangements, Hungary's adoption of the Schengen *acquis* potentially threatened to breech its EU-encouraged 1996 treaty with Romania to maintain free cross-border contacts for minorities.[53] Moreover, EU security-related regimes threaten to challenge those of other European security institutions. For example, full application of the Schengen *acquis* in Central and Eastern Europe may challenge the proper implementation of the Council of Europe's conventions on minority protection.[54] Similarly the EU's Charter of Fundamental Rights, important in promoting democratisation, tolerance and respect for human and minority rights, potentially competes with the provisions of the European Convention on Human Rights.[55] This is particularly poignant given that CEEC support for the Council of Europe is much stronger than in the West, owing both to the Council's speedy post-1990 embrace of CEECs and to its pan-European scope providing norms that help stabilise CEEC neighbours that have little prospect of joining the EU.

The EU and South-Eastern Europe

EU difficulties in developing security in the CEECs were put into perspective by successive crises in the Balkans that were brought about by the long-predicted dissolution of Yugoslavia.[56] These constituted both the most dramatic post-Cold War threat to European security and the greatest challenge to its security architecture.[57] And this was no more so than for the EC/EU, driven as it was by Yugoslavia's bordering on some member states, fear of instability spreading and concern that failure to act in its own backyard would jeopardise its credibility as a security actor. The latter would be particularly damaging given the ongoing preparation for the TEU, the Union's relative impotence in the Middle East peace process, and especially its poor collective performance in the Gulf War.[58]

From 1990 tensions in Yugoslavia became acute. Multi-party elections set against a backdrop of economic crisis saw Serbia and Montenegro return communist leaders but the other republics elect centre-right parties. The rotating presidency also ran into trouble and the long-extant external source of Yugoslav cohesion, the threat of the USSR, faded. Against this background the EC extended diplomatic support for the continuance of a single Yugoslav state, which made geo-strategic sense. A centrally controlled Yugoslavia promised greater Balkan stability than did several new undeveloped states in its stead. It also avoided the implosion of a federation at a critical time for Gorbachev's USSR and for European integration and assuaged EC member state sensitivities about their own internal secessionist problems, such as France and Corsica, Britain and Northern Ireland, and Spain and the Basque country. The EC encouraged this objective by combining diplomatic efforts with what might be termed 'carrot and conditionality' measures in an attempt to substitute its own benign influence for the cohesion formerly provided by the Soviet threat. Specifically, it held out promises of increased economic co-operation, an extension of the PHARE programme and the long-term prospect of full EU membership. To qualify, however, Yugoslavia had to remain a single state and develop a market economy, multi-party elections and legally codified guarantees of human rights.

The EC intensified its diplomatic efforts in 1991, particularly once Slovenia and Croatia declared their independence in June. The EC immediately decided at its Luxembourg Summit to dispatch the troika to mediate a peaceful resolution. A fragile cease-fire was brokered in Slovenia, owing not least to possible EC economic sanctions, and on 8 July 1991 the Community began the Brioni Accords. Hailed by German Foreign Minister Genscher as proof of the Community's ability to act,[59] these provided for the resumption of the Yugoslav presidential rotation, a three-month suspension of declarations of independence and a return of all army units to barracks. They were complemented by the dispatch of the European Community Monitoring Mission (ECMM). Seen as possibly the most successful part of the EU's involvement in the Yugoslav crisis,[60] the ECMM primarily monitored cease-fires but was also a useful vehicle of moral pressure and a source of field intelligence.

The EC met deepening crisis from September 1991 with further diplomatic initiatives, the application of sanctions and the provision of humanitarian aid. In September 1991 it set up a peace conference at The Hague under the chairmanship of Lord Carrington. In 1992 this was superseded by a jointly run EC–UN international conference and by the Vance–Owen Peace Plan, arguably the closest that a European-sponsored initiative came to effecting a resolution of the crisis. Concomitantly, the EC underlined its determination to force a negotiated settlement through its endorsement of a UN arms embargo on Yugoslavia, suspension in November 1991 of a trade and co-operation agreement with Yugoslavia and imposition of economic sanctions on Serbia and Montenegro on 1 June 1992. It also ratcheted-up its moral pressure on Serbia. EC member states collectively withdrew their ambassadors from Belgrade and orchestrated Serbia's expulsion from the CSCE. Furthermore, despite progressively ceding the diplomatic initiative to the UN and, more especially, the US and the Contact Group, the EC provided important humanitarian relief, especially after the creation in 1993 of its Humanitarian Office (ECHO).[61] One of the first CFSP joint actions in autumn 1993 supported the convoying of much-needed humanitarian aid to Bosnia and Herzegovina. Also, the EU assumed responsibility in 1994 for the administration of Mostar. Supported by the WEU in a policing and security role, it managed at least to maintain a fragile peace and to assist limited reconstruction, especially in the country's Muslim sector.[62]

Cast in this light, EC/EU performance in the Yugoslav crisis constituted 'an honest attempt at finding a solution . . . [and] made a substantial contribution to alleviating suffering and to preparing the way for the eventual accord reached at Dayton'.[63] Yet this masks a catalogue of problems that cumulatively made EC/EU handling of the Yugoslav dissolution arguably the single most damaging issue for prospects of a genuine CFSP and for EU credibility as a security actor.[64] This can be seen in four aspects: the recognition controversy, internal division, institutional shortcomings and a 'capabilities-expectation gap' in the fulfilment of declared objectives.

The question of whether, and then how, to recognise the independence of the breakaway republics is illustrative of how the EC was hamstrung by disagreement amongst its member states and lost credibility as a consequence. The

EC's initial consensus about maintaining a single Yugoslav state quickly dissolved as Croatia and Slovenia pushed for independence. Put crudely, Germany sympathised with calls for independence, not least because of its large Croatian *émigré* community, the precedent of German reunification and Bavaria's particularly close ties with Croatia and Slovenia through the Alpe-Adria association. Indeed, over 50 per cent of German investments in Yugoslavia were vested in Slovenia and Croatia. France preferred to work with the Serbs to effect a peaceful resolution based on a single Yugoslav state, a stance underpinned by fears of separatist demands precipitating wider instability and of Croatian and Slovenian independence encouraging a *Mitteleuropa* under German influence.[65] As for Britain, it agreed with maintaining the territorial integrity of Yugoslavia but generally preferred not to get involved in another potential 'Northern Ireland'. Worse still, EC member states divided into two broad camps, each of which sought to legitimise its position in international law. Hence Britain, France, Greece and Spain, all plagued by their own internal separatist movements, supported maintenance of the Yugoslav federation in line with Principles III (inviolability of borders), IV (territorial integrity) and VI (non-intervention in the internal affairs of a sovereign state) of the Helsinki Final Act. Germany headed a group more sympathetic to the aspirations of Croatia and Slovenia in line with Principle VIII – the guarantee to self-determination.[66]

It is thus difficult to demur from the conclusion that whatever success the EC enjoyed in 1991 was 'achieved in the shadow of a shambles'.[67] Ultimately, in an act that made a mockery of Maastricht commitments to a CFSP, Foreign Minister Genscher announced on 16 December 1991 Germany's intent to recognise Croatia and Slovenia, unilaterally if necessary. It did so on 23 December. Were this not bad enough, EC attempts to cover its disarray further undermined its credibility. Collective recognition of the breakaway republics was to be conditional upon their meeting certain criteria, including that borders be altered only by peaceful means, protection be afforded to refugees and ethnic minorities, human rights be observed and adherence to the Nuclear Non-proliferation Treaty be ensured. The Badinter Committee was then to deliver assessments of compliance or otherwise on 14 January 1992. Yet having set this up, the EC proceeded to compromise its own procedures. For example, the Badinter Committee reported that Croatia did not have in place the necessary constitutional safeguards for minority rights. Its decision not to make this an explicit reason against extending recognition was rendered academic by Germany's unilateral recognition on 23 December.[68] Still more contentious were the cases of Bosnia and Herzegovina and of the FYROM. The former was granted recognition despite its failure to satisfy Badinter Committee guidelines.[69] The latter met the EC's criteria but recognition was deferred owing to a Greek veto imposed nominally on grounds of FYROM's potential territorial claims on Greek Macedonia.[70] In short, the EC shifted in a matter of months from supporting a single Yugoslavia to recognising the independence of a number of its constituent parts and did so in an *ad hoc* manner that publicly demonstrated its internal divisions and incurred further humiliation through the Badinter Committee débâcle. As one observer damningly concluded, EC recognitions 'were startling in that they contravened most of the recognizing countries' own rules for recognition. The new states did not have uncontested control of their territories; in some cases minority-dominated and at least some other regions opposed independence; all the recognitions contravened the stipulations of the Helsinki Accords that sanctified post-war European boundaries.'[71]

The recognition controversy was symptomatic of an enduring EC problem: the unwillingness of its member states to abide by the principles of the newly agreed CFSP and to act consistently as a collective. Germany's much-criticised stance on recognition was far from an isolated example of unilateralism. On 28 June 1992 French President Mitterand unexpectedly flew to Sarajevo in an effort to break a siege there and to open the airport to humanitarian supplies. Britain promptly castigated his 'playing "cavalier seul"' and his undermining of EC unity through a unilateral national initiative.[72] Also, it has been suggested that irrespective of an EC and UN arms embargo on Yugoslavia, from 1991 covert German, US and allied military aid and materials were funnelled to Croatia and Muslim Bosnia.[73] Even more dramatic was the Greek decision in February 1994 to impose a unilateral trade embargo on the FYROM. Demanding that the republic change its name, constitution and national symbols to prove that it had no territorial ambitions on Greek Macedonia, Greece closed its northern port of Thessaloniki and effectively sealed the FYROM off from all EU trade.[74] Interestingly, the European Commission fought a damaging losing battle before the European Court of Justice to compel Greek lifting of the blockade.[75] Furthermore, the longer the Yugoslav crisis went on, then the more prone leading EC member states were to marginalise the Community in preference for the UN, NATO and, especially, the Contact Group. It is poignant in this context that one of the interesting retrospective debates about the international handling of Yugoslavia's dissolution is actually not whether, but just how early, the EC became eclipsed and ceased to function as a single entity in the crisis.[76]

Member state discord also helped to highlight the inadequacy of the EC's institutional machinery, especially in crisis management. The events of 1991 in particular revealed that EC officials were inexperienced mediators[77] and that the impact of Community diplomacy was hindered by its rotating presidency.[78] Insistence on a single Yugoslav state rather than belated EC acceptance of a single entity was an inflexible position that probably contributed to tensions,[79] both by reinforcing Serb intransigence and propelling would-be breakaway republics upon more extreme paths to independence. Similarly, EC recognition of Croatian independence probably encouraged Bosnia and Herzegovina to follow suit.[80]

The complex Maastricht pillar structure caused further complications as the EU became mired in internal competency disagreements. For example, the joint action in autumn 1993 regarding convoying humanitarian supplies to Bosnia and Herzegovina before the winter embarrassingly fell foul of a six-month internal wrangle over whether the appropriated ECU 48 million should be serviced from the Community budget or by the member states.[81] Also, despite the potential role accorded to the WEU in the Maastricht Treaty as 'an integral part of the development of the Union',[82] links between the two bodies were insufficiently developed. For instance, EU administration of Mostar was severely circumscribed by its inability to coerce reluctant parties on the ground and by WEU officials responding not to EU but to WEU instructions.

Finally, the EC endured a damaging expectation–capabilities gap. Certainly it was able to exert considerable economic influence over Yugoslavia and its constituent parts. The EC accounted for over 50 per cent of Yugoslav trade[83] and was responsible for two major aid packages – its own scheme worth $800 million[84] and a G24 aid programme totalling some $4.1 billion.[85] However, the Yugoslav crisis painfully revealed EC weaknesses as a civilian power both in preventative diplomacy and especially in situations of armed conflict. Without a credible military force to back its diplomacy, the EC had little influence on the ground and this often compromised its well-intentioned initiatives. The Brioni Accords were used by rival factions less to engage in negotiation than to consolidate their relative political and military positions. Similarly, the positive contribution of the ECMM was limited by member state wrangling over how it would be funded and whether it should be armed, and especially by EC inability to create the conditions on the ground that would allow it to maximise its role.[86] Moreover, technically available forces under the WEU were not deployed amid a Franco-British stand-off about the wisdom of French preferences for providing an interpositionary European military force.[87] That this was ultimately provided through the dispatch to Croatia of a United Nations Protection Force, authorised on 21 February 1992 under UN Security Council Resolution 743, does little to counter David Owen's castigation of the EC approach in spring that year as another 'Munich'.[88]

It is, of course, possible to counter-argue that the EC, as distinct from its WEU member states, did what it could in the absence of military tools. However, this ignores the expectation element of the capabilities–expectation gap and here EC/EU mismanagement of the Yugoslav crisis was perhaps most culpable. Its geographic proximity, economic influence and long-established relationship with Yugoslavia all created reasonable expectation that the EU would be responsible for addressing the security problems there. Indeed, the US repeatedly declared Yugoslavia to be a European responsibility and supported initial EC attempts to maintain a single Yugoslav state.[89] However, EC officials massively and unrealistically raised expectations about the Community's capacity to deal successfully with unfolding events. Jacques Poos, Luxemburg's Foreign Minister, gave the most celebrated expression of such hubris. Speaking as chair of the EC's Foreign Affairs Council of Ministers in June 1991, he proclaimed the 'hour of Europe' and declared that 'if one problem can be solved by the Europeans, it is the Yugoslav problem. This is a European country and it is not up to the Americans. It is not up to anyone else.'[90] In fairness, he was far from alone. Even Commission President Delors seemingly anticipated a prestige and credibility-raising EC solution to a European security problem, warning in summer 1991 that American engagement would be regarded as meddling in European affairs: '[w]e do not interfere in American affairs; we hope they will have enough respect not to interfere in ours'.[91] The contrast between this expectation-generating rhetoric and the EC's rapid eclipse by other actors amid spiralling crisis was enormously damaging. WEU Secretary-General Van Eekelen captured this admirably in February 1993: 'our credibility has fallen very low in the Balkans . . . We are looking for the US to take the lead again.'[92]

The US did eventually take the lead and sponsored a peace settlement through the Dayton Accords which were signed on 21 November 1995, albeit not before severe transatlantic tension, manifest threats to NATO's credibility and France's Jacques Chirac forcing of Clinton's hand by threatening to withdraw French peacekeepers in the absence of stronger action.[93] However, this was far from the end of either Yugoslavia's travails or EU involvement in the Balkans. Dayton required a massive international effort in nation-building, both to maintain the peace and to reconstruct civil society slowly. While NATO's Implementation Force (IFOR) and subsequent Stabilisation Force (SFOR) were charged with the former, the EU was invited to co-ordinate the economic reconstruction of Bosnia and Herzegovina.

This task was clearly laden with security implications and was undertaken by the EU on a bilateral and, especially after the later Kosovo War, regional level. Herein it has made heavy use of economic incentives and conditionality. The PHARE programme, which provided Bosnia and Herzegovina with $1 billion during 1996–99, contains conditions that include democratisation and respect for human rights. Similarly the EU's OBNOVA initiative, set up in 1996 specifically in support of the Dayton Accords, was tied in part to the reconstruction of civil society in Bosnia and Herzegovina and to the development of regional co-operation in the western Balkans.[94] Additionally, in the wake of the Kosovo War, ECHO performed emergency humanitarian functions and the EU began its Police Mission (EUPM) in Bosnia and Herzegovina on 1 January 2003. Also, the Commission both headed the department of the UN mission in Kosovo charged with reconstruction and development and provided political guidance to the European Agency for Reconstruction, which finances sustainable reconstruction and development projects.[95]

The EU also became centrally involved in two ongoing major regional initiatives. The first of these is the Stability Pact for South-Eastern Europe, adopted in Cologne on 10 June 1999 and involving more than forty partner countries and international organisations.[96] Again security matters were prominent, explicit goals including enhanced regional co-operation, prevention of further violent conflicts and the creation of proper foundations for democratisation. Indeed, work was divided into three tables, one of which was dedicated solely to security issues. This was in turn divided into two sub-tables, one on JHA matters, which included asylum, organised crime and security institutions, and the other on security and defence, which included military and defence reform, arms control and de-mining.[97]

The second, even more important EU Balkan initiative has been its Stabilisation and Association Process, which includes Albania, Bosnia and Herzegovina, Croatia, Federal Republic of Yugoslavia and the FYROM. Herein the EU seeks to exert significant influence on the region through its preponderant economic position and an assumption that the principal motivation for reform in these countries is a credible prospect of full EU membership, which the Feira European Council offered in June 2000.[98] The SAP thus combines aid, dialogue, technical advice, trade preferences and eventually contractual relationships in a step-by-step process towards membership.[99] Again, conditionality and enhanced regionalism are hallmarks of the framework, and security issues are firmly embedded in EU objectives. For example, SAP conditions include full compliance with the Dayton peace settlement and the development of regional co-operation. The Commission, in addition to emphasising general stability and respect for human rights and democratic principles, also specifically flags the importance of JHA co-operation in combating organised crime, illegal immigration and trafficking.[100] Indeed, the supporting Community Assistance for Reconstruction, Development and Stabilisation programme (CARDS) dedicates approximately 10 per cent of its budget to JHA matters.[101]

EU diplomatic activity has been instrumental in damping down further unrest in the Balkans too. In 1997 civil war threatened in Albania as its government and economy collapsed amid fraudulent pyramid schemes. The EU's rhetorical response demonstrated a steep learning curve, officials studiously avoiding either hostages to fortune or raising false expectations. There seemed to be some practical improvement too. The Commission quickly organised international aid, while Italy, under UN Security Council Resolution 1101 of 28 March 1997, led Operation Alba – a 7,000-strong multinational protection force designed to safeguard aid supplies and to re-establish a viable police force.

Similar positive outcomes were achieved in the FYROM and Montenegro. In the former, intense EU and US pressure prevented full-scale war by bringing ethnic Macedonian and Albanian communities together under the Ohrid Framework Agreement, signed on 13 August 2001. NATO's 4,000-man UK-led Operation Essential Harvest collected weapons from Albanian insurgents in FYROM. Subsequently the EU utilised CARDS funding and, together with the OSCE, provided monitors under the protection of NATO's Task Force Fox to oversee the process of peace and constitutional reform.[102] The EU also launched Operation Concordia upon expiry of the NATO operation on 31 March 2003, which is the first ever EU military peace-support operation.[103] As for Montenegro, the EU successfully applied pressure to counter drives for its independence from Serbia, not least for fear of destabilising Kosovo where the international community had denied full independence.[104] On 14 March 2002, in the wake of intensive efforts by EU High Representative for CFSP Solana, agreement was reached whereby the Yugoslav federation became a loose union of Serbia and Montenegro.

A cautionary note should, however, be sounded lest it appear that the EU has successfully addressed all of the problems highlighted by the Yugoslav dissolution. In Montenegro it is quite possible that it has bought time rather than found a resolution, for under the terms of the agreement Montenegro can exercise a right of opt-out after three years. Also, nation-building in Bosnia and Herzegovina and the wider reconstruction of the western Balkans has proven a difficult and expensive task from which there is no obvious exit strategy. At the turn of the millennium the holding operation in Bosnia and Herzegovina ran at about $9 billion per year.[105] Post-1996 programmes in Bosnia and Herzegovina and Kosovo in particular have experienced fragmentation, overlap, misallocation of resources and contradictory targets,[106] something in part acknowledged by the European Commission's attempts to streamline the Balkan Stability Pact to make it more complementary with the SAP. The EU also struggled amid bureaucratic shortcomings in late 1999 to disburse the large quantities of pledged reconstruction aid and the Stability Pact 'suffered for a long time from a lack of content and credibility'.[107] Even the European Commission conceded in its 2003 SAP Second Annual Report that '[o]rganised crime and corruption are endemic in the region', that the countries involved had a generally poor implementation record and that progress was both slow and 'sometimes more due to international input and pressure rather than a willingness or ability of the countries themselves to take ownership of and drive forward the process'.[108]

As for situations in which military tools have been necessary, the EU has again been generally found wanting, irrespective of its Amsterdam Treaty ambitions regarding the Petersberg tasks. That international intervention was speedier in Kosovo than in the early dissolution of Yugoslavia owed much to the facts of extant NATO deployments and that US concern about exit strategies had been rendered academic by its reluctant but seemingly inexorable rolling prior commitment to the Balkans.[109] There were, of course, serious transatlantic differences, notably over the issue of ground troops, which one commentator captured thus: '[t]he EU is as hesitant, NATO as unwilling, Russia as reluctant and the US as much a solo player as ever'.[110] Nevertheless, NATO's 78-day air assault eclipsed the EU and through the overwhelming US contribution demonstrated the relative military incapacity of EU member states. Even the operation in Albania in 1997, hailed as demonstrating 'the potential for combining EC/EU instruments' and as 'a model for the EU peacekeeping role prescribed in the Amsterdam Treaty',[111] saw the OSCE take the lead and demonstrated continued EU divisions and inter-institutional difficulties.[112] There was no consensus for the WEU to mount an intervention on behalf of the EU. Instead it fell to Italy, as the country most affected by Albania's haemorrhaging of refugees, to fashion a coalition of the willing that included non-EU states such as Turkey and Romania. Moreover, even when a small WEU contingent was deployed to train local police, its Secretary-General, Jose Cutileiro, publicly emphasised that it did so independently of the EU.[113]

The EU and the European security architecture

The EU's efforts to stabilise Central and South-Eastern Europe must be seen in the context of the sheer enormity and complexity of the challenge. Its mixed record clearly owes in part to problems of internal competence, to inconsistent national co-ordination and to evolving but sometimes inadequate institutional structures. However, this picture is further complicated by a European security architecture comprising principally Cold War institutions competing to reinvent themselves sufficiently to secure post-Cold War roles in a radically changed security environment.

The warm afterglow of the 1989 velvet revolutions and hopes of a new world order encouraged visions of a new pan-European security system rooted in an inclusive architecture of interlocking institutions. With Cold War rigidities swept away there appeared to be greater 'interaction opportunities' through which mutual confidence could be built and shared norms and common values developed.[114] There was even a collection of existing institutions through which potentially those norms could be propounded, confidence-building measures developed and military and economic security extended. Indeed, there was much talk of a new collective security system,[115] albeit that not everyone was convinced by liberal institutionalists' claims about the ability of institutions to modify state behaviour sufficiently.[116]

Interestingly the EC at its Strasburg European Council Summit in December 1989 laid claim to the Community being 'the corner-stone of a new European architecture',[117] pretensions rooted in its own internal ambitions and a new security agenda that emphasised increasingly non-traditional elements in which the EC was expected to excel.[118] Within this task it would work alongside the Council of Europe, NATO, C/OSCE, UN, WEU and financially based institutions that would play a role in channelling reconstruction funds to Central and South-Eastern Europe. These included the IBRD, the EIB, in which the EU was the majority shareholder, and the new EU-sponsored European Bank for Reconstruction and Development (EBRD). Working together it was possible that a sense of inclusiveness could be exported to the strategically homeless, normative congruence could be established and maintained, and concerns could be met as to ensuring coherence within, and complementarity between, the economic and military security domains.[119]

The early 1990s, however, witnessed the opportunity for interlocking institutions squandered and EU claims upon a leading role in the security architecture challenged as the various institutions embarked upon a Darwinian struggle for post-Cold War survival. One of the first consequences of this was duplication of effort, increased overlap of competencies and weakened co-ordination. EU security ambitions made it a leading culprit in this respect. As it developed more systematic political co-operation it 'inevitably started to move into security-related areas such as OSCE policy and disarmament'.[120] Its growing involvement in election monitoring led it to significant overlap with

OSCE and UN competencies. Also its democracy promotion strategies, provision of technical and legal assistance within its Europe Agreements, and JHA initiatives such as increased border guard co-operation led the EU to overlap increasingly with the Council of Europe.[121] Furthermore, and much more controversially, its pretensions in the TEU to the eventual framing of a common defence policy, French-led aspirations for an ESDI separable from the transatlantic relationship and EU expansion into aspects of hard security through the Amsterdam Treaty's incorporation of the Petersberg tasks threatened overlap with NATO and friction with the US.

This overlap and duplication were exacerbated by the post-Cold War re-inventions of other institutions. The WEU sought to escape its enforced hibernation of forty years by carving out a niche role between the EU and NATO,[122] expanding beyond territorial defence into the Petersberg tasks and developing outreach programmes to the CEECs. For instance, it became actively involved in developing arms control and understandings and in measures to implement the Conventional Forces in Europe Treaty verification regime. In April 1990 the WEU instructed also its Secretary-General to engage in contacts with newly democratic states in Central and Eastern Europe, including Poland, Hungary, Bulgaria, Romania, Czechoslovakia and the three Baltic states. These relationships were formalised at the June 1992 Petersberg Council through the creation of a Forum for Consultation and later through Associate Memberships.[123] Meantime, the CSCE transformed itself into a regional organisation under Chapter VIII of the UN Charter, moved from being a temporary conference to the status of a permanent organisation in January 1995 and began extending its competencies beyond norm setting and into operational activities. Hence it was that the EU's Balladur Plan, as initially feared by some EU member states such as Germany, so duplicated OSCE activities that eventually the EU ceded to it the responsibility for overseeing the various agreements made. Furthermore, the C/OSCE made potential incursions into harder aspects of security when its 1992 Helsinki document *The Challenges of Change* mandated it to undertake peacekeeping operations.[124]

Concomitantly, EU failure to cope with the Yugoslav crisis dragged the UN into European security affairs to an unprecedented degree[125] and NATO confounded predictions of its demise by embarking upon a dramatic re-invention.[126] NATO's intergovernmental framework retained a wider appeal than the EU, not least because of national sovereignty concerns, as a vehicle for deterring the renationalisation of defence policies. Its New Strategic Doctrine, unveiled on 8 November 1991, also saw it accept responsibilities far beyond the domain of collective defence and enter spheres of activity hitherto the realm of other organisations.[127] For example, that NATO Secretary-General Manfred Wörner signalled support of the CSCE as one of the main tenets of NATO's security effort in Central and Eastern Europe[128] did not disguise that the New Strategic Doctrine marked an incursion into the CSCE's soft security competencies. Later, NATO nullified the WEU's advantage of potential geographic deployment when, propelled by warnings to go 'out of area' or out of business, it moved beyond the restrictions of Article 5. Its first such military action was to shoot down four Bosnian-Serb aircraft that had violated the UN no-fly zone over Bosnia and Herzegovina in February 1994. Finally, NATO embarked upon its own outreach programmes to the CEECs. From the tentative North Atlantic Co-operation Council (NACC), NATO moved at its January 1994 summit in Brussels to its Partnership for Peace scheme (PFP).[129] This, despite being a holding operation, was hailed by President Clinton as also changing 'the entire NATO dialogue so that now the question is no longer if NATO will take on new members, but when and how'.[130] The first formal enlargement followed in March 1999, and in November 2002 the NATO Prague Summit approved further accession negotiations with a view to another seven members joining in 2004.[131]

Problems generated by this extensive architectural reform for the EU and for effective European security management were heightened by four principal factors. First, the processes of reform and especially the question of enlarging institutional memberships were driven in part by exogenous factors. Foremost of these were deteriorating security conditions, most obvious in the Balkans, and the expectations of the newly independent states. Fear of exclusion, coupled with the benefits of inclusion, drove the majority of CEECs and states further afield to seek either membership of, or preferential links with, the established European security institutions. This post-1990 ' "ideology" in favour of membership'[132] became a defining force in the different enlargement debates. For example, in October 1995 Estonian Defence Minister Andrus Öövel cited NATO as the primary vehicle for providing guaranteed security and the EU as a vehicle for economic progress.[133]

Second, there were the questions of overlapping memberships and scopes. The UN was global, NATO transatlantic and the OSCE, Council of Europe, WEU and EU all regional. OSCE and Council of Europe memberships were much more inclusive than either NATO or the EU. Moreover, processes of enlargement threatened to accentuate differentiated memberships and generate difficulties in inter-institutional relationships. For example, a NATO Enlargement Study published on 28 September 1995 affirmed all members' agreement that the defence memberships of the WEU and NATO be kept in-line – not least to ease US fears of indirect commitments to non-NATO states via WEU membership. Yet this was not legally binding. Besides, after the June 1993 Copenhagen Summit the EU was committed to its own enlargement programme and had already invited in the Maastricht Treaty all EU members to become full or observer members of the WEU.[134]

Third, and most problematic for EU attempts to establish itself as the cornerstone of the security architecture, the evolution of 'alternative architectures' confounded aspirations of an effective interlocking of institutions.[135] Worse still, the leading EU states were principal proponents of these different architectural preferences. Germany, in line with its post-WW2 tradition of civilian power and principled multilateralism, favoured a pan-European collective security arrangement to be orchestrated through an augmented C/OSCE.[136]

Britain disagreed, consistently promoting instead NATO's primacy and emphasising common transatlantic values as a substitute binding agent in the absence of an immediate threat.[137] As for France, in line with traditional Gaullist resentment of US dominance, it preferred an ESDI that was distinct and separable from NATO. Herein its aspirations for a re-invigorated WEU and for its potential role in developing the EU as a counterpoise to the US and NATO brought it into profound disagreement with Britain, the latter traditionally seeing the WEU as a bulwark to keep defence issues out of the EU.[138] Indeed, Anglo-French disagreement was largely responsible for WEU inaction both in Yugoslavia in 1991/92 and in Albania in 1997.

If this were not complicated enough, the preferences of the US and Russia cut across those of the leading EU powers. US demands for enhanced European burden-sharing prompted cautious American endorsement of ESDI and concomitant warnings against European ambitions that potentially threatened NATO primacy and American influence in Europe. Caution about potential Russian *revanchism* and EU assertion also inclined Washington to strengthen and reform NATO, to retain America's privileged institutional positions and to contain Russian security-architectural ambitions that would accord it status equal to the US. Moreover, although anxiety about a 'Weimar Russia' and European instability drove Washington to pursue policies of engagement with Russia,[139] these were predominantly channelled bilaterally rather than through European institutions. As for Russia itself, the policies of Yeltsin and Primakov in particular were geared especially to countering American and NATO influence and retaining Russian spheres of influence. Russia consequently called for the establishment of some type of European Security Council, prioritised existing institutions in which it enjoyed full member status, especially the C/OSCE, and opposed adamantly NATO expansion. Hence, at the December 1994 Budapest OSCE Summit Russia proposed, albeit with predictable failure, that NATO and the CIS be placed under OSCE control and be run through a directorate of major powers.[140]

The final architectural problem for the EU was the tendency of its member states either to exploit institutional polyphony as a tool of individual national interests or to operate outside institutions as and when it suited them. Of the latter, Western (mis)management of the Balkans imbroglio affords numerous examples. Greece unilaterally imposed sanctions on FYROM in 1994 and Germany's stance in the recognition controversy over Croatia and Slovenia was doubly symbolic so soon after the Maastricht Treaty's announcement of a CFSP. Also, formation of the Contact Group represented both the apparent failures of established institutions and a *de facto* resort to continued great power politics within European security. A similar message, though less overt, was conveyed through the so-called Quint, which in the Balkans often seemed to influence heavily the outcome of EU discussions.[141]

As for state exploitation of multiple security institutions, the crisis in Bosnia provides a case in point. European NATO members acquiesced to US pressure within that organisation to increased air strikes designed to relieve pressure on the UN 'safe haven' of Bihac. However, they tied their agreement to UN author-isation, which was subsequently withheld – a predictable outcome given a Security Council in which Britain and France held potential vetoes and Russia and China were known to be opposed to NATO action. Britain and France consequently appeased the US within NATO whilst using their positions in other fora to secure their own interests by scuttling the plan and thereby avoid-ing their ground forces incurring increased danger from collateral damage by, and/or Serb reprisals for, air strikes.[142] Set in this context, the views of Alyson Bailes in 1996, then a British Foreign and Commonwealth Office official and later Political Director of the WEU, are particularly poignant: 'if complex, overlapping security institutions can be shown to contribute to diversity and flexibility in solutions, the British will generally be content to maintain and even elaborate upon their "beautiful variety" '.[143]

Rather than the EU leading an interlocking security architecture it seemed that the extensive and competitive re-invention of existing Western security institutions through the 1990s encouraged institutional paralysis. Initial optim-ism was replaced by fears of interblocking and even gridlocking[144] institutions in which responsibilities, roles and purposes were increasingly blurred and security outcomes increasingly inefficacious. The lack of institutional co-ordination was painfully demonstrated when, in order to monitor and eventu-ally enforce UN sanctions imposed against Serbia in May 1992, the WEU and NATO undertook simultaneous and separate patrols in the Adriatic.[145] Problems were evident, too, in the relationship between mandate and opera-tional activities. For example, by 1995 there was acute tension between NATO and the UN over the latter's need to mandate every NATO air strike. Indeed, this paralysing dual key system formed one element of UN Secretary-General Kofi Annan's 'stunning institutional *mea culpa*' in 1999 as he sought to draw lessons from the Yugoslav experience.[146] Even peace plans have been seen in the context of the struggle for security leadership in Europe with former EU negotiator David Owen suggesting in 1995 that the Vance–Owen deal was obstructed by the US in order to maintain its predominance in European security.[147]

On a positive note, some rationalisation of the security architecture did take place from the mid-1990s as a consequence of lessons drawn from security management in Central and South-Eastern Europe. EU strengths as a provider of economic security, a promulgator of norms and supplier of technical assist-ance were all recognised and there developed improved soft security co-ordination between it and other institutions and countries, notably with the US following conclusion of the NTA. Conversely, its shortcomings in crisis management and inability either to maintain internal cohesion or to agree peacekeeping underscored the continuing imperative of NATO and of a US presence in European security.[148] This had direct and indirect benefits. First, NATO re-established its credentials as Europe's primary security institution, at least in its harder dimensions such as peacekeeping and peacemaking. Second, NATO's deeper involvement in Bosnia stimulated significant developments in the emerging security architecture.[149] European impotence was perversely re-assuring to the US and sufficiently embarrassing to the Europeans to induce important changes of attitude. The OSCE, shown to be inclusive but of limited effectiveness, was accorded legitimator functions but also, in relative terms, pushed towards the margins of operational soft security. Also the US could, at least temporarily, advance the CJTF concept without fears for its leadership in European security. And France had to accommodate itself to NATO in the face of the obvious incapacity of the WEU to provide then a practical alternative.[150] Together with the further demonstration of European military impotence in Kosovo, this in turn made possible the Anglo-French St Malo agreement and subsequent EU commitment to the EURRF.

Further architectural simplifications followed. Within the gaggle of financial institutions charged with providing for CEEC and Balkan reconstruction and political transformation, the EBRD struggled to deliver and became somewhat eclipsed by the EIB.[151] More prominent has been the squeezing-out of the WEU owing to the re-established primacy of NATO and strengthened ambitions of the EU. By 2000 the 'cherry-picking' of WEU assets[152] had begun, albeit the first ever joint WEU–NATO crisis management exercise, CMX/CRISEX 2000, indicated that much needed to be done with regard to NATO–EU interface. Removal of all but one reference to the WEU in the Nice Treaty likewise por-tended WEU obscurity as the EU assumes responsibility for all but its collective defence provisions.[153]

However, the architectural debate, together with the EU role within it, remains inconclusive and contentious. This is most obvious in the continued jockeying for position by the leading security institutions. The OSCE, despite its clear deficiencies, retains significant support and ambitions. For example, at its November 1999 Istanbul Summit it adopted a Charter for European Secur-ity in which it outlined a security architecture based on inter-organisational co-operation in which the OSCE enjoyed a co-ordinating role.[154] More politically charged is the reinvigorated debate about the possible de-coupling of the Atlantic Alliance as a consequence of new-found EU determination to press ahead with its EURRF and commitment to the Petersberg tasks. This question divides analysts and constitutes the single most important factor in determin-ing the evolving architecture and the EU's place within it.[155] While the trans-atlantic capabilities gap encourages an informal de-coupling, political messages currently carry greatest salience. On the one hand, leading NATO figures such as Lord Robertson, European Commission officials and Atlanticist EU member states anxiously attest to the compatibility and complementarity of NATO and the EURRF. On the other, Gaullist rhetoric of an autonomous European defence pillar, reflecting a view that the EURRF might do for French policy what the WEU failed to, simultaneously encourages fears of de-coupling and threatens to unhinge the Anglo-French rapprochement by affronting Britain's Atlanticist preferences.[156] Likewise, European desires for greater autonomy are fed by uncertainty about US commitment to Europe, particularly post-September 11, and by provocative statements such as US National Security

Adviser Condoleezza Rice's pre-election suggestion for transatlantic burden-sharing whereby Europeans would concentrate on peacekeeping while the US dedicated resources to potential major war contingencies in Asia and the Gulf.[157] Furthermore, even if NATO and EURRF 'complementarians' should win out in that debate, there remains the issue of autonomous EU decision-making. It is difficult to see that any nation, let alone the US, would accept being dragged into military commitments through a process over which it exerted no control. It is equally difficult to see how, set in the context of Euro-pean dependence on US power in the Balkans and continued low EU defence spending, the EU will in the foreseeable future have the necessary independent capabilities to manage all potential eventualities in a Petersberg intervention. The obvious danger is that the EU exercises its proven capacity to develop insti-tutions but fails to develop the necessary operational capabilities to do much effective with them.

Three final, interrelated issues further impact upon the EU's place in the evolving security architecture: the mandate for, and legitimacy of, action and the credibility of institutions to deliver upon rhetorical commitments. These issues carry particular poignancy for the EU on account of its mixed legal com-petencies, foundation in international law and questions about its legitimacy, especially in the context of democratic accountability.[158] In principle the most inclusive security institutions, the UN and the OSCE, have assumed legitim-ator functions, with the EU, WEU and NATO pledging their support in effect-ing operational dimensions. Hence, for example, the ECMM was deployed to Yugoslavia in July 1991 at the request of the CSCE. However, the other organisations have reserved their right to act in the absence of an OSCE or UN mandate. The most obvious instance of this to date was NATO's military inter-vention without a UN mandate in the Kosovo War, albeit that Bosnia had earlier revealed problems in reconciling NATO's own integrity of command with the higher mandating authorities of the UN.[159]

This mandate issue is entwined with an increasingly vigorous debate about contemporary limitations of sovereignty, the obligations of the international community and whether institutions can determine legitimacy satisfactorily so as to act as 'mandators'. For example, British Prime Minister Blair 'legitimised' NATO's intervention without a UN mandate in Kosovo in terms of 'a just war, based not on territorial ambitions but on values'.[160] Even UN Secretary-General Kofi Annan mused on the relationship between legitimacy and institu-tional mandates: '[o]n the one hand, is it legitimate for a regional organization to use force without a UN mandate? On the other, is it permissible to let gross and systematic violations of human rights, with grave humanitarian conse-quences, continue unchecked?'[161]

Finally, Europe's security institutions have become increasingly exposed, none more so than the EU, by the propagation of common values both to develop security within Central and South-Eastern Europe and as a substitute cohesive force within Western institutions in the absence of a common threat. Such expansive use of values has proven very effective and a key aspect of the

EU's normative power. The flip side of this strategy is that critical questions of credibility consequently arise wherever and whenever those values are challenged. In such circumstances moral equivalency and an ineffective defence of values compromise their worth and seriously erode the credibility of the institutions that espouse them. The EU experienced this to devastating effect in Yugoslavia when the naïve hubris of 'the hour of Europe' drained away, together with EU credibility, into the Balkan quagmire.

Conclusion

Central and South-Eastern Europe proved to be a baptism of fire for EU aspirations to be the cornerstone of the post-Cold War European security architecture. Geographical proximity, the relative disinterest of the US, EU economic and normative power and the sometimes naively bold rhetoric of EU officials all conspired to raise security expectations of the Union. Concomitantly, the environmental legacy of planned economies, the implosion of Yugoslavia, migratory pressures and new opportunities for trans-border crime all combined to expand the range and type of security challenges that the EU faced in this region. How well it managed these expectations and challenges reveals much about its strengths and weaknesses as a European security actor.

Perhaps its greatest success has been its stabilisation of the applicant CEECs and its export of economic security to that region. Herein its normative power and especially the enlargement process have enabled the EU to influence positively the expectational environment of CEECs and to develop anticipatory socialisation. The enlargement process also demonstrated the EU's ability to develop coherent external policies that involve extensive cross-pillar co-ordination, despite inevitable disputes about the budget, institutional reform and member state preferences as to which CEECs to admit in the 'first wave'. Also, insistence on prior acceptance of the entire *acquis* has, especially after the added requirements of the Amsterdam Treaty, transferred EU norms and its internal security regime beyond extant borders, albeit at a cost of drawing new discriminatory divisions between the acceding countries of 2004 and those left behind. Moreover, as Croatia's formal application for EU membership on 21 February 2003 indicates, the EU may in the future be able to exert a similar promotion of security through the enlargement process in South-Eastern Europe.

Thus far, however, the EU has been less successful in South-Eastern Europe. It is, of course, possible to relativise its performance here. At the onset of troubles, CFSP was in its infancy and the whole sorry tale of Yugoslav dissolution contains 'innumerable villains, few heroes'.[162] Nevertheless, it revealed painfully EU limitations both as a civilian power and as a collective entity, especially as a number of member states pursued unilateral policies and favoured other institutions such as the UN, NATO and the Contact Group. Only in the aftermath of fighting in Bosnia and in Kosovo did the EU re-emerge as a leader in nation-building, the regeneration of civil society and the export of economic security.[163] And even here progress has been tentative and fragile, as exemplified by the assassination of Serbian Prime Minister Zoran Djindjic in March 2003, the expansion and diversification of the Balkans drugs trade[164] and the fact that the region continues to haemorrhage would-be immigrants and asylum seekers.

The EU's development and performance as a European security actor has thus been inconsistent, at times contentious and, above all, incomplete. Its disproportionate influence over relatively backward states aspiring to EU membership, coupled with measures such as readmission agreements, have opened it to charges of developing a 'Fortress Europe' that guards EU internal security and exports the problems and costs of security challenges to those beyond its perimeter wall. Its determination to become a leading regional security actor has also exacerbated the institutional overlap within the European security architecture. Perversely, this has further empowered its member states to use institutional polyphony to their own ends at a time when the discourse of European security politics oscillates between competing concepts of common and collective security and strategic calculations. Moreover, although the EU has made something of a recovery as a European security actor since the dark days of Yugoslavia, this is due only in part to its internal reforms, enhanced legal competence and improved cross-pillar co-ordination. Equally, if not more telling, have been the progressive rationalisation of the European security architecture, the reassertion of NATO and US leadership and the growing trend towards *ad hoc* groupings of the willing to lead peacekeeping and peace-making missions, such as Operation Alba. Even in the EU's own backyard, the delayed arrival of the 'hour of Europe' must seemingly continue to wait upon the outcome of the renewed transatlantic architectural debate and whether the EURRF can realise EU ambitions beyond the boundaries of soft security.

Notes

1 Baev, P.K. (1999) 'External Interventions in Secessionist Conflicts in Europe in the 1990s' *European Security* 8 (2) p. 22.

2 Between October 1992 and December 1994 alone German authorities seized six illicit shipments of weapons grade nuclear material and in 1999 human trafficking in Europe was worth $3–4 billion per annum. Lee, R. (1997) 'Recent Trends in Nuclear Smuggling' in *Russian Organized Crime: The New Threat?*, Williams, P. (ed.), London: Frank Cass, 1997, p. 110; Gardner, A.L. (2001) 'From the Transatlantic Declaration to the New Transatlantic Agenda' in *Ever Closer Partnership*, Philippart, E. and Winand, P. (eds), New York: Peter Lang, p. 92; figures from *The Economist*, cited in Joutsen, M. (2001) 'Cross-Border Crime Patterns Between

Eastern Europe and the European Union' in *Cross-Border Crime in a Changing Europe*, Van Duyne, P.C., Ruggiero, V., Scheinost, M. and Valkenburg, W. (eds), New York: Nova Science Publishers, p. 23.

3 European Commission (1990) *The European Community and its Eastern Neighbours*, Luxembourg: Office for the Official Publications of the European Communities, p. 5.

4 Piening, C. (1997) *Global Europe: The European Union in World Affairs*, London: Lynne Rienner Publishers, note 18, p. 91.

5 For example, the EC concluded a general agreement on trade in industrial goods with Romania in 1980, and that same year upgraded relations with Tito's Yugoslavia to a preferential trade and co-operation agreement.

6 These included with Hungary (September 1988), Czechoslovakia (December 1988), Poland (September 1989), the USSR (December 1989) and Bulgaria and the GDR (May 1990).

7 Pfaff, W. (1993) 'Is Liberal Internationalism Dead?' *World Policy Journal* 10 (3) p. 5.

8 European Commission, *The European Community and its Eastern Neighbours*, p. 10.

9 For an interesting investigation of this psychology of insecurity see Smoke, R. (ed.) (1996) *Perceptions of Security: Public Opinion and Expert Assessments in Europe's New Democracies*, Manchester: Manchester University Press.

10 Rosencrance, R. (1998) 'The European Union: A New Type of International Actor' in *Paradoxes of European Foreign Policy*, Zielonka, J. (ed.), The Hague: Kluwer Law International, p. 22.

11 These were Hungary (31 March 1994), Poland (5 April 1994), Romania (22 June 1995), Slovak Republic (27 June 1995), Latvia (13 October 1995), Estonia (24 November 1995), Lithuania (8 December 1995), Bulgaria (14 December 1995), Czech Republic (17 January 1996), and Slovenia (10 June 1996).

12 Belgian Prime Minister Wilfred Martens cited by Buchan, D. (1993) *Europe: The Strange Superpower*, Aldershot: Dartmouth Press, p. 33; Grant, C. (1994) *Inside the House that Jacques Built*, London: Nicholas Brealey, p. 143. Austria, Finland and Sweden subsequently joined the EU in 1995. Norway was prevented from doing so by a 'no' vote in a national referendum.

13 http://europa.eu.int/comm/enlargement/arguments/index.htm.

14 Eisl, G. (1999) 'EU Enlargement and Co-operation in Justice and Home Affairs' in *Back to Europe: Central and Eastern Europe and the European Union*, Henderson, K. (ed.), London: UCL Press, p. 180.

15 Bretherton, C. and Vogler, J. (1999) *The European Union as a Global Actor*, London: Routledge, p. 142.

16 UN report in 1998 cited by Sander, H. (2000) 'Towards a Wider Europe: Eastern Europe's Rocky Road Into the European Union' in *Rewriting Rights in Europe*, Hancock, L. and O'Brien, C. (eds), Aldershot: Ashgate, p. 144.

17 Sjursen, H. (1999) 'Enlargement and the Common Foreign and Security Policy: Transforming the EU's External Identity?' in *Back to Europe*, Henderson (ed.), p. 40.

18 See next chapter for these dimensions. See also for an overview: Sedelmeier, U. and Wallace, H. (2000) 'Eastern Enlargement: Strategy or Second Thoughts?' in *Policymaking in the European Union*, Wallace, H. and Wallace, W. (eds), Oxford: Oxford University Press, pp. 435–40.

19 http://europa.eu.int/comm/enlargement/intro/criteria.htm.

20 Hailbronner, K. (2000) *Immigration and Asylum Law and Policy of the European Union*, Boston: Kluwer Law International, p. 26.

21 For detail on EU readmission agreements with CEECs see Lavenex, S. (1999) *Safe Third Countries: Extending the EU Asylum and Immigration Policies to Central and Eastern Europe*, Budapest: Central European University Press; Lavenex, S. (1998) 'Asylum, Immigration and Central-Eastern Europe: Challenges to EU Enlargement' *European Foreign Affairs Review* 3 pp. 275–94.

22 Sperling, J. (1999) 'Enlarging the EU and NATO' in *Europe in Change. Two Tiers or Two Speeds: The European Security Order and the Enlargement of the European Union and NATO*, Sperling, J. (ed.), Manchester: Manchester University Press, p. 10.

23 For Agenda 2000 see: http://europa.eu.int/comm/agenda2000/index_en.htm; Avery, G. and Cameron, F. (1998) *The Enlargement of the European Union*, Sheffield: Sheffield Academic Press, pp. 101–39.

24 Avery and Cameron, *The Enlargement of the European Union*, p. 43; Grabbe, H. and Hughes, K. (1998) *Enlarging the EU Eastwards*, London: Royal Institute for International Affairs, pp. 58 and 114.

25 Van Oudenaren, J. (1999) 'EU Enlargement: The Return to Europe' in *Europe Today: National Politics, European Integration, and European Security*, Tiersky, R. (ed.), Oxford: Rowman and Littlefield Publishers, p. 442.

26 The conference also included Cyprus, Turkey and, upon reactivation of its application, Malta.

27 Interestingly, a Eurobarometer public opinion survey in May 2002 found that 60 per cent of respondents tended to agree that enlargement secures peace in Europe. Special Eurobarometer 56.3, May 2002, http://www.europa.int/comm/public_opinion/enlargement_en.pdf.

28 Eurobarometer findings in April 2003 for the ten acceding countries put average public support for CFSP at 67 per cent and for CESDP at 71 per cent. Figures from Eurobarometer, http//:www.europa.int/comm/public_opinion/archives/notes/cfspapr03_en.pdf.

29 Measures taken include holding municipal elections, direct elections for state president, legislation on minority languages and the creation of various bodies for overseeing human and minority rights.

30 Gower, J. (2000) 'The Charter of Fundamental Rights and EU Enlargement: Consolidating Democracy or Imposing New Hurdles?' in *The EU Charter of Fundamental Rights: Text and Commentaries*, Feus, K. (ed.), London: Federal Trust, p. 230.

31 Slocock, B. (1999) ' "Whatever Happened to the Environment?": Environmental Issues in the Eastern Enlargement of the European Union' in *Back to Europe*, Henderson (ed.), pp. 164–5.

32 Pelkmans, J. and Murphy, A. (1991) 'Catapulted Into Leadership: The Community's Trade and Aid Policies *vis-à-vis* Eastern Europe' *Journal of European Integration* **14** pp. 125–51; L. Whitehead cited in Pridham, G. (2002) 'EU Enlargement and Consolidating Democracy in Post-Communist States – Formality and Reality' *Journal of Common Market Studies* **40** (5) p. 954.

33 Nello, S.N. and Smith, K.E. (1998) *The European Union and Eastern Enlargement: The Implications of Enlargement in Stages*, Aldershot: Ashgate, p. 55.

34 Flockhart, T. (1995) 'The Dynamics of Expansion: NATO, WEU, and EU' *European Security* **5** (2) p. 211.

35 Avery and Cameron, *The Enlargement of the European Union*, p. 123.

36 The eight states in question are the Czech Republic, Estonia, Hungary, Latvia, Lithuania, Poland, the Slovak Republic, and Slovenia. Cyprus and Malta are also set to join on 1 May 2004. Bulgaria and Romania hope to join by 2007.

37 Apapa, J., Boratynski, J., Emerson, M., Gromadzki, G., Vahl, M. and Whyte, N. (1991) 'Friendly Schengen Borderland Policy on the New Borders of an Enlarged EU and Its Neighbours', p. 9, 6–7 July 1991, Centre for European Policy Studies, http://www.ceps.be.

38 Unattributed, 'Border Controls "Set to Remain"' *European Voice*, 12 September 2002.

39 Joutsen, M. (2001) 'Cross-Border Crime Patterns Between Eastern Europe and the European Union' in *Cross-Border Crime in a Changing Europe*, Van Duyne et al. (eds), p. 19.

40 This is perhaps not surprising given studies suggesting that over a fifteen-year period Germany is likely to receive between two and six million migrants from EU CEEC members. Sinn, H.W. and Werding, M. (2001) 'Immigration Following EU Eastern Enlargement' *CESIFO Forum* **2** (2) p. 40.

41 Vandamme, L. (December 2001) 'Schengen and Integration of Schengen in the European Union With a View to Enlargement' *Collegium* **22** p. 118. For an indication of how human rights groups have been alarmed that post-September 11 EU anti-terrorist measures have reinforced the trend towards harder border and immigration policies see Human Rights Watch (November 2001) 'Human Rights Implications of European Union Internal Security Proposals and Measures in the Aftermath of the 11 September Attacks in the United States', http://www.hrw.org/press/2001/11/eusecurity-memo.htm.

42 Geddes, A. (2000) *Immigration and European Integration: Towards a Fortress Europe?*, Manchester: Manchester University Press, pp. 171–2.

43 Imbusch, K. (2000) 'Regime Export and Institutional Change? The Governance of EU-Enlargement in Justice and Home Affairs', paper given at the Workshop 'Governance by Enlargement' Program, Darmstadt University of Technology, 23–25 June 2000; Lippert, B. and Becker, P. (1998) 'Structured Dialogue Revisited: The EU's Politics of Inclusion and Exclusion' *European Foreign Affairs Review* **3** p. 345.

44 Dhian, M.S. and Philippart, E. (25 October 2001) 'JHA and Enlargement: A Plea For a Core Acquis Test' *Challenge Europe*, European Policy Centre, http://www.theepc.net/challenge/challenge_detail.asp?.

45 For EU states exporting immigration problems to neighbouring states see, amongst others, Lavenex, S. (1998) ' "Passing the Buck": European Refugee Policies Towards

Central and Eastern Europe' *Journal of Refugee Studies* **11** (2) pp. 126–45; Eisl, 'EU Enlargement and Co-operation in Justice and Home Affairs', p. 173.

46 Peers, S. (2003) 'Readmission Agreements and EC Migration Law' *Statewatch Analysis* **17**, http://www.statewatch.org/news/2003/may/12readmission.htm.

47 ECRE Observations on the Presidency Conclusions of the European Union Council Meeting, 21 and 22 June 2002, 27 June 2002, http://www.ecre.org/statements/seville.shtml.

48 Apapa, J. (2001) 'Enlargement and an Area of Freedom, Security and Justice: Striking a Better Balance' *Challenge of Europe*, European Policy Centre, http://www.theepc.net/challenge/challenge.detail.asp.

49 Since the entry into force of the Amsterdam Treaty the EC has been able to conclude readmission agreements in its own right.

50 Leonard, D. (20 September 2001) 'Schengen Poses Tough Hurdle For Candidates' *European Voice*, http://www.knoweurope.net/cgi/quick/full_rec?action.

51 Apapa, 'Enlargement and an Area of Freedom, Security and Justice: Striking a Better Balance', n.p.

52 Kovács, P. (March 2002) 'The Schengen Challenge and its Balkan Dimension' *Centre for European Policy Studies Brief* **17** p. 2, http://www.ceps.be. Sensitivity to this issue is heightened by the fact that not all states beyond new EU borders will be treated equally. Croatia, for example, already enjoys visa-free status with Schengen member countries.

53 Apapa et al., 'Friendly Schengen Borderland Policy', p. 10.

54 Kovács, 'The Schengen Challenge and its Balkan Dimension'.

55 Gower, 'The Charter of Fundamental Rights and EU Enlargement', pp. 234–5.

56 Yugoslavia's collapse had been predicted intermittently from Tito's death in 1980. Edwards, G. (1997) 'The Potential and Limits of the CFSP: The Yugoslav Example' in *Foreign Policy of the European Union: From EPC to CFSP and Beyond*, Regelsberger, E. et al., London: Lynne Rienner, p. 190; Lucarelli, S. (2000) *Europe and the Breakup of Yugoslavia*, Boston: Kluwer Law International, pp. 15–18.

57 The full story of the Yugoslav crises is beyond the scope of this book. Nevertheless, there is a burgeoning literature on the topic, with useful starting points including Gow, J. (1997) *Triumph of the Lack of Will: International Diplomacy and the Yugoslav War*, London: Hurst and Company; Lucarelli, *Europe and the Breakup of Yugoslavia*; Woodward, S. (1995) *Balkan Tragedy: Chaos and Dissolution after the Cold War*, Washington D.C.: Brookings Institute; Ullman, R.H. (ed.) (1996) *The World and Yugoslavia's Wars*, New York: Council of Foreign Relations; Danchev, A. and Halverson, T. (eds) (1996) *International Perspectives on the Yugoslav Conflict*, Basingstoke: Macmillan.

58 Peterson, J. and Sjursen, H. (eds) (1998) *A Common Foreign and Security Policy for Europe?*, London: Routledge, p. 171; Salmon, T. (1992) 'Testing Times for European Political Cooperation: The Gulf and Yugoslavia' *International Affairs* **68** (2) p. 248; Soetendorp, B. (1999) *Foreign Policy in the European Union*, London: Longman, p. 128.

59 Edwards, G. (1992) 'European Responses to the Yugoslav Crisis: An Interim Assessment' in *Toward Political Union: Planning a Common Foreign and Security*

Policy in the European Community, Rummel, R. (ed.), Oxford: Westview Press, p. 168.

60 Gow, J. (1999) 'Security and Democracy: The EU and Central and Eastern Europe' in *Back to Europe*, Henderson (ed.), p. 26.

61 ECHO operates within the EC pillar, works in close conjunction with NGOs and is charged with responsibility for humanitarian aid and reconstruction. The Contact Group was set up in April 1994 and comprised Russia, France, Germany, Britain and the US.

62 Spence, A. and Spence, D. (1998) 'The Common Foreign and Security Policy from Maastricht to Amsterdam' in *Foreign and Security Policy in the European Union*, Eliassen, K.A. (ed.), London: Sage, p. 56. See also Cameron, F. (1999) *The Foreign and Security Policy of the European Union*, Sheffield: Sheffield Academic Press, pp. 50–5.

63 Piening, *Global Europe*, p. 195.

64 White, B. (2001) *Understanding European Foreign Policy*, Basingstoke: Palgrave, p. 106.

65 Lepick, O. (1996) 'French Perspectives' in *International Perspectives on the Yugoslav Conflict*, Danchev and Halverson (eds), p. 78.

66 Anderson, S. (1995) 'EU, NATO and CSCE Responses to the Yugoslav Crisis: Testing Europe's New Security Architecture' *European Security* 4 (2) p. 333.

67 Gow, *Triumph of the Lack of Will*, p. 65.

68 Caplan has suggested that Germany's unilateral recognition was motivated by suspicion that Croatia would not meet the necessary conditions and its consequent desire to circumvent the Badinter Committee's opinions. Caplan, R. (1995) 'The EU's Recognition Policy Towards Republics of Former Yugoslavia', seminar paper, cited by Von Hippel, K. (2000) *Democracy by Force*, Cambridge: Cambridge University Press, p. 132.

69 For example, the Badinter Committee's stipulated full referendum on independence was compromised by a large-scale Bosnian Serb boycott. This boycott did not, however, deter Bosnia and Herzegovina, having already proclaimed sovereignty in October 1991, from declaring independence from the former Yugoslavia on 3 March 1992.

70 For a fuller exposition of Greece's underlying objections see: Gow, *Triumph of the Lack of Will*, footnote 32, pp. 78–9.

71 Jacobsen, C.G. (1995) 'Yugoslavia's Successor Wars Reconsidered' *European Security* 4 (4) p. 658.

72 Wood, P.C. (1994) 'France and the Post-Cold War Order: The Case of Yugoslavia' *European Security* 3 (1) p. 139.

73 Jacobsen, 'Yugoslavia's Successor Wars Reconsidered', p. 668.

74 The Greek blockade cost FYROM approximately $58 million per month. Glenny, M. (1996) 'The Macedonian Question' in *International Perspectives on the Yugoslav Conflict*, Danchev and Halverson (eds), p. 143.

75 Smith, H. (2002) *European Union Foreign Policy: What It Is and What It Does*, London: Pluto Press, p. 121. Greece finally lifted its trade blockade in 1995 and the

two countries agreed to normalise relations, despite continued disagreement over the FYROM's use of 'Macedonia'.

76 Peterson and Bomberg have argued that the creation of the Contact Group marked the point at which 'the EU essentially ceased to function as a single entity on policy towards Bosnia'. Others see this as happening much earlier. Soetendorp emphasises the failure of the EC, amid an Anglo-French standoff, to agree upon use of the WEU to intervene in 1991/92 and Whitman suggests that the EU became very much a 'secondary actor' in Yugoslavia from UN involvement in 1991. Peterson, J. and Bomberg, E. (1999) *Decision-Making in the European Union*, Basingstoke: Macmillan, p. 243; Soetendorp, *Foreign Policy in the European Union*, p. 142; Whitman, R.G. (1999) 'CFSP After Enlargement' in *The Enlargement of the European Union: Issues and Strategies*, Price, V.C., Landau A. and Whitman, R.G., London: Routledge, p. 157.

77 Bretherton and Vogler, *The European Union as a Global Actor*, p. 178.

78 Edwards, 'The Potential and Limits of the CFSP', pp. 191–92; Spence and Spence, 'The Common Foreign and Security Policy From Maastricht to Amsterdam', p. 56.

79 Gow, J. (1991) 'Deconstructing Yugoslavia' *Survival* 33 (4) pp. 305–6; Gow, 'Security and Democracy', p. 24.

80 For more on the possible contribution of EC policy to exacerbating the Balkan situation see Peterson and Bomberg, *Decision-Making in the European Union*, p. 243.

81 Monar, J. (1997) 'The Financial Dimension of the CFSP' in *Common Foreign and Security Policy*, Holland, M. (ed.), London: Pinter, pp. 38–9.

82 http://europa.eu.int/abc/obj/treaties/en/entr2f.htm#Article_J.4.

83 Salmon, 'Testing Times for European Political Cooperation', p. 248.

84 Gow, 'Security and Democracy', p. 25.

85 Gow, *Triumph of the Lack of Will*, p. 49.

86 Blair, A. (1994) 'What Happened in Yugoslavia? Lessons for Future Peacekeepers' *European Security* 3 (2) pp. 344–5.

87 For deadlock over whether the WEU should intervene in 1991/92 see Duke, S. (1996) 'The Second Death (Or the Second Coming?) of the WEU' *Journal of Common Market Studies* 34 (2) p. 180; Kintis, A. (1997) 'The EU's Foreign Policy and the War in the Former Yugoslavia' in *Common Foreign and Security Policy*, Holland (ed.), pp. 150–1.

88 As cited by Rieff, D. (1995) *Slaughterhouse: Bosnia and the Failure of the West*, New York: Simon and Schuster, p. 29. Owen called in 1992 for NATO airstrikes to defend Bosnia and Herzegovina against the Serbs. See his open letter to British Prime Minister John Major, 30 July 1992, published in the *Evening Standard* and reprinted in Owen, D. (1995) *Balkan Odyssey*, New York: Harcourt Brace, pp. 14–16. In similar vein see the opinion of former US ambassador to Yugoslavia Zimmermann, W. (1996) *Origins of a Catastrophe: Yugoslavia and its Destroyers – America's Last Ambassador Tells What Happened and Why*, New York: Times Books, pp. xi–xii.

89 In 1991 the US invoked the Nickles amendment against the whole of Yugoslavia, which suspended aid and support for money raising on the international market. Examples of American declarations of Yugoslavia as a European responsibility

include Secretary of State James Baker's 'We don't have a dog in this fight' and Secretary of State Warren Christopher's reiteration in May 1993 that Yugoslavia was at heart a European problem. Walker, M. (2000) 'Variable Geography: America's Mental Maps of a Greater Europe' *International Affairs* **76** (3) p. 460; Drew, E. (1994) *On the Edge: The Clinton Presidency*, New York: Simon and Schuster, p. 162.

90 Jacques Poos cited in Smith, C.J. (1996) 'Conflict in the Balkans and the Possibility of a European Union Common Foreign and Security Policy' *International Relations* **13** (2) p. 1.

91 Delors cited by Allin, D.H. (2002) *NATO's Balkan Interventions*, Adelphi Paper 347, London: Oxford University Press for the International Institute for Strategic Studies, note 6, p. 102.

92 Cited in Anderson, 'EU, NATO and CSCE Responses to the Yugoslav Crisis', p. 346.

93 Chirac's threat to withdraw French peacekeepers effectively promised to activate an earlier US promise to cover a UN withdrawal of UNPROFOR should it become necessary, for which NATO had drawn up contingency plan OpPlan 40-104 that required 20,000 US ground troops. Daalder, I.H. (2000) *Getting to Dayton: The Making of America's Bosnia Policy*, Washington D.C.: Brookings Institute Press, *passim*; Holbrooke, R. (1998) *To End a War*, New York: Random House, pp. 64–70. US aversion to deploying American ground troops meant reliance on NATO air-power. However, it has been suggested that the NATO bombing campaign was perhaps more symbolic than decisive and that the ending of the conflict owed more to concessions made at Dayton to Serb war aims, especially acceptance of an ethnically cleansed *Republika Srpska*. Bozo, F. (2003) 'The Effects of Kosovo and the Danger of Decoupling' in *Defending Europe: The EU, NATO and the Quest for European Autonomy*, Howorth, J. and Keeler, J.T.S. (eds), Basingstoke: Palgrave, p. 62; Bildt, C. (2000) 'Force and Diplomacy' *Survival* **42** (1) p. 144; Allin, *NATO's Balkan Interventions*, p. 40.

94 Kotios, A. (2001) 'European Policies for the Reconstruction and Development of the Balkans' in *The Development of the Balkan Region*, Petrakos, G. and Totev, S. (eds), Aldershot: Ashgate, pp. 242–3.

95 'European Commission Adopts Annual Programme for Kosovo', 25 April 2003, http://europa.eu.int/comm/external_relations/see/news. The EUPM follows on from the UN International Police Task Force and acts in support of the Dayton objectives. It comprises 500 police officers drawn from all fifteen EU member states plus eighteen non-EU states.

96 Participants: EU member states and the Commission, Albania, Bosnia and Herzegovina, Croatia, FYROM, Bulgaria, Hungary, Romania, Slovenia, Turkey, Canada, Japan, Norway, Russia, Switzerland, the US, UN, OSCE, UN High Commissioner for Refugees, Council of Europe, NATO, OECD, WEU, IBRD, EBRD, EIB, the Black Sea Economic Cooperation, Central European Initiative, Royaumont process, South Eastern European Cooperation Initiative, South Eastern Europe Cooperation Process. The Federal Republic of Yugoslavia joined later, on 26 October 2000, after lifting of sanctions.

97 For more details and an assessment of progress in security-related measures see http://www.stabilitypact.org; Pandurevic, N. (2001) 'Security Aspects of the Stability Pact for South Eastern Europe' *Security Dialogue* **32** (3) pp. 311–24.

98 In 2001 the EU accounted for 55 per cent of western Balkan trade and after enlargement the Commission anticipates that 70 per cent of western Balkan trade will be with the EU. European Commission (2003) 'Stabilisation and Association Process for South East Europe Second Annual Report', COM (2003) 139 final, 26 March 2003, pp. 5 and 11.

99 Since 2000 exports from SAP countries have largely entered the EU on a basis even more preferential than those enjoyed by CEEC candidate countries. 'The EU's Relations with South Eastern Europe (Western Balkans)', http://europa.eu.int/comm/external_relations/see/index.htm.

100 'The EU's Actions in Support of the Stabilisation and Association Process', http://europa.eu.int/comm/external_relations/see/actions/sap.htm.

101 European Commission, 'Stabilisation and Association Process for South East Europe Second Annual Report', Annex 1, p. 23.

102 For an analysis of EU policy towards the crisis in FYROM see Piana, C. (2002) 'The EU's Decision-Making Process in the Common Foreign and Security Policy: The Case of the Former Yugoslav Republic of Macedonia' *European Foreign Affairs Review* 7 pp. 209–26.

103 The operation is small-scale, comprising a budget of €6.2 million and 350 military personnel drawn from thirteen EU member states and fourteen non-EU countries. It draws on NATO assets and capabilities, is based on UN Security Council Resolution 1371 and is scheduled to last for six months.

104 Roberts, E. (1999) 'Montenegro: Trouble Ahead' *World Today* 55 (12) pp. 11–14.

105 Bennett, C. (1999) 'Bosnia: New Opportunities' *Security Dialogue* 30 (3) p. 281.

106 Kotios, 'European Policies for the Reconstruction and Development of the Balkans', p. 276; Daianu, D. and Veremis, T. (eds) (2001), *Balkan Reconstruction*, London: Frank Cass, p. 1.

107 Allin, *NATO's Balkan Interventions*, p. 88. For similar doubts see: Kotios, 'European Policies for the Reconstruction and Development of the Balkans', p. 263; Gligorov, V. (2001) 'Notes on the Stability Pact' in *Balkan Reconstruction*, Daiano and Veremis (eds), pp. 18–19.

108 European Commission, 'Stabilisation and Association Process for South East Europe Second Annual Report', pp. 2, 3 and 8.

109 At Dayton the US insisted on a one-year mandate for IFOR. On 15 November 1996 Clinton committed 8,500 US troops to the subsequent SFOR until June 1998. In February 1998 NATO resolved upon an open-ended commitment. Even the George W. Bush administration has accepted a for-as-long-as-it-takes ethos in the form of an 'all in together, all out together' format. SFOR consequently remains in place, albeit troop levels were reduced to approximately 12,000 by the close of 2002. Bildt, C. (1997–98) 'There is no Alternative to Dayton' *Survival* 39 (4) pp. 19–21; Daalder, I.H. (1997–98) 'Bosnia after SFOR: Options for Continued US Engagement' *Survival* 39 (4) pp. 5–18; Schulte, G. (1998) 'SFOR Continued' *NATO Review* 2 pp. 27–30; http://www.cia.gov/cia/publications/factbook/geos/bk.html.

110 Bildt cited by Baev, 'External Interventions in Secessionist Conflicts in Europe in the 1990s', p. 41. For more on the EU and Kosovo see Mahncke, D. and Bayerl, A. (eds) (2001) *Old Frontiers – New Frontiers: The Challenge of Kosovo and its*

Implications for the European Union, Bern: Peter Lang; Deighton, A. (2000) 'The European Union and NATO's War over Kosovo: Towards the Glass Ceiling?' in *Alliance Politics, Kosovo and NATO's War: Allied Force of Forced Allies?*, Martin, P. and Brawley, M.R. (eds), New York: Palgrave, pp. 57–74.

111 Bretherton and Vogler, *The European Union as a Global Actor*, p. 213.

112 For an analysis of the EU role in Albania see Di Feliciantonio, S. (1999) 'EU Foreign Policy and Albania' *European Foreign Affairs Review* 4 (4) pp. 519–36. For the OSCE role in Albania see Ahrens, G.H. (2001) 'Albania: Status Report' in *The Operational Role of the OSCE in South-Eastern Europe*, Ghebali, V.Y. and Warner, D. (eds), Aldershot: Ashgate, pp. 30–6.

113 Cutileiro, J. (1997) Letter in *The Economist* 344 (8031) 23 August 1997, p. 8.

114 For more on interaction capacity in the context of structuring international relations see Buzan, B., Jones, C. and Little, R. (1993) *The Logic of Anarchy: Neorealism to Structural Realism*, New York: Columbia University Press, pp. 66–80.

115 For example: Kupchan, C.A. and Kupchan, C.A. (1991) 'Concerts, Collective Security, and the Future of Europe' *International Security* 16 (1) pp. 114–61; Flynn, G. and Scheffer, D.J. (1990) 'Limited Collective Security' *Foreign Policy* 80 pp. 77–101; Ullman, R. (Autumn 1990) 'Enlarging the Zone of Peace' *Foreign Policy* 80 pp. 102–20.

116 This theoretical debate is beyond the remit of this book but interesting insights can be found in Keohane, R.O. and Martin, L.L. (1995) 'The Promise of Institutionalist Theory' *International Security* 20 (1) pp. 39–51; Snyder, J. (1990) 'Averting Anarchy in the New Europe' *International Security* 14 (4) pp. 5–41; Kupchan, C.A. and Kupchan, C.A. (1995) 'The Promise of Collective Security' *International Security* 20 (1) pp. 52–61; Russell, R. (1995) 'The Chimera of Collective Security in Europe' *European Security* 4 (2) pp. 241–55; Zelikow, P. (1992) 'The New Concert of Europe' *Survival* 34 (2) pp. 12–30; Joffe, J. (1992) 'Collective Security and the Future of Europe: Failed Dreams and Dead Ends' *Survival* 34 (1) pp. 36–50; Mearsheimer, J. (1994/95) 'The False Promise of International Institutions' *International Security* 19 (3) pp. 5–49.

117 As cited in Bretherton and Vogler, *The European Union as a Global Actor*, p. 145.

118 Hill, C. (1998) 'Closing the Capabilities-Expectation Gap?' in *A Common Foreign and Security Policy for Europe?*, Peterson and Sjursen (eds), pp. 20–1.

119 Sperling, J. and Kirchner, E. (1997) *Recasting the European Order: Security Architectures and Economic Cooperation*, Manchester: Manchester University Press, p. 16.

120 Bailes, A.J.K. (1999) speech to St Anthony's College, 'Under a European Flag? From WEU to EU', 29 November 1999.

121 The Council of Europe has predominantly retained its original role as a pan-European promoter of democracy, cultural understanding and respect for human and ethnic rights. Its normative approach was epitomised in its European Charter for Regional or Minority Languages and the Framework Convention on the Protection of National Minorities. It has also expanded its activities to include principles of law enforcement and training of lawyers, civil servants and judiciary. Tarschys, D. (1995) 'The Council of Europe: The Challenge of Enlargement' *The World Today* 51 (4) pp. 62–4.

122 For example, Secretary-General William Van Eekelen publicly located the WEU between NATO and the European institutions and at 'the heart of a dynamic two-fold process' of their reform. Van Eekelen, W. (1992) 'WEU's Post-Maastricht Agenda' *NATO Review* **40** (2) p. 15.

123 For more details see Croft, S., Redmond, J., Rees, G.W. and Webber, M. (1999) *The Enlargement of Europe*, Manchester: Manchester University Press, pp. 99–104.

124 http://www.osce.org/docs/english/1990-1999/summits/hels92e.htm.

125 By 1994 the annual cost of UN Balkans intervention was greater than the total spent on thirty UN peace operations world-wide since 1948. Blair, 'What Happened in Yugoslavia?', p. 349.

126 For but two of the many predictions of NATO's demise see Mearsheimer, 'Back to the Future', p. 52; Lodgaard, S. (1992) 'Competing Schemes for Europe: The CSCE, NATO and the European Union' *Security Dialogue* **23** (3) p. 58.

127 For details see NATO (1999) 'The Alliance's Strategic Concept, 8 November 1991' in *NATO Handbook Documentation*, Brussels: NATO Office of Information and Press, pp. 281–300.

128 Wörner, M. (1992) 'A Vigorous Alliance – A Motor for Peaceful Change in Europe' *NATO Review* **40** (6) p. 7.

129 Opinions about the value of PFP have varied from US Senator Richard Lugar's 'policy for postponement', through US Ambassador to NATO Robert Hunter's 'magic bullet', to US Assistant Secretary of State for Europe Richard Holbrooke's verdict that 'PFP has become an integral part of the European Security scene'. Lugar, R.G. (1995) 'NATO Enlargement and US Public Opinion', speech at Center for Strategic and International Studies Conference on 'NATO's Role in European Security', Washington D.C., 3 March 1995; Hunter, R.E. (1999) 'NATO at Fifty. Maximising NATO: A Relevant Alliance Knows How to Reach' *Foreign Affairs* **78** (3) p. 194; Holbrooke, R.C. (1995) 'America as a European Power' *Foreign Affairs* **74** (2) p. 44. For analysis of PFP see (1996) *Cooperation and Partnership for Peace: A Contribution to Euro-Atlantic Security in the 21st Century*, Whitehall Paper Series, London: RUSI for Defence Studies; Rühle, M. and Williams, N. (1996) 'Partnership for Peace After NATO Enlargement' *European Security* **5** (4) pp. 521–8; De Santis, H. (1994) 'Romancing NATO: Partnership for Peace and East European Stability' *Journal of Strategic Studies* **17** (4) pp. 61–81; Borawski, J. (1995) 'Partnership for Peace and Beyond' *International Affairs* **71** (2) pp. 233–46; Williams, N. (1996) 'Partnership for Peace: Permanent Fixture or Declining Asset?' *Survival* **38** (1) pp. 98–110.

130 Clinton cited in George, B. and Borawski, J. (1995) 'Continental Drift' *European Security* **4** (1) p. 12.

131 The countries in question are Bulgaria, Estonia, Latvia, Lithuania, Romania, Slovakia and Slovenia.

132 Croft, S. (2000) 'The EU, NATO and the Return of the Architectural Debate' *European Security* **9** (3) p. 13.

133 Öövel, A. (1996) 'Estonian Defence Policy, NATO and the European Union' *Security Dialogue* **27** (1) p. 65.

134 For more on the enlargement of Europe's security institutions see Croft et al., *The Enlargement of Europe*.

135 Croft, 'The EU, NATO and the Return of the Architectural Debate', p. 5.

136 For more on national differences regarding the role of OSCE see Borawski, J. (2000) 'Revisiting the Common European Home: A Rejoinder' *Security Dialogue* **31** (1) pp. 85–90.

137 For example, Secretary of State for Defence Malcolm Rifkind launched his 'Atlantic Community' concept in December 1994 in which he called for a re-enforcement of free trade, parliamentary and popular contacts as well as security co-operation between Europe and North America.

138 Bailes, 'Under a European Flag?'.

139 For an exploration of the Russia-Weimar analogy see Hanson, S.E. and Kopstein, J.S. (1997) 'The Weimar/Russia Comparison' *Post-Soviet Affairs* **13** (3) pp. 252–83.

140 Mlyn, E. (1996) 'The OSCE, the United States and European Security' *European Security* **5** (3) pp. 439–40.

141 The Quint comprises Britain, Germany, France, Italy and the US. For details see Gegout, C. (2002) 'The Quint: Acknowledging the Existence of a Big Four-US *Directoire* at the Heart of the European Union's Foreign Policy Decision-Making Process' *Journal of Common Market Studies* **40** (2) pp. 331–44. For a discussion of *directoires* in the EU's CFSP see Keukeleire, S. (2001) 'Directoires Within the CFSP/CESDP of the European Union: a Plea for "Restricted Crisis Management Groups"' *European Foreign Affairs Review* **6** (1) pp. 75–101.

142 Wright, J. (1997) 'European Security – Post-Bosnia' *European Security* **6** (2) p. 5.

143 Bailes, A.J.K. (1996) 'European Defence and Security: The Role of NATO, WEU and EU' *Security Dialogue* **27** (1) p. 56.

144 Baev, 'External Interventions in Secessionist Conflicts in Europe in the 1990s', p. 30; Lindley-French, J. (2002) 'In the Shade of Locarno? Why European Defence is Failing' *International Affairs* **78** (4) p. 799.

145 This embarrassing situation was later corrected through Operation Sharp Guard, run under a joint NATO–WEU Military Committee. Schulte, G.L. (1997) 'Former Yugoslavia and the New NATO' *Survival* **39** (1) p. 30.

146 Allin, *NATO's Balkan Interventions*, p. 26.

147 On this theme Jacobsen has argued that US sympathy for Bosnian Muslims led it to repeated friction with EU countries, to the point that its intervention has been seen to 'effectively sabotage occasional European, UN [and former President Carter's December 1994] attempts to explore compromise solutions'. Gow has argued that American reluctance to implement the Vance–Owen plan was key in its failure, and Hoffmann argues that it 'was as if there was a need to demonstrate that the Europeans could not succeed without US help'. Jacobsen, 'Yugoslavia's Successor Wars Reconsidered', p. 660; Gow, *Triumph of the Lack of Will* pp. 258–59; Hoffmann, S. (1997) 'The United States and Europe' in *Eagle Adrift: American Foreign Policy at the End of the Century*, Lieber, R.J. (ed.), New York: Longman, p. 190.

148 For the importance of the US presence in allowing the EU to overcome past patterns of insecurity and promote collective gain see Rühle, M. and Williams, N.

(1997) 'Why NATO Will Survive' *Comparative Strategy* **16** (1) p. 113; Kagan, R., 'Power and Weakness', http://www.atlanticcommunity.org.

149 Aybet, G. (2000) *A European Security Architecture after the Cold War*, Basingstoke: Macmillan, p. 196; Bozo, F. (2003) 'The Effects of Kosovo and the Danger of Decoupling' in *Defending Europe*, Howorth and Keeler (eds), p. 62.

150 For an analysis of the French shift of position see Grant, R.P. (1996) 'France's New Relationship With NATO' *Survival* **38** (1) pp. 62–5; Menon, A. (1995) 'NATO the French Way. From Independence to Cooperation: France, NATO and European Security' *International Affairs* **75** (1) pp. 19–34.

151 Sperling and Kirchner, *Recasting the European Order*, note 43, p. 27.

152 Howorth, J. (2000) 'Britain, France and the European Defence Initiative' *Survival* **42** (2) p. 41.

153 Duke, S. (2001) 'CESDP: Nice's Overtrumped Success?' *European Foreign Affairs Review* **6** p. 157.

154 Charter for European Security, www.osce.org/docs/english/1990-1999/summits/istachart99e.htm. Text reproduced in Ghebali and Warner (eds), *The Operational Role of the OSCE in South-Eastern Europe*, pp. 113–31.

155 For a convenient contrast of conclusions see Menon, A. (2003) 'Why ESDP is Dangerous and Misguided for the Alliance' in *Defending Europe*, Howorth and Keeler (eds), pp. 203–18; Howorth, J. (2003) 'Why ESDP is Necessary and Beneficial for the Alliance' in ibid., pp. 219–38. See also Hunter, R.E. (2002) *The European Security and Defence Policy: NATO's Companion – Or Competitor*, Pittsburgh: RAND.

156 For more on Franco-American relations see Robinson, S. (2000) 'France Could Split NATO, Clinton Aide Warns', *Daily Telegraph*, 21 January 2000; Gordon, P.H. (2000) 'The French Position' *The National Interest* **61** pp. 57–65; Petras, J. and Morley, M. (2000) 'Contesting Hegemons: US–French Relations in the "New World Order"' *Review of International Studies* **26** (1) pp. 49–68.

157 Gordon, M.R. (2000) 'Bush Would Stop U.S. Peacekeeping in Balkan Fights' *New York Times*, http://query.nytimes.com/gst/abstract.html?res=F30D15FF355A0C728EDDA90994D8404482.

158 EU legitimacy, of course, is a hotly debated issue and has numerous facets beyond democratic accountability. For example, Allen and Smith argue that through the concept of international 'presence' it is possible to show that the EU has 'considerable structure, salience and legitimacy in the process of international politics'. Alternatively Feldman sees the notion of reconciliation as a basic legitimising factor for the EU, both internally and externally. Allen, D. and Smith, M. (1991) 'Western Europe's Presence in the Contemporary International Arena' in *The Future of European Political Cooperation*, Holland, M. (ed.), Basingstoke: Macmillan, p. 116; Feldman, L.G. (1999) 'Reconciliation and Legitimacy: Foreign Relations and the Enlargement of the European Union' in *Legitimacy and the European Union: The Contested Polity*, Banchov, T. and Smith, M.P. (eds), London: Routledge, pp. 66–90.

159 For the legal dimensions of the Kosovo campaign see Guicherd, 'International Law and the War in Kosovo', pp. 19–34.

160 Prime Minister Blair (1999) 'Doctrine of International Community', speech in Chicago, 22 April 1999, www.fco.gov.uk/news.

161 Annan, K.A. (1999) 'Two Concepts of Sovereignty' *The Economist* 18 September 1999, pp. 49–50.

162 Hitchcock, W.I. (2003) *The Struggle For Europe*, London: Profile Books, p. 380. Critiques of Western institutions in Yugoslavia include Freedman, L. (1994–95) 'Why the West Failed', *Foreign Policy* 97 pp. 53–69.

163 The EU has been the largest single donor to the western Balkans. From 1991 to 2002 it provided more than €6 billion and has allocated €4.65 billion under CARDS for the period 2000–06.

164 Joutsen, M. (2001) 'Cross-Border Crime Patterns Between Eastern Europe and the European Union' in *Cross-Border Crime in a Changing Europe*, Van Duyne, P.C., Ruggiero, V., Scheinost, M. and Valkenburg, W. (eds), New York: Nova Science Publishers, p. 19.

CHAPTER 7

The EU's economic relations with its European and Mediterranean neighbours

In stark contrast to the difficult situation that the Union has found itself in as a security actor in Europe, it has long been established as the continent's principal economic force. The sheer size of its economy means that the EU simply cannot be ignored – neither as a market nor as a competitor. Also, neighbouring states frequently find the external economic implications of essentially inwardly-focused EU policy decisions magnified by their geographical proximity. Moreover, EU enlargement processes often cut across extant extra-EU preferential trading relationships, redirect trade and FDI flows and project EU economic influence ever further across Europe. For example, formal EU relations with the western Balkans[1] are a recent development, the CIS have never enjoyed the intensity of relations with the EU as those experienced by the CEECs and at present only Finland and Greece share land borders with any country belonging to the two former groups. The May 2004 enlargement, however, will move both sets of countries much closer to the EU, with the Union physically bordering not only on Russia, Albania and the FYROM, as it currently does, but also on Ukraine, Belarus, Serbia and Montenegro and Croatia.[2]

It is thus not surprising that nearly all of Europe's countries, and most of the Union's Mediterranean neighbours, have entered into contractual agreements with the ECs. Indeed, the only political entities in Europe that are not contractually linked to the ECs or the EU are Monaco and the Vatican.[3] However, the type of contractual relationship varies substantially, as does the nature of the countries and country groupings with which association agreements have been struck. There is an array of strictly bilateral agreements, ranging from an exchange of letters with Andorra[4] to a considerable number of agreements with Switzerland. There are also no less than five multilateral agreements: that of the European Economic Area, and those with the CEEC applicant states, the Mediterranean partners, the CIS associated countries and the western Balkans.

This chapter focuses on three of these country groupings and their respective agreements. It begins by examining the EEA in terms of transforming the

EC–EFTA relationship from potential rivalry to ever closer partnership and of its subsequent slide into relative obscurity. Second, as a complement to the investigation in Chapter Six of EU–CEEC security relations, the economic aspects of the Europe Agreements are examined. Finally, the southern dimension, often overshadowed throughout the 1990s by the momentous events in, and challenges of, Central and Eastern Europe, is assessed in the context of the so-called Euro-Med Agreement.

The European Economic Area

The EEA, the virtual extension of the EU's SEM to the members of EFTA, is easily the closest economic association the Union has with any third country. In many ways, however, it also represents the one formal partnership in which the EU may have become the least interested. Explanations of this apparent contradiction lie in the complex history of relations between the countries involved and in post-Cold War developments.

The EEA is the latest stage in a long-standing process of collaboration between the ECs and EFTA – a free trade arrangement initiated by Britain in 1959. The UK, which originally had been party to the negotiations on plans for further European integration, left these talks in November 1955 when it became clear that the existing ECSC members wanted to move far beyond the British idea of a mere free trade area and establish instead not only a customs union but eventually even a common market.[5] Britain thus pursued its plans for a FTA with other partners and found Austria, Denmark, Norway, Portugal, Sweden and Switzerland interested. These seven countries subsequently signed the Stockholm Agreement and therewith created the European Free Trade Association. Subsequently, in 1961, a wide-ranging trade agreement was signed with Finland which in effect brought the country into the Association,[6] and in March 1970 Iceland was also admitted as a full member.[7]

At first glance EFTA looks like an arrangement to rival the ECs, which for some countries was initially part of its attraction. However, the location, trade patterns and diversity of EFTA members put them in an inferior position from the onset. Their geographical dispersion was a major handicap for the FTA, especially at a time when transportation costs held greater salience than they do currently. Also, EFTA membership did not obviate the need of member states to negotiate free trade arrangements with the ECs – and when they did so it was from a relatively weak position. The loose association between EFTA members meant that they negotiated with the ECs on an individual basis whilst the latter negotiated as a group. Moreover, that EEC integration outperformed EFTA in its early years suggested that the EFTA countries needed the ECs more than vice versa.

Not surprisingly, some EFTA countries were led to reconsider their position on membership by the combination of the ECs' economic achievement and the limited influence they gained *vis-à-vis* the Communities through mere association. As early as 1960 the British government had taken note of the perceptible first economic accomplishments of the EEC, whilst at the same time realising the limited potential of EFTA in the absence of a joint FTA with the Communities. In August 1961, the UK consequently applied to join the Communities in order to partake of the economic prosperity that the integration process had already brought (and promised to continue to bring) with it, and also to enable it to influence the future of the ECs, which could best be done from the inside. It was, however, exactly this last point which caused the French President Charles de Gaulle to veto British membership. He feared the implications of Britain's relationship with the US and that, once a member, the UK would try to dilute most of the initiatives towards 'ever closer union', in particular the envisaged CAP – a policy especially dear to the French.[8]

So, during the 1960s, whilst the ECs were busy integrating into a customs union and apparently unwilling to accept new members – at least for the time being – EFTA made steady progress on its programme of establishing a FTA in non-agricultural products, mainly industrial goods. This FTA was largely complete by the end of 1966. However, to the geographically dispersed EFTA countries, free trade only really made economic sense if it were extended also to include the ECs. After all, many of the Association's members had more intense economic relations with ECs countries than they had with fellow EFTA states.[9] Consequently they negotiated bilateral free trade agreements with the Communities, which came into force on 1 January 1973. Some EFTA states went even further: Britain, Denmark and Ireland became full ECs members that same day.[10] This had become possible following de Gaulle's departure from office, which removed the opposition to the widening of the ECs at Community level.

All this means that at the beginning of the year 1973 the foundations had been laid for a sixteen-country free trade area in industrial goods and some processed agricultural products in Europe. By 1977, tariff and import duties had virtually disappeared between the ECs and the remaining seven EFTA countries.[11] Although widely regarded as a success, the scope of the joint FTA was nevertheless quite limited, and by the early 1980s both parties were ready to expand their relationship.[12] In 1984 the two organisations published a paper in which they committed themselves to intensifying their co-operation, with the eventual aim of creating a European economic space. What this meant was nothing less than extending the envisaged Single European Market programme to the members of EFTA.

Although both sides were heavily interested in this initiative, it brought a number of concerns. Many of the EFTA states found themselves in a situation similar to that they had faced some twenty years previously: remain outside the ECs but accept the deal on the conditions set by it, or seek membership in order to have a say in shaping its future. However, again, the Communities decided for them: they wanted to get the SEM established before accepting additional members. Besides, with the accession of Greece, Spain and Portugal (another EFTA defector), there were already enough interests to be considered and potential disagreements to be reconciled. The project to establish a European economic space was consequently held on the backburner until the third enlargement had been dealt with, the SEA ratified and the SEM programme successfully launched.[13] In January 1989, the President of the European Commission, Jacques Delors, invited EFTA to negotiate with the ECs a new and more extensive partnership. A couple of months later the Association accepted the invitation and negotiations began. They turned out to be quite difficult.

The main problem was that the two parties went into the talks with rather divergent ideas over how to go about enlarging the Communities' SEM to include the members of EFTA. The ECs, on the one hand, were not prepared to accept any changes to their established body of law, the *acquis communautaire*; nor did they want to grant extensive exceptions and derogations tailored to the needs of specific EFTA countries. They were also opposed to having EFTA countries involved in the Communities' decision-making processes. EFTA, on the other hand, demanded a full say in the matters covered by the EEA and for the Communities to adjust to certain individual national needs. Ultimately, though, the Communities largely got their way, with EFTA granted only a marginal role in the decision-making process of the EEA.[14] This owed to the lack of structures and experience within EFTA to conduct multilateral negotiations and to the ECs' stronger position on account of their size, institutional structures and experience of multilateral dialogue.

The talks were further complicated and prolonged by the fact that EFTA itself had not been able to establish common positions on all the issues that needed to be resolved in order to bring about the EEA. This meant that additional, bilateral agreements on such topics as state monopolies and fish and related products had to be concluded.[15] And as if all this had not delayed the whole process long enough, in 1991 the European Court of Justice objected to the draft treaty because the envisaged EEA court would have superseded the ECJ. To make the latter acceptable to the Luxembourg Court, substantial changes would have had to be made to the Communities' founding treaties. This, however, was something that the ECs had already ruled out and so the agreement had to be revised in line with the Court's concerns.[16]

In May 1992 the way was finally open for the ECs and the remaining EFTA members – Austria, Finland, Iceland, Liechtenstein,[17] Norway, Sweden and Switzerland – to sign the EEA Agreement. The original idea had been that the joint common market would get under way on 1 January 1993, the same day as the official starting date of the SEM. But, in a referendum on the EEA in December 1992, the Swiss people voted against ratification of the Agreement,[18] which forced the renegotiation of certain parts of the legal text[19] and delayed its implementation for another year. From 1 January 1994 the EEA has generally extended the 'four freedoms' of the SEM – the free movement of goods, services, labour and capital – to the six associated EFTA states, thereby effectively opening the SEM to them. Goods are now sold and bought across borders without any customs procedures; people move, live and work in any of the EEA member states; large parts of the service sector, including transport, are open for intra-EEA competition; and capital restrictions have been removed. The EEA Agreement even included so-called 'horizontal measures', such as social policy, consumer protection and environmental provisions. Notably, though, the Agreement excludes the entire field of agriculture and therewith the ECs' CAP.[20]

A number of new institutions have been established as part of the EEA arrangement, of which the EEA Council is the most powerful. It consists of the members of the Council of the EU, members of the European Commission and one member of the government of each of the associated EFTA states. The Council's task is to give political impetus to the implementation of the Agreement and to lay down general guidelines for the EEA Joint Committee. This latter institution consists of representatives from the contracting partners,[21] who have to ensure the effective implementation and operation of the Agreement – in other words, this institution deals with the day-to-day decisions to be made in connection with the EEA.[22] In addition, two advisory bodies have been created at EEA level: a joint parliamentary committee and a consultative committee.[23]

EFTA, which prior to the negotiations to set up the EEA had not had an organisational structure, also set up a few institutions. The EFTA Surveillance Authority is responsible for the implementation of EEA decisions and the adherence to competition rules within the associated EFTA countries. In this respect, this Authority can be regarded as EFTA's counterpart to the EU's Commission. It consists of one member from each of the EFTA countries bar Switzerland. The EFTA Court fulfils a similar task to the ECJ by dealing with disputes over EEA provisions between the Surveillance Authority and the individual EFTA member. Finally, the EFTA Standing Committee is the place where the associated members meet to discuss and prepare themselves for meetings of the EEA's Joint Committee.[24]

What are the advantages and disadvantages of this enlarged common market for the EU and the associated countries? To the EFTA states, the EEA represents a major transition from being part of a FTA in non-agricultural goods to having access to large sectors of the economy of seventeen other European nations, including the right to live, learn and work there – inside the largest integrated economic area in the world. And they have achieved this without joining what in 1993 became the European Union. Having said this, the disadvantage of the EEA deal for the associated EFTA countries has been that they have had to accept large parts of the Union's *acquis* without having much influence over it. To some of them this amounted to a catch–22 situation: either they stayed outside the EU as an officially independent state but at the price of having little influence over substantial provisions governing their economies, or they gained such influence but at the cost of losing a degree of their national sovereignty. Because this dilemma had been clear already during the negotiations of the EEA Agreement, five of the EFTA countries had already sought membership of the ECs/EU. The Swiss application was suspended following the negative outcome of the EEA referendum there. But four other countries would have been accepted into the Union, had not a referendum in Norway also gone against closer links with the EU. So, on 1 January 1995, three EFTA states, Austria, Finland and Sweden, left that club and became members of the EU. Being inside, even if their relative position as one of, by now, fifteen members was limited, was preferable to staying outside and having only marginal influence on the legislation that affected substantial aspects of their economies.

The developments in connection with the EEA of the early to mid-1990s have had a fundamental influence on the way in which the EU assesses this joint common market. When plans for a European economic space were first debated, in the early 1980s, the ECs consisted of ten, later twelve, members and were only just beginning to develop the SEM initiative in response to the perceived productivity gap *vis-à-vis* the US and Japan. EFTA, with six comparatively highly developed and prosperous members, seemed an attractive partner in helping to boost the position of Europe in the world economy. Moreover, the ECs have always had an interest in EFTA – albeit more in some of its members than in others. Switzerland and Austria must be singled out in this context. Geographically sandwiched between Germany to the north, Italy to the south and France to the west, they represented a potential bridge between some of the ECs' largest national economies and were established trading partners of the Communities. Extending the single market to these countries was thus expected to further boost this relationship, with one of the most desired effects for the ECs being the opening of important transport links across the Alps.

This interest in EFTA continues, but the EEA, by far the closest economic relationship the EU keeps with any third country, has been sidelined by Switzerland's rejection of the EEA in 1992 and the accession to the EU of Austria, Finland and Sweden in 1995. The reason for this becomes obvious when trade patterns and volumes are considered. In 2001 EFTA as a whole accounted for 10.6 per cent of all EU exports and the same share of its imports.[25] However, of this Switzerland accounted for 7.5 per cent of the EU's export market and 5.8 per cent of all imports to the Union.[26] Given the relative insignificance of the EEA's remaining EFTA members and concomitant upheavals in post-Cold War Europe, it is not surprising that EU attention switched away from the EEA and towards Central and Eastern Europe.[27]

The Central and Eastern European Countries

Although in strictly geographic terms many a country could be put into a category labelled 'Central and Eastern Europe', within the context of the EU there are exactly ten of these, namely: Poland, Hungary, the Czech Republic, Slovakia, Slovenia, Romania, Bulgaria, and the three Baltic states – Estonia, Latvia and Lithuania. What these states have in common is not only a past under socialist or communist rule but also the desire to join the European Union. For eight of them this should become a reality in May 2004. The other two, Bulgaria and Romania, still have to wait for a concrete date to be set – currently widely expected to be in 2007.

For the ECs the CEECs became a top priority even as the momentous events of the years 1989–91 were still unfolding. No sooner had they established fledgling democracies and begun the transformation of their economies, than Poland, Hungary and Czechoslovakia, commonly known as the 'Visegrád three', made it clear that they wanted quick membership of the ECs. It would provide insurance against a possible resurgence of internal and external threats, such as the strengthening of reactionary forces at home or renewed imperialist ambitions in Moscow or Belgrade. The Communities reacted swiftly. As early as August 1990 they offered the Visegrád three a special form of association by way of so-called Europe Agreements.[28] The particularly noteworthy aspect of these associations was that they implied the prospect of ECs membership for the associated countries.[29]

Linking the CEECs to the ECs by way of association made sense for the Communities. To begin with, association positively and constructively addressed the wishes and concerns of the ten without the Communities having to accept them as full members too soon. This way the ECs won valuable time, not only to complete a number of projects already under way, most prominently the SEM and EMU, but also to reform their institutional structures and procedures, which had originally been designed for a membership of six and were widely expected to be unsuitable for a membership of more than twenty. Association also made economic sense, as it opened new markets and provided new opportunities for investment for the ECs. A similar assessment would have come from the CEECs. Association linked them to the Communities with the clear prospect of future membership and brought with it economic advantages, such as preferential entry conditions to many of the ECs markets.

Between 1991 and 1996 the ECs/EU signed Europe Agreements with all ten CEECs.[30] Like all association agreements they represent the legal basis for the bilateral relations between the ECs/EU and the associated countries and establish a number of joint institutions: an Association Council, an Association Committee and a Parliamentary Committee. The principal difference compared to the EEA Agreement was that instead of one 'communal' institutional structure there were individual bilateral institutions between the EU and each of the CEECs. Apart from this, the institutions set up under the Europe Agreements work very much like those of the EEA. The Council consists of national ministers from the EU and the associated country as well as representatives from the Commission. It meets at least once a year and has as its main task to supervise the implementation of the Agreement. It can take binding decisions and also serves as a forum to settle disputes between the contracting partners. The Association Committee, which is staffed with officials from all parties involved, assists the Association Council in that it carries out the day-to-day work. Finally, the Parliamentary Committee serves to bring some democratic legitimacy to the process, even though this body has a strictly advisory role.[31]

The Europe Agreements, like all other association agreements of the ECs, were first and foremost about economic co-operation and, more specifically, improved access to the markets of the EU for the associated countries. On the trade front, they foresaw the establishment of bilateral FTAs within ten years. Although market access for agricultural goods was improved, quotas still remained in place. With the exception of textiles and clothing, and the products falling under the mandate of the ECSC, all quantitative restrictions on the import of industrial goods to the ECs were removed immediately. Tariffs were reduced on both sides, with the ECs doing this within five years whilst the CEECs were given the full ten-year period to do so.[32]

Despite the fact that the Europe Agreements represented a definite step towards greater trade liberalisation, they nevertheless incurred heavy criticism on account of continued protectionism in 'sensitive' products. It was argued that the restrictions on steel, textiles and agricultural goods affected the very products in which the CEECs had a comparative advantage and therefore the most potential to export. In light of such criticism, the EU undertook unilateral action to improve the situation and therewith speed up the liberalisation process.[33] The result of all these measures was that trade between the ECs and the CEECs rapidly increased.[34] The non-trade provisions of the Europe Agreements called for the progressive approximation of CEECs legislation to EU norms, including the Union's rules on competition. They also covered regulations concerning the movement of workers, the right of establishment and trade in services, as well as on payments and the movement of capital. However impressive this may sound, given the sensitive nature of these areas, the liberalising effects were actually quite limited. Most of the rules aimed at improving the situation of CEECs workers already inside the EU rather than trying to establish new flows of people.[35]

Association agreements are, however, not just about economics. They also contain provisions on a political dialogue between the partners involved. And since the particular feature of the Europe Agreements was the prospect of ECs membership for the CEECs, this issue dominated the political dialogue between the partners. Whilst the associated countries kept pushing for progress in this field, opinions on the subject were rather mixed inside the ECs. Traditional integrationists, such as France, were wary of too early and substantial a widening of the Communities' membership for fear that this might slow down the integration process. For very much the same reason the more Eurosceptical members, like Britain, supported enlargement. But they also supported it for the economic potential it promised, which was why Germany and other countries geographically located close to the CEECs, such as Italy and Greece, but also Denmark and later Austria, Finland and Sweden, were largely in favour of having these countries join the Communities too. However, because of their geographical proximity to the associated countries, these member states were not unreservedly pro accession. Many feared, for example, being swamped with cheap labour and products from the east.

In order to end such debates and deal with the situation in a more product-
ive manner, the European Council, meeting in Copenhagen in June 1993,
decided to invite the CEECs to join the Union on the proviso of their fulfilling
three criteria. First, the country in question had to have 'stable institutions
guaranteeing democracy, the rule of law, human rights and respect for and protection of minorities'. Second, it had to prove 'the existence of a functioning
market economy as well as the capacity to cope with competitive pressure and
market forces within the Union'. And finally it needed to have 'the ability to
take on the obligations of membership including adherence to the aims of political, economic and monetary union'.[36] Of the three, the last criterion was in
many ways the most demanding, as it required of the applicants nothing less
than the acceptance of the entire *acquis communautaire* and the according
alterations of their national legislation in order to make them compatible with
ECs law.

This was a colossal task, and not just because the CEECs had to work their
way through over forty years of ECs legislation, including the enormously
complex provisions on the SEM. Converging with the ECs was also a structural, and hence economic and political challenge. The CEECs were much
poorer than the ECs, mustering in terms of per capita GDP figures only around
a third of the Communities' average. There were also huge differences between
the CEECs too. While Slovenia and the Czech Republic already had per capita
GDPs of over 50 per cent of the ECs' average, Latvia had a GDP per head of
population of less than a fifth of the Communities' average.[37] Another big
structural difference was that all of the CEECs had larger agricultural sectors
than the ECs/EU had on average. While only 2.4 per cent of overall EU GDP[38]
was produced in the agricultural sector in 1994, the figure for the ten CEECs
was 8.6 per cent, with Romania and Bulgaria having much higher such figures
at 20.5 per cent and 13.9 per cent respectively in 1995. Even more striking
were the discrepancies in 1995 between the EU and the CEECs in terms of the
number of people employed in the agricultural sector. Whereas on average only
5.3 per cent of all employed in the EU worked in agriculture, a striking 22.5 per
cent of workers in the CEECs were still employed in this sector. In Romania
more than a third of all employed worked on the land (34.4 per cent), and
in the most populous member of the CEECs, Poland, some 26.9 per cent
did so.[39]

All this meant that the ten applicants needed a substantial transition period,
which suited the ECs for they needed internal reform if eastern enlargement
were not to end in disaster. Apart from a rigorous overhaul of institutions
and/or the way in which decisions were arrived at, reforms to the costliest
of the ECs' policies, i.e. CAP and Structural Policy, appeared overdue too –
especially in light of the serious structural differences between existing and
future members of the Communities. For the time being, however, the agenda
of the ECs was already quite packed. Following the eventual ratification of the
Maastricht Treaty in November 1993, EMU was the big issue that the existing
members wanted to complete before seriously thinking about admitting new
members, who would have been unlikely to qualify for this ambitious project

in any case. Besides, enlargement to Austria, Finland and Sweden was already in the pipeline. With fifteen members from 1995, the EU realised that institutional reform had become inevitable if the accession of up to thirteen more countries (Malta, Cyprus and Turkey were also waiting to be let in) was not to render it totally ineffective. The Commission consequently developed Agenda 2000, and an IGC on institutional reform in 1996 resulted in the 1997 Amsterdam Treaty. Although this produced some reforms, there proved to be insufficient political will to drive through the major institutional overhaul that many believed to be both long overdue and essential in view of impending further enlargement.

Meanwhile, the CEECs were making steady progress in their efforts to meet the Copenhagen criteria. This was all the more difficult as they were aiming at a moving target, for the EU continued its integration process unabated. However, by 1997 the time had arrived to give at least some of them a concrete perspective. Upon recommendations by the Commission in December 1997, the Council decided to start firm accession negotiations with five of the CEECs. In March 1998 talks began with Poland, Hungary, the Czech Republic (the larger of the two successor states of the Czech and Slovakian federation that split in 1993), Slovenia and Estonia – the frontrunners in the group of ten – and also with the Mediterranean island of Cyprus.[40] Splitting the CEECs into two groups was not uncontroversial. On the one hand, it clearly looked as if the EU favoured certain of its eastern neighbours over others. On the other hand, keeping them all together in one batch would have meant progress at the speed of the slowest of them. Since this was politically even less desirable, a decision was needed about who was to belong in the one group or the other. There was no doubt that Poland, Hungary and the Czech Republic would be among the frontrunners. Slovakia, the other Visegrád country, was not added due to serious doubts over its transition to democracy and the stability of its institutions.[41] Less obvious was why Estonia and Slovenia were chosen to join the three aforementioned CEECs in accession talks with the EU. This decision was highly political. Many of the CEECs have EU members acting as advocates for them. The Baltic states were supported by the Scandinavian members of the EU, Slovenia by its neighbour Austria, and Romania by France. Whilst Slovenia could prove relatively easily that it had stable democratic institutions, a largely functioning market economy and not insurmountable obstacles to adopting the Union's *acquis*, Romania clearly failed the last two criteria. As for Estonia, its institutions were in order and its economy stronger than Romania's, even if vulnerable to competitive pressures.[42]

All of this notwithstanding, talks continued with all ten CEECs. The only difference was that the frontrunners were negotiated with bilaterally and much more concretely. The remaining five, meanwhile, kept negotiating with the Commission in a multilateral setting and in less detail. In a first progress report, in November 1998, the Commission noted some economic problems in Slovenia and the Czech Republic but highlighted the progress in Latvia and, to an extent also, in Lithuania and Slovakia. A year later, in its next progress report, the Commission came to the conclusion that the other five CEECs had made enough progress towards meeting the Copenhagen criteria to render the 'two group approach' unnecessary.[43] Following the Helsinki European Council in December 1999, bilateral talks with the remaining five CEEC applicants then started in February 2000.[44]

While the applicants were busy adapting to the EU's *acquis*, the Union undertook steps towards institutional and policy reform necessary to enable it to cope with up to twelve new members.[45] Particularly pressing was the CAP, because under the existing rules financing the policy would have virtually bankrupted the Union once the new members with their large agricultural sectors had joined. The Commission also considered other key issues, including the EC budget, structural and cohesion funding allocations and pre-accession aid for the CEECs. However, a special summit in Berlin in March 1999 watered down significantly proposals contained in Agenda 2000. Britain and Spain led a successful rearguard action in protecting their benefits under Regional Policy, and France blocked radical reform to the guaranteed payment system within CAP. That the European Council declared their decisions sufficient to allow the CEECs into the Union was met with considerable scepticism amongst commentators. Particularly suspect was the freezing of the ECs budgetary ceiling to 2006 on the basis of two dubious assumptions, namely economic growth of at least 2.5 per cent and the willingness of the new members to accept smaller transfers from the Union's budget than their 'older' counterparts.[46] To make matters worse, further institutional reform, developed through another IGC from February 2000[47] and concluded at the European Council meeting in Nice in December that same year, was again piecemeal. The Nice Treaty, which finally came into force in February 2003 following ratification problems in Ireland,[48] was marked by bitter exchanges over re-weighting of votes within the Council of Ministers, resistance to the extension of QMV into 'sensitive' areas and Britain's refusal to surrender its budgetary rebate. Again, it is doubtful whether the institutional changes under Nice are adequate to ensure the smooth functioning of the EU once ten new members will have joined in May 2004.[49]

In its 2002 Strategic Report, the European Commission recommended that all but two of the CEECs, plus Cyprus and Malta, should be accepted as new members in 2004. Romania and Bulgaria were given the prospect of membership by 2007 but excluded from the 2004 enlargement because they were simply too far behind in transforming their economies and integrating the *acquis*. The official invitation to join the EU was then announced at the European Council meeting in Copenhagen in December 2002. Following the assent by the European Parliament, the accession treaty between the ten applicants and the fifteen existing members was signed in a ceremony in Athens in April 2003. With the positive outcome for membership in a referendum in Latvia on 20 September 2003 the ratification process has ended in the applicant countries, and if no problems occur in the ratification process within the existing member states of the EU, the Union will have a membership of twenty-five from 1 May 2004.

'Eastern enlargement', as the process is widely called, has dominated ECs/EU affairs for over a decade. During that time it has moved from being a largely external policy affair, to a position where it gradually transcended the external/internal policy divide, until finally becoming a primarily 'internal' affair. Despite the scheduled macro-enlargement of 2004, this process remains far from complete. Romania and Bulgaria await a formal date for entry and the Balkan countries are queuing up for membership – as Croatia's 2003 membership application clearly shows. Moreover, eastern enlargement is a part of a wider EU neighbourhood strategy. Turkey's application for full membership remains to be dealt with[50] and the post-Soviet Union CIS will attract increasing attention as their so-called 'partnership agreements' (association agreements without the membership option) develop. Furthermore, as shall be seen in the following section, there is another group of countries seeking to regain the attention of EU member states and the decision-makers in Brussels: the Union's Mediterranean partners.

The 'Euro-Med' relationship

Before the momentous events of 1989, the Mediterranean arena enjoyed the ECs' undivided attention as far as Association Policy with its immediate neighbours was concerned. The relationship between the ECs and the Mediterranean region is almost as old as the Communities themselves. The first association agreements with countries located around the Mediterranean Sea were signed as early as 1962 and 1963. Unlike the connection between the ECs and EFTA, which was one of equal partners negotiating FTAs in industrial goods, the relationship between the Communities and their southern neighbours was asymmetric in terms of both wealth and structural development. Indeed, it is precisely this relative underdevelopment that made the Mediterranean neighbours eligible for the trade concessions and aid provisions of the Communities' Association Policy. The only other group of countries with which such agreements were originally signed were the ACP countries, discussed in Chapter Nine.

The Mediterranean partners comprise the countries in Northern Africa, the Middle East, the Balkans and a couple of island states in the middle of the Mediterranean Sea. The easiest way to group them is by the way in which they are linked to the EU, although even this is complicated by certain relationships having progressed differently from others. In a very general sense, the following countries and groups of countries can be identified: the three applicant countries, Cyprus, Malta and Turkey; the original Yugoslavia; Israel; the countries of the Maghreb (Algeria, Libya, Mauritania, Morocco and Tunisia); and the members of the Mashreq (Egypt, Jordan, the Lebanon and Syria). Another entity later entered the picture: the Palestinian Authority governing the West

Bank and the Gaza Strip. Greece, Spain and Portugal were also part of EC Mediterranean policy prior to their accession to full membership.

The ECs have tried to construct a Mediterranean policy since as early as 1957 but the developments have been 'sporadic, reactive rather than progressive'.[51] The first set of Mediterranean association agreements was signed with countries that aspired to joining the Communities. Greece concluded one with the ECs in 1962, and Turkey did the same the following year. That same year, 1963, Morocco and Tunisia approached the ECs for similar arrangements – but it took six more years before preferential trade agreements were signed with these two countries. Also in 1969 the EEC granted preferential access to Israeli and Spanish citrus fruit exports, which was followed the next year by more general preferential trade agreements between the two countries and the EEC. These two latter arrangements proved to be quite controversial, firstly because Spain was still a dictatorship, and secondly because granting preferential treatment to Israel was regarded as an affront to the Arab world.[52]

The European Communities responded to criticism by offering preferential trade agreements to the other Mediterranean applicants. This led to a proliferation of agreements – with Egypt, Lebanon, Jordan, Syria, Malta, Cyprus and Yugoslavia[53] – which had two principal effects. Firstly, it enhanced the role of the Mediterranean area as an important political and economic arena for the ECs. Secondly, it quickly highlighted negative side-effects of having concluded so many different arrangements because some partners secured more favourable conditions than others. Politically, this was of course not particularly adroit, and as a consequence the ECs decided to reorganise the approach towards their Mediterranean partners.

The so-called 'Global Mediterranean Policy' (GMP) was born at the Paris Summit of European Heads of State and Government in 1972 – the first ever European Council meeting and the same gathering at which the overall concept of European political co-operation was adopted. The GMP was guided by three main objectives: compliance with the rules of GATT; consistency among the various existing agreements; and non-discrimination towards neighbouring countries. This said, the GMP developed more as a reaction to events than as a positively inspired policy.[54] Negotiations under the auspices of the GMP began in 1974 and resulted in a series of new agreements. The first country with which such an agreement was established was Israel in 1975. Co-operation agreements with the three Maghreb countries of Algeria, Morocco and Tunisia followed in 1976. And a year later, the four Mashreq countries, Egypt, Jordan, Lebanon and Syria, also concluded co-operation agreements.[55]

The principal aim of the GMP had been to create a free trade area in industrial goods between the EEC and each of the partner countries by 1977, albeit one that excluded 'sensitive products' such as textiles and clothing. The EEC had also envisaged preferential treatment for 80 per cent of each Mediterranean country's agricultural exports, but this ran foul of the Community's CAP. As soon as the associated countries began to export too many agricultural goods to the Community, the EEC took unilateral action against the country in question, such as the imposition of quantitative restrictions – hardly the most co-operative gesture of 'good neighbourliness'.[56] All in all, the GMP did not substantially change the previous situation. Whilst the aid payments received as part of the deal by the Mediterranean partners were welcomed, the value of the trade preferences was disappointing. Most Mediterranean countries continued to import more from the EEC than they were able to export to it, which must be largely attributed to EEC protectionism on trade in agricultural goods and other sensitive products.[57] In addition, the accession of Greece, Spain and Portugal to the ECs had detrimental effects on the other Mediterranean countries. These states brought into the EEC customs union markets that formerly competed for access with the products of other Mediterranean countries, such as wine, olive oil and citrus fruits.[58] The North African countries were further disillusioned with plans by the ECs to restrict migrant workers' entry to the Community in the run-up to the creation of the single market.[59]

Towards the end of the 1980s, it became increasingly clear that the high aims of the GMP had not been achieved. Many of the Mediterranean partners had hoped for the agreements to lead to more of a political dialogue. Pressure consequently mounted on the Communities to review the GMP, which finally happened in 1989 and led to the so-called New Mediterranean Policy (NMP).[60] New protocols were signed in 1990 and 1991 that reflected the ECs' free market approach to economic development and support for IMF and World Bank policies. The NMP offered around ECU 4.4 billion in grants and loans over five years to eight Mediterranean countries. A little over half of the money was allocated to Morocco, Algeria and Tunisia. The funds were aimed at supporting a number of issues, such as structural adjustment, private investment, access to the European market and a strengthening of economic and political dialogue.

The NMP had objectives that were more coherent than those of its predecessor, and although it was overtly targeted at supporting economic reform, its political overtones were more pronounced. The resources dedicated to the NMP were also substantially greater than those provided under the GMP (2.7 times greater), albeit that strict controls on agriculture and textile exports strongly resembled the previous regime.[61] However, the NMP scarcely got under way before other developments, both within and outside the Communities, fundamentally altered the background against which it had to be set. The collapse of the Berlin Wall, and all the developments that came in its wake, initially made other issues appear more urgent, perhaps even more interesting. This changed very quickly, though, once the bloody conflicts in the former Yugoslavia[62] and rising tensions inside some of the other Mediterranean countries, especially Algeria, required the Communities to remain active in the Mediterranean arena. Internal developments also helped in this respect. The ratification of the Maastricht Treaty meant that the new EU gained authority in the fields of CFSP and JHA. The former was immediately tested, in particular over Yugoslavia, as seen in Chapter Six. The latter quickly began to address questions of migration, be it of war refugees from Bosnia, or political and economic refugees from countries such as Algeria or Morocco.[63] And in October 1994 the European Commission published a paper calling on the EU to develop a more ambitious and comprehensive policy towards relations with the Mediterranean countries.[64]

This initiative led to the first ever EU–Mediterranean summit, held in Barcelona in November 1995, at which the fifteen EU member states met with eleven Mediterranean countries and representatives of the Palestinian Governing Authority.[65] The principal objective of the Conference was to be the first step towards a Euro-Mediterranean partnership. Contrary to the early signs, which indicated huge differences between the positions of such participants as Syria, Israel, Turkey, Morocco and Spain, the Conference actually turned out to be a success. The consequent 'Barcelona Declaration' called for a regular political dialogue amongst the signatories, greater EU aid for the southern Mediterranean states (ECU 4.685 billion until the end of 1999), and the control of migration, crime and drugs. It also referred to nuclear non-proliferation, anti-terrorism and self-determination.[66] Arguably the most significant breakthrough though, at least in the medium term, was a plan for free trade in industrial products by the year 2010.[67]

Commentators from the southern European countries generally regarded the results achieved at the Barcelona conference as a success. In France and Spain, some even talked of a new era in history having begun. In the Mediterranean countries outside the European Union, however, disappointment quickly became the main tenor of comments, for it was widely suspected that free trade in industrial goods stood to benefit the EU more than the Mediterranean partners. Even worse was the realisation that the Barcelona deal neither opened the EU's agricultural market to their products nor contained any provisions on industrial development measures in the region.[68]

The Barcelona conference, just like all the previous attempts at co-operation between the ECs and their Mediterranean neighbours, was dominated by the demands and ideas of Community negotiators. The EU–Mediterranean relationship is asymmetric at the best of times, but on this occasion the hand of the Mediterranean countries was especially weak. They could count on little support from most northern EU member states, not least because these clearly prioritised the CEECs and eastern enlargement. This strengthened the hand of the EU's southern members in shaping the discussions. However, although these were traditionally the most vocal advocates of the EU paying more attention to its southern periphery and were primary movers behind the Barcelona process, they were equally determined to protect their economic interests. The Mediterranean countries therefore appear both to have had little choice but to agree to what was on offer and to have been somewhat 'betrayed' by their main champions within the EU. It is no coincidence that France and Spain were clearly most pleased by the outcome of the Barcelona Declaration. Their agricultural sectors would be unaffected whilst their most pressing concerns about increasing migration from the Northern African countries, terrorism and drug trafficking, were addressed.

Apart from annual follow-up meetings and a number of other, more sporadic contacts between the partners,[69] there have been three main developments in EU–Mediterranean relations since the conclusion of the Barcelona conference. The first of these was the joining of the Euro-Mediterranean Agreement of the Palestinian Authority in 1997, which reflected more EU concern about the Middle East peace process than it did its economic interests. Then, secondly, a new financial perspective came into force in 2000. In real terms this meant a slight increase in allocations to MEDA – the programme financing the Euro-Mediterranean Agreement – from €3.4 billion during the period 1995–99 to €5.4 billion for the period 2000–06.[70] The third development is the prospect of Libya joining the Agreement. Following the extradition of the two suspects in the Lockerbie air-crash investigation, the country was already allowed observer status at the 1999 Stuttgart Mediterranean Conference (one of the follow-ups to Barcelona).[71] Now that all UN sanctions against the country have been lifted, the way looks open for it to join the Euro-Mediterranean Agreement.[72]

The EU's relationship with its Mediterranean partners may not be headline-grabbing material but it is an important piece in the big jigsaw puzzle that is the Union's external relations. While the FTA between the EU and its remaining ten Mediterranean partners[73] will bring undoubted economic benefits, it is not intended to be an end in itself. Rather it is meant as a means to accelerate economic and social development in the partner countries, to improve the standard of living there, and to reduce the welfare gap between the Union and its Mediterranean partners.[74] If all this were to be realised, the Mediterranean countries would hopefully be more stable – economically, socially and polit-ically. Concomitantly, the EU would consolidate its economic interests and advance its politico-security agenda in terms of reducing economic refugees, terrorism and unrest on its doorsteps. This is clearly a prospect worth working towards – top of the priority list or not.

Conclusion

The EU is linked to all its neighbours in Europe and its periphery by way of association of one sort or another. Rather than simply being agreements on economic co-operation, they all have clear political dimensions too. As has been seen, though, the EU addresses different demands and requirements in a differentiated way. The EEA was originally meant to extend the 'four free-doms' across the Alps and into Scandinavia. When the Swiss people rejected the EEA and Austria, Sweden and Finland joined the EU itself, the whole pro-ject lost much of its appeal to the Union. The challenge in connection with the CEECs was to support their transition to democracy and the establishment of market economies there so that they would be peaceful and stable neighbours who, at the same time, promised enormous economic potential from which both sides stood to benefit. Rather than mere association of the traditional kind, meaning trade concessions and aid payments, the CEECs were satisfied with nothing less than the prospect of eventual EU membership.

By contrast, the Euro-Med Partnership is the one still based on a more traditional association deal. Even here, though, things have moved on from mere trade concessions and aid to a more structured approach envisaging one large FTA between the Mediterranean countries and the EU. In fact, this last point is actually the common denominator in the EEA, Europe and association agreements. In the early years of the ECs, association agreements were signed with individual countries on a case-by-case basis. Over time, countries were put into different groups, such as 'EFTA' or 'Mediterranean' and, later, 'CEECs'. For a while, this categorisation simply meant that the ECs would sign similar agreements with countries belonging to one and the same grouping. More recently, however, the ECs have encouraged members of respective groups to link themselves. EFTA remained a FTA until the EEA came into force. Since then, the three associated EFTA members have had a quasi-common market with one another as well. In a similar vein, the CEECs are not contractually linked to one another but will become so through EU membership.

Differential treatment by the EU of its neighbours is likely to continue. As seen in the previous chapter, the western Balkans countries are linked to the EU by way of so-called stabilisation and association agreements,[75] which contain a perspective for eventual membership. The CIS does not have this perspective and is linked instead to the Union by so-called partnership associations. Likewise, few Mediterranean partners can hope for full EU membership. Malta and Cyprus are notable exceptions, and the case of Turkey is still undecided. Nevertheless, EU Association Policy is developing widespread benefits for both the Union and the associated countries. Moreover, the EU seems increasingly determined to push the groupings to form FTAs amongst themselves, therewith continuing its recent policy of encouraging co-operation between the association partners as much as to link them to itself.[76] Were this successful then the EU might even establish a pan-European FTA (at least in industrial goods) that stretches into northern Africa and well into central Asia – a very ambitious project indeed.

Notes

1 These are designated by the EU as Albania, Bosnia and Herzegovina, Croatia, the Former Yugoslav Republic of Macedonia, and Serbia and Montenegro.

2 For further information on the links that currently exist between the EU and the CIS countries and the western Balkans, see http://europa.eu.int/comm/trade/issues/bilateral/regions/cis/index_en.htm; http://europa.eu.int/comm/external_relations/see/index.htm.

3 This should not be interpreted as meaning that no links between the two micro-states and the EU exist. Quite the opposite is the case: they are extremely closely integrated into the Union's economic system, including EMU – as shown by them issuing their own euro-coins. But this close relationship is provided by their historically close links with France and Italy respectively, which apparently make the need for contractual agreements with the ECs/EU redundant.

4 See http://europa.eu.int/comm/external_relations/andorra/intro/index.htm.

5 For more details on this, see Dinan, D. (1994) *Ever Closer Union? An Introduction to the European Community*, Basingstoke: Macmillan, p. 32.

6 The country formally joined EFTA in 1986, see Heidensohn, K. (1997) *Europe and World Trade*, London: Pinter, p. 88.

7 Bannock, G., Baxter, R.E. and Davis, E. (1987) *The Penguin Dictionary of Economics*, 4th edn, London: Penguin Books, p. 140.

8 For more information on the unsuccessful British application for ECs membership, see Dinan, *Ever Closer Union?*, p. 40.

9 This was the case in particular with the two Alpine members of EFTA, Austria and Switzerland, who, not least due to their geographic location, were strongly linked to the economies of the FRG, Italy and France.

10 Norway had also applied to join the Communities and been accepted, but its people rejected the idea in a referendum in 1972.

11 Heidensohn, *Europe and World Trade*, p. 88.

12 Nelsen, B.F. (2000) 'European Economic Area (EEA)' in *Encyclopedia of the European Union*, Dinan, D. (ed.), Basingstoke: Macmillan, p. 197.

13 See Dent, C.M. (1997) *The European Economy: The Global Context*, London: Routledge, p. 108.

14 Nelsen, 'European Economic Area (EEA)', p. 197.

15 For a full list of Protocols annexed to the EEA Agreement, see http://secretariat.efta.int/Web/EuropeanEconomicArea/EEAAgreement/EEAAgreementProtocols.

16 For more details on the history of the EEA, see Nelsen, 'European Economic Area (EEA)', p. 197.

17 Liechtenstein, although associated from the start through its customs union with Switzerland, had become a full member in 1991. See Heidensohn, *Europe and World Trade*, p. 88.

18 See http://europa.eu.int/comm/external_relations/eea/index.htm.

19 Including, in particular, how to allow Liechtenstein to become part of the EEA without having to sever its long-standing and close economic links with the Swiss Confederation.

20 For a much more comprehensive account, see Nelsen, 'European Economic Area (EEA)', p. 198.

21 Formally, the European Community and – until its expiry – the ECSC are/were also party to the EEA Agreement, see Preamble to the Agreement on the European Economic Area, http://secretariat.efta.int/Web/EuropeanEconomicArea/EEAAgreement/EEAAgreement.

22 For more details, see Articles 89–94 EEA Agreement, ibid.

23 Heidensohn, *Europe and World Trade*, p. 93.

24 For more detail and additional information on the institutions of EEA and EFTA, see ibid., p. 93.

25 EFTA, http://europa.eu.int/comm/trade/bilateral/data.htm.

26 Switzerland's importance is further substantiated when looking at FDI figures. In 2000, 9.8 per cent of all FDI inflows to the EU had their origin in Switzerland, which itself received 7.6 per cent of all FDI from the EU. In terms of FDI stocks by the year 2000, 14.9 per cent of all FDI inside the EU had come from Switzerland, and the country accounted for 6.6 per cent of all FDI by the EU. Respective figures for EFTA as a whole are only insignificantly higher. FDI figures from 'Switzerland' and 'EFTA' at http://europa.eu.int/comm/trade/bilateral/data.htm.

27 Of the three remaining EFTA members of the EEA Liechtenstein is tiny with less than 34,000 inhabitants, and Iceland, although considerably larger with a population of around 290,000, still only accounted for 0.01 per cent of all EU exports and 0.03 per cent of all imports to the EU in the year 2000. Norway was the EU's eighth most important export market, with a share of 2.7 per cent, and its sixth most important import market, with 4.4 per cent of the total in 2001. See http://europa.eu.int/comm/external_relations/lichtenstein/intro/index.htm; Iceland, http://europa.eu.int/comm/trade/bilateral/data.htm; Norway, ibid.

28 Dinan, *Ever Closer Union?*, pp. 477–8.

29 Weidenfeld, W. and Wessels, W. (eds) (2002) *Europa von A bis Z*, 8th edn, Bonn: Bundeszentrale für politische Bildung, p. 393.

30 December 1991: Poland, Hungary and Czechoslovakia (but the latter was never enacted due to the country's break-up); February 1993: Romania; March 1993: Bulgaria; October 1993: Czech Republic and Slovakia; June 1995: Estonia, Latvia, Lithuania; June 1996: Slovenia. See: Dinan, D. (2000) 'Europe Agreements' in *Encyclopedia of the European Union*, Dinan (ed.), p. 176.

31 Sedelmeier, U. and Wallace, H. (2000) 'Eastern Enlargement: Strategy or Second Thoughts?' in *Policy-Making in the European Union*, Wallace, H. and Wallace, W. (eds), 4th edn, Oxford: Oxford University Press, p. 437.

32 For a more detailed description, see ibid., pp. 436–7.

33 Grabbe, H. and Hughes, K. (1998) *Enlarging the EU Eastwards*, London: Pinter, p. 32.

34 Trade between the ECs of twelve members and the six original CEECs (CEE6), the Visegrád four (after the split between the Czech and Slovak Republics) plus Romania and Bulgaria (the Baltic states, as parts of the former Soviet Union, and Slovenia as a former Yugoslav republic were added later) grew tremendously during the early 1990s, with a 47 per cent jump of exports to the CEE6 and an increase of 30 per cent in the imports from there in 1990, and respective figures of 16 per cent each for 1991, and 28 per cent and 22 per cent for 1992. See: ibid., p. 12. Growth rates remained impressive. So, for instance, between 1993 and 2001, trade between the EU and Poland, the largest of the CEECs, increased more than three-fold. During the same period, trade with the Czech Republic, the second largest of the EU's trading partners inside the CEECs, even grew four-fold. The largest increases in trade between the EU and individual CEECs between 1993 and 2001 were a

ten-fold jump in imports from Estonia, and a multiplication of exports to Lithuania by more than six. The lowest growth rates were with Slovenia, even though the trade with this former Yugoslavian republic still doubled during this period. This can be explained by the different history of this country and the already more open economy of the former Yugoslavia, compared to the countries formerly under the influence of the Soviet Union. Respective figures can be found at http://europa.eu.int/comm/trade/bilateral/data.htm.

35 Van Oudenaren, J. (2000) 'Central and Eastern European States (CEES)' in *Encyclopedia of the European Union*, Dinan (ed.), p. 37.

36 'The European Union and the World', www.delguy.cec.eu.int/en/eu_global_player/3.htm.

37 Figures from 1995, based on the EU of fifteen member states. Source: Mayhew, A. (1998) *Recreating Europe*, Cambridge: Cambridge University Press, n.p.

38 Calculations include Austria, Finland and Sweden.

39 Grabbe and Hughes, *Enlarging the EU Eastwards*, p. 97.

40 Van Oudenaren, 'Central and Eastern European States (CEES)', p. 39.

41 The man mostly held responsible for Slovakia's lack of progress in this field is former Prime Minister Vladimir Meciar. See Synovitz, R. (1999) 'Slovakia: Economic Reforms Necessary For EU Membership Talks', http://www.rferl.org/nca/features/1999/06/F.RU.990604115313.html.

42 Many observers have stated that another reason for accepting more countries than Poland, Hungary and the Czech Republic as frontrunners concerned the limited NATO enlargement in 1999. See Chapter Six for details.

43 'Composite Paper: Reports on Progress Towards Accession by Each of the Candidate Countries', p. 39. See http://europa.eu.int/comm/enlargement/report_10_99/pdf/en/composite_en.pdf.

44 Jones, R.A. (2001) *The Politics and Economics of the European Union: An Introductory Text*, 2nd edn, Cheltenham: Edward Elgar, p. 472.

45 Next to the CEECs, the EU was also negotiating accession with Cyprus and Malta. Turkey, although officially granted applicant status at the 1999 Helsinki Summit, had not advanced quite that far yet.

46 See, for instance, Sedelmeier, U. and Wallace, H. (2000) 'Eastern Enlargement: Strategy or Second Thoughts?' in *Policy-Making in the European Union*, Wallace and Wallace (eds), p. 453.

47 'Presidency Conclusions Helsinki European Council 10 and 11 December 1999', http://europa.eu.int/rapid/start/cgi/guesten.ksh?p_action.gettxt=gt&doc=DOC/99/16|0|RAPID&lg=EN.

48 See http://europa.eu.int/abc/treaties_en.htm.

49 See, for instance, 'Nice Treaty' at http://news.bbc.co.uk/2/hi/in_depth/europe/euro-glossary/1230330.stm.

50 For details on the ECs'/EU's enlargements, see 'Enlargement of the European Union', http://www.wikipedia.org/wiki/Enlargement_of_the_European_Union.

51 Lister, M. (1997) *The European Union and the South*, London: Routledge, p. 3.

52 Ibid., p. 84.

53 Ibid.

54 Ibid.

55 Dent, *The European Economy*, pp. 126–7.

56 See Lister, *The European Union and the South*, p. 85.

57 Ibid., pp. 85–6.

58 See Pelkmans, J. (1997) *European Integration: Methods and Economic Analysis*, Harlow: Longman, p. 320; also Bretherton, C. and Vogler, J. (1999) *The European Union as a Global Actor*, London: Routledge, p. 154.

59 Lister, *The European Union and the South*, p. 86.

60 Dent, *The European Economy*, p. 130.

61 Lister, *The European Union and the South*, pp. 87–8.

62 Yugoslavia had, of course, been one of the EEC's Mediterranean partners. The latest trade agreement with the Socialist Federal Republic of Yugoslavia had come into force in 1983. Under the agreement, most Yugoslavian industrial products entered the Community free of customs duties, quantitative restrictions, or measures having equivalent effect – even though many were subject to import ceilings. Yugoslavia itself was obliged to grant the Community most-favoured nation status in trade. The agreement extended to co-operation in the fields of industrial co-operation, energy, transport, tourism, environment, and fishing. When civil war broke out in Yugoslavia, the commercial preferences were first suspended, and then completely cancelled in November 1991.

63 Rhein, E. (2002) 'Die Europäische Union und der Mittelmeerraum' in *Europa-Handbuch*, Weidenfeld, W. and Wessels, W. (eds), Bonn: Bundeszentrale für politische Bildung, p. 702.

64 Dent, *The European Economy*, p. 130.

65 As a leading force in the Middle East peace process, the US attended as an observer.

66 Lister, *The European Union and the South*, pp. 88–9.

67 Rhein, 'Die Europäische Union und der Mittelmeerraum', pp. 703–4.

68 Lister, *The European Union and the South*, p. 89.

69 Behrendt, S. and Neugart, F. (2002) 'Mittelmeerpolitik' in *Europa von A bis Z*, Weidenfeld and Wessels (eds), p. 307.

70 http://europa.eu.int/comm/external_relations/euromed/meda.htm#2.

71 http://europa.eu.int/comm/external_relations/euromed/#Libya.

72 See, for instance, 'U.N. Lifts Sanctions On Libya', 12 September 2003, http://www.cbsnews.com/stories/2003/09/01/attack/main571001.shtml.

73 Algeria, Egypt, Israel, Jordan, Lebanon, Morocco, the Palestinian Authority, Syria, Tunisia and Turkey, plus perhaps Libya.

74 Rhein, 'Die Europäische Union und der Mittelmeerraum', p. 708.

75 http://europa.eu.int/comm/external_relations/see/news/ip03_860.htm.

76 Lippert, B. (2002) 'Mittel- und Osteuropa / Südosteuropa / Neue Unabhängige Staaten' in *Europa von A bis Z*, Weidenfeld and Wessels (eds), pp. 299–305.

The EU and global security

In March 1991 Commission President Jacques Delors urged that the EC look beyond the security horizons of the new Europe and recognise that naked ambition, national uprising, underdevelopment and WMD proliferation presented global challenges that needed to be met if potentially dangerous situations, destabilisation and conflict were to be countered.[1] Twelve years later, and set against the chastening background of EU disarray over US-led pre-emptive military intervention in Iraq, Javier Solana published the outline of what at the December 2003 European Council Summit in Brussels should become the EU's first ever Global Security Strategy.[2] According to Solana, in an era of globalisation the EU faces three principal threats: international terrorism, WMD proliferation and failed states. To address these the EU should exercise its particular ability to contribute to security and stability in its immediate neighbourhood, help construct an international order based on effective multilateralism and further develop the capability, coherence and will to act in pursuit of its strategic objectives.[3]

No one chapter in a book can hope to capture the rich tapestry of EU security interests and programmes beyond the Euro-Atlantic area. Instead, this chapter addresses three key themes developed in Solana's global EU security vision within a Eurasian context. First, it examines the EU's security relationship with Russia as a vital element in the declared objective of promoting 'a ring of well-governed countries to the East of the European Union and on the borders of the Mediterranean'.[4] Second, in line with the emphasis on building key strategic partnerships and integrating countries into the international community, it examines the EU's security relationship with China (PRC), Asia's rising regional power and leading example of the marriage between market economy and communist leadership. Finally, the issue of the EU and failed states is considered in the context of North Korea (DPRK), which President George W. Bush identified within his 'axis of evil' and Solana's Security Paper cited as a danger to regional security and WMD non-proliferation.[5] Afghanistan and Iraq may have dominated post-September 11 headlines, but a nuclear-capable DPRK poses a security challenge of a different order.

Engaging the Bear – EU–Russia security relations

The call in Solana's Security Paper for the development of a strategic partnership with Russia was new only insofar as it placed it within the broader objective of extending the zone of security around Europe. The EU had previously acknowledged repeatedly, such as in its Common Strategy on Russia in 1999, the critical importance to European security of EU–Russia co-operation and of Russia's development as a stable, democratic and prosperous country.[6] Exactly what claim Russia has to such security significance has traditionally been ascribed to three factors, namely the atom, the veto and its location.[7] For the EU, Russia's UN Security Council membership, regional influence and dual status as a leading Eurasian state and bridge between Europe and Asia make it an attractive potential partner in conflict prevention and crisis management, especially in areas adjacent to Russia, in the Balkans and the Middle East.[8] This EU aspiration is encouraged by its often being closer to Moscow's position than Washington's on issues such as Iraq, sanctions policy toward Cuba, US NMD, Iran and the Arab–Israeli conflict. Russia's influence and sensitivity to interference in the CIS also makes essential its co-operation in addressing so-called frozen conflicts such as Abkhazia, Nagorno-Karabakh, Ossetia and Transdniestria.[9]

EU enlargement accorded Russia's geo-strategic location added salience in European security matters. First, lengthening direct EU–Russia borders raised security spill-over concerns. For instance, the Commission cites soft security threats emanating from Russia as including nuclear safety, organised crime, illegal immigration and environmental pollution.[10] Second, EU enlargement cuts across established Russian interests and privileges in CEECs and encroaches upon the Russian diaspora. Some 15–20 million Russians reside outside Russia in the CIS. Kaliningrad has become a sensitive test-case for EU–Russian co-operation as Lithuanian and Polish accession in 2004 leaves the 900,000-strong exclave completely surrounded by EU territory.[11] Third, the 2004 enlargement creates a sensitive eastern zone between the EU and Russia of Moldova, Ukraine and Belarus. These countries are important to Russia, strategically, economically and politically. Moreover, Moldova experiences internal conflict over the Transdniestria issue, Belarus is potentially engaged in some form of 'union' with Russia, and the Ukraine remains stranded between its engagement of the EU and NATO[12] and its ties with Russia, especially through its energy dependence.

As for the atom, Russia's nuclear power status warrants attention on counts both of WMD non-proliferation and of environmental security. For example, although Russia notes in its Foreign Policy Concept the importance of persuading India and Pakistan to accede to the CTBT and the Treaty on the Non-proliferation of Nuclear Weapons (NPT),[13] it is also a supplier of nuclear technology and products. Contracts include those with India for the Tamil Nadu nuclear reactor and those with Iran for the nuclear plant at Bushehr. Likewise, there is a need to combat the smuggling of nuclear materials from

Russia, to safeguard and progressively destroy WMD stockpiles and to guard against the dangerous decaying legacies of the Soviet Empire. Russia's ageing nuclear reactors potentially risk another Chernobyl and its economic weakness means an inability either to maintain satisfactorily or to decommission its nuclear-powered fleet and WMD arsenal. Furthermore, owing to systematic long-term environmental neglect and its status as a leading energy producer, Russia is both a source of serious environmental degradation and pollution and a potentially key partner in regional and global environmental management. For instance, the Kyoto Protocol cannot become effective and binding until ratified by at least 55 countries representing 55 per cent of the developed countries' greenhouse gas emissions as calculated in 1990. At the time of writing, 104 countries representing more than two-thirds of the world population have done so, but cumulatively they accounted for 43.9 per cent of 1990 emissions. Russia's non-ratification thus far gives it a pivotal position, for it accounted for 17.4 per cent of 1990 emissions.

Russia's attraction and importance to the EU as a security partner have been accentuated by three more recent factors: growing *de facto* EU responsibility for dealing with Russia; the war on terrorism; and Russia's significance in the promotion of effective multilateralism, especially in light of Moscow's opposition to the Bush administration's unilateralism. The former factor stems not only from EU enlargement but also from a relative downgrading of US focus on Russia – a process traceable back to Clinton's quiet shelving of 'strategic partnership' in favour of a less ambitious normalisation of US–Russian relations. Aside from anti-terrorism, WMD and NATO, Washington's reasons to maintain a sustained engagement of Moscow are steadily declining, so much so that it has been suggested that '[f]ar from having the *wrong* policy toward Russia, the United States may cease to have one at all'.[14] As for a EU–Russia partnership in the promotion of multilateralism, there is a strong coincidence of interest between the EU's culture of multilateralism and Russia's increasingly pragmatic adjustment to an evolving post-imperial role. Russia's Foreign Policy Concept sees as a challenge and a threat the emergence of a unipolar structure and in its 'World Concept for the 21st Century' cites the importance of renouncing claims to global dominance and of the development of a multipolar world order.[15] Herein Russia has further argued that '[m]ultipolarity objectively calls for shifting emphases to multilateral security fora'[16] and stressed the importance of the 'development and strengthening of strategic partnership between Russia and the EU'.[17]

Finally, the international response to September 11 has made Russia's co-operation more essential across a range of counter-terrorism activities. These include providing bases for military action, specialist military and intelligence contributions, legal co-operation and enforcement, and financial controls. Indeed, the OECD Financial Action Task Force on Money Laundering placed Russia on the list of non-co-operating countries in 2000 and kept it there until June 2003.[18] From the EU perspective, Putin's generally strong support for most aspects of post-September 11 counter-terrorism has been doubly propitious. First, as the Commission noted, it has provided an opportunity for enhanced

EU–Russia co-operation on issues such as money laundering.[19] Second, it has led to a substantial improvement in the tone and reality of US–Russia and NATO–Russia relations.[20] For instance, in January 2003 the Bush administration authorised $450 million within the Co-operative Threat Reduction (Nunn-Lugar) Program to facilitate work on a chemical weapons destruction facility at Shchuch'ye in Russia.[21] Similarly, Russian reaction to NATO's announcement at its November 2002 Prague Summit of another round of enlargement was 'almost anti-climactic'.[22] This upturn in US–Russia relations eases the fears of some EU member states of EU–Russia engagement cutting across the EU–US relationship.

In pursuing its security relations with Russia, the EU has adopted a largely incremental and long-term approach that combines multi-level, functional and institutional dimensions. The keystone of EU–Russia co-operation is the 1994 Partnership and Co-operation Agreement (PCA),[23] which provided for political dialogue on matters of common concern that included security issues. However, economic concerns were preponderant[24] and actual security ties were stimulated somewhat later by prospective eastern enlargement and the EU's 1999 Common Strategy on Russia.[25] That same year Russia responded with its Medium-term Strategy for Development of Relations between the Russian Federation and the European Union, and President Putin subsequently offered the prospect of prac-tical steps to 'create new, higher forms, of co-operation between Russia and the EU'.[26]

The EU and Russia have consequently developed incrementally dense and ever-expanding networks for security dialogue and consultation. These were initially most prominent within multilateral fora such as the Contact Group and the IMF, which granted Moscow its largest ever financial assistance package of $17.1 billion following Russian economic collapse in 1998. From the late 1990s, however, bilateral security networks have developed rapidly to include six-monthly EU–Russia summits, annual co-operation councils, co-operation committees and numerous sub-committees.[27] The EU–Russia Summit in October 2000 in Paris announced the opening of consultations on security and defence matters and of bilateral co-operation in crisis management. Russia subsequently became the first non-EU state to have regular monthly meetings with the EU's Political and Security Committee. Prompted by the development of CESDP, it was decided at the May 2002 EU–Russia Summit in Moscow that steps would be taken to establish military contacts and the development of a common approach to crisis management. And at the EU–Russia Summit in May 2003 it was agreed to strengthen ties by upgrading the Co-operation Council to the status of a Permanent Partnership Council. This mirrored the consolidation of NATO–Russia ties through the establishment in 2002 of the NATO–Russia Council, with the so-called 'NATO at 20' agreement giving Russia equal status in discussions of issues relating to terrorism, WMD, rescue operations and so forth.[28]

The expanding EU–Russia security dialogue reflects mutual sensitivity towards the implications of EU enlargement and broad commonality in their respective security agendas. Both the EU's Common Strategy on Russia and Russia's Medium-term Strategy for Development of Relations between the Russian Federation and the European Union highlight issues such as fighting international terrorism, drug and human trafficking, transnational organised crime, money laundering, nuclear safety and WMD non-proliferation.[29] The enhanced dialogue reflects, too, the range of EU activities in helping to combat these mutual security problems. ECHO has channelled humanitarian aid since the mid–1990s into the Caucasus, especially Chechnya, and emergency food aid was provided to Russia between March 1999 and April 2000 to alleviate the crisis caused by its economic collapse. The EU also runs good-governance programmes designed to encourage democratisation and the development of civil society grounded in the rule of law. These include the European Initiative for Democracy and Human Rights in Russia, which can finance human rights, democratisation and conflict prevention activities in partnership with NGOs and other international organisations. In addition, EU aid, particularly through the Technical Assistance to the Commonwealth of Independent States pro-gramme (TACIS), has exhibited a strong emphasis on nuclear safety and WMD non-proliferation. Between 1991 and 2003 the EU afforded Russia over €2 bil-lion in technical assistance through TACIS, and the 1999 programme annual report revealed that more had been devoted therein to nuclear safety and envir-onmental projects than to any other sector.[30] The priority areas within the 2000 TACIS Regulation again included the promotion of civil society, nuclear safety and environmental protection and envisaged multi-annual programming to 'ensure that it reflects wider policy issues, such as . . . foreign and security policy'.[31]

EU policies have been developed with Russia at the international, national and sub-national levels and include both own projects and those pursued in collaboration with other international actors. For example, on 17 December 1999 the EU agreed a CFSP joint action on a co-operation programme for non-proliferation and disarmament in the Russian Federation. This assists Russia to implement the Chemical Weapons Convention, which it signed in 1997 with a commitment to destroy a stockpile of 40,000 tons over ten years.[32] Also, on 27 June 2002 the G8 launched its Global Partnership Against the Spread of Weapons of Mass Destruction. It had a pledged budget line of $20 billion over ten years and was targeted first and foremost at helping Russia to dismantle WMD stockpiles.[33] And on 21 May 2003 an international agreement was reached on a Multilateral Nuclear Environmental Programme in Russia (MNEPR). An EC budget contribution of €40 million is designed to help clear up radioactive waste in north-west Russia and to facilitate co-operation regarding the safety of spent nuclear fuel, radioactive waste management and the decommissioning of nuclear submarines and icebreakers.[34] As for sub-national schemes, the most developed is the EU's Northern Dimension project which forms part of a proximity policy that has slowly integrated Russia into trans-border security governance and exported EU norms and notions of civil society to north-west Russia. The second Action Plan (2003–06) continues security themes such as environment issues, Kaliningrad, cross-border co-operation, the fight against organised crime and nuclear safety, with TACIS continuing to support on-site assistance to nuclear plants in the Leningrad region and in the Kola Peninsular.[35]

Just how effective EU policies have been in building a co-operative security relationship with Russia is difficult to assess with any certainty, particularly given the relatively fluid positions on both sides. Russia has to contend with multiple EU voices and frequent institutional and policy reforms/innovations. Conversely, the orientation of Russian foreign and security policy is far from uncontested and the processes of internal reform remain inconclusive. Nevertheless, there is much to be positive about. EU objectives of integrating Russia into multilateral fora and bilateral dialogue are well-developed. In addition to its established international memberships, Russia has joined the Council of Europe, IMF, G8, Contact Group and the Quartet on the Middle East. It has become involved in IFOR, KFOR and peacekeeping operations in the CIS in association with the OSCE, and is due to provide a contribution to the EU Police Mission in Bosnia and Herzegovina. Furthermore, extensive networks have been developed between the EU and Russia for security discussion, and Moscow has been both generally supportive of CESDP and keen to establish an input.[36]

Although EU measures lack the profile of bilateral US–Russia security co-operation, such as the Strategic Offensive Reductions Treaty which commits them to reduce by two-thirds their deployed long-range nuclear warheads by 2012, they have nevertheless played important roles in developing environmental and border security, nuclear safety, democratisation and WMD non-proliferation. In fact, the combination of functional, institutional and multilevel programmes has enabled the EU to be far more intrusive in Russian affairs than any other external actor.[37] At a base level, Russia's need of EU investment capital, management skills and technology, coupled with the EU's status as Russia's leading trade partner, has left Moscow little choice but to tolerate EU normative intrusion and to accept trade-offs to further its own interests. In 2000 the EU accounted for 25 per cent of Russian imports and 35 per cent of its exports and this is anticipated to increase after enlargement in 2004 to around 50 per cent of Russian trade turnover.[38] Together with Putin's recognition of the EU as a key strategic partner and pragmatic willingness to align with Euro-Atlantic structures, this has produced a more co-operative environment in recent times. It was consequently possible in May 2003, for instance, to expand plans unveiled at the EU–Russia Summit of May 2001 for a Common European Economic Space to include also 'a common space of freedom security and justice, a space of co-operation in the field of external security . . . [and] a space of research and education, including cultural aspects'.[39]

EU policies have carried added weight owing to the use of conditionality being underpinned by the asymmetric nature of the EU–Russia relationship, in terms both of economic power and of relative need.[40] The Commission has, for example, tied Russian ambitions to increase nuclear-generated electricity sales to the EU to consideration of progress on safety standards, including the decommissioning of older reactors.[41] Also, the EU has used targeted aid and conditionality to back its repeated pressure within the PCA for Russia to respect human rights, promote the development of media pluralism and ensure appropriate conduct in Chechnya. The PCA contains conditionality clauses linked to Russian commitment to democracy and respect for human rights and only came into operation in 1997 because the European Parliament suspended ratification in 1995 in protest against Russian human rights violations in Chechnya. Similarly, set against a background of renewed conflict in Chechnya, the EU Helsinki Summit decided in December 1999 to reduce TACIS aid to Russia and to redirect some allocated funds into democracy promotion programmes.[42]

Yet, despite all of this, EU policies and approaches have suffered limitations. Its Northern Dimension, for instance, lacks specific agreements and approved budget lines[43] and risks becoming lost amid a surfeit of Russia instruments.[44] This danger is accentuated by growing points of overlap with the US Northern European Initiative (NEI) and between EU–Russia and NATO–Russia co-operation, such as disarmament issues and programmes of technical assistance and nuclear and environmental safety.[45] More seriously, the scope for EU influence is limited, particularly with regard to domestic developments in Russia.[46] Although the 1999 EU Common Strategy on Russia specifically offers a strategic partnership 'based on shared democratic values',[47] how far that commonality extends is questionable. A case in point is EU democracy and good governance promotion. Some query whether Western concepts of law can be transplanted successfully into Russia[48] – and thus far Russia has not developed a political culture compatible with European standards.[49] It is also possible that the Putin regime is trying to modernise Russia on an authoritarian-technocratic basis in which Russian 'illiberal' or 'contained' democracy will remain at odds with European values.[50] Indeed, in December 2001 the Commission expressed concern about the lack of media pluralism, possible political intolerance and weak civil society, concluding that '[t]he actual respect of human rights principles in Russia continues to lag behind the country's formal commitments'.[51] That the EU–Russia Summit in November 2002 conspicuously failed to force the issue of Russian policy in Chechnya only underlined the EU's limited purchase over Moscow, especially given the latter's extra international leverage on account of its anti-terrorism assistance.[52]

These value differences extend into the international realm and suggest a degree of instrumentality and uncertainty about EU–Russia security relations. Whereas EU multilateralism is generally a reflection of its own values and embraces concepts such as humanitarian interventionism, Russia remains wedded to state sovereignty and tends to see multilateralism in terms of power-balancing rather than of transcending Westphalian structures. Russia's Foreign Policy Concept explicitly rejects humanitarian intervention.[53] Its Medium-term Strategy for Development of Relations between the Russian Federation and the European Union links the evolution of its position on the European defence identity and practical security co-operation to the possible 'counterbalance, inter alia, [of] the NATO-centrism in Europe'.[54] It also seems that, given that problems of inter-operability limit potential military benefits, CESDP is viewed in some Russian quarters in terms of political advantage *vis-à-vis* balancing NATO[55] or even of de-coupling the EURRF from NATO. Although there is increasing recognition that this is unlikely to happen, such aspirations are certainly in line with Russia's declared objective 'to ensure pan-European security by the Europeans themselves without both isolation of the United States and NATO and their dominance on the continent'.[56]

EU–Russian co-operation in promoting multilateralism is consequently far from assured. Russian opposition to military action in Bosnia, Kosovo and Iraq indicates that this is likely to be especially vulnerable in interventionist scenarios. This is, again, partly explicable in terms of value differences. Russia insists on a UN mandate for military intervention and on traditional concepts of international law regarding the inviolability of state sovereignty, albeit being prepared to capitalise on US precedents where it suits its interests.[57] Meantime the EU accepts notions of limited sovereignty and, while committed to the principles of the UN Charter, has reserved its right to act without a UN mandate in pursuit of the Petersberg tasks.[58] Russia's staunch defence of what it regards as its spheres of influence only adds to these problems. Its sensitivity was demonstrated during the Kosovo War by the dash by a Russian military unit from Bosnia to take control of Pristina airport before NATO could get there.[59] Moscow has ensured, too, that peacekeeping operations in the CIS are either wholly Russian or Russian-led and has vowed to oppose possible EU attempts to hamper economic integration in the CIS, in particular through its maintaining 'special relations' with individual CIS countries to the detriment of Russian interests. It has even suggested that 'the development of partnership with the EU should contribute to consolidating Russia's role as a leading power in shaping up a new system of interstate political and economic relations in the CIS area'.[60] In this context Solana's recommendation in June 2003 that the EU should take a stronger interest in the problems of the southern Caucasus[61] is potentially highly sensitive.

EU–Russia security dialogue is, it seems, open to charges of the 'triumph of process over policy'[62] and of being symptomatic of 'the deficit of common foreign policy within EU internal policy making'.[63] The EU approach to Russia in the first half of the 1990s at least was characterised by reactivism and incoherence.[64] It has subsequently been seen to have indulged its 'institutional fetishism' in building new constructs rather than substantive policy,[65] whilst concomitantly breaking rhetorical commitments not to draw new divisions across Europe.[66] Although Russia has traditionally been more sanguine about EU than NATO enlargement, it is understandably sensitive about Euro-Atlantic integration processes that it considers 'often pursued on a selective and limited basis'[67] and about the negative consequences of EU expansion, such as discriminatory visa and border regimes.[68] EU enlargement not only heightens the sense of Russian exclusion but also, together with NATO enlargement, has seemingly initiated an 'inexorable process' of separating Europe into 'insiders' and 'outsiders'.[69] Former Russian spheres of interest are absorbed into the EU and the increasing significance of JHA in EU policies towards Russia draws new dividing lines, especially with the erection of Schengen borders.[70] Moreover, the different instruments used towards, and importance attributed to, EU relationships with former communist countries further this impression of division. Commission officials are keen to argue that Russia has *de facto* become a privileged partner of the EU,[71] but the PCA is clearly less advantageous than the Europe Agreements. Coupled with the contrasting emphases of PHARE and TACIS, this reveals a differentiated approach that by the mid-1990s was seen to have established 'a new institutional demarcation' between former communist countries of Europe.[72] A similar hierarchy of EU concern may also be distinguished within evolving CESDP measures, where provisions for co-ordination are much more developed with EU candidate countries and non-EU NATO members than with Russia.

The real challenge is how to develop EU–Russia security relations in ways that minimise Russia's sense of exclusion and maximise co-operation in areas of mutual security interest. It is reasonable to criticise the relative lack of substantive policy emerging from the plethora of EU–Russia institutional contacts and networks. Yet this needs to be placed in context. It is only quite recently that either side began to pay attention to their security relationship, rather than their economic relationship. More significantly, ambivalence is evident in the approach of both sides. For Russia the EU is one key element in a multi-vector foreign and security policy that seeks also to exploit the advantages of its membership of leading multilateral fora, especially the UN Security Council, key bilateral relationships and Russia's status as a leading Eurasian state and the largest country of the CIS.[73] Russian rhetoric of multipolarity, with Russia as a distinct if enfeebled pole, has faded since the days of Prime Minister Primakov. In its stead there has evolved a pragmatic Russian alignment with Euro-Atlantic structures in the absence of rational alternatives.[74] However, that Yeltsin and Putin have steered Russia in a European direction[75] does not necessarily mean that Russia is resolved upon a pro-Western policy.[76] The 'liberal westernizers' who predominated in the government immediately after Russia became independent have faded[77] and Russia has sought to consolidate its Asian position through, for example, becoming a full ASEAN dialogue partner in July 1997 and joining the Asia-Pacific Co-operation Forum in 1998. Moreover, Russia's Foreign Policy Concept notes disillusion about initial post-Cold War hopes for Russia's international treatment and the need to develop relations with India and, especially, China.[78]

As for the EU, Russia is an important but difficult security partner. It is too big to integrate and too close to ignore. The commonality of values is limited and the objectives for co-operation often differ, despite common security interests. Moreover, their preferred European security architectures differ. Russia emphasises the UN and the OSCE where its influence is greatest, albeit Moscow has become less sanguine about the latter's potential following its impotence in

Kosovo. In contrast, the EU generally prioritises the transatlantic security relationship and the compatibility of NATO and the CESDP, albeit that some of
its member states differ in their emphases. This in turn introduces unacceptable
risks for the EU in being seen to overly develop its relationship with Moscow,
especially *vis-à-vis* the evolving CESDP – risks that are accentuated by uncertainty about the instrumentality or otherwise of Russia's Western orientation,
its openness to Western norms and the sustainability and direction of its internal reforms.[79] Indeed, at the May 2002 EU–Russia Summit External Relations
Commissioner Patten put the onus on Russia, linking security co-operation to
the question of just how 'European' Russia is willing to become.[80] The flip side,
of course, is how open to Russia does the EU wish to be, with some commentators detecting an anxiety to push Russia aside in a friendly way 'so that it does
not walk on the "European" lawn'.[81]

The EU and China

EU security interests in Asia were evident throughout the Cold War and subsequently expanded in line with the post-Cold War diversification of the security
agenda. That said, the development of a strategic EU role in, and contribution
to, Asian security lagged significantly behind acknowledged interests. Only in
1994 did the Commission's 'Towards a New Asia Strategy' set out potential
EU contributions to regional stability in terms of promoting democracy and
human rights, regional conflict resolution, non-proliferation and arms control.[82] Seven years later, the Commission went further in its 'Europe and Asia:
A Strategic Framework for Enhanced Partnerships' by declaring a fundamental
EU objective as being to '[c]ontribute to peace and security in the region and
globally, through a broadening of our engagement with the region'.[83]

The EU approach to doing this has been to emphasise the importance of
regional co-operation structures such as ASEM, ASEAN, the ASEAN Regional
Forum and the South Asian Association for Regional Co-operation. Concomitantly, however, the cohesive weakness of such structures has encouraged the
EU to develop extensive bilateral relationships too.[84] Herein some Asian countries have greater salience in security terms than others, and in this respect it is
little surprise that Solana's Security Paper singled out China as a target for EU
strategic partnership. As the Commission noted, 'a country the size of China is
both part of the problem and the solution to all major issues of international
and regional concern'.[85] For example, China's rapid development and status as
the world's second largest energy consumer and third largest producer is of
major significance for air pollution, climate change and bio-diversity. China
also generates security problems associated with widespread poverty such
as organised crime, illegal immigration and trafficking. In 1998 China had an
estimated 130 million people living below the World Bank's poverty line and it

is thought that some 200,000 Chinese migrants are annually smuggled illegally by organised rings into various countries.[86] That destinations include EU member states was both highlighted in the June 2000 Dover tragedy, when fifty-eight Chinese would-be immigrants died, and reflected in the recommendation by the General Affairs Council in November 2002 that the EU should intensify relations with China with a view to concluding a readmission treaty.

Beyond the specifics there are, from the EU perspective, two critical security questions about China. First, as a rising regional power that has around 20 per cent of the global population, covers a land mass almost three times that of the EU and has enjoyed twenty years of an estimated 10 per cent annual economic growth,[87] how will China seek to exercise its growing influence? For instance, Beijing has developed improved relations with Russia and negotiated with the Central Asian republics a series of military confidence-building measures through the Shanghai Co-operation Organisation, which includes China, Russia, Kazakhstan, Kyrgyzstan, Tajikistan and Uzbekistan. Nevertheless, it still has unresolved border disputes with India, Russia, Tajikistan and over the Islands of Spratly, Senkaku and, most problematically, Taiwan. Growing Chinese pressure on the Malacca Straits has also prompted joint US–Indian naval patrols. Second, as a nuclear power, leading communist state and an established member of the UN Security Council, on what terms will China develop its engagement with the international community? Its conduct is liable to be a growing factor in the effectiveness or otherwise of EU preferences for multilateralism and will impinge directly not only on Asian security but on European interests as diverse as environmental security, WMD non-proliferation, trafficking in human beings, organised crime, money laundering and anti-terrorism. Moreover, China's established international relationships have a major bearing on some of Asia's most pressing and dangerous security issues. For example, Beijing has the closest relationship of any state with Kim Jong-il's unstable and nuclear-capable North Korean regime, especially since the collapse of the Soviet Union. Also, China and India are strategic competitors and Beijing has aligned itself with Pakistan ever since the 1962 Sino-Indian border war. This means that China could exert potentially constructive influence over a volatile Pakistan that might assist both international anti-terrorism and the calming of Indo-Pakistan tensions. It means too, however, that for over two decades China has been supporting Islamabad in ways that include the provision of nuclear materials and missiles. Pakistan's nuclear plants at Kahuta, Khushab and Chasma were all built with Chinese assistance. China has also provided not only enriched uranium and nuclear bombs but also delivery systems in the form of ready-to-launch M-9 (Ghaznavi/Hatf), M-11 (Shaheen), and a number of Dong Feng 21 (Ghauri) ballistic missiles.[88]

The EU's relationship with China is much longer established than that with Russia, dating back to the opening of diplomatic relations in 1975 in the wake of China's Cultural Revolution and the onset of its open-door policy. In 1978 a trade and co-operation agreement was signed, two years later China secured access to the EC's Generalised System of Preferences and in 1985 an augmented

Trade and Economic Co-operation Agreement was concluded. As these agreements indicate, for a long period EU interest was primarily economic and the
US dealt principally with Cold War security issues. After the Cold War, though,
and especially following the Commission's 'Towards a New Asia Strategy',
security issues were incrementally incorporated into EU–China dialogue.

The EU's constructive engagement of China on security issues combines a
range of activities that include multilateral and bilateral dialogue, development
aid, technical assistance, food aid, exchange schemes, and encouragement and
assistance in entering key multilateral fora. Ambitions for the bilateral EU–
China relationship were laid out in a Commission communication on 'Building
a Comprehensive Partnership with China', which was adopted on 25 March
1998. The Commission called for upgraded political dialogue, further integration of China into the world economy, raising the EU's profile in China, and
support for socio-economic reform in accordance with principles of sustainable development and the transition to a civil society based on the rule of
law and respect for human and minority rights. Moreover, priority areas for
security dialogue were listed as including enhanced co-operation to promote
further reconciliation between North and South Korea, clear demonstration
of EU determination to see a peaceful resolution of the Taiwan issue and the
identification of ways of promoting multilateral security dialogues for conflict
prevention in regional and international issues. The EU–China relationship
was further seen as instrumental in supporting multilateral efforts to limit
arms proliferation and exports and to encourage disarmament – including
the Missile Technology Control Regime code of conduct, CTBT, support for
the Ottawa process on landmines and the commencement of negotiations on
a Fissile Material Cut-Off Treaty.[89]

According to the Commission, the EU has progressively developed 'a sophist-
icated multi-faceted and dynamic relationship with China' that is based on
sustainable development, integration into the world economy, the fight against
poverty and the promotion of democracy, human rights and the rule of law.[90]
The diversity of Sino-European contacts is certainly difficult to dispute. The
EU, in various formats, comes together with China regularly in global and
regional multilateral fora such as the UN, ASEM and ARF. Annual EU–China
summits began in 1998, there is an ongoing multilevel human rights dialogue,
and bilateral discussions on illegal migration and trafficking in human beings
have been initiated, the first high-level consultations being held in October
2000. The EU has also used development co-operation extensively and select-
ively to promote its security interests by targeting economic and technical co-
operation funds at specific areas designed to promote the rule of law, social
reform and good governance. The raft of associated EU assistance programmes
includes the EU–China Legal and Judicial Co-operation Programme, the
Training Programme on Village Governance and the EC–China network on
the ratification and implementation of UN Covenants. Furthermore, environmental co-operation is regarded as 'a key area of bilateral cooperation with
China'. Some 30 per cent of the EC 2002–06 China budget is devoted to

sustainable development and the EC–China Environmental Management Co-operation Programme helps channel EU knowledge and expertise into helping to control and then reverse environmental degradation.[91]

The EU's engagement of China has paid dividends on certain security issues. The Commission bemoans the fact that the EU's extensive activities in China receive little attention in Europe.[92] Yet it is precisely the low-profile nature of its involvement that has allowed it to develop progressively its influence inside China and activities ranging from environmental security through to the promotion of good governance and civil society. More prominently, the EU has encouraged and facilitated China's entry into some of the world's key multilateral fora, notably full WTO membership, which was finally secured on 12 December 2001 after a fifteen-year wait. There has likewise been generally good EU–China co-operation over Hong Kong and Macao, which became Special Administrative Regions (SARs) upon their reversion to Chinese sovereignty on 1 July 1997 and 20 December 1999 respectively. Commission annual reports indicate both satisfaction that China treats the SARs in accordance with the agreed 'one country, two systems' principle and a deepening of EU relations with them, such as the conclusion of readmission agreements in 2002.[93] Furthermore, the EU has helped to bind China into WMD non-proliferation regimes. China signed the NPT in 1992, the CTBT in 1996 and also concluded the China–Euratom Co-operation Agreement on the Peaceful Use of Nuclear Energy. The significance of this should not be understated for the non-proliferation regime generally, and for Asian stability specifically, given the tense relationship between China and Taiwan, Chinese WMD support of Pakistan and the nuclear weapons programmes of North Korea, India and Pakistan. Indeed, India's Prime Minister, Atal Behari Vajpayee, specifically cited China as a major reason for his country's adopting the nuclear option.

Nevertheless, although the diversity of the EU's relationship with China stands out among its Asian relations,[94] its most intense aspects concern trade and the security dimension remains underdeveloped. This is explained partially by structural constraints. First, China and the EU each have security priorities within their respective regions that rank higher than both their bilateral relationship and interregional co-operation. The shift from 'cold war geopolitics to multipolar geoeconomics' has changed the terms of reference for EU–China relations.[95] As a consequence Sino-European relations have become arguably more distant than during the Cold War when each shared a fear of the Soviet Union and the US finally opened relations with China in an effort to exploit its differences with the USSR.[96] The EU has subsequently prioritised security concerns in Central and Eastern Europe and Euro-Atlantic security structures. China, however, has become preoccupied with its massive project of internal reform, consolidating its Asian influence and searching for means to counterbalance American Asia-Pacific power. This rationale helps explain China's conclusion with Russia of a Common Declaration on Strategic Partnership in April 1996 and the decision to follow this up, in 1997, with a joint Declaration on a Multipolar International System.[97]

The absence of an overriding imperative has hampered the security relationship in issues beyond easy agreement and in action other than declaratory diplomacy. Key security issues such as Taiwan remain omnipresent yet confined principally to the margins of EU–China dialogue. Beijing can accept EU declarations in favour of a peaceful settlement and its nominal support of the PRC's 'one China policy'. Meantime the EU hedges by cultivating informal relations with the Taipei regime, a stance encouraged by developing trade links and especially by US support for Taiwan and the potential for escalation between the PRC and Taiwan.[98] It was, for example, scarcely coincidental that China's entry into the WTO was closely followed by Taiwan's on 1 January 2002. Furthermore, EU priorities elsewhere, combined with the sheer size of China, impose additional constraints upon the influence of EU projects within China. For example, in 1998 EU food aid to the whole of Asia totalled ECU 81 million while the Russian Federation alone received five times that amount.[99] As for China specifically, EC budget grants for co-operation with China for the five-year period 2002–06 total approximately €250 million. This represents just 1 per cent of net ODA devoted to China and, as the Commission concedes, is 'undoubtedly low, compared to the size of the challenges China faces, and to the resources available to other donors'.[100]

The other principal source of frustration in EU–China security relations is value differences. These are arguably even more important than structural constraints. They affect fundamentally the terms on which China chooses to engage the international community and its Asian neighbours. They also impact negatively on both EU–China relations and on the practical impact of EU policies towards China. This can be seen particularly in divergent Sino-European attitudes towards national sovereignty and over democratisation and human rights issues.

EU–China differences over national sovereignty carry clear implications for regional and international security management. Whereas the EU is seemingly committed to transcending the Westphalian model of the states system in its European locale,[101] post-Cold War Chinese foreign policy has in many respects exhibited the type of great power calculations prevalent in Europe during the nineteenth century.[102] This limits both the potential for transferring EU security concepts and arrangements to the Asian theatre and the prospects of fora such as ASEM and the ARF developing into anything substantially more binding than international informal meetings for the discussion of Asian and global security. For example, in arguing that the ARF should evolve from confidence-building to preventative diplomacy and eventually conflict resolution, the Commission noted in July 2003 that it 'would prefer a quicker pace for this planned evolution' than most Asian members seemingly wanted.[103] In this respect, Chinese and general Asian sensitivity towards non-intervention in their internal affairs is especially poignant. Thus, while the Commission cites Paragraph 12 of the Asia–Europe Co-operation Framework (2000) as not constraining political dialogue *a priori* on the principle of non-interference in internal affairs, other ASEM members note that the same clause stresses that

ASEM 'political dialogue should be conducted on the basis of mutual respect, equality, promotion of fundamental rights and, in accordance with the rules of international law and obligations, non-intervention, whether direct or indirect, in each other's internal affairs'.[104]

The EU and China, rather like the EU and Russia, are also liable to be divided over sovereignty-related interpretations of international law and over the importance of a UN mandate for international interventionism. As noted previously, the EU has not bound EURRF action in pursuit of the Petersberg tasks unreservedly to a UN mandate. Also, Solana's Security Paper cautiously stresses pre-emptive engagement and a security concept that, owing to processes of globalisation, frequently draws the first line of EU defence abroad. Although any future EU Petersberg missions are unlikely to be in China's sphere of influence, Beijing will almost certainly oppose any action that diminishes its influence as a permanent member of the UN Security Council. Furthermore, experience suggests that Beijing is irreconcilable to Western doctrines of limited sovereignty and humanitarian intervention. It opposed NATO intervention in Bosnia and Kosovo and the US-led coalition against Iraq in 2003. It even briefly broke its dialogue with the EU during the Kosovo War in the aftermath of NATO's accidental bombing of the Chinese Embassy in Belgrade.

Interestingly, Solana's Security Paper elevates the significance of values in the development of international peace and security. Resonating of democratic peace theory, it asserts that '[t]he best protection for our security is a world of well-governed democratic states. Spreading good governance, dealing with corruption and abuse of power, establishing the rule of law and protecting human rights are the best means of strengthening the international order.'[105] Cast in this light, EU–China tensions over human rights and internal governance are particularly noteworthy. The EU has a long-established human rights dialogue with China and has repeatedly expressed its concern for human rights generally and for minority rights specifically, most notably in Tibet and Xinjiang. In this respect, it has augmented bilateral dialogue with cautious pressure through international fora such as the UN and by contributing to projects designed to liberalise Chinese civil society. The EU also imposed economic sanctions in response to the most public demonstration of Chinese human rights abuse, the Tiananmen Square massacre of pro-democracy protestors on 4 June 1989, albeit that the measures were relatively minor and largely confined to an embargo on arms sales and military co-operation. In fact, it appears that the EU has progressively developed a twin-track approach that sees a degree of high-level confrontation over human rights issues and lower-level co-operation and training exercises to improve the civil and legal culture in China.[106]

Nevertheless, the limits both of EU influence on Beijing and of the practical results of EU programmes are clear. Chinese culture differs from the EU's in its interpretation of individual rights, responsibility and freedoms. One consequence is that China has chosen carefully the types of agreement that it has been willing to enter into with the EU. As a result the practical impact of EU conditionality has been limited, a product underpinned further by China's lack of economic dependence on the EU. For example, China became the world's seventh largest trading nation in 2000 and the second largest recipient of FDI. Although the EU was China's largest single source of FDI, excluding Hong Kong, it also ran a record trade deficit of €44.4 billion in a total two-way trade relationship worth €95 billion.[107]

The lack of EU progress was conceded by the Commission in its call in 2001 for a more results-orientated human rights dialogue and observation that in China there is 'still a wide gap between generally accepted international standards and the human rights situation on the ground'.[108] In explanation it went on to note that 'China is not always an easy partner for the EU. Its political system is unlike that of most other major third countries with which the EU has significant and growing relations.'[109] While this is undoubtedly true, some NGOs and human rights pressure groups have been less charitable in their judgements. They see EU anxiety to capitalise on Chinese trade opportunities as having led it to sideline difficult issues such as human rights. They point to the lack of action regarding China's recent use of the 'war on terrorism' as a pretext to step up its campaign against Uighur separatists in the Xinjiang province,[110] and especially to the consistent EU failure since 1997 to take on the China issue at the United Nations Commission on Human Rights (UNCHR). As one activist noted in respect to Tibet, '[t]he EU clearly neither possesses the courage or political will to make an objective defence of the Tibetan people's rights, despite expressions of profound concern'.[111]

The EU and failed states: the case of North Korea

Failed states, backlash states, rogue states, states of concern: the post-Cold War terminology has differed but the essential concerns about, and dilemmas arising from, these types of state have remained relatively consistent. In 1994 US National Security Advisor Anthony Lake listed characteristics of backlash states as including non-acceptance of certain norms, such as democratic institutions, peaceful conflict resolution, collective security and free market economies.[112] Nine years later Solana's Security Paper resonated with similar themes: '[a] number of countries have placed themselves outside the bounds of international society. Some have sought isolation; others persistently violate norms of domestic governance or of international behaviour.' That it went on to note the desirability of such countries rejoining the international community was axiomatic. The part that raised familiar and difficult questions was the assertion that '[t]hose [states] who are unwilling to do so should understand that there is a price to be paid, including in their relationship with the European Union'.[113]

How to deal with failed states is one of the key and most contentious contemporary security questions, especially in a post-September 11 environment that blurs distinctions between failed states, WMD, non-proliferation and international terrorism. Should these regimes be contained and isolated through punitive measures such as economic sanctions and their exclusion from the leading international financial institutions and other multilateral fora? Should regime reform be promoted through policies of engagement, such as conditional humanitarian, development and economic programmes, and through their assimilation into multilateral fora and the global economy? Or should pre-emptive military action be taken to remove forcibly recalcitrant regimes that fail to conform to predominant international norms? And if so, how is such intervention to be justified, on what mandate is action to be taken and how is the aftermath to be controlled such as to avoid residual insecurity and potentially unsustainable long-term military and economic commitments? After all, Bosnia, Kosovo and Iraq fundamentally divided the EU and the international community along a number of these fault-lines and there still appears to be a continuing dearth of exit strategies.

Another question arising from Solana's Security Paper is what 'price' the EU can exact from a state that fails to abide by predominant international norms? Or, put another way, how much international influence can the EU exert to effect regime reform or regime change? Answers are not simple. Nor perhaps, given the current confluence of EU enlargement, security innovation and prospective constitutional reform stemming from the European Convention, are they fully formed. Solana's Security Paper highlights the contribution of the EU and its member states in helping 'failed states back on their feet' in the Balkans, Afghanistan, East Timor and the Congo.[114] Yet, as has been seen, the EU performance in the Balkans, for example, was far from glorious, particularly pre-Dayton. Tellingly, Solana's Security Paper makes no mention of Iraq.

In this context North Korea represents a particularly interesting and difficult 'failed state' challenge to the EU and to the international community. Indeed, Solana's Security Paper explicitly notes that regional insecurity such as the Korean Peninsular and North Korea's nuclear activities impact on European interests directly and indirectly.[115] Once described as 'the last glacier of the Cold War in Asia',[116] the Korean Peninsular retains the division established at the 38th parallel during the 1950–53 Korean War between the Republic of Korea in the South and the DPRK in the North. The potential security stakes have been and continue to be high, for the Peninsular lies at a confluence of great power interests and assumes a pivotal role in East Asian security. Technically, the US is still at war with the DPRK as fighting was ended in 1953 by armistice rather than by peace treaty. Some 37,000 US troops stand alongside South Korean forces to face a million-strong, but poorly equipped, North Korean army across a 4 km wide, 250 km long, de-militarised zone that is littered with more than a million landmines. In addition, North Korea has traditionally had tense relations with Japan and it borders on Russia and China. Moscow and Beijing were Cold War backers of the DPRK. Currently, each is seeking either to maintain or to develop its regional sphere of influence, neither is enamoured of the heavy US presence, and China regards the DPRK as a useful communist buffer between its borders and American influence in South Korea.[117]

In many respects Korea is symptomatic of the apparent lack of an East Asian security system that is acceptable to the leading regional powers.[118] What makes the DPRK a particularly pressing security issue, however, is the combination of its post-Cold War economic collapse, the established connection between its leader Kim Jong-il and terrorism, and the fact that his reclusive communist totalitarian regime is known to possess WMD and missile technology and use them to raise funds and to bargain with regional powers. North Korea is consequently regarded as a direct strategic threat, a source of regional instability and a potential perpetrator of WMD proliferation in terms of supplying both materials and delivery systems to state and non-state actors, including international terrorist groups.

None of the security scenarios in the Korean Peninsular are attractive. Were the North Korean regime to collapse, then it could be taken over by an even more hard-line group, which would increase the WMD threat. Alternatively, a more liberal and pro-Korean reunification leadership might emerge. This might ease WMD considerations, provided suitable control could be established over fissile materials and plant, but it would also generate different security problems. Regional economic fallout would be severe. Reunification in the Korean Peninsular would impose a burden on the South in excess of that absorbed by West Germany in its reunification with the East. The shock-waves would not only travel across an Asian region still recovering from the 1997–98 financial crisis but would be felt also throughout the global economy. China, in particular, might be destabilised at a critical point in its internal reforms and when it lacks full control over its own territories, notably Xinjiang where the separatist movement has been identified by China's leadership as the main threat to PRC stability.[119] Korean reunification would also allow US Asian influence to expand and to bear directly upon China's border and open it to potentially massive refugee flows. Even under existing conditions the PRC absorbs considerable numbers of North Korean illegal immigrants – some 200,000 in 2000 alone.

The most acute extant problem, however, concerns the possibility of nuclear war and WMD proliferation. The US anticipates an ICBM threat from North Korea,[120] and in 1993/94 the Clinton administration gave serious consideration to a pre-emptive military strike against DPRK nuclear facilities. In its December 2001 Nuclear Posture Review the Bush administration specified the DPRK as an 'immediate contingency' for which the US must be prepared to respond with nuclear force.[121] Indeed, North Korea's impact on regional stability is particularly pronounced. It is known to sell missiles to Middle Eastern countries including Egypt and Iran. Also, Pakistan and India are nuclear powers operating outside the NPT regime and who clashed conventionally in the 1999 Kargil conflict and mobilised 1 million men either side of the Kashmir Line of Control in 2002.[122] In 1997–98 the DPRK is believed to have exchanged No-Dong missiles with Pakistan in return for gas-centrifuge uranium enrichment technology.[123] Furthermore, the DPRK's successful ICBM test-launch over Japan in

1998 had a major destabilising effect, not least because, much to Chinese chagrin, it prompted Tokyo to agree to co-operate with Washington in developing a regional missile defence system.[124] A sustained DPRK drive to stockpile nuclear weapons, coupled with its proven capacity to deliver them, might provoke South Korea, Japan and even Taiwan into reconsidering their non-nuclear status.[125]

Throughout the Cold War the EC largely eschewed political contact with the DPRK, and the Commission traditionally rebuffed its repeated efforts to establish some form of trading relationship, in itself an interesting contrast to EC China policy given that they were both communist countries with poor human rights records. However, events unfolded during the 1990s in ways potentially conducive to EU general preferences for constructive engagement of revolutionary movements in order to promote moderation and slowly change attitudes.[126] First, the self-isolation of Kim Jong-il's regime became increasingly untenable. On the one hand, liberalisation of South Korea and its growing economic prosperity potentially increased DPRK internal tensions and its fears of the South. On the other, the DPRK lost a considerable source of patronage and economic well-being as a consequence both of the collapse of the Soviet Union and of China's normalisation and subsequent consolidation of relations with South Korea from August 1992.[127] Second, economic collapse and a series of natural disasters precipitated such serious food crises that the DPRK was forced to appeal for international assistance in 1995. It is estimated that famine killed over 1 million North Koreans and that the economy shrank by 50 per cent in the 1990s. Third, further encouraged by Kim Dae Jung's South Korean sunshine policy of reconciliation and engagement with the North, there was evidence of a thaw in North–South Korean relations.[128] For instance, in 1991 the North–South Agreement on Reconciliation, Non-Aggression, Exchanges and Cooperation was concluded, followed in 1992 by a North–South Declaration on a Non-Nuclear Korean Peninsular. Finally, the US Clinton administration concluded with the DPRK a Framework Agreement on 21 October 1994, a key part of which was measures to combat the destabilising consequences of the DPRK's decision to withdraw from the NPT. The Korean Peninsular Energy Development Organisation (KEDO) was subsequently set up in March 1995 under a scheme whereby the DPRK would freeze and eventually dismantle its graphite-moderated nuclear reactors in return for the supply by an international consortium of two light water reactors and interim energy supplies (heavy fuel oil).

The initial EU response to the opportunities presented for the constructive engagement of a failed state was ambiguous, caught between international and moral pressure to act, its focus on internal reform and CEEC enlargement, and fears of extracting too little from the DPRK in return for assistance. EU humanitarian assistance began in 1995 and between 1997 and 2001 the Commission provided some €168 million worth of food aid through bilateral means, the World Food Programme and NGOs. On 22 May 1997 the EU also initialled the terms of its entry into KEDO with financial obligations broadly comparable to those of the US. Leon Brittan, then Commission Vice-President, hailed this as both a commitment to fostering stability in Korea and as 'a strong signal of the importance it [Europe] attaches to strengthening political and security ties in Asia'.[129] Less sympathetically, though, EU entry into KEDO has been seen as reluctant and explained as being due principally to American pressure.[130]

The pace of EU engagement seemingly quickened following the first ever inter-Korean summit in June 2000, which Commission President Prodi both welcomed and saw as a possible catalyst for further Commission action to encourage the opening of North Korea to the outside world.[131] On 14 May 2001 the EU duly established diplomatic relations with North Korea, news welcomed by the South Korean Foreign Ministry as a positive contribution 'to achieving peace and stability on the Korean Peninsular and improving inter-Korean relations'.[132] More substantively, that same month the troika of Patten, Solana and Swedish Prime Minister Persson secured from North Korean leader Kim Jong-il pledges to extend a moratorium on missile testing, to restrain missile technology exports and to open discussions on human rights.

The Commission thus claims that '[t]he EU has contributed to peace and stability on the Korean Peninsular through its actions in the field of humanitarian and food assistance, its contribution to the KEDO project and by beginning a dialogue with Pyongyang'.[133] Herein its policies of engagement with a 'failed state' conform to its general preference for economic and humanitarian aid and market access as inducements that reward good behaviour. Hence progress at the inter-Korean summit in 2000 was followed in 2001 by an EU relaxation of restrictions on North Korean textile exports and the onset of a limited programme of technical assistance.[134] There is also evidence of conditionality, both on the ground and in EU strategy. Thus ECHO succeeded in securing from the DPRK Letters of Understanding for projects that included an EC clause stipulating minimum humanitarian standards. Likewise, the EC Country Strategy Paper states that 'assistance to North Korea for sustainable economic and social development must go hand in hand with respect for democratic principles and human rights and prospects of regional peace and stability'.[135]

The critical question remains, though, of just how influential and effective EU policies have been in modifying the behaviour of an economically beleaguered DPRK regime that has simultaneously become more dangerous and more responsive.[136] North Korea has certainly embarked on a series of internal reforms and a gradual opening up to the outside world. In 2000 it attended the seventh meeting of ARF, in July 2002 it formally abrogated its command economy and in September 2002 Kim Jong-il opened the way for developing relations with Japan. He admitted and apologised for the North Korean kidnap of Japanese citizens during the 1970s,[137] and during the first ever visit by a Japanese Prime Minister to Pyongyang, Koizumi both apologised for the harshness of Japanese inter-war colonisation of Korea and offered a multi-billion dollar aid package as part of the normalisation process.[138]

However, these reforms have been thrust upon North Korea by economic crisis and follow broadly the Chinese, rather than the EU, economic model. In fact, the regime remains firmly in control and EU activities have been hampered by structural obstacles within the DPRK, such as restrictions on movement and the absence of a clear development policy. Also, differences with other international actors, notably the US, have impeded the EU's approach. For example, the Commission cites the DPRK's integration into the world economy as a 'necessary condition for economic and social development' but notes also that the hard-line US attitude is a leading obstacle to the DPRK securing membership of international financial institutions.[139] Furthermore, the practical impact of EU conditionality appears to have been very limited. Indeed, some EU member states and NGOs have attacked the Commission for giving North Korea too many enticements without getting enough in return for human rights.[140] Even the Commission's Country Strategy Paper (2001–04) concedes that the DPRK's human rights record remains poor and that, although it has become party to the UN Covenant on Economic, Social and Cultural Rights and the Convention on the Rights of the Child, these obligations seem not to be observed.[141]

This question of EU influence or impotence in handling North Korea has recently become acute. Six months after the EU established diplomatic ties with the DPRK, US Under-Secretary of State for Arms Control and International Security John Bolton accused North Korea of having broken the Biological and Toxin Weapons Convention.[142] Matters took a further dramatic downturn in October 2002 when the DPRK admitted, under US pressure, to conducting a clandestine nuclear weapons programme in contravention of its obligations under the NPT, North–South Declaration on a Non-Nuclear Korean Peninsular and the Agreed Framework underpinning KEDO. On 12 December Pyongyang announced that it was restarting its 5-MW reactor and resuming construction of its 50 and 200 MW reactors. It subsequently expelled International Atomic Energy Authority (IAEA) inspectors on 27 December, formally withdrew from the NPT on 10 January 2003 and pulled out of the 1992 agreement on a nuclear-free Korean Peninsular.

The consequent crisis has shown the grave limitations of EU international influence over both the DPRK and the regional powers there. Its gradual engagement of North Korea during the 1990s appears to have induced little or no modification in Pyongyang's behaviour, with Kim Jong-il's ongoing brinkmanship largely mirroring that of his father's during 1993–94. The EU also lacks the leverage necessary to make an effective contribution to the international crisis management of the DPRK. Its principal response has been declaratory. On 19 November 2002 the General Affairs and External Relations Council requested that the DPRK dismantle its nuclear programme in a verifiable manner and warned that failure to do so would jeopardise the future of EU–DPRK relations. Food and humanitarian assistance was to be left in place but the Commission and the member states were urged to review their North Korean activities, including technical assistance and trade measures.[143] On 11 February 2003 the EU reaffirmed that it considered 'the NPT as the cornerstone of the global nuclear non-proliferation regime'.[144] And at its Thessaloniki Summit in June 2003, the EU again called on North Korea to

' "visibly, verifiably and irreversibly dismantle its nuclear programme" and to start complying with its international non-proliferation obligations'.[145]

This declaratory diplomacy might send the right signals to other states about EU values. Such moral suasion, however, has little purchase on a regime that does not share EU norms, orientates its diplomacy primarily towards the US and leading Asian powers, and has a history of 'strategic deception' – signing agreements to convey reliability but purposefully cheating on them to its own advantage.[146] Nor does EU–China dialogue seem to have had any discernible influence on Beijing's approach to North Korea, again reflecting the limits of EU influence over the PRC and the frustration of one of its stated objectives for security co-operation. The EU did agree within KEDO, under heavy US pressure, to apply economic sanctions on Kim Jong-il's regime by suspending oil shipments to North Korea from December 2002. Again, though, neither this nor possible suspension of EU trade and technical assistance is likely to force a change of policy upon Pyongyang. EU–North Korean trade is small, EU imports totalling just €73 million in 1999, and its humanitarian aid is significantly less than that of some other donors.[147] For example, DPRK–China trade exceeded $700 million in 2002 and China reportedly provides 30 per cent of total outside assistance to North Korea, 38 per cent of its imports and 70–90 per cent of its energy supplies.[148]

It thus seems that the EU can exert marginal influence at best in the international management of Kim Jong-il's 'failed state' and that the 'price' it can exact in reprisal for North Korean disregard for international norms is correspondingly small. This is perhaps an inevitable consequence of what one inside commentator has noted as its paying 'insufficient attention . . . to the situation in North Korea, the tensions in the Korean Peninsular, and the importance of Korea for the security of East Asia'.[149] Financial participation in KEDO and the accompanying right to vote have both proven a poor substitute for an established policy[150] and seemingly condemned the EU to repeat its spectator role adopted during the 1993–94 crisis. Meantime Pyongyang's latest manoeuvrings will be negotiated between the Bush administration's policy of tailored containment and the preferences of the other key regional powers for a less confrontational approach.[151] Indeed, US Secretary of State Colin Powell underscored this, and by implication EU impotence, in a press conference in February 2003: 'we are prepared to address these issues with North Korea in a multilateral context in which China and other nations can participate. It is a matter for China, it's a matter for South Korea, it's a matter for Japan, it's a matter for Russia, it's a matter for the United Nations, the IAEA, and it is a matter for the United States.'[152]

Conclusion

The EU's security relationships with Russia, China and North Korea reveal a broadly common EU approach. Whether dealing with a democratising and market-orientating neighbouring state, a distant communist regional power or a failed state, the EU has consistently pursued policies of engagement rather than of strategic competition or containment. It has also pursued a multilateralist agenda, emphasising in each case the importance, and facilitating the process, of their integration into regional and global multilateral fora and their incorporation into international security arrangements, such as the NPT, CTBT and UN human rights covenants. In each case, too, it has sought to combine institutional, technical and functional dimensions within multilevel policies designed to build confidence, develop co-operation and modify behaviour in ways reflective of its own values. Furthermore, it has consistently used cross-pillar policy instruments and combined positive dialogue, trade and aid incentives with conditionality and, in exceptional cases, political and economic sanctions.

Even in the era of globalisation, however, geography exerts a differentiating influence in terms of policy priorities and components. The EU has generally been slow to develop its Eurasian security relationships, having prioritised instead the CEECs and successive Balkan crises. Also, of Russia, China and North Korea, the EU seems to have focused its recent enhanced security efforts on neighbouring Russia, even though the failed state of North Korea arguably constitutes a greater immediate threat to regional security and WMD proliferation. As for differences in policy approaches, EU enlargement and Russia's neighbour status has meant both that greater resources have been dedicated to the EU–Russia relationship and that JHA measures have been far more prominent therein.

Perhaps most interesting though, in the context of Solana's pursuit of strategic partnerships with Russia and China and the importance attributed to dealing with failed states, is that the EU has met varying degrees of opposition to its policies and achieved very different levels of influence and effectiveness. Its influence seems greatest *vis-à-vis* Russia, principally owing to its dominant economic position but also to more direct EU–Russia common security concerns and their greater, if still limited, normative congruence. In all three states, however, EU human rights dialogue and democratisation programmes have been contentious and of limited impact. Moreover, none of these states share EU acceptance of limited sovereignty and humanitarian interventionism. This would suggest that EU security relationships with these countries are for the foreseeable future liable to be rooted more in traditional coincidences of interest than in an emerging consensus on post-Westphalian norm-based global governance.

Finally, these EU–Eurasian security relationships indicate that the EU, leaving aside particularly strong historical connections between member states and third countries, exerts progressively less influence the further a country is from Europe and the less it either shares EU norms or depends on EU trade/aid. Even allowing for the dangers of extrapolating from specific examples and the importance of EU contributions to multinational security regimes, this suggests that, although the EU has established itself as a global economic actor and clearly has global security interests, as a security actor it is still primarily regional. Moreover, its influence is greatest with those actors either already in, or aspiring to enter, the international system of which the EU is both part and promoter. Failed states such as North Korea, though, are often distant and elect to operate outside the bounds of international society, which suggests in turn that the EU's ability in dealing effectively and pre-emptively with them is liable to remain limited in scenarios other than voluntary reconstruction.

Notes

1 Delors, J. (1991) 'European Integration and Security' *Survival* **33** (2) p. 100.

2 Italy elected to anticipate application of the decision taken under the Treaty of Nice, and binding from 2004 onwards, to hold meetings of the European Council in Brussels rather than in national venues. http://www.ueitalia2003.it/EN/Presidenza/coselaPresidenza/.

3 Solana, J. (2003) 'A Secure Europe in a Better World', SO138/03.

4 Ibid.

5 Bush also conceded in summer 2002 a personal loathing of North Korean leader Kim Jong-il. Woodward, B. (2002) *Bush at War*, New York: Simon and Schuster, p. 340.

6 Common Strategy of the European Union on Russia, 4 June 1999, Luxembourg: Official Journal of the European Communities, L 157/1, 24 June 1999.

7 Legvold, R. (2001) 'Russia's Unformed Foreign Policy' *Foreign Affairs* **80** (5) p. 63.

8 Common Strategy of the European Union on Russia, 4 June 1999; European Commission (2001) Country Strategy Paper for Russia, 27 December 2001.

9 Baev, P.K. (1999) 'External Interventions in Secessionist Conflicts in Europe in the 1990s' *European Security* 8 (2) p. 29; Lynch, D. (2002) 'Separatist States and Post-Soviet Conflicts' *International Affairs* 78 (4) pp. 831–48.

10 European Commission, Country Strategy Paper for Russia, 27 December 2001.

11 For Kaliningrad see especially Baxendale, J., Dewar S. and Gowan, D. (eds) (2000) *The EU and Kaliningrad: Kaliningrad and the Impact of EU Enlargement*, London: Federal Trust.

12 The Ukraine has concluded a partnership and co-operation agreement with the EU and both a PFP programme and a Charter on a Distinctive Partnership with NATO.

13 The Foreign Policy Concept of the Russian Federation, 28 June 2000, p. 11, http://www.bits.de/EURA/Russia052800.pdf.

14 Sestanovich, S. (1997) 'Why the United States has no Russia Policy' in *Eagle Adrift: American Foreign Policy at the End of the Century*, Lieber, R.J. (ed.), New York: Longman, p. 164.

15 The Foreign Policy Concept of the Russian Federation, 28 June 2000, p. 1; Russian Federation – Concept of the World in the 21st Century, http://www.bits.de/frames/database.htm.

16 Russian Federation – Concept of the World in the 21st Century.

17 Medium-term Strategy for Development of Relations between the Russian Federation and the European Union (2000–2010), 1999, unofficial translation, http://europa.eu.int/comm/external_relations/russia/russian_medium_term_strategy/.

18 See Financial Action Task Force on Money Laundering, Annual Report, 20 June 2003, p. 25.

19 European Commission (2001) Country Strategy Paper for the Russia Federation, 27 December 2001, p. 6.

20 For example, Washington benefited during the Afghanistan intervention from Russia's restraint over US troop deployments in Central Asia, significant intelligence assets and on-ground influence with the anti-Taliban Northern Alliance. For more details see Stent, A. (2002) 'American Views on Russian Security Policy and EU–Russian Relations', paper for the IISS/CEPS European Security Forum, http://www.eusec.org/stent.htm.

21 'Bush Approves Resumed Funding for Destruction of Soviet Arms', 14 January 2003, US Office of International Information Programs. The Bush administration's FY2003 budget request for $1.04 billion for Cooperative Threat Reduction CTR programmes marked a 37 per cent increase on the previous year. The International Institute for Strategic Studies (2002) *The Military Balance, 2002–2003*, London: Oxford University Press, p. 15.

22 Trenin, D. (Spring 2002) 'Silence of the Bear' *NATO Review*, http://www.nato.int/docu/review.htm.

23 European Commission (1994) Partnership and Cooperation Agreement with Russia, http://www.europa.eu.int/comm/external_relations/russia/intro/index.htm.

24 Gower, J. (2000) 'The EU and Russia: The Challenge of Integration Without Accession' in *Enlarging the European Union: The Way Forward*, Gower, J. and Redmond, J. (eds), Aldershot: Ashgate, p. 168; Webber, M. (2001) 'Third-Party Inclusion in European Security and Defence Policy: A Case Study of Russia' *European Foreign Affairs Review* 6 p. 409.

25 Friis, L. and Murphy, A. (2000) 'Enlargement: A Complex Juggling Act' in *The State of the European Union, Vol. 5*, Cowles, M.G. and Smith, M. (eds), Oxford: Oxford University Press, pp. 199–200.

26 Putin cited by Timmermann, H. (2000) 'European–Russian Partnership: What Future?' *European Foreign Affairs Review* 5 (2) p. 167.

27 For an overview of the pre-2000 EU–Russia framework see Gower, J. (2000) 'Russia and the European Union' in *Russia and Europe: Conflict or Cooperation?*, Webber, M. (ed.), New York: St Martin's Press, pp. 66–98.

28 The NATO–Russia Council replaces the NATO–Russia Permanent Joint Council (PJC) and acts 'as a mechanism for consultation, consensus-building, co-operation, joint decision and joint action, in which the individual Allies and Russia will work as equal partners on a wide spectrum of Euro-Atlantic security issues of common interest'. 'NATO–Russia Relations', http://www.nato.int/docu/facts/nato-rus.htm.

29 Medium-term Strategy for Development of Relations between the Russian Federation and the European Union (2000–2010); Common Strategy of the European Union on Russia, 4 June 1999.

30 European Commission (2000) The TACIS Programme Annual Report 1999, COM (2000) 835 final, 20 December 2000; http://www.europa.eu.int/comm/external_relations/russia/intro; Commission, Country Strategy Paper for Russia, 27 December 2001, p. 12.

31 European Commission, The TACIS Programme Annual Report 1999.

32 Council Joint Action establishing a European Union Cooperation Programme for Non-proliferation and Disarmament in the Russian Federation, 1999/878/CFSP, 17 December 1999.

33 Kananaskis Summit Document: The G8 Global Partnership Against the Spread of Weapons of Mass Destruction, 27 June 2002, http://www.useu.be/Categories/Defense/June2702WeaponsRussia.html.

34 MNEPR membership: EC, EURATOM, Russia, Norway, Finland, Sweden, Denmark, UK, Netherlands, Germany and Belgium. Signature of MNEPR, 21 May 2003, IP/03/724, http://europa.eu.int/comm/external_relations/russia/intro/ip03_724.htm.

35 EU Northern Dimension membership comprises the EU fifteen plus Poland, Norway, Iceland, Russia and the Baltic states. For further details see Frank, C. (September 2002) 'The Northern Dimension: Added Value or Redundancy?', conference paper, http://www.edc.spb.ru/conf2002/home.html.

36 Rontoyannia, C. (2002) 'So Far, So Good? Russia and the ESDP' *International Affairs* 78 (4) pp. 813–30.

37 De Spiegeleire, S. (2002) 'Recoupling Russia: Staying the Course. Europe's Security Relationship with Russia', paper prepared for the IISS/CEPS European Security Forum, Brussels, 14 January 2002.

38 'The EU's Relation with Russia: EU–Russian Trade', http://www.europa.eu.int/comm/external_relations/Russia/intro/trade.htm.

39 EU–Russia Summit, St Petersburg, 31 May 2003, http://europa.eu.int/comm/external_relations/russia/sum05_03/js.htm. For the Common European Economic Space between Russia and the EU see Samson, I. (2002) 'The Common European Economic Space Between Russia and the EU: An Institutional Anchor for Accelerating Russian Reform' *Russian Economic Trends* 11 (3) pp. 7–15.

40 Russia's share of EU external trade in 2000 accounted for just 4.4 per cent of imports and 2.1 per cent of exports. 'The EU's Relation with Russia: EU–Russian Trade', http://www.europa.eu.int/comm/external_relations/Russia/intro/trade.htm.

41 Commission, Country Strategy Paper for Russia, 27 December 2001, p. 5.

42 Portela, C. (May 2001) 'EU–Russia Co-operation in the Security Domain: Problems and Opportunities', BITS Research Note 01.2.

43 Frank, 'The Northern Dimension: Added Value or Redundancy?'; Malfliet, K. (September 2002) 'Russia and the European Union in a Wider Europe: New Openings and Old Barriers', http://www.edc.spb.ru/conf2002/home.html.

44 Kivikari, U. (2002) 'The Northern Dimension – One Pillar of the Bridge Between Russia and the EU' *Russian Economic Trends* **11** (3) pp. 26–30.

45 Portela, 'EU–Russia Co-operation in the Security Domain: Problems and Opportunities'. The NEI is a US government cross-border programme designed to encourage economic and security co-operation amongst the nations of the Nordic and Baltic region and to associate them with the US and the EU. Within this involving north-west Russia is a key objective in encouraging US–Russia co-operation in regional bodies, including military to military co-operation. The NEI also supports the Council of Baltic Sea States regional environmental objectives and efforts to combat organised crime. Gfoeller, T.C. (2000) 'Diplomatic Initiatives: An Overview of the Northern European Initiative' *European Security* **9** (1) pp. 98–104.

46 Mahncke, D. (2001) 'Russia's Attitude to the European Security and Defence Policy', *European Foreign Affairs Review* **6** p. 436.

47 Common Strategy of the European Union on Russia, 4 June 1999.

48 Malfliet, 'Russia and the European Union in a Wider Europe'.

49 Leshoukov, I. (2000) 'Beyond Satisfaction: Russia's Perspectives on European Integration', IEI Discussion Paper C26.

50 Timmermann, 'European–Russian Partnership: What Future?', p. 173; Zakaria, F. (1997) 'The Rise of Illiberal Democracy' *Foreign Affairs* **76** (6) pp. 22–43.

51 Commission, Country Strategy Paper for Russia, 27 December 2001, p. 4.

52 Tompson, W. (2002) 'Begging Ends' *World Today* **58** (2) p. 17; Cronin, D. (2003) 'Rights and Wrongs' *European Voice*, 16 January 2003, p. 59. Criticism was such that External Relations Commissioner Patten felt compelled to issue a rebuttal. Patten, C. (2002) 'Declarations as Regards the EU–Russia Summit and the Situation in Chechnya', 12 November 2002, http://www.europa.eu.int/commission/external_relations/news/patten/IP02_1655.htm.

53 The Foreign Policy Concept of the Russian Federation, 28 June 2000, http://www.bits.de/EURA/Russia052800.pdf.

54 Medium-term Strategy for Development of Relations between the Russian Federation and the European Union (2000–2010).

55 Zhurkin cited by Deighton, A. (2002) 'The European Security and Defence Policy' *Journal of Common Market Studies* **40** (4) p. 733.

56 Medium-term Strategy for Development of Relations between the Russian Federation and the European Union (2000–2010).

57 On 12 September 2002 Putin wrote to the OSCE and UN threatening Russian preemptive strikes against neighbouring Georgia for harbouring Chechen terrorist groups. Lynch, D. (2003) *Russia Faces Europe*, Chaillot Paper 60, Paris: EU Institute for Security Studies, pp. 13–14.

58 Ortega, M. (2001) *Military Intervention and the European Union*, Chaillot Paper 45, Paris: Institute for Strategic Studies, p. 107.

59 For Russia and Kosovo see Levitin, O. (2000) 'Inside Moscow's Kosovo Muddle' *Survival* **42** (1) pp. 130–40.

60 Medium-term Strategy for Development of Relations between the Russian Federation and the European Union (2000–2010).

61 Solana, 'A Secure Europe in a Better World'.

62 Webber, M. (2001) 'Third-Party Inclusion in European Security and Defence Policy: A Case Study of Russia' *European Foreign Affairs Review* 6 p. 417.

63 Malfliet, 'Russia and the European Union in a Wider Europe'.

64 Allen, D. (1997) 'EPC/CFSP, the Soviet Union, and the Former Soviet Republics: Do the Twelve Have a Coherent Policy?' in *Foreign Policy of the European Union: From EPC to CFSP and Beyond*, Regelsberger, E., Wessels, W. and de Schoutheete de Tervarent, P. (eds), London: Lynne Rienner Publishers, p. 233.

65 De Spiegeleire, 'Recoupling Russia'.

66 Common Strategy of the European Union on Russia, 4 June 1999; Commission, Country Strategy Paper for Russia, 27 December 2001, p. 3.

67 The Foreign Policy Concept of the Russian Federation, 28 June 2000, p. 3.

68 Medium-term Strategy for Development of Relations between the Russian Federation and the European Union (2000–2010).

69 Light, M., Löwenhardt, J. and White, S. (2000) 'Russian Perspectives on European Security' *European Foreign Affairs Review* 5 (4) p. 491.

70 For example, Poland has declared that as of July 2003 it will impose visa requirements on citizens from Russia, Ukraine and Belarus.

71 Wright, Richard (2000) 'Prospects for EU–Russia Economic Relations', speech by Head of the European Commission Delegation to Russia at the RECEP conference, 20 December 2000.

72 Gower, 'The EU and Russia', p. 168.

73 The Foreign Policy Concept of the Russian Federation, 28 June 2000, p. 4; Medium-term Strategy for Development of Relations between the Russian Federation and the European Union (2000–2010).

74 Mangott, G. (2000) 'A Giant on its Knees: Structural Constraints on Russia's Global Role' *International Politics* 37 p. 479; Lynch, *Russia Faces Europe*, pp. 9 and 12.

75 Baranovsky, V. (2000) 'Russia: A Part of Europe or Apart from Europe?' *International Affairs* 76 (3) pp. 443–58.

76 For a contrary argument in which Putin's strong Western engagement is seen as a new strategy rather than tactics in Russian foreign policy see Trenin, D. (2002) 'A Russia-within-Europe: Working Toward a New Security Arrangement', paper prepared for the IISS/CEPS European Security Forum, Brussels, 14 January 2002.

77 Light et al., 'Russian Perspectives on European Security', p. 493.

78 The Foreign Policy Concept of the Russian Federation, 28 June 2000, pp. 1 and 11.

79 For a discussion of evolving Russian attitudes towards a European or Eurasian identity see Sakwa, R. (2002) *Russian Politics and Society*, London: Routledge, pp. 362–64; Trenin, D. (2002) *The End of Eurasia: Russia on the Border Between Geopolitics and Globalization*, Moscow: Carnegie Endowment for International Peace.

80 Patten, C. (2002) speech at the European Business Club Conference, 28 May 2002, http://www.europa.eu.int/external_relations/news/patten/sp02_235.htm.

81 A. Rahr (Head of Russia/CIS Research Department of the German Foreign Policy Association) cited by Osinskaya, D. (2003) 'EU Does Not Want Russia Walking on Its "European" Lawn' *Rosbalt News*, 30 June 2003, http://www.rosbaltnews.com.

82 European Commission (1994) 'Towards a New Asia strategy', COM (94) 314 final, 13 July 1994, http://www.iias.nl/asem/offdocs/docs/Towards_a_New_Asia_strategy.pdf.

83 European Commission (2001) 'Europe and Asia: A Strategic Framework for Enhanced Partnerships', COM (2001) 469, 4 September 2001.

84 Nuttall, S. (1998) 'European and Asian Policies' in *Europe and the Asia Pacific*, Maull, H., Segal, G. and Wanandia, J. (eds), London: Routledge, p. 175.

85 European Commission (2001) 'EU Strategy Towards China: Implementation of the 1998 Communication and Future Steps for a More Effective EU Policy', Communication for the Commission to the Council and the European Parliament, COM (2001) 265 final, 15 May 2001, p. 7.

86 European Commission, Working Document, Country Strategy Paper: China, 2002–2006, p. 18.

87 Ibid., p. 12.

88 Malik, M. (2002) 'China, Pakistan and India: Nervous Neighbours' *The World Today* 58 (10) p. 21.

89 European Commission, 'EU Strategy Towards China', p. 9.

90 European Commission, Country Strategy Paper: China, 2002–2006, p. 23.

91 Ibid., p. 27; 'China: European Commission Approves Country Strategy Paper 2002–2006', IP/02/349, 1 March 2002, http://europa.eu.int/comm/external_relations/china/csp/index.htm.

92 European Commission, 'EU Strategy Towards China', p. 19.

93 The Hong Kong agreement was initialled in November 2001 and signed as the first ever EC–third country readmission agreement on 28 November 2002. The EC–Macao agreement was initialled on 18 October 2002. European Commission (2002) 'Hong Kong Special Administrative Region: Fourth Annual Report – 2001', Report from the Commission to the Council and the European Parliament, COM (2002) 450 final, 5 August 2002; European Commission (2002) 'Macao Special Administrative Region: Second Annual Report – 2001', Report from the Commission to the Council and the European Parliament, COM (2002) 445 final, 31 July 2002.

94 Wiessala, G. (2002) *The European Union and Asia Countries*, London: Sheffield Academic Press, p. 104.

95 Dent, C. (1999) *The European Union and East Asia: An Economic Relationship*, London: Routledge, p. 149.

96 For the change in US policy toward China see Kim, I.J. (1987) *The Strategic Triangle: China, the United States and the Soviet Union*, New York: Paragon House; Harding, H. (1992) *A Fragile Relationship: The United States and China Since 1972*, Washington D.C.: Brookings Institute.

97 Between 1997 and 2001 Russia supplied 91.5 per cent of China's import of major conventional weaponry. From SIPRI (2002) *SIPRI Yearbook 2002*, p. 376.

98 In 2001, for example, the Bush administration considered selling advanced-capability theatre missile defence to Taiwan. Ibid., p. 510.

99 Smith, H. (2002) *European Union Foreign Policy: What It Is and What It Does*, London: Pluto Press, p. 207.

100 European Commission, Country Strategy Paper 2002–06: China, p. 24; 'China: European Commission Approves Country Strategy Paper 2002–2006'.

101 Leifer, M. (1998) 'European and Asian Policies' in *Europe and the Asia Pacific*, Maull, Segal and Wanandia (eds), p. 199.

102 Shambaugh, D. (1994) 'Growing Strong: China's Challenge to Asian Security' *Survival* **36** (2) pp. 43–59.

103 European Commission (2003) 'Communication from the Commission: A New Partnership with South East Asia', COM (2003) 399/4, 9 July 2003. For a discussion of problems inherent in 'parachuting' Western concepts of security management and governance into Asia see Baker, N. and Sebastian, L.C. (1995) 'The Problem With Parachuting: Strategic Studies and Security in the Asia/Pacific Region' *Journal of Strategic Studies* **18** (3) pp. 15–31.

104 European Commission, 'Communication from the Commission: A New Partnership with South East Asia'; Reiterer, M. (2002) 'The Asia–Europe Meeting (ASEM): The Importance of the Fourth ASEM Meeting in the Light of 11 September' *European Foreign Affairs Review* **7** (2) footnote 9, p. 135. For more on ASEM see also Lim, P. (2001) 'The Unfolding Asia-Europe (ASEM) Process' in *The European Union and East Asia: Interregional Links in a Changing Global System*, Preston, P.W. and Gilson, J. (eds), Cheltenham: Edward Elgar, pp. 91–108.

105 Solana, 'A Secure Europe in a Better World'.

106 Yahunda, M. (1998) 'European and Asian Policies' in *Europe and the Asia Pacific*, Maull, Segal and Wanandia (eds), p. 191.

107 European Commission (2001) 'EU Strategy Towards China', p. 12.

108 Ibid., p. 10.

109 Ibid., p. 7.

110 Human Rights Watch (2003) 'Asian Security Talks Risk Giving Green Light to Repression: Human Rights Abused in Name of Fighting Terrorism', 16 June 2003, http://www.hrw.org/press/2003/06/asean061603.htm.

111 Unattributed (2002) 'Tibet NGOs Slam Political Apathy by European Union on China at the UNCHR', 10 April 2002, http://www.tibet.com/NewsRoom/unchr-2.htm.

112 Lake, A. (1994) 'Confronting Backlash States' *Foreign Affairs* **73** (2) pp. 45–55.

113 Solana, 'A Secure Europe in a Better World'.

114 Ibid.

115 Ibid.

116 Baker, J. (1991) 'America in Asia: Emerging Architecture for a Pacific Community' *Foreign Affairs* **70** (5) p. 13.

117 For example, Russia and China each harbour concerns about the US Asian-Pacific presence, which is symbolised by the 1996 US–Japan Security Agreement.

118 Acharya, A. (1999) 'A Concert of Asia' *Survival* **41** (3) p. 84.

119 Dillon, M. (2002) 'China and the US Bases in Central Asia' *The World Today* **58** (7) p. 15.

120 Cited in: *SIPRI Yearbook 2002*, p. 482.

121 US Department of Defense (2001) 'Nuclear Posture Review', submitted to Congress 31 December 2001, p. 16, http://www.globalsecurity.org/wmd/library/policy/dod/npr.htm.

122 Despite the recent resumption of diplomatic relations, security tensions and risks remain high between India and Pakistan, especially given the absence of nuclear risk reduction measures and the unresolved Kashmir issue. Roy-Chaudhury, R. (2003) 'Hand of Friendship' *World Today* **59** (6) p. 22.

123 Samore, G. (2003) 'The Korean Nuclear Crisis' *Survival* **45** (1) p. 10.

124 Khoo, N. (2003) 'Time for Action' *The World Today* **59** (7) p. 15.

125 For US–North Korean relations and the history of nuclear and missile proliferation in Korea see Kim, S. (ed.) (1998) *North Korean Foreign Relations in the Post-Cold War Era*, New York: Oxford University Press; Albright, D. and O'Neill, K. (eds) (2000) *Solving the North Korean Nuclear Puzzle*, Washington D.C.: Institute for Science and International Security.

126 Smith, *European Union Foreign Policy*, p. 143.

127 In 2001 China overtook the US to become South Korea's largest trading partner with two-way trade of over $40 billion. Shambaugh, D. (2003) 'China and the Korean Peninsular: Playing for the Long Term' *Washington Quarterly* **26** (2) p. 49.

128 Roh Moo Hyun succeeded Kim Dae Jung in December 2002 elections in South Korea on a platform of continuing his predecessor's sunshine policy.

129 The EU formally entered KEDO in September 1997. Brittan, L. (1997) cited in 'European Union to Join North Korea Nuclear Security Body', 22 May 1997, http://www.eurunion.org/news/press/1997-2/pr34-97.htm.

130 Peterson, J. (1998) 'Introduction' in *A Common Foreign Policy for Europe? Competing Visions of CFSP*, Peterson, J. and Sjursen, H. (eds), London: Routledge, p. 13.

131 Statement by European Commission President Prodi on Korean Peninsular: North-South Summit, IP/00/625, 15 June 2000, http://europa.eu.int/comm/external_relations/south_korea/intro/ip_00_625.htm.

132 Unattributed (2001) 'EU to Open Ties With North Korea', 14 May 2001, http://www.cbsnews.com/stories/2001/05/14/world.

133 European Commission, The EC-Democratic People's Republic of Korea (DPRK) Country Strategy Paper 2001–2004, p. 7.

134 Textile quota ceilings were raised by around 60 per cent in 2001. European Commission, National Indicative Programme for People's Republic of Korea 2002–2004, p. 4

135 European Commission, The EC-Democratic People's Republic of Korea (DPRK) Country Strategy Paper 2001–2004, p. 18.

136 Clark, I. (2001) *The Post-Cold War Order: The Spoils of Peace*, Oxford: Oxford University Press, p. 118.

137 Kang, D. (2003) 'The Avoidable Crisis in North Korea' *Orbis* **47** (3) pp. 495–510; Laney, J. and Shaplen, J. (2003) 'How to Deal with North Korea' *Foreign Affairs* **82** (2) p. 17.

138 Wall, D. (2002) 'North Korea and China' *The World Today* **58** (12) p. 21.

139 European Commission, The EC-Democratic People's Republic of Korea (DPRK) Country Strategy Paper 2001–2004, pp. 3 and 18.

140 Anderson, S. (2001) 'The Changing Nature of Diplomacy: The European Union, the CFSP and Korea' *European Foreign Affairs Review* **6** p. 477.

141 European Commission, The EC-Democratic People's Republic of Korea (DPRK) Country Strategy Paper 2001–2004, p. 8.

142 Bolton, J.R. (2001) Remarks to the 5th Biological Weapons Convention RevCon Meeting, 19 November 2001, http://www.state.gov/t/us/rm/janjuly/6231.htm.

143 General Affairs and External Relations Council (2003), http://europa.eu.int/comm/external_relations/north_korea/intro/gac.htm#nk191102; 'North Korea: Commission Grants EUR 9.5 Million in Emergency Humanitarian Food Aid for Children', IP/03/20, 8 January 2003, http://europa.eu.int/comm/external_relations/north_korea/intro/ip03_20.htm.

144 EU Statement on DPRK, 11 February 2003, http://www.delkor.cec.eu.int/en/whatsnew/dprk.htm.

145 Dempsey, J. (2003) 'Big Powers Get Behind EU Foreign Policy', http://www.financialtimes.printthis.clickability.com.

146 Cha, V.D. and Chang, D.C. (May/June 2003) 'The Korea Crisis' *Foreign Policy*, p. 22.

147 European Commission, The EC-Democratic People's Republic of Korea (DPRK) Country Strategy Paper 2001–2004, p. 10.

148 Cha and Chang, 'The Korea Crisis', p. 23.

149 Nuttall, 'European and Asian Policies', p. 180.

150 Grand, C. (2000) *The European Union and the Non-Proliferation of Nuclear Weapons*, Chaillot Paper 37, Paris: Institute for Security Studies, p. 26.

151 At the time of writing the Bush administration insisted that North Korea dismantle its nuclear weapons programme as a prelude to bilateral negotiations. However, at the Russia–China Summit in Beijing in December 2002, Jiang and Putin demonstrated considerable solidarity and it seems highly unlikely that either would join a coercive and confrontational US approach to Pyongyang. Shambaugh, 'China and the Korean Peninsular', p. 54; Laney and Shaplen, 'How to Deal With North Korea', pp. 16–30.

152 Press Conference Secretary Colin L. Powell St Regis Hotel Beijing, China, 24 February 2003, http://www.uspolicy.be/Issues/NorthKorea/northkorea.htm.

CHAPTER 9

The EU as a global economic actor

In stark contrast to its relatively new role and variegated performance as a global security actor, the European Union, and especially the ECs, can reflect upon a much longer history of economic relationships that span virtually the entire globe. Its most intensive bilateral extraterritorial economic partnership – that with the US – has been examined in Chapter Five. How the Union has associated itself with its neighbouring countries in Europe and on its periphery has been the subject of Chapter Seven. Other economic links, of differing intensities, include those with Canada,[1] Australasia,[2] the Gulf Co-operation Council (a group of six countries in the Gulf region),[3] and with Iran, Iraq and Yemen.

This chapter demonstrates the global economic reach of the EU by examining three relationships in detail: the EU's relations with the ACP group of countries; its links to the Far East, mainly Japan but also China and ASEAN; and its economic relations with the countries of Latin America. This is no random choice. The ACP countries enjoy the longest and closest contractual link with the ECs of any country outside Europe. Japan has long been the Communities' second-largest economic competitor after the US, although its position has been to an extent usurped by a number of other countries in the region, formerly often referred to as the Asian Tigers. Some of these countries got together as the Association of South-East Asian Nations with which the EU has established close links. These days, however, the undisputed contender for the title of regional economic superpower of the future is China – already the Union's second most important market for imports.[4] Finally, another important economic region for the EU is Latin America. This is reflected in the number and variety of relations the Union keeps with individual countries in the region, such as Mexico and Chile, and with country groupings like Mercosur, Central America and the Andean Community.

The EU–ACP connection

The relationship between the ACP group of countries and what is now the EU dates back to the early years of the EEC. When the Treaty of Rome establishing the European Economic Community was signed in 1957, some member states still had colonies and otherwise dependent countries and territories,[5] and the decolonisation process was only just gathering pace. Initially, the dependencies were linked to the EEC by way of special association agreements containing a combination of aid, trade and political co-operation. The overall aim of association was 'to promote the economic and social development of the countries and territories and to establish close economic relations between them and the Community as a whole'.[6]

This kind of association, based on Articles 131–136 of the original EEC Treaty (now Articles 182–188 EC Treaty[7]), must not be confused with the association agreements signed between the ECs/EU and fully independent and sovereign third countries, based on Articles 228 and 238 EECT (now Articles 300 and 310 ECT). The latter, on which the associations discussed in Chapter Seven are also based, became the appropriate instruments once the former colonies had gained independence. However, even though the legal basis for relations with the ACP changed, the spirit and the objectives of the associations were maintained.[8] Following independence, the relationship between the ECs and the former colonies was put on a new formal footing under the so-called Yaoundé Conventions. The first of these was signed between the six original EEC members and seventeen African states plus Madagascar in Yaoundé, Cameroon, in July 1963; the follow-up in July 1969 came into effect on 1 January 1971.

The number of former colonies with EC connections increased substantially as a consequence of the first enlargement of the European Communities – especially given UK membership in 1973. In 1975, the first of the so-called Lomé Conventions was signed between the then nine EEC members and 46 ACP countries in the capital of Togo, which gave it its name. Like its predecessors, the first Lomé Convention also aimed at co-operation in trade and financial as well as technical assistance. It is usually seen also as the *de facto* start of the EEC's Development Policy – despite the absence of any explicit competencies in this field. Gradually, though, the Community has acquired both the instruments and the financial framework that could bear any comparison with the measures used by the member states themselves.[9] Three more Lomé Conventions were concluded with an ever-increasing number of ACP countries: Lomé II in 1979 with 58 ACP states, Lomé III in 1984 with 65 ACP partners, and the last of these sort of conventions, Lomé IV, with 68 ACP countries in 1989, extended to 70 ACP states in 1995.[10] Before looking at how the relationship between the EU and its by now 77 ACP partners has changed since Lomé IV expired in February 2000, it is useful to see how the Lomé Conventions used to work in order to allow for comparisons with the new arrangements.

As far as trade was concerned, Lomé IV foresaw free access to the ECs' markets for 99 per cent of all ACP products, though sensitive products were still excluded from this provision – such as those that fall under the intervention mechanisms of the CAP. ACP countries themselves were allowed to impose tariffs on imports from the EU, as long as they fell within the rules of the most-favoured nation principle – in other words, as long as they did not discriminate against the ECs in favour of other industrial countries. On the Development Policy side, one of the most important instruments of the collaboration between the ECs and ACP countries, developed within the framework of the Lomé Conventions, was a system aimed at stabilising the revenue from exports for the partner countries. This system was called STABEX and basically assured the ACP states a minimum income from around forty agrarian products, which represented the most important export goods for the developing countries. If export revenues fell below the average income of previous years, the ECs used to balance out this loss either by way of a temporary ('bridging') loan, or with a non-refundable grant. But they only did so up to a certain maximum amount and under certain given preconditions. A similar system was in place for mineral exports, called SYSMIN.[11] Other chapters of the Convention concerned themselves with issues such as the third-world debt question, environmental considerations and human rights. The financial framework for the fourth Lomé arrangement amounted to around ECU 27 billion between 1990 and 2000.[12] This money used to be administrated via the European Development Fund, which is not part of the EU budget, but exists outside the Community financial framework. The last point highlights the different roles played by the ECs under the provisions of the Lomé Conventions: whilst they had direct competency in the field of trade policy, they only had more of a supervisory role when it came to the Development Policy parts of the Conventions.

The actual effects of collaboration between the EU and the ACP countries under the auspices of the Lomé Conventions were not particularly satisfactory. The share of ECs trade with the ACP countries halved in only twenty years, declining from more than 7 per cent in 1975 to between 3 and 4 per cent in the mid-1990s. Other problems were the collapse of the prices for raw materials, upon which so many developing countries relied, and increasing debt levels of many ACP countries. According to a 1995 report by the European Court of Auditors, none of the annual STABEX payments for the first three years of Lomé IV were sufficient to bridge the gap between loss of income from exports and the income levels from the previous years. Between 1990 and 1992 only just over 40 per cent of the (justified) claims could be met. In some areas not even the basic food supplies could be ensured any more.

All this left observers wondering whether other approaches might not be more suitable to help bring the ACP countries – and the poorest amongst them in particular – out of the disadvantaged situation in which they still found themselves. Two more radical alternatives to the Lomé arrangements were possible. One was the 'trade instead of aid' idea. This represents the liberal approach: free trade completely, and allow the ACP countries to specialise in what they can produce best and therewith establish their place in the global division of labour. It may be argued that the EU had already opened 99 per cent of its markets to goods coming from the now 77 ACP countries. But it must not be forgotten that the crucial agricultural sector was still partly closed for imports from the ACP countries and that the real problem for these countries would have come from the requirement for reciprocity, i.e. to open their markets too. The alternative would have been for the EU to commit itself to a much more substantial aid programme for the associated ACP countries. However, this was never likely because it would have required a substantial upgrading of the EU's Development Policy and, more difficult still, firm budgetary commitments. The EU was divided over internal fiscal arrangements, there was little willingness to increase development aid payments to ACP partners, and, as seen in Chapter Seven, the CEECs and the Union's Mediterranean neighbours were much higher on the Union's list of priorities. So, of the two alternatives, the first always looked the more likely option. Besides, the EU had to reform its ACP regime in accordance with the trade liberalisation rules of the WTO.

Although the ACP countries were sceptical about a substantial departure from the previous arrangement,[13] the EU succeeded in its demand for a new chapter to be opened in EU–ACP relations. The general principles for the future relationship between the Union and its ACP partners were agreed between representatives from the two sides in two meetings in December 1999 and February 2000. The resultant EU–ACP partnership agreement was then signed in Cotonou (Benin) a few months later in June. The new approach places more emphasis on the issue of free trade between the ACP countries themselves. To this end they have been split into several country groupings with the aim of achieving regional free trade by the year 2008. For the interim period, WTO-compliant transitional arrangements keep the existing preferential EU–ACP trade relationship in place. The Cotonou Agreement is to last for twenty years in the first instance. On the development aid side, it provides for €13.5 billion of aid for the first five years, which is in addition to the €9 billion under-spent from previous programmes.[14] But rather than being merely about trade and aid, the new EU–ACP partnership, based on the Cotonou Agreement, also has a profoundly political angle. All in all, it is based on five interdependent pillars, namely: 'a *political dimension* . . . ; *participation* . . . ; *a poverty-reduction strategy*; a *new framework for economic and trade co-operation* . . . ; and *reform of financial co-operation*'.[15]

These rather vague headlines warrant fuller investigation. The political dimension is based on a 'comprehensive, balanced and deep political dialogue leading to commitments on both sides'.[16] This dialogue is supposed to take place mainly within the institutional framework which consists of the EU–ACP Council of Ministers, a Committee of Ambassadors and the EU–ACP Joint Parliamentary Assembly. Of the three, the joint Council of Ministers is the most powerful. It 'conducts the political dialogue and adopts policy guidelines by taking decisions that are essential for [the] proper implementation of the provisions of the Cotonou Partnership Agreement. . . . [It also] examines and settles any Cotonou matter likely to impede the effective and efficient implementation of the Agreement or to constitute an obstacle to the achievement of its objectives'.[17] The Council of Ministers consists of the members of the Council of the European Union, members of the European Commission and one member from each ACP government, who meet once a year unless an extraordinary meeting is needed.[18]

The day-to-day work of monitoring the implementation of the Agreement and the progress towards achieving its objectives, as well as any other task with which the Council of Ministers may have entrusted it, is carried out by the Committee of Ambassadors. This body brings together the permanent representatives of the EU's fifteen member states, a representative from the European Commission, and the head of mission to the EU of each ACP country. The Committee of Ambassadors meets regularly.[19] The third of the EU–ACP institutions is the Joint Parliamentary Assembly, consisting of equal numbers of EU and ACP representatives, currently 77 members of the EP and one member each from the national parliaments of the 77 ACP countries.[20] Although the Joint Parliamentary Assembly is a purely consultative body, it is nevertheless an important part of the overall political dialogue that is to take place inside and outside the institutional framework, at national, regional and ACP level.[21] The Cotonou Agreement assigns to the political dialogue a key role within its political dimension. Permanent and intense contacts, discussions and debates are designed to promote initiatives and strategies that address issues such as conflict prevention or conflict resolution, and therewith contribute to peace and political stability across the EU–ACP partnership. Respect for human rights, democratic principles, the rule of law and good governance are essential principles in the political dimension of the Agreement and are to be assessed regularly within the political dialogue framework.[22]

The second pillar of the Cotonou Agreement concerns participation.[23] This derives very much from the political dialogue and the demand that this should not be restricted to the joint institutions of the partnership, or to the various layers of government within the member states. The aim here is to ensure that civil society and economic and social players can be involved in the process too. To this end they are to be, first of all, informed about the EU–ACP partnership, especially within the ACP countries. Following on from this, they are to be consulted on the economic, social and institutional reforms and policies supported by the EU and should remain involved within the subsequent processes. Finally, networking links between ACP and EU actors are to be encouraged in order to facilitate the involvement of non-state actors in the political processes of the Cotonou partnership.[24]

Pillar number three of the new EU–ACP relationship contains strategies for future development. Poverty reduction and ultimately its eradication, sustainable development, and the progressive integration of the ACP countries into the world economy are singled out as the central objective of EU–ACP cooperation.[25] According to the EU, '[t]he Agreement proposes for the first time a global strategy for development which will require the Community, Member

States and ACP partners to work together to establish a consolidated and effective strategic framework and to measure progress according to results'.[26] Three areas for support were singled out: economic development, social and human development, and regional co-operation and integration.

Economic development focuses on the development of and investment in private sectors; macro-economic and structural policies and reforms such as improved and disciplined fiscal and monetary policies; and specific aspects such as, for instance, the development of training systems, property rights issues and tourism development.[27] Social and human development refers to the social sectors and respective policies in the partner countries; 'youth issues', such as children's rights and the rights of girls, the right to an education, and the reintegration of children and internally displaced peoples in post-conflict situations; and also the promotion of cultural development.[28] Finally, regional co-operation and integration is to encourage the gradual integration of the ACP countries into the world economy and the promotion of regional economic and political co-operation and integration.[29] In addition, the development strategy of the Agreement also contains provisions on so-called cross-cutting issues, such as gender, here mainly the role of women; natural resources and the environment; and institutional development and capacity building, meaning nothing less than supporting the establishment of democratic structures and procedures.[30]

The fourth pillar of the Cotonou Agreement deals with the new framework for the economic relationship between EU and ACP countries. To enable trade to contribute more (and more directly) to development, the partners agreed to overhaul completely their previous trade relations. Whereas these were formerly based on non-reciprocal trade preferences granted by the ECs to ACP exports, the partners now agreed to enter into much more balanced economic integration agreements through new, WTO-compatible trading arrangements aimed at progressively removing barriers to trade between them and enhancing co-operation in all areas related to trade, including trade in services, competition policies and the protection of intellectual property rights.[31] To this end, the EU has begun to negotiate so-called economic partnership agreements (EPAs) with ACP countries willing to engage in a regional economic integration process. The EPAs are intended to consolidate regional integration initiatives within the ACP, and to provide an open, transparent and predictable framework for goods and services to circulate freely. The expectation is that these measures will increase the competitiveness of the ACP countries and ultimately facilitate their transition towards full participation in a liberalising world economy.[32]

The fifth and last pillar of the Cotonou Agreement concerns financial co-operation between the partners. It is guided by such principles as flexibility and efficiency, accountability, the rewarding of performance, and the inclusion also of non-state actors. The EDF instruments, which were judged to be too complex and rigid, were changed. There are two new instruments, one for providing grants and the other for providing risk capital and loans to the private sector[33] called the Investment Facility (IF). The former aims at supporting long-term development and has been given €10 billion from the ninth EDF (running from 2000 to 2005),[34] plus €1.3 billion for regional programmes. The IF, which replaces the Lomé IV risk capital and interest-rate subsidy facilities, is managed by the EIB and works on the basis of €2.2 billion from the ninth EDF. Since it is meant to function as a revolving fund, meaning that the returns accruing from its operations are expected to flow back into it, the IF is intended to be self-sustaining and therefore not to require any further EDF capital.[35] Financial co-operation under the Cotonou Agreement also involves reform of the way in which resources are allocated, including the criteria underlying respective allocations, and an extensive performance assessment procedure.[36]

It can thus be said that the Cotonou Agreement represents a substantial departure from the Lomé Conventions – at least in spirit. As far as substance is concerned, a lot still needs to be done before 2008, the year in which the WTO waiver for the continuation of the Lomé trade preferences will finally expire.[37] By then, the new EPAs will have to have been concluded between the EU and either individual ACP members or groups of them, aimed at bringing about nothing less than a revolution in their economic relationships. In accordance with the rules of the WTO, these relationships are not only to be guided by the principle of reciprocity but also, unlike the situation under the old regime, through a multilateral approach. Against this background, the negotiations of the EPAs between the EU and the ACP countries were officially launched in Brussels on 27 September 2002.[38] There it was agreed that subsequent negotiations ought to be divided into two phases.

The first of these phases took just over a year and was negotiated at an all-EU–ACP level given that the subject matter concerned all parties involved. Meetings at ambassadorial and technical level covered, for instance, the development dimension of the EPAs, market access, agriculture and fisheries, services, legal issues and trade-related areas. A joint EU–ACP report at the end of this first phase identified areas of agreement between the partners but also some issues where this had proven elusive. On 2 October 2003, the second phase of the negotiation process towards the conclusion of bilateral or multilateral EPAs got under way. Two regions had signalled their willingness to launch EPA negotiations with the EU: the Economic Community of Western African States (ECOWAS) and the Central African Economic and Monetary Community (CEMAC). ECOWAS was founded in 1975 and consists of fifteen member states, which are the eight members of the West-African Economic and Monetary Union (WAEMU) – Benin, Burkina Faso, Côte d'Ivoire, Guinea-Bissau, Mali, Niger, Senegal and Togo – plus Cape Verde, Gambia, Ghana, Guinea, Liberia, Nigeria and Sierra Leone. The principal objective of ECOWAS is to establish an EMU and to promote more generally integration in all fields of economic activity. All this may sound quite impressive but, given that some of the projects still in the pipeline include a FTA, a CET and a single currency, ECOWAS clearly has some way to go to meet its own objectives. On the other hand, an EPA with the EU is likely to give the regional integration process a fillip. Besides, WAEMU is already a good way ahead of its partners within ECOWAS. Set up in 1994, its members share a common currency (the CFA franc), pursue a common economic and monetary policy, and have had a customs union since 1 January 2000. Its next aim is to develop a common market allowing the free flow of goods, services, capital and people, including the right of establishment. CEMAC, the other group of ACP countries ready to enter into EPA negotiations with the EU, is a customs and monetary union formed by six countries: Cameroon, the Central African Republic, Chad, the Republic of Congo, Gabon, and Guinea Equatorial. São Tomé and Príncipe is linked to CEMAC by way of a free trade arrangement and will therefore be part of the EPA negotiations with the EU.[39]

Although reform of the EU–ACP relationship is ongoing, it would be naive to believe that the process will be smooth and not encounter major difficulties. The aims that the partners have set themselves in the Cotonou Agreement are high and similar objectives have been regular features of each and every ECs–ACP contractual arrangement from the early days of the European integration process. However, this time around the prospects are enhanced as economic reforms appear inevitable. With the WTO in place, a new and 'higher' authority has been created by whose rules the EU must abide – eventually.

The EU and the Far East

In 1994, the European Commission published its first strategy paper on Asia (as a whole continent). This new approach either replaced or substantially upgraded earlier agreements to create a more formalised dialogue with China, Japan, India, South Korea and ASEAN.[40] Nominally, this dialogue spans economics, politics and security and is conducted at all levels, ranging from talks between low-ranking officials and experts to bilateral and multilateral summit meetings of top politicians. In reality, though, the EU–Asia relationship has traditionally been, and continues to be, foremost about economics.[41] Three EU Far Eastern partners have been selected for discussion here. These are Japan, the world's third greatest economic force and for many years the EU's principal economic partner in Asia; ASEAN because of its close institutional connection with the EU and its being the Union's second most important economic associate in Asia; and finally China, which, as the economic superpower of the future, has begun to challenge the positions of Japan and ASEAN within the hierarchy of EU economic relationships.

For decades, economic issues dominated the connection between Japan and what is now the EU. This is unsurprising given Japan's status as one of the most important trading partners of the ECs. By far the largest economy in Asia, Japan has long been the EU's third largest export market and even its second most important market for imports world-wide.[42] The domination of economic issues in the relationship began to change when, following the first EC–Japan summit, the two put their linkage on a formal footing. This was done through the 'Joint Declaration on Relations between the European Community and its Member States and Japan', signed in The Hague in 1991. It remained the basis of the bilateral EC/EU–Japan relationship until a successor agreement was signed in 2001.

The 1991 Joint Declaration started a regular dialogue between the two parties 'on major international issues, which are of common interest to both . . . be they political, economic, scientific, cultural or other'.[43] It was agreed to hold annual consultations, either in Europe or in Japan, between the Japanese Prime Minister, the President of the European Council and the President of the European Commission. In addition to these meetings at the highest political level, annual meetings were held between the Commission and the Japanese government at ministerial level, as well as six-monthly talks between the troika of EU foreign ministers, the Commissioner for External Relations and the Japanese Foreign Minister.[44]

Arguably the most tangible outcomes of this formalised relationship, and the regular discussions it brought with it, were felt in the field of economics. The trade relationship had not always been a happy one. The root cause of problems had been Japanese protectionism *vis-à-vis* European trade and FDI. For decades Japan had pursued a mercantilist policy of encouraging exports whilst strictly limiting imports. This naturally resulted in a substantial Japanese trade surplus with the EU, an EU trade deficit with Japan and a series of trade disputes. Matters improved once a gradual opening of Japanese markets was induced by a combination of enhanced dialogue and, more especially, the Asian economic crisis, the creation of the WTO and the realisation that Japan was suffering as a consequence of the structural rigidities of its own system.[45]

However, the EU was convinced that this limited opening still left scope for further improvement in the bilateral relationship. In December 2001, the two parties agreed on what they called 'An Action Plan for EU–Japan Cooperation', entitled 'Shaping Our Common Future'.[46] Therein, they undertook to progress their relationship 'from consultation to joint action'.[47] This encompassed not only the field of economics but also the political relationship, the strengthening of which was explicitly stated as a 'priority objective' of the two partners.[48] In all, the Action Plan addressed four principal objectives: promoting peace and security, strengthening the economic and trade partnership, coping with global and societal challenges, and bringing together people and cultures.[49]

Taking these objectives in reverse order, the latter is meant to 'breathe life into the EU–Japan relationship', which, according to the Action Plan, could only be realised through 'people-to-people links'.[50] In more concrete terms this means: extending existing contacts in the academic field, ranging from schools to universities and research institutions; adding to them exchange schemes offering periods of vocational training and/or work experience; and, more generally, encouraging contacts and exchange programmes across civil society as a whole.[51]

The third objective of the Action Plan, addressing global and societal challenges, included a number of issues. Given that the Joint Action Plan was published shortly after the terrorist attacks of 11 September 2001, combating international terrorism unsurprisingly topped their common agenda in this field. Other challenges to be tackled together included: international crime and drug trafficking, global environmental problems, and common societal and demographic challenges, such as gender equality and the problem of ageing populations. These challenges were to be met in various ways, such as political and judicial co-operation to fight terrorism and international crime, and technological and scientific collaboration to address environmental questions. The Action Plan also recognised that the global nature of some societal problems and demographic developments required EU–Japanese joint action to be developed alongside multilateral dialogue designed to establish international co-operation in addressing shared problems.[52]

Like all such bilateral papers, the Joint Action Plan for EU–Japan Co-operation was, ultimately, largely a declaration of intent. Few would expect all the aims and objectives to be met. Yet one area in which the prospects for actually meeting them are reasonable is the field of trade and commerce. Although the Action Plan refers to vague goals such as 'advancing the global economy', 'strengthening the international monetary and financial system', and 'fighting poverty', there are specific provisions in which the two partners have such a vital mutual interest that change can already be detected. Arguably the most visible of these is progress in the bilateral trade and investment partnership.[53]

The volume of trade in goods between the two partners has increased tremendously over the last twenty years or so, with ECs exports to Japan growing more than eight-fold between 1980 and 2001 and imports from Japan to the Communities growing 'merely' by a factor of just under five during the same period. Within this, however, the Commission has remained highly critical of continuing high levels of Japanese protectionism, especially in traditional industries.[54] This is unsurprising given that the EU ran a trade deficit of over €30,000 million in 2001, albeit with a slight amelioration given a surplus of around €6,500 million in EU trade in services with Japan during the same year.[55] More surprising has been that the response has thus far been much more constructive and less antagonistic than past, often successful, ECs/EU resort to GATT and later the WTO.

One such initiative was the Mutual Recognition Agreement that came into force in January 2002. The aim of the MRA is the reduction in the cost of certifying products for conformity with the technical regulations of both the EU and Japan. The MRA enables the exporter to test and certify products against the regulatory requirements of the other party, but on its own territory before exporting. As the other country recognises the test, no additional procedures are required, therewith speeding up the process and generally saving cost. The MRA between the EU and Japan covers products in four specific areas: pharmaceuticals, chemicals, telecommunication equipment and electrical equipment. The European Commission estimates that the MRA with Japan could cover trade worth more than €21,000 million per year, thereby saving exporters up to €400 million annually.[56] It has to be expected that such reduction of red-tape will encourage and ultimately increase trade.

Another important aspect of the economic relationship between the EU and Japan is the two-way Regulatory Reform Dialogue, previously known as the Deregulation Dialogue. The EU has naturally argued for greater Japanese openness and deregulation to overcome structural obstacles to trade and FDI[57] and to re-energise Japan's economy and thereby its attraction as an economic partner, through access to foreign capital and expertise. In this the EU has again had some success, not least because Japan has been forced to address its well-documented economic travails.[58] Whereas in 2000 inflows of FDI from Japan into the EU were a fifth higher than outflows of FDI from the EU to Japan, a year later more than two and a half times as much FDI went from the EU to Japan than the other way around. However, there is still some way to go in the EU's quest for a more balanced FDI relationship with Japan, both in relative and absolute terms. For instance, in absolute figures, Japanese companies had more than one-fifth more FDI stocks in the EU than EU businesses held in Japan in 2001. In relative terms, Japanese FDI stocks accounted for 5.1 per cent of all FDI stocks in the EU, whilst EU FDI in Japan comprised a mere 2.3 per cent of all FDI stocks there by the end of the same year.[59]

Japan's apparent U-turn on international trade and related issues is reflected also in closer co-operation with the EU on multilateral trade[60] and greater agreement on the spill-over benefits of free trade in terms of peace and stability, the latter being the first objective of the EU–Japan Joint Action Plan. The two have thus begun to work more closely together in the WTO to liberalise the international economy and in international fora such as the UN to promote and protect common concerns that include human rights, WMD non-proliferation and international law. They also work together in Asian regional multilateral arrangements, notably ASEM and the ARF.[61] The latter was created in 1994 and, with a membership of twenty-three countries, is explicitly concerned with informal multilateral dialogue on regional security in the Asia-Pacific region.[62] The former was founded in 1996 with an overall objective of strengthening Europe–Asia ties and has a current membership of twenty-five states plus the European Commission. Its mandate is broader than that of the ARF, including as it does dialogue on political, economic and cultural issues, and is developed through biannual summit meetings and annual ministerial gatherings.[63]

One subset of the ARF with which the ECs have particular links, spanning over twenty years, is the ASEAN group of South-East Asian countries. The first formal link between the two country groupings was established with the signing of a co-operation agreement in 1980 between the then nine members of the ECs and the original five members of ASEAN: Indonesia, Malaysia, the Philippines, Singapore and Thailand. Brunei and Vietnam, which joined ASEAN in 1984 and 1995 respectively, have since also been incorporated into the EU–ASEAN Agreement. In a similar vein, protocols to incorporate Laos and Cambodia, which joined ASEAN in 1997 and 1999, were signed with the EU in 2000 and are currently being ratified. Myanmar cannot currently participate in EU–ASEAN co-operation schemes because the EU has refused to negotiate an extension of its co-operation agreement with that country on grounds of its lack of democracy and respect for human rights.[64]

The EU–ASEAN relationship is nominally concerned primarily with political dialogue, which is conducted through regular biannual ministerial meetings and through post-ministerial conferences that immediately follow the annual ASEAN meeting and the ARF gatherings. Nevertheless, in a paper published in 2001 and entitled 'Europe and Asia: A Strategic Framework for Enhanced Partnerships', the European Commission referred to ASEAN first as a key economic and only then also as a political partner. That the relationship between EU and ASEAN is at least as much about economics as it is about politics is shown by what might be called the 'institutional structure' of the EU–ASEAN partnership. The EC–ASEAN Joint Co-operation Committee is a committee of officials that regularly meets every eighteen months and has as its task the promotion and review of activities deriving from the co-operation agreement. Over time it has thus developed a number of sub-committees that deal with economic and economic-related issues, including trade and investment, economic and industrial co-operation, and science and technology.[65] The economic importance of ASEAN to the EU is also reflected in its having been collectively the Union's second most important trade and investment partner in Asia after Japan for many years. Moreover, the EU–ASEAN trade relationship is more balanced than that between the EU and Japan, and EU investors have for some time been able to hold more FDI stocks in ASEAN countries than in Japan.[66]

In recent years, China has begun to challenge the relative significance of both Japan and ASEAN to the EU. The European Commission estimates two-way trade between the Communities and China to have increased more than forty-fold between 1978 and 2002.[67] Admittedly, this impressive statistic owes much to the low base from which China started. Nevertheless, latest available figures (2001–02)[68] show that China has in recent years moved up the ranks to become the EU's second most important source of imports after the US, having overtaken ASEAN in 2001 and even Japan in 2002. Given the substantial trade deficit that the EU has run up with China over the decades, the situation as far as export destinations for EU trade is concerned looks slightly different. Here China is still a less important partner than Japan and ASEAN were in 2001 and 2002. Indeed, combined export and import figures for 2001 show Japan still ahead of ASEAN and China in terms of its percentage share of EU trade. However, few doubt China's ascendancy as a regional economic power. Given the enormous growth rates of imports from China alone, the 0.1 per cent lead of ASEAN over China in 2001 looks likely to have been overtaken in 2002. Even the 0.7 per cent gap between China and Japan might have been closed, for, although no firm figures to substantiate this claim fully have yet been published, the Commission refers in its most recent publications to China as the EU's second largest non-European trading partner after the US.[69]

The economic and commercial links between China and what is now the EU predate their bilateral political dialogue by many years and have recently regained centre stage, a development encouraged by substantial political and economic reforms in China itself and by its accession to the WTO in 2001. This has had mixed results for the EU so far. It has benefited greatly from Chinese opening to FDI. The European Commission estimates that over the past five years an average of US$4.2 billion of FDI from the EU has been invested in China, bringing stocks of EU FDI to over US$33.9 billion.[70] This may still not be quite as much as the EU has invested in ASEAN or Japan, but it already represents more than the EU's FDI stocks in Japan in 2001.[71] The trade picture, however, looks less encouraging for the EU. The EU's trade deficit with China is its largest with any country in the world, and dialogue over market access, coupled with China's membership of the WTO, is only slowly opening the potentially largest market in the world for EU products.[72] Indeed, while the EU's economic links with ASEAN are the oldest of the three Far Eastern relationships looked at, and those with Japan traditionally the most intensive, it is the relationship with China that offers the EU the greatest future potential and challenges.

The EU's economic links with Latin America

Links between Latin America and what is now the EU date back to the 1960s. Since then the ECs/EU have developed relations between the two continents in a number of fora, which the European Commission puts into two broad categories: 'bi-regional' and 'specialised dialogues'. Although this looks as if it might distinguish between multilateral and bilateral approaches, the particular difference lies not so much in which country is being dealt with but rather in what the relationship is all about. In this respect, bi-regional relationships are about institutionalised political dialogues and two such links have been established under this headline: between the EU and the Rio Group and between the EU and Latin America and the Caribbean (LAC). The Rio Group was formed in 1986 by Argentina, Brazil, Colombia, Mexico, Panama, Peru, Uruguay and Venezuela. In 1990, Chile, Ecuador, Bolivia and Paraguay joined, and in 2000 Costa Rica, El Salvador, Guatemala, Honduras, Nicaragua and the Dominican Republic also became members, together with a representative of the Caribbean Community and Common Market, Caricom (at the time of writing: Guyana).[73] The Rio Group thus comprises all Latin American countries, is connected to Caricom and was first engaged by the ECs in political dialogue in 1990.[74] The two sides have since met at ministerial level roughly every two years.[75] In June 1999, the political dialogue with LAC was intensified with a summit meeting between the heads of state and government from the region and the EU in Rio de Janeiro. Here a strategic partnership between the EU and all of Latin America and the Caribbean, not only Caricom, was inaugurated.[76] A second summit subsequently took place in Madrid in 2002 and a third has been scheduled for 2004 in Mexico.[77]

Next to these bi-regional relationships, the EU also maintains what the Commission refers to as 'specialised dialogues' with countries and country groupings in Latin America. What is 'special' about these dialogues is that they are more concerned with economics, especially trade and FDI, than with politics. The EU has established such dialogues with five entities: Mercosur, the Andean Community, Central America and the two countries that are not part of any of these clubs, namely Mexico and Chile. The levels of co-operation under respective agreements differ quite substantially, ranging from GSP access to the EU's market for Andean and Central American countries to quite far-reaching free trade agreements with Chile and Mexico.[78]

Arguably the least developed of the EU's economic relationships with Latin America is the one with the Central American group of countries, consisting of Guatemala, El Salvador, Honduras, Nicaragua, Costa Rica and Panama. Established in 1984 as the San José Dialogue, it started mainly as a political discussion forum to support democratisation and peace in the region. Although the EU is the group's second most important trade and investment partner after the US, EU exports to the region – mostly industrialised goods – amount to less than 0.5 per cent of all EU exports world-wide. The commercial relationships between the partners are dominated by the so-called 'drugs regime' of the GSP, which aims to support the region's efforts to combat drug production and trafficking. However, whilst this special regime provides duty-free access to the EU's markets for all industrial products, it only does so for some agricultural goods. Given that Central America exports mainly agricultural goods to the EU it is questionable just how effective the drugs regime is. On a more positive note, the EU has over recent years managed to increase substantially its FDI in Central America.[79]

The alliance between the ECs and the Andean Community (CAN) is much older than that with Central America, stretching back over thirty years. Despite this, the economic link between the EU and Venezuela, Colombia, Ecuador, Peru and Bolivia is little more advanced than that with Central America. The origins of the ECs–CAN partnership can also be traced back to a political dialogue, but here the fight against drugs has been, and remains, the priority objective of the relationship. This has been echoed in the economic arena. Apart from the fact that CAN was the first Latin American region to receive development aid from the Union, the region has also benefited from the 'drugs GSP', possibly to greater effect. The European Commission claims that exports from CAN to the EU have grown by 60 per cent between 1990 and 2000, and that some 90 per cent of products exported by CAN to the EU were exempted from customs duties.[80] The EU's trade relationship with CAN also appears to be slightly more intense than that with Central America. The Union exports around 0.8 per cent of its total to the region. When it comes to FDI, the EU is the leading investor in CAN, accounting for more than a quarter of the total investment there, albeit that the amounts invested are substantially smaller than those put into Central America.[81]

A different case altogether is Mercosur, a fledgling common market formed in 1991 by Argentina, Brazil, Uruguay and Paraguay. Less than a year after its inception, the ECs signed an agreement with the four members to provide technical and institutional support to further its development. Whilst progress with the integration process has been erratic and slow within Mercosur, the link between the EU and its southern American counterpart has developed substantially. Since 1996, the relationship between the two has been governed by an Interregional Framework Co-operation Agreement. The principal aim of this agreement was to start negotiations on yet another one – an accord that would lead to the creation of a free trade area, in both goods and services, between the two entities. It was not, however, until June 1999 that negotiations on the latter project were given the go-ahead at an EU–Mercosur meeting in Rio de Janeiro. Since then, progress has been much more tangible. After a preliminary exchange of thoughts in Brussels in November 1999, where basic rules for negotiations and a timetable were agreed, the first full round of negotiations between the two partners was held on 6 and 7 April 2000 in Buenos Aires. Since then another ten rounds of similar talks have taken place, roughly two to three times a year. The eleventh and latest so far was held between 2 and 5 December 2003 in Brussels. Currently, at least another four meetings are scheduled for 2004 to bring about the conclusion of the long-awaited free trade area between the two entities – possibly at a meeting in October 2004.[82]

The EU and Mercosur might thus be quite close to a comprehensive free trade agreement. This can only be mutually beneficial as their economic links are already quite well developed. The EU is both Mercosur's principal trading partner and its biggest source of FDI. Around 50 per cent of all EU FDI in Latin America goes to Mercosur – in total around 7 per cent of all outgoing EU FDI in 2001. FDI stocks in Mercosur even comprise 7.5 per cent of all EU stocks abroad. In terms of trade, exports to and imports from Mercosur amount to around 2.5 per cent each of the EU's respective global figures. The southern American group was consequently the Union's ninth most important export market and tenth most important source of imports in 2001, and there is clear scope to intensify further this trade and investment relationship. That this potential may be delayed is due, primarily, to the EU's simultaneous avowed commitment to international trade liberalisation and its discriminatory CAP, a problem underscored by the fact that agricultural goods accounted for a full 16 per cent of all EU imports.[83]

Two countries in Latin America with which the EU has already concluded free trade arrangements are Mexico and Chile. The EU–Mexico bilateral relationship is based on the 1997 'Economic Partnership, Political Co-ordination and Co-operation Agreement' that entered into force in October 2000. Apart from a political dialogue, the economic aspects of this accord foresaw the establishment of a FTA in goods and services, the mutual opening of procurement markets, and the liberalisation of capital movements and payments. Also included in the agreement was the adoption of rules concerning competition and intellectual property rights. According to the European Commission, the FTA 'covers an unprecedented broad spectrum of economic aspects. It includes a full liberalization of industrial products by 2003, for the EC, and by 2007 – with a maximum 5 per cent tariff applied by 2003 – for Mexico, a substantial liberalization for agricultural and fisheries products and, as regards rules of origin, a satisfactory balance between EC policy of harmonization and market access considerations.'[84] The FTA between the EU and Chile is even more recent than the one with Mexico. Negotiations started in April 2000 and a new association agreement was signed between the two partners in November 2002. At present, its provisions on trade and institutional issues have been applied provisionally since February 2003. This brings the EU into line with a number of other countries with which Chile has concluded FTA agreements in recent years, including Canada, Mexico, South Korea, most of the major South American countries, and the US.[85]

The EU has thus substantially deepened its economic relationships in Latin America in the post-Cold War era. The free trade agreements with Mexico and Chile are the first such comprehensive trade accords with any country outside the EU's immediate vicinity. Indeed, they seem to be the Union's preferred means of developing its economic relationships in the future – as the Mercosur negotiations clearly reflect. However, where such agreements appear beyond immediate reach, as with CAN and Central America, the EU still promotes trade liberalisation and regionalism. Of this its support for Mercosur's objective of establishing its own common market is a good example.[86]

Conclusion

This selective examination of some of the EU's world-wide economic relationships underlines its established credentials as a global economic superpower. Its economic presence can be felt at every level, from the sub-state through to the international and the global. It has a vast and ever expanding and intensifying cobweb of relationships that criss-cross the world. And it is at the heart of efforts to liberalise international markets and to manage processes of economic globalisation.

More interesting still are the ways in which the EU operationalises its global economic presence and the objectives that it pursues. It pushes its global trade liberalisation agenda through the WTO, a forum that has given it additional leverage, if also some occasional embarrassment. This same agenda is pursued on a bilateral, multilateral and regional basis and through the terms and conditions contained within its vast array of economic relationships. The Cotonou Agreement, for instance, demonstrates EU commitment to fostering free trade not only between itself and its partners but also among its partners.

Furthermore, the EU has used, and continues to use, its formidable tools of economic coercion against those that flout their free trade commitments.

The examination of EU relationships with the Far East, Latin America and the ACP countries also indicates that the Union's commitment to global trade liberalisation is both problematic and even less an ultimate objective than it is a contributory factor in the pursuit of larger goals. The most obvious problem is the hypocrisy of the EU preaching free trade whilst retaining a seemingly devout attachment to its own discriminatory structures, notably the arcane CAP. Also, despite being a global economic superpower, the EU's economic influence is still more pronounced in some regions of the world than in others and its relationships with some countries, such as China, are more difficult than with others. Furthermore, the EU's economic relationships increasingly form part of a much stronger and clearly articulated EU ambition to develop its global politico-security influence. Engagement and socialisation underpin strongly EU promotion of free trade and its economic relationships increasingly evince the Union's normative agenda as it binds its economic partners, big and small, into what are ultimately formalised political processes at the bilateral and multilateral levels.

Notes

1 For details, see http://europa.eu.int/comm/external_relations/canada/intro/index.htm.

2 Australia and New Zealand, see
   http://europa.eu.int/comm/external_relations/asia/reg/aus.htm.

3 Saudi Arabia, Kuwait, Bahrain, Qatar, United Arab Emirates, Oman, see
   http://europa.eu.int/comm/external_relations/gr/index.htm.

4 In 2001, see WTO, 'International Trade Statistics 2002',
   http://www.wto.org/english/res_e/statis_e/its2002_e/chp_3_e.pdf.

5 The member states in question were: Belgium, France, Italy and the Netherlands. A list of the overseas countries and territories linked to the EEC by way of association was annexed to the Treaty of Rome (Annex IV). See Article 131, EEC Treaty (1957).

6 Article 131, EEC Treaty (1957). More concrete objectives were listed in Article 132, EECT (1957).

7 The Founding Treaties and the TEU were renumbered with the coming into force of the Treaty of Amsterdam in 1999.

8 See http://europa.eu.int/comm/trade/bilateral/acp/index_en.htm.

9 Legally, the EC only gained its own Development Policy with the ratification of the Treaty on European Union in November 1993. Since then, the EU has had a clearly defined role in addition to the ones played by the member states themselves (Article 177–181 [formerly 130u–130y] ECT).

10 See http://europa.eu.int/comm/trade/bilateral/acp/index_en.htm.

11 For more details on STABEX and SYSMIN, see Dinan, D. (ed.) (2000) *Encyclopedia of the European Union*, Basingstoke: Macmillan, p. 445.

12 See Lister, M. (1997) *The European Union and the South: Relations with Developing Counties*, London: Routledge, p. 134.

13 See, for instance, Harding, G. (1999) 'Bid to Narrow Gap in Lomé Talks' *European Voice* 5 (5) p. 10; or Harding, G. (1999) 'WTO Has Yet to Win Over ACP States' *European Voice* 5 (33) n.p.

14 'ACP–EU ministerial meeting' *European Voice* 6 (6) p. 30.

15 Jones, R.A. (2001) *The Politics and Economics of the European Union: An Introductory Text*, 2nd edn, Cheltenham: Edward Elgar, pp. 421–2.

16 Article 8, Cotonou Agreement, http://www.acpsec.org/gb/cotonou/pdf/agr01_en.pdf.

17 Unattributed (September–October 2002) 'The ACP–EU Council of Ministers Explained' *The Courier ACP–EU* **194**, http://europa.eu.int/comm/development/body/publications/courier/courier194/en/en_018_ni.pdf.

18 See Article 15, Cotonou Agreement.

19 Article 16, ibid.

20 For the particular details of the Joint Parliamentary Assembly, see Article 17, ibid.

21 See (2001) 'The Cotonou Agreement' *Europe on the Move*, Luxemburg: Office for Official Publications of the European Communities, http://www.delsur.cec.eu.int/en/eu_and_acp_countries/cotonou/print.htm; also Article 8, Cotonou Agreement.

22 Article 8, Cotonou Agreement; see also 'The Cotonou Agreement'.

23 Article 2, Cotonou Agreement.

24 See 'The Cotonou Agreement'.

25 Article 19, Cotonou Agreement.

26 'The Cotonou Agreement'.

27 The detailed provisions are to be found in Articles 21–24, Cotonou Agreement.

28 See Articles 25–27, ibid. Current figures of officially recognised 'persons of concern' are available at http://www.unhcr.ch/cgi-bin/texis/vtx/statistics.

29 Articles 28–30, Cotonou Agreement.

30 Articles 31–33, ibid.

31 For a complete list, see 'The Cotonou Agreement'.

32 European Commission (August 2002) 'Bilateral Trade Relations: ACP Countries (77)', http://europa.eu.int/comm/trade/bilateral/acp/index_en.htm.

33 Jones, *The Politics and Economics of the European Union*, p. 422.

34 See Aussenwirtschaft Österreich (September 2001) 'EDF – European Development Fund', http://www.wko.at/awo/services/drittstaaten/edf.htm.

35 'The Cotonou Agreement'.

36 For more details on respective reforms, see ibid.

37 Unattributed (November 2001) 'EC–ACP Cotonou Waiver Finally Granted' *Bridges Weekly Trade News Digest* 5 (39) http://www.ictsd.org/weekly/01-11-15/story2.htm.

38 European Commission (2002) *Economic Partnership Agreements: Start of Negotiations*, Brussels, European Communities.

39 European Commission (October 2003) 'EU–ACPs: Opening of Trade Negotiations with West and Central Africa', http://europa.eu.int/rapid/start/cgi/guesten.ksh?p_action.gettxt=gt&doc=IP/03/1334|0|RAPID&lg=EN&display=.

40 European Commission, 'Asia Relations', http://europa.eu.int/comm/external_relations/asia/rel/index.htm.

41 Algieri, F. (2002) 'Asienpolitik' in *Europa von A bis Z*, 8th edn, Weidenfeld, W. and Wessels, W. (eds), Bonn: Bundeszentrale für politische Bildung, p. 67.

42 European Commission (May 2003) 'EU–Japan Economic and Trade Relations', http://europa.eu.int/comm/external_relations/japan/intro/eco_trade_relat.htm.

43 European Commission (May 1991) 'Joint Declaration on Relations between the European Community and its Member States and Japan', http://europa.eu.int/comm/external_relations/japan/intro/joint_pol_decl.htm.

44 For more details of the 1991 Joint Declaration, see ibid.

45 European Commission, 'EU–Japan Economic and Trade Relations'.

46 European Commission (2001) 'Shaping Our Common Future – An Action Plan for EU–Japan Cooperation', http://europa.eu.int/comm/external_relations/japan/summit_12_01/actionplan.pdf.

47 European Commission, 'EU–Japan Economic and Trade Relations'.

48 European Commission, 'The EU's Relations with Japan – Overview', http://europa.eu.int/comm/external_relations/japan/intro/index.htm.

49 European Commission, 'Shaping Our Common Future', p. 2.

50 Ibid., p. 3.

51 Ibid., p. 21.

52 Ibid., pp. 14–20.

53 Ibid., pp. 9–13.

54 European Commission, 'EU–Japan Economic and Trade Relations'.

55 European Commission, 'Bilateral Trade Relations', http://europa.eu.int/comm/trade/bilateral/data.htm.

56 European Commission (May 2003) 'Mutual Recognition Agreement' *The EU's Relations with Japan,* http://europa.eu.int/comm/external_relations/japan/intro/mra.htm.

57 For a brief introduction of the way in which the economy has traditionally been influenced by the state in Japan, see Dicken, P. (1998) *Global Shift: Transforming the World Economy*, 3rd edn, London: Paul Chapman, pp. 121–5.

58 European Commission, 'EU–Japan Economic and Trade Relations'.

59 European Commission, 'Bilateral Trade Relations'.

60 Delegation of the European Commission in Japan (2002) 'EU–Japan Economic and Trade Relations', http://jpn.cec.eu.int/english/eu-relations/e3-03.htm.

61 European Commission, 'Shaping Our Common Future', p. 4.

62 ARF membership: the ten countries belonging to ASEAN, Indonesia, the Philippines, Thailand, Vietnam, Malaysia, Singapore, Brunei, Myanmar, Laos and

Cambodia; the twelve so-called ASEAN dialogue partners, Australia, Canada, China, North Korea, South Korea, US, India, Japan, Mongolia, New Zealand, Russia and the EU; plus one ASEAN observer, Papua New Guinea. For more details on the ARF, see European Commission (March 2003) 'ASEAN Regional Forum (ARF)', http://europa.eu.int/comm/external_relations/asean/intro/arf.htm.

63 Membership: the fifteen EU member states, European Commission, Brunei, China, Indonesia, Japan, South Korea, Malaysia, the Philippines, Singapore, Thailand and Vietnam. For more information on ASEM, see European Commission (October 2003) 'The Asia Europe Meeting (ASEM) – Overview', http://europa.eu.int/comm/external_relations/asem/intro/index.htm.

64 European Commission (January 2003) 'The EU-ASEAN Partnership' *The EU's Relations with ASEAN – Overview*, http://europa.eu.int/comm/external_relations/asean/intro/index.htm.

65 Ibid.

66 For details, see European Commission, 'Bilateral Trade Relations'.

67 European Commission (September 2003) 'The EU's China Policy' *The EU's Relations with China – Overview*, http://europa.eu.int/comm/external_relations/china/intro/index.htm.

68 See European Commission, 'China Trade Statistics', http://trade-info.cec.eu.int/doclib/cfm/doclib_type.cfm?type=9; also European Commission (2003) 'EU Trade with Main Partners 2001 (Mio euro)', http://europa.eu.int/comm/external_relations/andean/doc/trade/eutrade03.pdf; and European Commission (2001) 'EU Trade with Main Partners 2000 (Mio euro)', http://europa.eu.int/comm/external_relations/peru/intro/perumainp.pdf.

69 European Commission, 'The EU's China Policy'.

70 Ibid.

71 European Commission, 'Bilateral Trade Relations'.

72 European Commission, 'The EU's China Policy'.

73 Grupo de Río, 'Información Básica sobre el Mecanismo Permanente de Consulta y Concertación Política – Grupo de Río', http://www.rree.gob.pe/domino/nsf/GrupoRio.nsf/MarcoGeneralGR?OpenFrameSet.

74 European Commission, 'Chronology of EU–Latin America and EU–Caribbean Relations' *History of the EU–Latin America–Caribbean Relations*, http://europa.eu.int/comm/world/lac/chrono_en.htm.

75 European Commission (June 2003) 'Overview' *The EU's Relations with Latin America*, http://europa.eu.int/comm/external_relations/la/index.htm#1a.

76 For a list of the EU's LAC partners, see http://europa.eu.int/comm/world/lac/map_en.htm.

77 European Commission, 'Overview' *The EU's Relations with Latin America*.

78 Ibid.

79 European Commission (October 2003) 'Overview' *The EU's Relations with Central America*, http://europa.eu.int/comm/external_relations/ca/index.htm.

80 European Commission (September 2003) 'Overview' *The EU's Relations with the Andean Community*, http://europa.eu.int/comm/external_relations/andean/intro/index.htm.

81 European Commission, 'The EU and Andean Community', http://europa.eu.int/comm/world/lac/and_en.htm; European Commission, 'Overview' *The EU's Relations with the Andean Community*.

82 European Commission (September 2003) 'Overview' *The EU's Relations with Mercosur*, http://europa.eu.int/comm/external_relations/mercosur/intro/index.htm; European Commission (November 2003) 'EU–Mercosur: Trade Minister Agrees Roadmap for Final Phase of Free Trade Negotiations', http://www.europa.eu.int/comm/external_relations/mercosur/intro/ip03_1544.htm.

83 European Commission, 'The EU and Mercosur', http://europa.eu.int/comm/world/lac/merc.htm; European Commission, 'Bilateral Trade Relations'.

84 European Commission (February 2003) 'Overview' *The EU's Relations with Mexico*, http://europa.eu.int/comm/external_relations/mexico/intro/index.htm.

85 European Commission (April 2003) 'Overview' *The EU's Relations with Chile*, http://europa.eu.int/comm/external_relations/chile/intro/index.htm.

86 European Commission, 'Overview', *The EU's Relations with Latin America*.

CHAPTER 10

Conclusion

This book began with avowed aims of examining what the EU has done primarily within post-Cold War international relations, of assessing what happened and of asking what this tells us of the EU as an international actor. The preceding chapters have dealt principally with the first two of these aims. They have examined the EU's economic and security relationships with other regions and actors and placed these in the contexts of EU external relations competencies and of key changes within the international system, especially the implications of the collapse of the Cold War and processes of globalisation. What remains is to draw some conclusions about the EU in international relations and factors likely to help determine its future evolution as an international actor.

Perception and reality

Perception has for centuries been a critical element in determining international relations. International actors, based on very incomplete information, seek to predict what a state (traditionally) is likely to do. What are its capabilities? What drives its foreign policies? What does past precedent suggest of its likely future conduct? Similarly, the population of a state will, either directly or indirectly, help determine the national interest, foreign policy principles and the capacity of a state to fulfil its objectives. Both processes build expectations and involve drawing comparisons between one state and another in terms such as relative strength and typology of political leadership.

The importance to the EU of international perception is no less than for a state. In fact, it is arguably more important, for as an involving *sui generis* entity it possesses none of the traditional advantages accorded to states, such as popular support based around national identity or membership of many international organisations. At the extreme, people lay down their lives for their country. The EU can make no such claim – nor should it necessarily seek to do so. Instead it must seek new forms of legitimacy and foster the trust both of the peoples of its member states and of other international actors. However, this is a task made doubly difficult by the vagaries of perception and misperception. First, the EU's building process has made it prone to spectacular failures, especially in CFSP. Consider, for instance, the Balkan crises of the early 1990s and the severe splits within the EU over Iraq in 2002–03. These too often obscure the considerable, if lower profile, successes of the EU in its external relations. In addition, the difficulties for the EU in developing a positive international perception are compounded by media assessments of 'newsworthiness'. In this respect, coverage of its failures or of acrimonious debate surrounding its future often far outweigh that accorded to important and successful technical or incremental developments made by the EU in its external relations.

More significant still is that judgements of the EU are often based on false comparisons. As we have seen, the EU has at its disposal an impressive range of external relations instruments. This encourages the temptation to compare the EU's management of its external relations with that of states, and to judge its effectiveness accordingly. This same danger is encouraged by the rhetoric of politicians and bureaucrats and the gross simplifications frequently embedded in media coverage of the EU. Statements such as Jacques Poos's 'hour of Europe' at the onset of the Balkan crises encourage false expectations of EU capabilities and recklessly endanger its slowly accrued credibility. The propensity of member state governments to scapegoat the EU to justify unpopular policies or lack of action to domestic constituencies likewise contributes to a false impression of EU autonomy/responsibility in its external relations. The same can be said to result from frequent unsophisticated media treatment of the EU as a somehow autonomous entity empowered with great authority over its member states.

The reality is much different. The EU is far from a single entity that dictates the actions of its member states. The member states have hitherto ensured that the EU does not have recourse to all the external relations tools traditionally held by a state, most notably military force. Perhaps more significantly, EU external relations are marked by a constant battle for competencies, both between the member states and the different EC institutions and between the different EC institutions themselves. This is most obvious in the accelerated programme of treaty revisions in recent years but is just as important in the day-to-day interactions of EC institutions and the rulings of the ECJ. Consider, for instance, the importance of the latter in extending Commission authority within EU external environment policy. The consequences of this constant negotiation of competence are most starkly reflected in the absurd, at least from the perspective of the effective co-ordination of external relations instruments, divisions of EU foreign policy in the TEU pillar structure.

It is instructive here to reconsider the caricature of the EU as 'an economic giant, a political dwarf, and a military worm'.[1] As interesting a sound-bite as this may be, it is naturally replete with problems. Take, for instance, the distinction between international presence and effective international action. EU wealth, trade relationships and central position in global financial institutions justify its ascribed status as an economic giant. Likewise, its potential economic power accords it preponderance in most of its economic relationships. Yet, as we have seen, this giant is still far from complete and frequently experiences grave co-ordination difficulties. The SEM remains unfinished, the eurozone is liable for a time at least after the 2004 enlargement to comprise only approximately half of the EU membership, and EU competencies are arranged such that even in areas of pooled sovereignty it can be a slow and cumbersome actor. Matters can, of course, be still worse in areas of concurrent or member state competence.

In terms of political and military standing, the EU has far greater international presence than the Belgian Foreign Minister's caricature allows for. It is true that there is no EU army and that US military capacity dwarfs that of EU member states. Nevertheless, as noted in Chapter Three, collective EU military expenditure considerably exceeds that of the Middle East, Africa, Asia and Oceania. Also, Britain and France are nuclear powers, five EU member states were in the top eight suppliers of major conventional weaponry for the period 1997–2001, and in 2001 three of the world's top six military spenders were EU members. Furthermore, EU member states play leading roles in international organisations such as NATO, and the creation of the EURRF represents a key commitment by them to strengthening the EU's capacity to deliver upon its commitment to the Petersberg tasks. As for political presence, this is potentially formidable. The EU has a global network of diplomatic representation. The Commission maintains in its own right 123 delegations and offices to third countries world-wide and five to international organisations. This is augmented by the use of special representatives, troika missions and recourse to the global web of member state national embassies and their memberships of international organisations and regimes, many of which the EU is excluded from in its own right as a non-state actor. In fact, the EU has twice the number of diplomats in five times the number of embassies compared to the US.[2] Moreover, the EU benefits from the special relationships that its members enjoy with third parties, these often being legacies of Europe's imperial age.

With regards to the EU operationalising its military and political presence, it is fair to say that at best the Union's military dimension is putative. The WEU has been largely squeezed out of the European security architecture and successive crises in the Gulf and the Balkans revealed both the difficulties in arriving at collective EU positions on military force and grave shortcomings in transposing military expenditure into military capabilities appropriate to post-Cold War demands. Much now rests on the fate of the EURRF. Politically, the picture has been more encouraging, especially when one looks beyond narrow equations of EU foreign policy with CFSP. This is not to say that CFSP has itself not delivered a number of successes. It has, ranging from election monitoring through to establishing common EU positions on international treaties.

However, the EU's political power is best demonstrated by considering cross-pillar activities and its growing use of conditionality within its external relations. This is most obvious and effective in the context of enlargement strategy, where the degree of EU political intrusion into the internal affairs of applicant states has been truly remarkable.

This dissection of the caricature of the EU as 'an economic giant, a political dwarf, and a military worm' is not to argue that it contains no truths. The point is to demonstrate the importance when assessing EU performance in international relations of avoiding either being seduced by convenient simplifications or judging it in the same way that one might draw conclusions about states or even about other international organisations. This is no easy task. There is a natural tendency to view things through the prism of what is known, this being primarily states in terms of international relations – something further encouraged by the raging and unresolved debates about how to conceptualise the EU. Nevertheless, it is an essential task because it is key to understanding the EU's performance of its international relations and to arriving at balanced interpretations of its strengths and shortcomings.

A global EU foreign policy

Throughout this book it has been seen that the EU has available a panoply of external relations instruments. It has been seen, too, that it is seemingly determined to augment these further through stronger cross-pillar co-ordination and the potential to draw upon military instruments. This begs the questions of what guides EU external policy, whether EU instruments are sufficient to deliver a global foreign policy and to what purpose these instruments are to be harnessed. As Javier Solana declared in April 2002, '[a] more effective Europe in the foreign policy field requires that we clearly identify our common interests, that we have a consistent and clear message, and that we have the policy instruments to support this message'.[3]

EU foreign policy is clearly informed by the extrapolation of domestic norms to the EU level and the consequent delimitation of what actions can and cannot be regarded as legitimate. It is informed, too, by the principles of peace and reconciliation that underpinned the development of post-war integration and, in Jean Monnet's terms, the associated attempt to 'civilise international relations'. There is consequently a strong sense of the EU being different from other international actors on account both of its post-Westphalian construct based on the voluntary pooling of national sovereignty and of its shared values, common laws, cultural identity and social market, which embraces liberal capitalism but retains notions of welfare and solidarity. And it is further guided by the structure of the EU itself whereby the search for consensus is strongly embedded and member states both guard national autonomy in foreign policy and help determine the instruments available to the EU. One consequence has been a mitigation of the less desirable excesses of *realpolitik* and strong emphasis on 'soft' instruments and coalition building. The need to maintain the support of fifteen, soon to be twenty-five, different governments, national parliaments and sets of media likewise minimises the impact of particularist interests and maximises the importance of a 'principled' EU foreign policy.[4]

The EU's ability, even desire, has been weak to verbalise a coherent guiding ethos drawn from these different impulses. Nevertheless, it is possible to distinguish a broadly agreed core set of principles. These include international peace and security, sustainable development and the encouragement of a multipolar world order.[5] It is also possible to see a set of 'sanctioned' actions being derived from these principles that form the basis of EU foreign policy. These include the importance of international law, solidarity with the poorest countries, and multilateralism, engagement and containment rather than 'might is right' politics and confrontation. Moreover, they have been complemented in their ethical salience by the growing trend in post-Cold War international relations towards the conflation, even indivisibility, of values and interests. For instance, in June 2003 Solana emphasised that 'the quality of international society depends on the quality of the governments that are its foundation. The best protection for our security is a world of well-governed democratic states.'[6]

Herein Solana effectively summed up the EU's general approach to realising its foreign policy objectives, namely projecting its principles beyond its borders and persuading others to share them. This is not to say that the EU countries collectively, or member states individually, do not prioritise their own interests over avowed values. Consider, for example, the unilateral Greek blockade of the FYROM and EU protectionism of agriculture through the CAP. Nevertheless, basing its foreign policy upon the projection of its own values avoids the EU many potential embarrassments in the pursuit of an ethically orientated agenda. Its promotion of liberal capitalist democracy, the rule of law and human rights is both legitimated by widespread endorsement of these values within the EU and serves EU interests in line with democratic peace theory and the expansion of global free trade. Likewise, its commitment to multilateralism and multipolarity is both principled and serves the *realpolitik* calculations of its member states, which welcome the inherent additional leverage in their efforts to manage international relations and to influence the production of international law. The EU does, therefore, have a set of broadly agreed principles that guide its foreign policies and which to the outside world, especially given its lack of direct military capacity, lead to its appearing more ethically driven and less suspect than do states, including, ironically, its own member states.

Turning to the question of whether the EU has the capacity to deliver upon a global foreign policy, this seems banal at first sight. It clearly has a significant global presence and a 'Mr Nice Guy' image in international relations on account of its devout multilateralism and its traditionally non-coercive approach to its external relations. This image is encouraged both by EU actions frequently reflecting its principles and by comparison with other leading powers, notably the US. EU solidarity with the world's poorest nations, for instance, is reflected in its accounting for more than half of global ODA, its web of bilateral and multilateral trade and aid relationships, and its ambitious commitments at the Monterrey International Conference on Financing for Development. Similarly, its commitment to international consensus building and the development of international law is reflected in its support of the Kyoto Protocol, the CTBT, the Ottawa convention on APLMs, the ICC and so forth. That the US has thus far declined to accept any of these international agreements reinforces the positive image of the EU. The same can be said of increasingly marked transatlantic differences over unilateralism and multilateralism, the appropriate use of military force and the relative merits of engagement and confrontation.

Since the end of the Cold War the EU has also significantly developed its external policy tools and its willingness to harness its global economic presence and operational power to political and security objectives. This is most obvious in its increased use of conditionality. EU agreements carry all sorts of prerequisite commitments on the part of the third party, ranging from acceptance of the entire EU *acquis* to more limited obligations such as respect for human rights. Increasingly, also, the EU is using its economic preponderance to encourage (or, depending on one's point of view, coerce) countries into readmission agreements as it seeks to manage the human and security implications of migration. Just as significant, though, is its role within the WTO in the pursuit of a just international economic order that promotes global free trade in ways that embrace sustainable development and solidarity. Furthermore, the EU has strengthened its co-ordination in terms both of developing common positions from fifteen national foreign policies and of applying packages of external instruments. TEU provisions significantly strengthened the obligations of member states to co-ordinate their positions, which has been reflected both in the increasing use of instruments such as common positions and joint actions and in greater coherence on issues such as the Middle East peace process. As for the packaging of instruments, the best example is the enlargement process, which over time has seen a judicious use of CFSP, JHA and EC instruments. The SAP is also a prime example of how the EU has improved the co-ordination of its external relations instruments and promoted multilateral frameworks.

In addition, the EU has been engaged in a frantic effort, especially after the Anglo-French St Malo agreement, to develop its capacity for honouring the ambitious commitments stemming from its assumption in the Amsterdam Treaty of responsibility for the Petersberg tasks. The most rapid progress herein has been in building institutional capacity for conflict prevention, crisis management and conflict resolution. This ranges from the creation of the Policy Planning and Early Warning Unit and Political and Security Committee through to the Rapid Reaction Mechanism and the Commission's development of a Checklist for Root Causes of Conflict.[7] Indeed, conflict prevention has become a pivotal concept through which the EU has merged interests and ideals in a way that provides CFSP with a core common purpose around which member states can coalesce. As for crisis management, the EU has begun to develop CESDP to enable it to act in the event that prevention fails. Most high-profile herein have been the declared objectives of, and commitments to, the EURRF and the development of mechanisms for EU–NATO and EU–third party interface and co-operation. As early as December 2001 the Laeken European Council declared CESDP to be operational and in March 2003 the EU undertook in Macedonia its first ever military peace-support mission.

Clearly, therefore, the EU has both world-wide presence and acts at a global level in numerous dimensions of external relations. As has been seen, it is a forceful and formidable promoter and defender of its economic interests, both within its bilateral and multilateral trade relations and through the WTO. Particularly high-profile have been its clashes with the US over issues as diverse as steel, GMOs and bananas. It has also developed as a pole of stability and as an exporter of security, most prominently *vis-à-vis* Central and Eastern Europe but also with respect to the Balkans and the southern and eastern Mediterranean. And it is strongly engaged with the fight against international terrorism, the containment, engagement and reconstruction of rogue and failed states, and the promotion of democracy, human rights and sustainable development on a global scale. In short, the EU, particularly in the post-Cold War era, has taken major steps towards meeting Solana's prerequisites for an effective global foreign policy. There has been a greater identification of common interests, there has been a discernible and relatively consistent message about EU foreign policy principles and preferred means, and policy instruments have both been developed and progressively better co-ordinated in the pursuit of EU objectives.

Challenges to a global EU foreign policy

Accepting that the EU acts at a global level and has taken great strides in developing improved co-ordination and foreign policy instruments does not imply that the EU is either always effective or even that it is 'complete' as a foreign policy actor. Throughout this book it will have become apparent that the EU is still much more accomplished and formidable as an economic actor than it is as a politico-security actor. It will also have become evident that while the EU can and does act effectively on a global scale in its economic relations, as an international security actor it is most effective on a regional rather than on a global level. The further the distance from Europe, the less its attraction as a pole of stability is felt and the more difficult the EU finds it to maintain internal cohesion and to project decisive influence. Indeed, the challenges to the EU becoming a rounded global actor are significant and might, for convenience, be crudely divided into three clusters: institutional, instrumental and ideational.

At present the EU suffers in its external relations from its limited ability to project a coherent identity, the TEU pillar system, and the constant process of institutional reform and the battle for competencies. With regard to the former, the EU enjoys a surfeit of leaders and a deficit of leadership. The creation of a High Representative for CFSP has increased the 'visibility' of the EU in international relations. However, there is also the EU Commissioner for External Relations, the Commission President and numerous other commissioners whose portfolios have strong external relations dimensions, notably the commissioners for trade, development and the environment. Then, of course, there is the European Council and all the different national heads of government and their foreign policy bureaucracies. Moreover, the difficulties presented by this are aggravated by third-party attempts to 'divide and conquer' by circumventing the EU and dealing instead with national capitals, a strategy employed notably by the Bush administration in the lead-up to military intervention in Iraq in 2003.

Competency is also a key factor in limiting the effectiveness of EU foreign policy. Constant shifts in competency exacerbate the difficulties faced by third parties in understanding the EU policy-making system and in maintaining appropriate channels of dialogue and co-operation. More significantly, competency determines which actors control which facets of EU external relations and how these are conducted. This can be a major limitation on EU effectiveness as an international actor, even in the economic realm where the EU is enormously influential and integration is most developed. Consider, for instance, trade policy. The Commission is empowered to negotiate on behalf of the Union but its effectiveness is sometimes compromised by the lack of flexibility inherent in the EU's complex decision-making machinery. This has led repeatedly to difficulties in multilateral negotiations and especially within the GATT/WTO. Moreover, it is a problem exacerbated both by the refusal of EU member states to cede sovereignty in certain dimensions of trade policy and by the fungibility of policy areas, such as trade and environment policies.

As for the present structure of EU activities, the TEU pillar arrangement constitutes an additional obstacle to the effectiveness of EU foreign policy. First, it is a concrete symbol of the artificial division of EU external relations activities. Second, there exists a plethora of different actors and policy-making procedures in each of the three pillars. This limits the EU's ability to react swiftly to international events and hinders the cross-pillar co-ordination of external relations instruments. Third, the 'pillarisation' of EU external activities has had the effect, through delimiting fields of activity and competence, of limiting spill-over and processes of communitaurisation. Indeed, the determination of some member states to protect sovereignty by insulating the JHA and CFSP pillars from the EC pillar is reflected in their careful control of Commission responsibilities. Moreover, the damage that can be done to EU credibility as a foreign policy actor by the sensitivity of competence issues was demonstrated by the embarrassing delays in supplying humanitarian aid to Bosnia and Herzegovina in 1993–94. Although this was agreed as a joint action within CFSP, the EU was unable to implement it with the speed necessary on account not least of the anxiety of some member states to prevent the

EP acquiring pillar two influence through its control over EC non-compulsory expenditure.

Turning to a consideration of EU external relations instruments, three of the pressing issues are co-ordination, speed of delivery and type, all of which are related to considerations of institutional structures, competency divisions and, above all, the political will of the member states. Co-ordination has two principal facets, namely the co-ordination of EU external relations instruments and the co-ordination of EU foreign policy activities with those of the member states and other international actors. Recent Commission Country Strategy Papers and the Stabilisation and Association Process in the Balkans indicate a more holistic EU approach to its international relations in which it marshals a range of instruments in the pursuit of not just economic but also political and security objectives. Nevertheless, much needs to be done in terms of effective programme development and implementation, including improved cross-pillar co-ordination and ensuring adequate resources, appropriate budget lines and the necessary monitoring capacity. This task is made more challenging still by problems of consistency and duplication stemming from the often loose co-ordination of EU and member state activities. As has been seen, Development Policy is a good example of this, where, for reasons of national sensitivity *vis-à-vis* protecting historical privileged relationships and autonomy of action, member states have insulated the majority of their ODA from EC control and insisted upon parallel competencies. In addition, the EU's ability to ensure co-ordination and consistency in its external relations is limited by its complex hybrid structure and its exclusion as a non-state actor from many international organisations.

The speed at which the EU can formulate, equip and execute external relations actions is also a major determinant in its international effectiveness. Initiatives such as extending the use of QMV and the introduction of constructive abstention and enhanced co-operation all reflect justified concern about the ability of the EU to be both sufficiently proactive and able to respond quickly to international events. Its decision-making process can be laborious and, especially where unanimity is required, entail a search for consensus that is often both time-consuming and prone to produce lowest common denominator outcomes. Even where the Commission is empowered to negotiate on behalf of the Union, tightly defined mandates often reduce flexibility and require reference back to the Council of Ministers for clarification and/or a broadening of the mandate. One consequence is that the EU frequently performs better where its objectives can be pursued slowly through incremental steps than in crisis situations that demand quick policy and implementation responses. This partially explains why its most spectacular failures have been in crisis situations, such as during the dissolution of the Yugoslav federation. It also helps explain EU preferences for engagement and containment strategies and its increasing focus on conflict prevention activities, where its ability to call upon a whole range of 'soft' instruments gives it a clear advantage over organisations such as NATO.

This naturally leads to the issue of what type of external relations instruments the member states are prepared to equip the EU with. A central question here is how far are they prepared to go in enhancing the coercive capacity of the EU? The answer is unclear. On the one hand, the use of political conditionality has developed rapidly. For instance, the EU suspended aid fifteen times to developing world recipients from 1990–98 on account of the breaking of democratisation commitments.[8] Also, the TEU made economic sanctions much easier to apply by giving them a specific legal base and clarifying their link to CFSP. Furthermore, the development of CESDP and member state pledges to the EURRF underpin EU ambitions to evolve significantly its crisis management and conflict resolution capabilities. While there is no likelihood of an EU armed force, that the Union has recourse to military instruments is a major development and one that was practically inconceivable during the Cold War.

On the other hand, major doubts remain about the willingness or ability of EU member states to underwrite a more coercively empowered EU. It is telling of member state determination to limit the EU that the Nice Treaty effectively separated security and defence through its incorporation into the EU of most elements of the WEU other than its mutual defence clause. As for the EURRF, many of the Headline Goals remain unfulfilled and the political will, even ability, of the member states to increase their commitments continues to be questionable. At one extreme Denmark secured in the TEU an opt-out of any future EU defence issues. Many other states face severe constraints on military spending as a result of the Stability and Growth Pact, prospective costs of the planned 2004 macro-enlargement of the Union, and pressing domestic priorities such as social welfare. In addition, Atlanticist-oriented EU states in particular remain anxious that augmentation of EURRF capabilities should not be at the expense of NATO pre-eminence. Cast in this light, scepticism about the Laeken declaration is well-justified, as are predictions of 2012 at the earliest for the EURRF to be able to perform the entire range of Petersberg tasks.

Just as poignant is the question of how willing member states are to channel their foreign policies within the EU, rather than outside it? The answer seems policy, issue and even time dependent. While international trade policy is largely pursued through the EU as a matter of course, certain elements of it are closely guarded by member states. Development Policy is overtly and consistently pursued within and outside the EU. And CFSP can deliver a common strategy on Russia but fall apart spectacularly on what ought to be straightforward issues, such as the January 2003 débâcle over whether Zimbabwean President Robert Mugabe ought to be allowed to attend Franco-African and EU–African summits in Europe. Moreover, the EU has encountered particular problems in crisis situations, the management and resolution of which it is nevertheless, even consequently, seemingly determined to develop its capabilities in.

In June 2003 Solana warned that '[i]n a crisis there is no substitute for unity of command'.[9] This is true, but concerns for national sovereignty, EU competency divisions, the diversity of national concerns and the plethora of different actors within EU external relations all mitigate against its realisation within the EU. The experience of post-Cold War crises generally indicates a re-nationalisation of foreign policies in crisis situations and even a re-emergence of 'great power' politics. Iraq 2002–03 saw the EU largely circumvented by both the US and its own member states, some of which adopted high-profile, if opposed, stances, whilst others 'connived at their own irrelevance' in the knowledge that any attempt to forge a common position within CFSP would be both futile and possibly even more damaging to the EU than not trying at all.[10] Equally noteworthy has been the prominence of *directoires* in crisis situations. Especially interesting are the Contact Group and the Quint, membership of which included non-EU members but which still exerted heavy influence over CFSP positions.

The final set of challenges to a global EU foreign policy is less tangible but arguably even more important and difficult to meet. Ideational issues go to the core of the EU as an international actor. They affect its structures, instruments and cohesion, for these ultimately depend upon what its member states want the EU to be able to do in international relations. They affect, too, its international conduct, for that conduct is determined heavily by the norms and assumptions of its member states. They also pose key questions. If some version of Huntington's 'clash of civilisations' is to be avoided, how should the EU construct its international relations with countries and even movements that do not share its normative assumptions? What do member states want the EU to do in international relations? General answers to this are, of course, easy. They want it to protect, promote and project values of democracy, respect for human rights, solidarity, sustainable development, multilateralism, free trade, the rule of law and so forth. They want for it also to directly safeguard and pursue their national interests, such as maximising the benefits from a globalising international economy and promoting regional and international security. In addition, they want to draw upon the EU as a power-multiplier within their national foreign policies.

The universality of values and the implications of processes of globalisation both impel the EU to assume global responsibilities and to develop the capabilities necessary to fulfil them. But this raises the questions of how the EU should do these things and, in turn, what end form should the EU take? This is a dilemma frequently couched in terms of the EU being a superpower, a superstate or both – and is one that its member states cannot agree how to resolve. Britain is in the vanguard of EU member states that want the EU to be able to act as a superpower, projecting its power and influence across the globe in the pursuit not just of interests but also of universal values. However, members such as Germany and the Scandinavian countries are generally much less enamoured with the EU acting as a traditional superpower, not least due to historical legacies of European conflict and domination. Conversely, Britain is also at the forefront of EU member states that are strongly opposed to a federal Europe. Meantime, Germany and France lead the original six for which a federal Europe is much more acceptable. This raises the further interesting question of whether the EU can be a superpower, even of an extremely militarily limited kind, without becoming a super-state? It also portends that the EU is unlikely to develop rapidly towards either 'destination', not least because the Anglo-French relationship that is key to EU progress in the security domain cuts across the Franco-German relationship that drives general integration, and because both are cut across by national relationships with the US.

Despite this ideational irresolution, the EU is beginning to change its character as an international actor. First, the development of CESDP and the associated EURRF challenges notions of, and preferences for, the EU as a civilian power. Indeed, some already see this as having spelt the end of the vision of a civilian norm-based community.[11] Second, much greater use of political conditionality indicates new-found resolution to link and advance EU economic, political and security interests in a more coherent way. In some cases this has been undoubtedly beneficial and successful. EU enlargement strategy, for instance, has been highly intrusive yet both constructive in terms of preparing the next enlargement and largely consensual. However, greater assertiveness also potentially risks the EU's established international standing in that the abuse, or perceived abuse, of asymmetric relationships, such as in the Cotonou Agreement, could create the impression of a new imperialism. The putative military dimension in particular might also transform international opinion of the EU from being 'Mr Nice Guy' to something more akin to the distrust and resentment presently reserved for the US. Moreover, as the examples of Russia, China and North Korea indicate, the EU has considerably more difficulties in dealing with actors that do not share its norms than with those that do.

The latter point feeds in directly to potential problems in the EU's pursuit of a heavily value-laden series of external relations policies. First, universal values recognise no national borders, which means logically that the EU is liable both to incur criticism wherever it does not act in their defence and to come into conflict with states that do not share such universal values. Humanitarian interventionism, for instance, has repeatedly exposed differences between the EU and key countries such as Russia over legitimacy of action and the balance between human rights and national sovereignty. Second, EU foreign policies are predicated on assumptions about multilateral institutionalism, democracy and the transferability of the EU experience. Put crudely, democracies do not fight each other, institutions have socialising as well as power-enhancing effects and the EU model of regional integration can be adapted to work elsewhere. Hence the EU is keen to socialise and engage states such as China through membership of liberal capitalist and essentially Western fora such as the WTO. Yet none of these assumptions have been proven and many worry that to 'extrapolate this solidarity to a much larger group of states in a wholly new geo-politics would be to divorce political science completely from history'.[12] Moreover, it implies a proselytising of values somewhat different in content to those of the US but in a style akin to much-resisted American exceptionalism. While this does not suggest that the EU is driving a 'clash of civilisations', it does indicate the critical importance of, and particular difficulties in, the EU working across normative divides.

The future of the EU as a global actor

Attempting to predict the EU is a notoriously hazardous occupation. Few, for example, foresaw negative referenda results in Denmark and Ireland over the TEU and Nice Treaty respectively. Also, at the time of writing, the Convention on the Future of Europe is putting forward ideas for reform and development across a whole range of EU activities, including external representation and the possible abolition of the TEU pillar structure. For now, therefore, it seems prudent to conclude simply with some probable developments in the EU's international relations and an indication of known factors liable to mediate its evolution as a global actor.

In April 2002 Chris Patten declared of the EU that '[w]e are trying to move from a foreign policy of strong nouns and weak verbs to something more substantive, more muscular, more focused, that can have more impact'.[13] This process is likely to continue. Member states can support it regardless of whether they favour an EU superpower or an EU super-state. Collectively they are stronger than individually and they do have common interests in promoting peace, free trade, democracy, international security and so forth. Improving the co-ordination of EU external relations instruments and of the activities of the EU and its member states is liable to be encouraged also by the possibilities inherent for saving scarce resources. Furthermore, the EU can be variously an accelerator and a manager of processes of globalisation, functions that it is in the interest of the member states to enhance.

It is also likely that, despite the potential geographic ambition of the EURRF, the EU will for some time continue to be a global economic actor but a primarily regional security agent. This is not to say that it will not seek additional influence and involvement in global security. Political conditionality will remain a key and possibly increasingly controversial feature of EU international relations, and the EU will continue trying to build and shape international security norms, dialogue, agreements and law. Nevertheless, its security priorities and primary role will be in Europe and contiguous areas. This is driven by extant EU strengths and by the implications of the pending 2004 enlargement and is reflected in the EU's 'Good Neighbourhood' strategy, which focuses on building a ring of well-governed countries to the east of the Union and on the borders of the Mediterranean.[14]

One thing that is not likely to change is EU attachment to multilateralism, international law, engagement and coalition building as preferred mechanisms through which to pursue its objectives. These are obvious means not only of promoting a well-ordered and stronger international society but also afford arguably the best approach to containing the US. They are also core values of the EU itself and widely supported by its member states and citizens. Even during the 2002–03 débâcle over Iraq, opposing EU member states remained in agreement over the importance of a UN mandate for intervention. Less charitably of course, and as often alleged by the US in particular, multilateralism can provide a convenient cover either for inaction or for avoiding onerous burdens and difficult decisions.

What factors are likely to mediate the future direction and capabilities of the EU as an international actor? One consideration will be legitimacy, including the impact of international law and of the relationship between the EU and its citizens. Crises such as Kosovo, September 11 and Iraq have posed serious challenges to international law and widespread recognition that it must evolve in response. How what Patten has called the 'global rule book'[15] is adapted, and with what degree of international consensus this is done, will affect the EU considerably in its international relations. Also, there are evolving international fora to whose rules the EU is legally responsible and which delimit its actions, most obviously the WTO. As for the relationship between the EU and its citizens, the very limited role of the EP beyond pillar one activities leads to calls for increasing its power to provide greater accountability in EU external relations. Concomitantly, national governments are constantly aware of their accountability to their publics and this helps determine their commitments and approach to the EU and its external relations. In addition, TEU and Nice referenda have demonstrated the limits of permissive consensus and the consequent need to build popular support for EU activities in general, not just in external relations.

The transatlantic context is also likely to mediate heavily the EU's future development and conduct as an international actor. This is inevitable given US *hyperpuissance* but is accorded added salience by the high level of interdependence, historical, language and value ties, and different member state relationships with the US. Contrast, for instance, the often prickly relationship between Washington and Paris with the much closer Anglo-American relationship. The US factor is immediately obvious in intra-EU differences over the NATO–EURRF relationship, America's informal seat at the EU table through structures such as the Contact Group and the Quint, and the increasing US penchant under the George W. Bush administration for dealing with and, where necessary, dividing EU national capitals. The US factor is likewise obvious in international trade and global economic management. The EU and the US are the world's two leading economic powers and their co-operation or confrontation has had, and will continue to have, enormous implications. Moreover, the EU and US are highly influential in the upholding and development of international law and norms. For instance, the Bush administration's doctrine of pre-emptive self-defence and *de facto* reconceptualisation of sovereignty has provided a major challenge to the EU and to international law.

Equally important, however, are the underlying trends in transatlantic relations, about which debate is heated and possible consequent scenarios numerous. For example, were the Bush administration's assertive unilateralism to persist, then the EU member states may be persuaded to enhance EU capabilities further in order to contain the US and to protect multilateralism. Also, how much leadership is the US prepared to share with, or cede to, the EU as the latter expands its international capabilities and commitments? The burden-sharing debate and US ambivalence over the EURRF indicate that Washington does not necessarily see a direct relationship between greater EU commitments and reduced US leadership, a scenario that is unacceptable to the EU.

Another critical factor likely to affect the EU's future evolution in international relations is its enlargement, both the pending 2004 round and future obligations, such as those undertaken in the SAP. With new frontiers come obvious new external relations challenges, ranging from migration and new environmental threats through to trying to adapt further the European security architecture and avoiding drawing new dividing lines around EU frontiers. With new members also come new foreign policy cultures and national interests. One consequence is potential greater difficulty in devising and maintaining common EU positions. Another is that major reform of the decision-making apparatus will be needed if an often already inflexible and slow EU is to avoid institutional paralysis. Also, it is by no means assured that states in the 2004 wave will either continue their largely acquiescent attitude once EU membership has been secured or that their different foreign policy orientations will not exacerbate existing intra-EU tensions. For example, the majority of acceding countries either have recently become members of NATO, or are set to do so. They are thus liable to be sensitive to US opinion and to any weakening of transatlantic ties and NATO as a consequence of EURRF development. Furthermore, enlargement will tax scarce resources and demand that hard choices be made at the EU and national levels. This has obvious implication for projects such as the EURRF, ensuring adequate funding for, and monitoring capabilities of, external programmes, overseas representation and so forth. Indeed, prospective battles over institutional reform, Britain's budgetary rebate, EMU criteria, the EC budget ceiling and relative shares of cohesion and regional development funds all presage the possibility that the EU will become more introverted for a period.

Most significant of all, however, to the EU's future and conduct as an international actor will be the attitudes of its member states. They may not be absolute gatekeepers of integration but they remain the most important determinant in integration generally and in EU international relations specifically. One of the critical factors will be how well or how badly the leading member states co-ordinate and co-operate with one another. For instance, Anglo-French rapprochement in the St Malo declaration was the single most important reason for the significant development of the EU's security ambitions and capabilities from the late 1990s. Conversely, there is likely to be a significant loss of momentum as a result of the Iraq crisis aligning the Franco-German relationship against Britain, Spain and Italy. Whether or not bridges can be built quickly will be even more important to the EU's external relations development as an enlarged Union is likely to see both the growing importance of *directoires* and an increasing tendency to see smaller member states forming constellations around the larger ones.

It is also the case that the member states will determine all sorts of issues vital to the EU's performance of its international relations, including the resources available to it, the extent to which QMV will be expanded to expedite decision-making, and what areas of activity the EC will and will not be allowed competence and participation in. The EU's credibility as an international actor will also be strongly affected by national foreign policies, including the extent to which member states agree and follow CFSP positions and are able to resist exploiting institutional polyphony to their individual interests. After all, international credibility is hard won and easily lost, particularly for the EU as an emerging and unique actor, and it can ill-afford national assertions such as German unilateral recognition of Croatia, the Greek blockade of the FYROM and French posturing over Robert Mugabe's visit to Europe in 2003. Furthermore, if the EU is to develop capabilities such as the EURRF sufficient to match its sometimes expansive, even universal and moralistic rhetoric, then the member states are going to need to increase their political, economic and military contributions substantially.

In short, the most important determinant of all is political will. One dimension of this is the willingness or otherwise of other international actors to recognise the EU as a legitimate international actor in its own right. Much more decisive, though, is the political will of the EU member states. For the EU to be a truly effective international actor, and to be able to transpose its enormous international presence into operational power, it needs them to have a common will, a common vision and trust. Yet, as has been seen throughout this book, a common vision is lacking beyond broad principles and objectives, there has often been a deficit of political will, and trust is a seemingly scarce commodity. In consequence, the EU is likely to continue to develop incrementally and erratically as an international actor. It will remain differentiated in its economic and politico-security scope and geographic reach. And its international ambitions and credibility will for some time remain at the mercy of international events and continually exposed to potentially damaging and frustrating mismatches between rhetorical commitments and the capabilities/ political will to meet them.

Notes

1 Belgian Foreign Minister, cited by McCormick, J. (2002) *Understanding the European Union*, Basingstoke: Palgrave, p. 197.

2 Solana, J. (2002) 'Europe's Place in the World: The Role of the High Representative', speech, Stockholm, 25 April 2002.

3 Ibid.

4 Smith, H. (2002) *European Union Foreign Policy: What It Is and What It Does*, London: Pluto Press, p. 271.

5 Lamy, Pascal (2002) 'Time to Give Teeth to Europe's Foreign Policy', speech by EU Trade Commissioner, 30 October 2002, The European Policy Centre, http://www.theepc.be/challenge/topdetail.asp?SEC=documents&S.

6 Solana, J. (June 2003) 'A Secure Europe in a Better World', SO138/03.

7 For details of the latter see http://europa.eu.int/comm/external_relations/cpcm/cp/list.

8 Smith, K.E. (1998) 'The Use of Political Conditionality in the EU's Relations with Third Countries: How Effective?' *European Foreign Affairs Review* 3 p. 267.

9 Solana, 'A Secure Europe in a Better World'.

10 Crowe, B. (2003) 'A Common European Foreign Policy After Iraq?' *International Affairs* 79 (3) p. 535.

11 Deighton, A. (2002) 'The European Security and Defence Policy' *Journal of Common Market Studies* 40 (4) p. 736.

12 Hill, C. (2001) 'The EU's Capacity for Conflict Prevention' *European Foreign Affairs Review* 6 p. 325.

13 Patten, C. (2002) 'Developing Europe's External Policy in an Age of Globalisation', speech at Central Party School, Beijing, http://www.europa.eu.int/comm/external_relations/news/patten/sp02_134.htm.

14 European Commission (2003) 'Communication from the Commission to the Council and the European Parliament: Wider Europe – Neighbourhood; A New Framework for Relations With Our Eastern and Southern Neighbours', COM (2003) 104 final, 11 March 2003.

15 Patten, C. (2002) Speech at the Plenary Session of the European Parliament, 4 September 2002, http://www3.europarl.eu.int/omk/omnsapir.so/debatsL5?FILE=20020904EN&LANGUE=EN&LEVEL=DOC&NUMINT=3-006&SEARCH=ORAT&LEG=L5.

Bibliography

Acharya, A. (1999) 'A Concert of Asia' *Survival* **41** (3) pp. 84–101.

Ahrens, G.H. (2001) 'Albania: Status Report' in *The Operational Role of the OSCE in South-Eastern Europe*, Ghebali, V.Y. and Warner, D. (eds), Aldershot: Ashgate.

Albright, D. and O'Neill, K. (eds) (2000) *Solving the North Korean Nuclear Puzzle*, Washington: Institute for Science and International Security.

Alder, E. and Barnett, M. (1998) 'Security Communities in Theoretical Perspective' in *Security Communities*, Alder, E. and Barnett, M. (eds), Cambridge: Cambridge University Press.

Alexander, M. and Garden, T. (2001) 'The Arithmetic of Defence Policy' *International Affairs* **77** (3) pp. 509–29.

Allen, D. (1997) 'EPC/CFSP, the Soviet Union, and the Former Soviet Republics: Do the Twelve Have a Coherent Policy?' in *Foreign Policy of the European Union: From EPC to CFSP and Beyond*, Regelsberger, E., Wessels, W. and de Schoutheete de Tervarent, P. (eds), London: Lynne Rienner Publishers.

Allen, D. and Smith, M. (1991) 'Western Europe's Presence in the Contemporary International Arena' in *The Future of European Political Cooperation*, Holland, M. (ed.), Basingstoke: Macmillan.

Allin, H. (2002) *NATO's Balkan Interventions*, Adelphi Paper 347, London: Oxford University Press for the International Institute for Strategic Studies.

Almond, M. (1994) *Europe's Backyard War: The War in the Balkans*, London: Mandarin.

Anderson, S. (1995) 'EU, NATO and CSCE Responses to the Yugoslav Crisis: Testing Europe's New Security Architecture' *European Security* **4** (2) pp. 328–53.

Anderson, S. (2001) 'The Changing Nature of Diplomacy: The European Union, the CFSP and Korea' *European Foreign Affairs Review* **6** (4) pp. 465–82.

Annan, K.A. (1999) 'Two Concepts of Sovereignty' *The Economist*, 18 September 1999, pp. 49–50.

Antweiler Jr., W. (1996) 'A Brief History of the General Agreement on Tariffs and Trade', http://pacific.commerce.ubc.ca/trade/GATT-rounds.html.

Apapa, J. (2001) 'Enlargement and an Area of Freedom, Security and Justice: Striking a Better Balance', Challenge of Europe, European Policy Centre, 18 October 2001, http://www.theepc.net/challenge/challenge.detail.asp.

Apapa, J., Boratynski, J., Emerson, M., Gromadzki, G., Vahl, M. and Whyte, N. (1991) 'Friendly Schengen Borderland Policy on the New Borders of an Enlarged EU and

Its Neighbours', p. 9, 6–7 July 1991, Centre for European Policy Studies, http://www.ceps.be.

Appleman Williams, W. (1972) *The Tragedy of American Diplomacy*, 2nd edn, New York: Dell Publishing.

Aristotelous, K. and Fountas, S. (1996) 'An Empirical Analysis of Inward Foreign Direct Investment Flows in the EU with Emphasis on the Market Enlargement Hypothesis' *Journal of Common Market Studies* **34** (4) pp. 571–83.

Åslund, A. (1999) 'Russia's Collapse' *Foreign Affairs* **78** (5) pp. 64–77.

Auerswald, D.P. (2001) 'The President, Congress and American Missile Defence Policy' *Defence Studies* **1** (2) pp. 57–82.

Ausland, J.C. (1996) *Kennedy, Khrushchev, and the Berlin–Cuba Crisis, 1961–64*, Oslo: Scandanavia.

Avery, G. and Cameron, F. (1998) *The Enlargement of the European Union*, Sheffield: Sheffield Academic Press.

Aybet, G. (2000) *A European Security Architecture after the Cold War*, Basingstoke: Macmillan.

Baev, P.K. (1999) 'External Interventions in Secessionist Conflicts in Europe in the 1990s' *European Security* **8** (2) pp. 22–51.

Bailes, A.J.K. (1996) 'European Defence and Security: The Role of NATO, WEU and EU' *Security Dialogue* **27** (1) pp. 55–64.

Baker, J. (1991) 'America in Asia: Emerging Architecture for a Pacific Community' *Foreign Affairs* **70** (5) pp. 1–18.

Baker, N. and Sebastian, L.C. (1995) 'The Problem With Parachuting: Strategic Studies and Security in the Asia/Pacific Region' *Journal of Strategic Studies* **18** (3) pp. 15–31.

Baldwin, D. (1997) 'The Concept of Security' *Review of International Studies* **23** (1) pp. 5–26.

Ball, D.A., McCulloch Jr., W.H., Frantz, P.L., Geringer, J.M. and Minor, M.S. (2004) *International Business: The Challenge of Global Competition*, 9th edn, Boston: McGraw-Hill.

Bannock, G., Baxter, R.E. and Davis, E. (1987) *The Penguin Dictionary of Economics*, 4th edn, London: Penguin Books.

Baranovsky, V. (2000) 'Russia: A Part of Europe or Apart from Europe?' *International Affairs* **76** (3) pp. 443–58.

Barry, C. (1996) 'NATO's Combined Joint Task Force in Theory and Practice' *Survival* **38** (1) pp. 81–97.

Bass, W. (1998) 'The Triage of Dayton' *Foreign Affairs* **77** (5) pp. 95–108.

Baxendale, J., Dewar, S. and Gowan, D. (eds) (2000) *The EU and Kaliningrad: Kaliningrad and the Impact of EU Enlargement*, London: Federal Trust.

Becker, J.J. (1998) 'Asserting EU Cohesion: Common Foreign and Security Policy and the Relaunch of Europe' *European Security* **7** (4) pp. 12–32.

Bennett, C. (1999) 'Bosnia: New Opportunities' *Security Dialogue* **30** (3) pp. 291–2.

Bennett, C. (2001–02) 'Aiding America' *NATO Review* **49** (4) pp. 6–7.

Bensahel, N. (1999) 'Separable But Not Separate Forces: NATO's Development of the Combined Joint Task Force' *European Security* **8** (2) pp. 52–72.

Berger, S. (2000) 'A Foreign Policy for a Global Age' *Foreign Affairs* **79** (6) pp. 22–39.

Bertram, C. (2000) 'Reforming Germany's Army', http://www.projectsyndicate.cz/dcs/columns/Bertram2000July.asp.html.

Bildt, C. (1997–98) 'There is no Alternative to Dayton' *Survival* **39** (4) pp. 19–21.

Bildt, C. (2000) 'Force and Diplomacy' *Survival* **42** (1) pp. 141–8.

Blair, A. (1994) 'What Happened in Yugoslavia? Lessons for Future Peacekeepers' *European Security* 3 (2) pp. 340–9.

Blair, A. (1999) *The Longman Companion to the European Union Since 1945*, London: Longman.

Blair, A. (2002) *Saving the Pound? Britain's Road to Monetary Union*, London: Prentice Hall.

Blinken, A.J. (1987) *Ally Versus Ally: America, Europe and the Siberian Pipeline Crisis*, New York: Praeger.

Blinken, A.J. (2001) 'The False Crisis Over the Atlantic' *Foreign Affairs* 80 (3) pp. 35–48.

Bolton, J. (2000) 'The End of NATO' *World Today* 56 (6) pp. 12–14.

BOND, 'EC Budget Lines: Background Info', http://www.bond.org.uk/eu/budglines.htm.

Borawski, J. (1995) 'Partnership for Peace and Beyond' *International Affairs* 71 (2) pp. 233–46.

Borawski, J. (2000) 'Revisiting the Common European Home: A Rejoinder' *Security Dialogue* 31 (1) pp. 85–90.

Boughton, J.M. (2001) *Silent Revolution: The International Monetary Fund 1979–1989*, Washington: IMF.

Bozo, F. (2003) 'The Effects of Kosovo and the Danger of Decoupling' in *Defending Europe: The EU, NATO and the Quest for European Autonomy*, Howorth, J. and Keeler J.T.S. (eds), Basingstoke: Palgrave.

Brenner, M. (1992), 'The EC in Yugoslavia: A Debut Performance' *Security Studies* 1 (4) pp. 586–609.

Bretherton, C. and Vogler, J. (1999) *The European Union as a Global Actor*, London: Routledge.

Buchan, D. (1993) *Europe: The Strange Superpower*, Aldershot: Dartmouth Press.

Buzan, B. (1983) *People, States and Fear*, London: Wheatsheaf Books.

Buzan, B. (1997) 'Security after the Cold War' *Cooperation and Conflict* 32 (1) pp. 5–28.

Buzan, B., Jones, C. and Little, R. (1993) *The Logic of Anarchy: Neorealism to Structural Realism*, New York: Columbia University Press.

Buzan, B. et al. (1990) *The European Security Order Recast*, University of Copenhagen: Pinter Publishers.

Calleo, D.P. (1987) *Beyond American Hegemony*, New York: Basic Books.

Calleo, D.P. (2001) 'Imperial America and its Republican Constitution' in *The New Transatlantic Agenda: Facing the Challenges of Global Governance*, Gardner, H. and Stefanova, R. (eds), Aldershot: Ashgate.

Cameron, F. (1999) *The Foreign and Security Policy of the European Union*, Sheffield: Sheffield Academic Press.

Carpenter, T.G. (ed.) (1995) *The Future of NATO*, London and Portland, Oreg.: Frank Cass.

Cecchetti, S.G. (2000) 'Who Should Care about the Euro–Dollar Exchange Rate Anyway?' *Occasional Essay on Current Policy Issues* 8, http://people.brandeis.edu/~cecchett/pdf/cpi8.pdf.

Cha, V.D. and Chang, D.C. (May/June 2003) 'The Korea Crisis' *Foreign Policy*, pp. 20–7.

Chicago Council on Foreign Relations, 'American Public Opinion and Foreign Policy', http://www.worldviews.org/detailreports/usreport/html.

Christopher, W. (Spring 1995) 'America's Leadership: America's Opportunity' *Foreign Policy*, **98** pp. 6–28.

Church, C.H. and Phinnemore, D. (2002) *The Penguin Guide to the European Treaties*, London: Penguin Books.

Clark, I. (2001) *The Post-Cold War Order: The Spoils of Peace*, Oxford: Oxford University Press.

Clarke, M. (ed.) (1995) *New Perspectives in Security*, London: Brassey's for the Centre for Defence Studies.

Clarke, M. and Cornish, P. (2002) 'The European Defence Project and the Prague Summit' *International Affairs* **78** (4) pp. 777–88.

Cole, A. (2001) *Franco-German Relations*, London: Pearson.

Committee for the Study of Economic and Monetary Union (1989) *Report on Economic and Monetary Union in the European Community*, Luxembourg: Office for Official Publications of the European Communities.

Council of the European Union (1999) Common Strategy of the European Union on Russia, 4 June 1999, Luxembourg: Official Journal of the European Communities, L 157/1, 24 June 1999.

Council of the European Union (1999) Council Joint Action Establishing a European Union Cooperation Programme for Non-proliferation and Disarmament in the Russian Federation, 1999/878/CFSP, 17 December 1999.

Council of the European Union (2001) Council Common Position of 27 December 2001 on the Application of Specific Measures to Combat Terrorism, Luxembourg: Official Journal of the European Communities, 28 December 2001, pp. 93–6.

Cox, M. (2002) 'American Power Before and After 11 September: Dizzy With Success?' *International Affairs* **78** (2) pp. 261–76.

Croft, S. (2000) 'The EU, NATO and the Return of the Architectural Debate' *European Security* **9** (3) pp. 1–20.

Croft, S., Redmond, J., Rees, G.W. and Webber, M. (1999) *The Enlargement of Europe*, Manchester: Manchester University Press.

Cronin, D. (2003) 'Rights and Wrongs' *European Voice: The European Union in 2003*, 16 January 2003, pp. 59–61.

Crowe, B. (2003) 'A Common European Foreign Policy After Iraq?' *International Affairs* **79** (3) pp. 533–46.

Daalder, I.H. (1997–98) 'Bosnia after SFOR: Options for Continued US Engagement' *Survival* **39** (4) pp. 5–18.

Daalder, I.H. (2000) *Getting to Dayton: The Making of America's Bosnia Policy*, Washington D.C.: Brookings Institute Press.

Daianu, D. and Veremis, T. (eds) (2001) *Balkan Reconstruction*, London: Frank Cass.

Danchev, A. and Halverson, T. (eds) (1996) *International Perspectives on the Yugoslav Conflict*, Basingstoke: Macmillan.

Danchev, A. (1997) 'On Friendship: Anglo-America at the Fin de Siècle' *International Affairs* **73** pp. 247–59.

De Santis, H. (1994) 'Romancing NATO: Partnership for Peace and East European Stability' *Journal of Strategic Studies* **17** (4) pp. 61–81.

De Spiegeleire, S. (2002) 'Recoupling Russia: Staying the Course. Europe's Security Relationship with Russia', paper prepared for the IISS/CEPS European Security Forum, Brussels, 14 January 2002.

Dedman, M. (1996) *The Origins and Development of the European Union 1945–95*, London: Routledge.

Deighton, A. (2000) 'The European Union and NATO's War over Kosovo: Towards the Glass Ceiling?' in *Alliance Politics, Kosovo and NATO's War: Allied Force of Forced Allies?*, Martin, P. and Brawley, M.R. (eds), New York: Palgrave.

Deighton, A. (2002) 'The European Security and Defence Policy' *Journal of Common Market Studies* **40** (4) pp. 719–41.

Delors, J. (1991) 'European Integration and Security' *Survival* **33** (2) pp. 99–109.

Dent, C. (1999) *The European Union and East Asia: An Economic Relationship*, London: Routledge.

Dent, C.M. (1997) *The European Economy: The Global Context*, London: Routledge.

Deutsch, K. et al. (1957) *Political Community and the North Atlantic Area*, Princeton: Princeton University Press.

Dhian, M.S. and Philippart, E. (2001) 'JHA and Enlargement: A Plea For a Core Acquis Test', Challenge Europe, European Policy Centre, 25 October 2001, http://www.theepc.net/challenge/challenge_detail.asp?

Dicken, P. (1998) *Global Shift: Transforming the World Economy*, 3rd edn, London: Paul Chapman.

Di Feliciantonio, S. (1999) 'EU Foreign Policy and Albania' *European Foreign Affairs Review* **4** (4) pp. 519–36.

Dillon, M. (2002) 'China and the US Bases in Central Asia' *The World Today* **58** (7) pp. 13–15.

Dinan, D. (1994; 2nd edn 1999) *Ever Closer Union?*, Basingstoke: Macmillan.

Dinan, D. (2000) *Encyclopedia of the European Union*, updated edn, Basingstoke: Macmillan.

Dobson, A.P. (1995) *Anglo-American Relations in the Twentieth Century: Of Friendship, Conflict and the Rise and Decline of Superpowers*, London: Routledge.

Dobson, A.P. (2002) *US Economic Statecraft for Survival 1933–1991*, London: Routledge.

Dobson, A.P. and Marsh, S. (2001) *US Foreign Policy since 1945*, London: Routledge.

Dockrill, S. (1991) *Britain's Policy for West German Rearmament 1950–55*, Cambridge: Cambridge University Press.

Drew, E. (1994) *On the Edge: The Clinton Presidency*, New York: Simon and Schuster.

Dubois, D. (2002) 'The Attacks of 11 September: EU–US Cooperation Against Terrorism in the Field of Justice and Home Affairs' *European Foreign Affairs Review* **7** (3) pp. 317–35.

Duchêne, F. (1972) 'Europe's Role in World Peace' in *Europe Tomorrow: Sixteen Europeans Look Ahead*, Mayne, R. (ed.), London: Fontana.

Duke, S. (1996) 'The Second Death (Or the Second Coming?) of the WEU' *Journal of Common Market Studies* **34** (2) pp. 153–69.

Duke, S. (2001) 'CESDP: Nice's Overtrumped Success?' *European Foreign Affairs Review* **6** (2) pp. 155–75.

Duke, S. (2001) 'After Nice: the Prospects for European Security and Defence', European Policy Centre, 2 March 2001, http://www.theepc.be/challenge/topdetail.asp.

Duke, S. (2002) 'CESDP and the EU Response to 11 September: Identifying the Weakest Link' *European Foreign Affairs Review* **7** (2) pp. 153–69.

Dumbrell, J. (2001) *A Special Relationship: Anglo-American Relations in the Cold War and After*, Basingstoke: Macmillan.

ECDPM (2001) 'Cotonou Infokit: Innovations in the Cotonou Agreement', http://www.oneworld.org/ecdpm/en/cotonou/04_gb.htm.

Economist (1997) Letter by Jose Cutileiro *The Economist* **344** (8031) 23 August 1997, p. 8.

Economist (2001) 'Solid, For How Long?' *The Economist* **360** (8240) 22 September 2001, p. 43.

Economist (2001) 'Old Friends, Best Friends' *The Economist* **360** (8239) 15 September 2001, p. 20

Economist (2001) 'We're With You, Sort Of' *The Economist* **360** (8240) 22 September 2001, p. 29.

Economist (2001) 'Good for the (French) President' *The Economist* **360** (8240) 22 September 2001, p. 44

Economist (2002) 'Afghan Prisoners: A Transatlantic Rift' *The Economist* **362** (8256) 19 January 2002, p. 42

Economist (2002) 'Bob Zoellick's Grand Strategy' *The Economist* **362** (8262) 2 March 2002, p. 57.

Economist (2002) 'A Survey of the Defence Industry' *The Economist* **364** (8282) 20 July 2002.

Economist (2003) 'Shrink-proof: Why America's Deficit is Hard to Turn Around' *The Economist* **368** (8342) 20 September 2003, pp. 14–17.

Economist (2003) 'The WTO Under Fire' *The Economist* **368** (8342) 20 September 2003, pp. 29–32.

Economist (2003) 'A Hitch to Recovery' *The Economist* **369** (8350) 15 November 2003, pp. 43–4.

Economist (2003) 'Hard Choices' *The Economist*, **369** (8350) 15 November 2003, p. 55.

Economist.com (2003) 'Scrapped', http://www.economist.co.uk/ agenda/displaystory.cfm?story_id=2261621&CFID=9092570&CFTOKEN=25f638f-59f64d42-0724-455e-be5c-62ddf83edf5d.

Edwards, G. (1984) 'Europe and the Falkland Island Crisis 1982' *Journal of Common Market Studies* **22** (4) pp. 295–313.

Edwards, G. (1992) 'European Responses to the Yugoslav Crisis: An Interim Assessment' in *Toward Political Union: Planning a Common Foreign and Security Policy in the European Community*, Rummel, R. (ed.), Oxford: Westview Press.

Edwards, G. (1997) 'The Potential and Limits of the CFSP: The Yugoslav Example' in *Foreign Policy of the European Union: From EPC to CFSP and Beyond*, Regelsberger, E. et al. (eds), London: Lynne Rienner.

Eisl, G. (1999) 'EU Enlargement and Co-operation in Justice and Home Affairs' in *Back to Europe: Central and Eastern Europe and the European Union*, Henderson, K. (ed.), London: UCL Press.

El-Agraa, A.M. (2001) *The European Union: Economics and Policies*, 6th edn, Harlow: Prentice Hall.

Eurobarometer (May 2002) Special Eurobarometer **56** (3), http://www.europa.int/ comm/public_opinion/enlargement_en.pdf

European Commission (1990) *The European Community and its Eastern Neighbours*, Luxembourg: Office for the Official Publications of the European Communities.

European Commission (1994) 'Towards a New Asia Strategy', COM (94) 314 final, 13 July 1994.

European Commission (1994) Partnership and Cooperation Agreement with Russia, 24 June 1994.

European Commission (1997) 'Implementing European Union Strategy on Defence-Related Industries', COM (97) 583 final.

European Commission (2000) The TACIS Programme Annual Report 1999, COM (2000) 835 final, 20 December 2000.

European Commission (2001) Communication from the Commission to the Council and the European Parliament, 'EU Strategy Towards China: Implementation of the 1998 Communication and Future Steps for a More Effective EU Policy', COM (2001) 265 final, 15 May 2001.

European Commission (2001) Country Strategy Paper for Russia, 27 December 2001.

European Commission (2001) 'Europe and Asia: A Strategic Framework for Enhanced Partnerships', COM (2001) 469, 4 September 2001.

European Commission (2001) 'Overview of EU Action in Response to the Events of 11 September and Assessment of their Likely Economic Impact', Brussels, 17 October 2001, DOC/01/15.

European Commission (2001) 'Shaping Our Common Future – An Action Plan for EU–Japan Cooperation', http://europa.eu.int/comm/external_relations/japan/summit_12_01/actionplan.pdf.

European Commission (2002) 'China: European Commission Approves Country Strategy Paper 2002–2006', IP/02/349, 1 March 2002.

European Commission (2002) Report from the Commission to the Council and the European Parliament, 'Hong Kong Special Administrative Region: Fourth Annual Report – 2001', COM (2002) 450 final, 5 August 2002.

European Commission (2002) Report from the Commission to the Council and the European Parliament, 'Macao Special Administrative Region: Second Annual Report – 2001', COM (2002) 445 final, 31 July 2002.

European Commission (2002) Economic Partnership Agreements: Start of Negotiations, Brussels, European Communities.

European Commission (2002) Report on United States Barriers to Trade and Investment.

European Commission (2003) 'Communication from the Commission: A New Partnership with South East Asia', COM (2003) 399/4, 9 July 2003.

European Commission (2003) 'Communication from the Commission to the Council and the European Parliament: Wider Europe – Neighbourhood; A New Framework for Relations With Our Eastern and Southern Neighbours', COM (2003) 104 final, 11 March 2003.

European Commission (2003) 'European Defence – Industrial and Market Issues', COM (2003) 113 final, 11 March 2003.

European Commission (2003) 'Stabilisation and Association Process for South East Europe Second Annual Report', COM (2003) 139 final, 26 March 2003.

European Commission (2003) Staff Working Document: Follow-up to the International Conference on Financing for Development (Monterrey – 2002), SEC (2003) 569, 15 May 2003.

European Commission, 'Composite Paper: Reports on Progress Towards Accession by Each of the Candidate Countries', http://europa.eu.int/comm/enlargement/report_10_99/pdf/en/composite_en.pdf.

European Commission, National Indicative Programme for People's Republic of Korea 2002–2004.

European Commission, The EC–Democratic People's Republic of Korea (DPRK) Country Strategy Paper 2001–2004.

European Commission, Working Document, Country Strategy Paper: China, 2002–2006.

European Convention, Final Report of Working Group VIII – Defence, CONV 461/02, 16 December 2002.

Everts, S. (2001) 'Unilateral America, Lightweight Europe?', Centre for European Reform, Working Paper.

Eyal, J. (2000) 'Britain's European Defence Debate: Cliché after Cliché' *RUSI Newsbrief* **20** (12) p. 127.

Falke, A. (2000) 'The EU–US Conflict Over Sanctions Policy: Confronting the Hegemon' *European Foreign Affairs Review* 5 pp. 139–63.

Featherstone, K. and Ginsberg, R.H. (1996) *The United States and the European Union in the 1990s: Partners in Transition*, Basingstoke: Macmillan.

Feis, H. (1970) *From Trust to Terror, 1945–50*, NewYork: W.W. Norton.

Feldman, L.G. (1999) 'Reconciliation and Legitimacy: Foreign Relations and the Enlargement of the European Union' in *Legitimacy and the European Union: The Contested Polity*, Banchov, T. and Smith, M.P. (eds), London: Routledge.

Feldstein, M. (1997) 'EMU and International Conflict' *Foreign Affairs* **76** (6) pp. 60–73.

Financial Action Task Force on Money Laundering (2003) Annual Report, 20 June 2003.

Flockhart, T. (1995) 'The Dynamics of Expansion: NATO, WEU, and EU' *European Security* 5 (2) pp. 196–218.

Flynn, G. and Scheffer, D.J. (Autumn 1990) 'Limited Collective Security' *Foreign Policy*, pp. 77–101.

Foster, E. (2000) 'The Minster's Salvation? German Military Reform' *RUSI Newsbrief* **20** (6) pp. 55–7.

Frank, C. (2002) 'The Northern Dimension: Added Value or Redundancy?', conference paper, http://www.edc.spb.ru/conf2002/home.html.

Frellesen, T. (2001) 'Processes and Procedures in EU–US Foreign Policy Cooperation: From the Transatlantic Declaration to the New Transatlantic Agenda' in *Ever Closer Partnership: Policy-making in EU–US Relations*, Philippart, E. and Winand, P. (eds), New York, Oxford: Peter Lang.

Freedman, L. (Winter 1994–95) 'Why the West Failed' *Foreign Policy*, pp. 53–69.

Freedman, L. (Spring 1998) 'International Security: Changing Targets' *Foreign Policy*, pp. 48–63.

Frieden, J.A. and Lake, D.A. (1995) *International Political Economy: Perspectives on Global Power and Wealth*, 3rd edn, London: Routledge.

Friis, L. and Murphy, A. (2000) 'Enlargement: A Complex Juggling Act' in *The State of the European Union, Vol. 5*, Cowles, M.G. and Smith, M. (eds), Oxford: Oxford University Press.

Fukuyama, F. (1992) *The End of History and the Last Man*, London: Hamish Hamilton.

Fursdon, E. (1980) *The European Defence Community: A History*, Basingstoke: Macmillan.

Gaddis, J.L. (1983) 'The Emerging Post-Revisionist Thesis on the Origins of the Cold War' *Diplomatic History* 7 pp. 171–90.

Gaddis, J.L. (1982) *Strategies of Containment: A Critical Appraisal of Postwar American National Security Policy*, New York: Oxford University Press.

Gaddis, J.L. (1997) *We Now Know: Rethinking Cold War History*, Oxford: Clarendon Press.

Gardner, A.L. (1999) *A New Era in US–EU Relations: The Clinton Administration and the New Transatlantic Agenda*, Aldershot: Ashgate.

Gardner, A.L. (2001) 'From the Transatlantic Declaration to the New Transatlantic Agenda' in *Ever Closer Partnership: Policy-making in EU–US Relations*, Philippart, E. and Winand, P. (eds), New York, Oxford: Peter Lang.

Gardner, R. (2000) 'The One Percent Solution: Shirking the Cost of World Leadership' *Foreign Affairs* **79** (4) pp. 2–11.

Gardner, R.N. (1980) *Sterling–Dollar Diplomacy in the Current Perspective*, New York: Columbia University Press.

Garthoff, R. (1994) *Détente and Confrontation: American–Soviet Relations from Nixon to Reagan*, Washington: Brookings Institute.

Garton Ash, T. (2003) 'Anti-Europeanism in America' *New York Review of Books*, 13 February 2003, http://www.nybooks.com/articles/16059.

Gearson, J.S. (1998) *Harold Macmillan and the Berlin Wall Crisis 1958–1962: The Limits of Interest and Force*, Basingstoke: Macmillan.

Geddes, A. (2000) *Immigration and European Integration: Towards a Fortress Europe?*, Manchester: Manchester University Press.

Gegout, C. (2002) 'The Quint: Acknowledging the Existence of a Big Four-US Directoire at the Heart of the European Union's Foreign Policy Decision-Making Process' *Journal of Common Market Studies* **40** (2) pp. 331–44.

Geiger, T. (1996) 'Embracing Good Neighbourliness: Multilateralism, *Pax Americana* and European Integration, 1945–58' in *Regional Trade Blocs, Multilateralism and the GATT*, Geiger, T. and Kennedy, D. (eds), London: Pinter.

General Secretariat of the African, Caribbean and Pacific Group of States (2000) *Cotonou Agreement*, http://www.acpsec.org/gb/cotonou/accord1.htm.

George, B. and Borawski, J. (1995) 'Continental Drift' *European Security* **4** (1) pp. 1–25.

George, S. (1998) *An Awkward Partner: Britain in the European Community*, Oxford: Oxford University Press.

Gfoeller, T.C. (2000) 'Diplomatic Initiatives: An Overview of the Northern European Initiative' *European Security* **9** (1) pp. 98–104.

Ginsberg, R.H. (2001) 'EU–US Relations after Amsterdam: "Finishing Europe" ' in *Ever Closer Partnership: Policy-making in EU–US Relations*, Philippart, E. and Winand, P. (eds), New York, Oxford: Peter Lang.

Glenny, M. (1996) 'The Macedonian Question' in *International Perspectives on the Yugoslav Conflict*, Danchev, A. and Halverson, T. (eds), Basingstoke: Macmillan.

Gligorov, V. (2001) 'Notes on the Stability Pact' in *Balkan Reconstruction*, Daiano, D. and Veremis, T. (eds), London: Frank Cass.

Goldstein, W. (ed.) (1986) *Reagan's Leadership and the Atlantic Alliance: Views From Europe and America*, London: Pergammon-Brassey.

Gordon, P. (1993) *A Certain Idea of France: French Security Policy and the Gaullist Legacy*, Princeton: Princeton University Press.

Gordon, P. (1994) 'The Normalization of German Foreign Policy' *Orbis* **38** (2) pp. 225–43.

Gordon, P. (1996) 'Recasting the Atlantic Alliance' *Survival* **38** (1) pp. 32–57.

Gordon, P. (2000) 'The French Position' *The National Interest* **61** pp. 57–65.

Gordon, P. (2000) 'Their Own Army?' *Foreign Affairs* **79** (4) pp. 12–17.

Gorg, H. and Ruane, F. (1999) 'US Investment in EU Member Countries: The Internal Market and Sectoral Specialization' *Journal of Common Market Studies* **37** (2) pp. 333–48.

Gow, J. (1991) 'Deconstructing Yugoslavia' *Survival* **33** (4) pp. 291–311.

Gow, J. (1997) *Triumph of the Lack of Will: International Diplomacy and the Yugoslav War*, London: Hurst and Company.

Gow, J. (1999) 'Security and Democracy: The EU and Central and Eastern Europe' in *Back to Europe: Central and Eastern Europe and the European Union*, Henderson, K. (ed.), London: UCL Press.

Gower, J. (2000) 'The Charter of Fundamental Rights and EU Enlargement: Consolidating Democracy or Imposing New Hurdles?' in *The EU Charter of Fundamental Rights: Text and Commentaries*, Feus, K. (ed.), London: Federal Trust.

Gower, J. (2000) 'The EU and Russia: The Challenge of Integration Without Accession' in *Enlarging the European Union: The Way Forward*, Gower, J. and Redmond, J. (eds), Aldershot: Ashgate.

Gower, J. (2000) 'Russia and the European Union' in *Russia and Europe: Conflict or Cooperation?*, Webber, M. (ed.), New York: St Martin's Press.

Grabbe, H. and Hughes, K. (1998) *Enlarging the EU Eastwards*, London: Pinter.

Grand, C. (January 2000) *The European Union and the Non-Proliferation of Nuclear Weapons*, Chaillot Paper 37, Paris: Institute for Security Studies.

Grant, C. (1994) *Inside the House that Jacques Built*, London: Nicholas Brealey.

Grant, R.P. (1996) 'France's New Relationship With NATO' *Survival* 38 (1) pp. 58–80.

Greenwood, C. (2002) 'International Law and the "War Against Terrorism"' *International Affairs* 78 (2) pp. 301–17.

Guay, T. and Callum, R. (2002) 'The Transformation and Future Prospects of Europe's Defence Industry' *International Affairs* 78 (4) pp. 757–76.

Guicherd, C. (1999) 'International Law and the War in Kosovo' *Survival* 41 (2) pp. 19–34.

Hailbronner, K. (2000) *Immigration and Asylum Law and Policy of the European Union*, Boston: Kluwer Law International.

Hanson, S.E. and Kopstein, J.S. (1997) 'The Weimar/Russia Comparison' *Post-Soviet Affairs* 13 (3) pp. 252–83.

Harding, H. (1992) *A Fragile Relationship: The United States and China Since 1972*, Washington D.C.: Brookings Institute.

Harris, R. (2001) 'Blair's "Ethical" Policy' *The National Interest* 63 pp. 25–36.

Heidensohn, K. (1997) *Europe and World Trade*, London: Pinter.

Heisbourg, F. (2000) 'Europe's Strategic Ambitions: The Limits of Ambiguity' *Survival* 42 (2) pp. 5–15.

Hill, C. (1993) 'The Capability-Expectation Gap, or Conceptualizing Europe' *Journal of Common Market Studies* 31 (3) pp. 305–28.

Hill, C. (1998) 'Closing the Capability-Expectations Gap?' in *A Common Foreign and Security Policy for Europe? Competing Visions of the CFSP*, Petersen, J. and Sjursen, H. (eds), London: Routledge.

Hill, C. (2001) 'The EU's Capacity for Conflict Prevention' *European Foreign Affairs Review* 6 pp. 315–33.

Hirsch Jr., E.D., Kett, J.F. and Trefil, J. (eds) (2002) *The New Dictionary of Cultural Literacy*, 3rd edn, Boston: Houghton Mifflin Company.

Hitchcock, W.I. (2003) *The Struggle For Europe*, London: Profile Books.

Hoffmann, S. (1997) 'The United States and Europe' in *Eagle Adrift: American Foreign Policy at the End of the Century*, Lieber, R.J. (ed.), New York: Longman.

Hogan, M. (1987) *The Marshall Plan: America, Britain and the Reconstruction of Western Europe, 1947–52*, Cambridge: Cambridge University Press.

Holbrooke, R. (1995) 'America as a European Power' *Foreign Affairs* 74 (2) pp. 38–51.

Holbrooke, R. (1998) *To End a War*, New York: Random House.

Holland, M. (2002) *The European Union and the Third World*, Basingstoke: Palgrave.

Howorth, J. (2000) 'Britain, France and the European Defence Initiative' *Survival* **42** (2) pp. 33–55.

Howorth, J. (2002) 'CESDP After 11 September: From Short-Term Confusion to Long-Term Cohesion?' *EUSA Review* **15** (1) pp. 1–4.

Howorth, J. (2003) 'Why ESDP is Necessary and Beneficial for the Alliance' in *Defending Europe: The EU, NATO and the Quest for European Autonomy*, Howorth, J. and Keeler, J.T.S. (eds), Basingstoke: Palgrave.

Hunter, R.E. (1999) 'NATO at Fifty. Maximising NATO: A Relevant Alliance Knows How to Reach' *Foreign Affairs* **78** (3) pp. 190–203.

Hunter, R.E. (2002) *The European Security and Defence Policy: NATO's Companion – Or Competitor*, Pittsburgh: RAND.

Huntington, S.P. (1991) 'America's Changing Strategic Interests' *Survival* **33** (1) pp. 3–17.

Huntington, S.P. (1993) 'The Clash of Civilizations' *Foreign Affairs* **72** (3) pp. 22–49.

Hurt, S. (2002) 'Co-operation and Coercion? The Cotonou Agreement between the European Union and ACP States and the end of the Lomé Convention' *Third World Quarterly* **24** (1) pp. 191–76.

Hyde-Price, A. (2002) ' "Beware the Jabberwock!": Security Studies in the Twenty-First Century' in *Europe's New Security Challenges*, Gärtner, H., Hyde-Price, A. and Reiter, E. (eds), London: Lynne Rienner Publishers.

Imbusch, K. (2000) 'Regime Export and Institutional Change? The Governance of EU-Enlargement in Justice and Home Affairs', paper given at the Workshop Governance by Enlargement Program, Darmstadt University of Technology, 23–25 June 2000.

International Institute for Strategic Studies (2001) *The Military Balance 2001–2002*, Oxford: Oxford University Press.

International Institute for Strategic Studies (2002) *The Military Balance 2002–03*, London: Oxford University Press.

International Monetary Fund (2003) 'World Economic Outlook', September 2003, http://www.imf.org.

Isaacson, W. (1992) *Kissinger: A Biography*, New York: Simon and Schuster.

Jacobsen, C.G. (1995) 'Yugoslavia's Successor Wars Reconsidered' *European Security* **4** (4) pp. 655–75.

James, H.J. and Stone, M. (eds) (1992) *When the Wall Came Down: Reactions to German Unification*, New York: Routledge.

Joffe, J. (1987) *The Limited Partnership: Europe, the United States, and the Burdens of Alliance*, Cambridge, Mass.: Ballinger.

Joffe, J. (1992) 'Collective Security and the Future of Europe: Failed Dreams and Dead Ends' *Survival* **34** (1) pp. 36–50.

Joffe, J. (Summer 2001) 'Who's Afraid of Mr Big?', *The National Interest*, http://www.nationalinterest.org/.

Jones, R.A. (2001) *The Politics and Economics of the European Union: An Introductory Text*, 2nd edn, Cheltenham: Edward Elgar.

Journal of Strategic Studies (1994) 'The Future of NATO', Special Edition of the *Journal of Strategic Studies* **17** (4).

Joutsen, M. (2001) 'Cross-Border Crime Patterns Between Eastern Europe and the European Union' in *Cross-Border Crime in a Changing Europe*, Van Duyne, P.C., Ruggiero, V., Scheinost, M. and Valkenburg, W. (eds), New York: Nova Science Publishers.

Kagan, R. (2002) 'Power and Weakness' *Policy Review* **118**, http://www.atlanticcommunity.org.

Kaldor, M. (2003) 'American Power: From "Compellance" to Cosmopolitanism?' *International Affairs* **79** (1) pp. 1–22.

Kang, D. (2003) 'The Avoidable Crisis in North Korea' *Orbis* **47** (3) pp. 495–510.

Kanner, A. (ed.) (2001) 'The European Union and the September 11th Crisis', Working Paper Series **1** (1), University of Miami, http://www.miami.edu/EUCenter/911workingpaper.pdf.

Kegley, C.W. and Raymond, G.A. (2002) *Exorcising the Ghost of Westphalia: Building World Order in the New Millennium*, Upper Saddle River, N.J.: Prentice-Hall.

Kegley Jr., C.W. and Wittkopf, E.R. (2001) *World Politics: Trend and Transformation*, 8th edn, Boston: Bedford/St Martin's.

Kennedy, P. (1988) *The Rise and Fall of the Great Powers*, London: Unwin Hyman.

Keohane, R.O. (1997) *After Hegemony: Cooperation and Discord in the World Political Economy*, Princeton: Princeton University Press.

Keohane, R.O. and Martin, L.L. (1995) 'The Promise of Institutionalist Theory' *International Security* **20** (1) pp. 39–51.

Keohane, R.O. and Nye, J.S. (eds) (1973) *Transnational Relations and World Politics*, Cambridge, Mass.: Harvard University Press.

Keohane, R.O. and Nye, J.S. (1988) 'Complex Interdependence, Transnational Relations and Realism: Alternative Perspectives on World Politics' in *The Global Agenda*, 2nd edn, Kegley Jr., C.W. and Wittkopf, E.R. (eds), New York: Random House.

Keukeleire, S. (2001) 'Directoires Within the CFSP/CESDP of the European Union: A Plea for "Restricted Crisis Management Groups"' *European Foreign Affairs Review* **6** (1) pp. 75–101.

Khoo, N. (2003) 'Time for Action' *The World Today* **59** (7) pp. 14–15.

Kim, I.J. (1987) *The Strategic Triangle: China, the United States and the Soviet Union*, New York: Paragon House.

Kim, S. (ed.) (1998) *North Korean Foreign Relations in the Post-Cold War Era*, New York: Oxford University Press.

Kintis, A. (1997) 'The EU's Foreign Policy and the War in the Former Yugoslavia' in *Common Foreign and Security Policy*, Holland, M. (ed.), London: Pinter.

Kissinger, H. (1977) *American Foreign Policy*, New York: W.W. Norton.

Kissinger, H. (2002) 'NATO's Uncertain Future in a Troubled Alliance', 1 December 2002, http://www.expandnato.org/uncertain.html.

Kivikari, U. (2002) 'The Northern Dimension – One Pillar of the Bridge Between Russia and the EU' *Russian Economic Trends* **11** (3) pp. 26–30.

Koch, A. (2002) 'Resistance Builds to US Muscle' *Jane's Defence Weekly* **37** (6) p. 19.

Kohnstamm, M. (2003) 'The Europe We Need', 13 February 2003, http://www.theepc.be/europe.

Kotios, A. (2001) 'European Policies for the Reconstruction and Development of the Balkans' in *The Development of the Balkan Region*, Petrakos, G. and Totev, S. (eds), Aldershot: Ashgate.

Kovács, P. (March 2002) 'The Schengen Challenge and its Balkan Dimension', Centre for European Policy Studies Brief, 17, p. 2, http://www.ceps.be.

Krauthammer, C. (1990/91) 'The Unipolar Moment' *Foreign Affairs* **70** pp. 23–33.

Krautscheid, A. (1997) 'Contemporary German Security Policy: A View from Bonn' Discussion Papers in German Studies IGS97/8.

Kupchan, C.A. (2000) 'In Defence of European Defence: An American Perspective' *Survival* **42** (2) pp. 16–32.

Kupchan, C.A. and Kupchan, C.A. (1991) 'Concerts, Collective Security, and the Future of Europe' *International Security* **16** (1) pp. 114–61.

Kupchan, C.A. and Kupchan, C.A. (1995) 'The Promise of Collective Security' *International Security* **20** (1) pp. 52–61.

Laffan, B. (1997) *The Finances of the European Union*, Basingstoke: Macmillan.

Lake, A. (1994) 'Confronting Backlash States' *Foreign Affairs* **73** (2) pp. 45–55.

Laney, J.T. and Shaplen, S.T. (2003) 'How to Deal With North Korea' *Foreign Affairs* **82** (2) pp. 16–30.

Lansford, T. (2001) 'Security and Marketshare: Bridging the Transatlantic Divide in the Defence Industry' *European Security* **10** (1) pp. 1–21.

Laumanns, U. (2001) 'The World Bank Group', www.luze.de/nmun/worldbank.pdf.

Lavenex, S. (1998) 'Asylum, Immigration and Central-Eastern Europe: Challenges to EU Enlargement' *European Foreign Affairs Review* **3** pp. 275–94.

Lavenex, S. (1998) ' "Passing the Buck": European Refugee Policies Towards Central and Eastern Europe' *Journal of Refugee Studies* **11** (2) pp. 126–45.

Lavenex, S. (1999) *Safe Third Countries: Extending the EU Asylum and Immigration Policies to Central and Eastern Europe*, Budapest: Central European University Press.

Lee, R. (1997) 'Recent Trends in Nuclear Smuggling' in *Russian Organized Crime: The New Threat?*, Williams, P. (ed.), London: Frank Cass.

Leffler, M.P. (1972) *A Preponderance of Power: National Security, the Truman Administration, and the Cold War*, Stanford, Calif.: Stanford University Press.

Leffler, M.P. (1984) 'The American Conception of National Security and the Beginnings of the Cold War, 1945–48' *American Historical Review* **89** pp. 346–81.

Legvold, R. (2001) 'Russia's Unformed Foreign Policy' *Foreign Affairs* **80** (5) pp. 62–75.

Leifer, M. (1998) 'European and Asian Policies' in *Europe and the Asia Pacific*, Maull, H., Segal, G. and Wanandia, J. (eds), London: Routledge.

Lepick, O. (1996) 'French Perspectives' in *International Perspectives on the Yugoslav Conflict*, Danchev, A. and Halverson, T. (eds), Basingstoke: Macmillan.

Leshoukov, I. (2000) 'Beyond Satisfaction: Russia's Perspectives on European Integration', IEI Discussion Paper C26.

Leuchtenburg, W.E. et al. (1979) *Britain and the United States: Four Views to Mark the Silver Jubilee*, London: Heinemann.

Levitin, O. (2000) 'Inside Moscow's Kosovo Muddle' *Survival* **42** (1) pp. 130–40.

Levitt, M. and Lord, C. (2000) *The Political Economy of Monetary Union*, Basingstoke: Macmillan.

Lieber, R.J. (2000) 'No Transatlantic Divorce in the Offing' *Orbis* **44** (4) pp. 571–84.

Light, M., Löwenhardt, J. and White, S. (2000) 'Russian Perspectives on European Security' *European Foreign Affairs Review* **5** (4) pp. 489–505.

Lim, P. (2001) 'The Unfolding Asia–Europe (ASEM) Process' in *The European Union and East Asia: Interregional Links in a Changing Global System*, Preston, P.W. and Gilson, J. (eds), Cheltenham: Edward Elgar.

Lindert, P.H. (1986) *International Economics*, 8th edn, Homewood, Ill.: Irwin.

Lindley-French, J. (2002) 'In the Shade of Locarno? Why European Defence is Failing' *International Affairs* **78** (4) pp. 789–811.

Lippert, B. and Becker, P. (1998) 'Structured Dialogue Revisited: The EU's Politics of Inclusion and Exclusion' *European Foreign Affairs Review* **3** (3) pp. 341–66.

Lister, M. (1997) *The European Union and the South*, London: Routledge.

Lodgaard, S. (1992) 'Competing Schemes for Europe: The CSCE, NATO and the European Union' *Security Dialogue* 23 (3) pp. 57–68.

Lord, C. (1996) *Absent at the Creation: Britain and the Formation of the European Community, 1950–52*, Aldershot: Dartmouth.

Lucarelli, S. (2000) *Europe and the Breakup of Yugoslavia*, Boston: Kluwer Law International.

Ludlow, P. (2001) 'Wanted: A Global Partner' *Washington Quarterly* 24 (3) pp. 163–71.

Lundestad, G. (1997) *Empire by Integration: The United States and European Integration 1945–1997*, Oxford: Oxford University Press.

Lynch, D. (2002) 'Separatist States and Post-Soviet Conflicts' *International Affairs* 78 (4) pp. 831–48.

Lynch, D. (2003) *Russia Faces Europe*, Chaillot Paper 60, Paris: Institute for Security Studies.

Lyons, G.M. and Mastanduno, M. (eds) (1995) *Beyond Westphalia? State Sovereignty and International Intervention*, Baltimore: Johns Hopkins University Press.

McAllister, R. (1997) *From EC to EU: An Historical and Political Survey*, London: Routledge.

McCalla, R.B. (1996) 'NATO's Persistence After the Cold War' *International Organization* 50 (3) pp. 445–75.

McCormick, J. (2002) *Understanding the European Union*, Basingstoke: Palgrave.

McGoldrick, D. (1997) *International Relations Law of the European Union*, London: Longman.

McGwire, M. (1994) 'National Security and Soviet Foreign Policy' in *Origins of the Cold War*, Leffler, M.P. and Painter, D.S. (eds), London: Routledge.

Mackie, J. (2001) 'Bringing Civil Society into Foreign and Security Policy', European Policy Centre, 28 February 2001, http://www.theepc.be/challenge/topdetail.asp?SEC=documents&S.

MacLeod, I., Hendry, I.D. and Hyett, S. (1996) *The External Relations of the European Communities*, Oxford: Clarendon Press.

Mahncke, D. (2001) 'Russia's Attitude to the European Security and Defence Policy' *European Foreign Affairs Review* 6 (4) pp. 427–36.

Mahncke, D. and Bayerl, A. (eds), (2001) *Old Frontiers – New Frontiers: The Challenge of Kosovo and its Implications for the European Union*, Bern: Peter Lang.

Major, J. (1999) *John Major: The Autobiography*, London: Harper Collins.

Malfliet, K. (2002) 'Russia and the European Union in a Wider Europe: New Openings and Old Barriers', September 2002, http://www.edc.spb.ru/conf2002/home.html.

Malik, M. (2002) 'China, Pakistan and India: Nervous Neighbours' *The World Today* 58 (10) pp. 20–2.

Mangott, G. (2000) 'A Giant on its Knees: Structural Constraints on Russia's Global Role' *International Politics* 37 (4) pp. 479–508.

Mann, G. (1990) *The History of Germany Since 1789*, London: Penguin.

Marsden, P. (2003) 'Afghanistan: The Reconstruction Process' *International Affairs* 79 (1) pp. 91–105.

Marsh, S. (2003) *Anglo-American Relations and Cold War Oil*, Basingstoke: Palgrave.

Marsh, S. (2003) 'The Dangers of German History: Lessons from a Decade of Post-Cold War German Foreign and Security Policy' *Perspectives on European Politics and Society* 3 (3) pp. 389–424.

Marsh, S. (2003) 'Blair, Britain and the Anglo-American Special Relationship' in *Britain Under Blair*, Tönnies, M. (ed.), Heidelberg: Universitätsverlag Winter.

Marsh, S. (2003) 'September 11 and Anglo-American Relations: Reaffirming the Special Relationship' *Journal of Transatlantic Studies* special issue **1**.1 pp. 56–75.

Mastanduno, M. (1997) 'Preserving the Unipolar Moment: Realist Theories and US Grand Strategy After the Cold War' *International Security* **21** pp. 44–98.

May, E.R. (ed.) (1993) *American Cold War Strategy: Interpreting NSC 68*, New York: Bedford Books.

Mayhew, A. (1998) *Recreating Europe*, Cambridge: Cambridge University Press.

Maynes, C.W. (1999) 'US Unilateralism and its Dangers' *Review of International Studies* **25** (3) pp. 515–18.

Mearsheimer, J. (1990) 'Back to the Future: Instability in Europe after the Cold War' *International Security* **15** (3) pp. 5–57.

Mearsheimer, J. (1994/95) 'The False Promise of International Institutions' *International Security* **19** (3) pp. 5–49.

Mee, C.L. (1984) *The Marshall Plan: The Launching of Pax Americana*, New York: Simon and Schuster.

Meiers, F.J. (2001) 'The Reform of the Bundeswehr: Adaptation or Fundamental Renewal?' *European Security* **10** (2) pp. 1–22.

Menon, A. (1995) 'NATO the French Way. From Independence to Cooperation: France, NATO and European Security' *International Affairs* **75** (1) pp. 19–34.

Menon, A. (2003) 'Why ESDP is Dangerous and Misguided for the Alliance' in *Defending Europe: The EU, NATO and the Quest for European Autonomy*, Howorth, J. and Keeler, J.T.S. (eds), Basingstoke: Palgrave.

Milward, A. (1992) *The European Rescue of the Nation State*, Berkeley: University of California Press.

Mlyn, E. (1996) 'The OSCE, the United States and European Security' *European Security* **5** (3) pp. 426–47.

Moens, A. in collaboration with Domisiewicz, R. (2001) 'European and North American Trends in Defence Industry: Problems and Prospects of a Cross-Atlantic Defence Market', Ottawa: International Security Research and Outreach Programme.

Monar, J. (1997) 'The Financial Dimension of the CFSP' in *Common Foreign and Security Policy*, Holland, M. (ed.), London: Pinter.

Morris, E. (1983) *Blockade: Berlin and the Cold War*, London: Hamilton.

Mundell, R.A. (1961) 'A Theory of Optimum Currency Areas', *American Economic Review* **51** pp. 657–65.

Nello, S.N. and Smith, K.E. (1998) *The European Union and Eastern Enlargement: The Implications of Enlargement in Stages*, Aldershot: Ashgate.

Newhouse, J. (1997) *Europe Adrift*, New York: Pantheon.

Noonan, M.P. (1999) 'Conservative Opinions on U.S. Foreign Policy' *Orbis* **43** (4) pp. 621–32.

North Atlantic Treaty Organisation (1999) *NATO Handbook Documentation*, Belgium: NATO Office of Information and Press.

North Atlantic Treaty Organisation, 'New Strategic Concept', http://www.nato.int/docu/comm/49-95/c911107a.htm.

North Atlantic Treaty Organisation, 'NATO–Russia Relations', http://www.nato.int/docu/facts/nato-rus.htm.

Nugent, N. (1999) *The Government and Politics of the European Union*, Basingstoke: Macmillan.

Nugent, N. (2003) *The Government and Politics of the European Union*, 5th edn, Basingstoke: Macmillan.

Nuttall, S. (1992) *European Political Co-operation*, Oxford: Clarendon Press.

Nuttall, S. (1998) 'European and Asian Policies' in *Europe and the Asia Pacific*, Maull, H., Segal, G. and Wanandia, J. (eds), London: Routledge.

Nye Jr., J.S. (2000) 'The US and Europe: Continental Drift?' *International Affairs* 76 (1) pp. 51–60.

Nye Jr., J.S. (2002) 'The American National Interest and Global Public Goods' *International Affairs* 78 (2) pp. 233–44.

Nye Jr., J.S. (2002) *The Paradox of American Power*, Oxford: Oxford University Press.

Öövel, A. (1996) 'Estonian Defence Policy, NATO and the European Union' *Security Dialogue* 27 (1) pp. 65–8.

Organisation for Security and Cooperation in Europe (1999) Charter for European Security, http://www.osce.org.

Ortega, M. (March 2001) *Military Intervention and the European Union*, Chaillot Paper 45, Paris: Institute for Security Studies.

Owen, D. (1995) *Balkan Odyssey*, New York: Harcourt Brace.

Pandurevic, N. (2001) 'Security Aspects of the Stability Pact for South Eastern Europe' *Security Dialogue* 32 (3) pp. 311–24.

Papacosma, S.V. and Heiss, M.A. (eds) (1995) *NATO in the Post-Cold War Era: Does it Have a Future?*, New York: St Martin's Press.

Patten, C. (2001) 'Devotion or Divorce?: The Future of Transatlantic Relations' *European Foreign Affairs Review* 6 (3) pp. 287–90.

Peers, S. (2003) 'Readmission Agreements and EC Migration Law' *Statewatch Analysis* 17, http://www.statewatch.org/news/2003/may/12readmission.htm.

Pelkmans, J. (1997) *European Integration: Methods and Economic Analysis*, Harlow: Longman.

Pelkmans, J. and Murphy, A. (1991) 'Catapulted Into Leadership: The Community's Trade and Aid Policies *vis-à-vis* Eastern Europe' *Journal of European Integration* 14 pp. 125–51.

Peterson, J. (2001) 'Shaping, not Making – The Impact of the American Congress on US–EU Relations' in *Ever Closer Partnership: Policy-making in EU–US Relations*, Philippart, E. and Winand, P. (eds), New York, Oxford: Peter Lang.

Peterson, J. and Bomberg, E. (1999) *Decision-Making in the European Union*, Basingstoke: Macmillan.

Peterson, J. and Sjursen, H. (1998) *A Common Foreign Policy for Europe? Competing Visions of CFSP*, London: Routledge.

Petras, J. and Morley, M. (2000) 'Contesting Hegemons: US–French Relations in the "New World Order"' *Review of International Studies* 26 (1) pp. 49–68.

Pfaff, W. (1993) 'Is Liberal Internationalism Dead?' *World Policy Journal* 10 (3) pp. 5–15.

Piana, C. (2002) 'The EU's Decision-making Process in the Common Foreign and Security Policy: The Case of the Former Yugoslav Republic of Macedonia' *European Foreign Affairs Review* 7 pp. 209–26.

Piening, C. (1997) *Global Europe: The European Union in World Affairs*, London: Lynne Rienner Publishers.

Portela, C. (2001) 'EU–Russia Co-operation in the Security Domain: Problems and Opportunities', BITS Research Note 01.2.

Pridham, G. (2002) 'EU Enlargement and Consolidating Democracy in Post-Communist States – Formality and Reality' *Journal of Common Market Studies* **40** (3) pp. 953–73.

Rees, G.W. (1998) *The Western European Union at the Crossroads: Between Trans-Atlantic Solidarity and European Integration*, London: Westview Press.

Regelsberger, C., Wessels, W. and de Schoutheete de Tervarent, P. (eds) (1997) *Foreign Policy of the European Union: From EPC to CFSP and Beyond*, London: Lynne Rienner Publishers.

Reiterer, M. (2002) 'The Asia–Europe Meeting (ASEM): The Importance of the Fourth ASEM Meeting in the Light of 11 September' *European Foreign Affairs Review* **7** (2) pp. 133–52.

Renwick, R. (1996) *Fighting With Allies*, New York: Times Books.

Ridley, N. (1991) *My Style of Government: The Thatcher Government*, London: Hutchinson.

Rieff, D. (1995) *Slaughterhouse: Bosnia and the Failure of the West*, New York: Simon and Schuster.

Roberts, C. (1999) 'Montenegro: Trouble Ahead' *World Today* **55** (12) pp. 11–14.

Roberts, G.K. (1994) 'Review Article: German Reunification' *West European Politics* **17** (4) pp. 202–7.

Robinson, P. (1999) 'The CNN Effect: Can the News Media Drive Foreign Policy?' *Review of International Studies* **25** (2) pp. 301–9.

Robson, P. (1998) *The Economics of International Integration*, 4th edn, London: Routledge.

Rontoyannia, C. (2002) 'So Far, So Good? Russia and the ESDP' *International Affairs* **78** (4) pp. 813–30.

Rosencrance, R. (1998) 'The European Union: A New Type of International Actor' in *Paradoxes of European Foreign Policy*, Zielonka, J. (ed.), The Hague: Kluwer Law International.

Roy-Chaudhury, R. (2003) 'Hand of Friendship' *World Today* **59** (6) pp. 22–3.

Rubenstein, R.L. (ed.) (1987) *The Dissolving Alliance: The United States and the Future of Europe*, New York: Paragon House.

Ruggie, J. (1993) 'Territorality and Beyond: Problematizing Modernity in International Relations' *International Organization* **47** (1) pp. 139–74.

Rühle, M. and Williams, N. (1996) 'Partnership for Peace After NATO Enlargement' *European Security* **5** (4) pp. 521–8.

Rühle, M. and Williams, N. (1997) 'Why NATO Will Survive' *Comparative Strategy* **16** (1) pp. 109–16.

Russell, R. (1995) 'The Chimera of Collective Security in Europe' *European Security* **4** (2) pp. 241–55.

Russian Federation, 'Russian Federation – Concept of the World in the 21st Century', available at http://www.bits.de/frames/database.htm.

Russian Federation, 'The Foreign Policy Concept of the Russian Federation', 28 June 2000, available at http://www.bits.de/EURA/Russia052800.pdf.

Sakwa, R. (2002) *Russian Politics and Society*, London: Routledge.

Salmon, T. (1992) 'Testing Times for European Political Cooperation: The Gulf and Yugoslavia' *International Affairs* **68** (2) pp. 233–53.

Samore, G. (2003) 'The Korean Nuclear Crisis' *Survival* **45** (1) pp. 7–24.

Samson, I. (2002) 'The Common European Economic Space Between Russia and the EU: An Institutional Anchor for Accelerating Russian Reform' *Russian Economic Trends* **11** (3) pp. 7–15.

Sander, H. (2000) 'Towards a Wider Europe: Eastern Europe's Rocky Road into the European Union' in *Rewriting Rights in Europe*, Hancock, L. and O'Brien, C. (eds), Aldershot: Ashgate.

Sapir, A. (2002) 'Old and New Issues in EC–US Trade Disputes', unpublished paper.

Schabas, W. (2001) *The International Criminal Court*, Cambridge: Cambridge University Press.

Schick, J.M. (1971) *The Berlin Crisis, 1958–1962*, Philadelphia: University of Philadelphia Press.

Schlesinger Jr., A. (1974) *The Imperial Presidency*, New York: Popular Library.

Schuller, F.C. and Grant, T.D. (2003) 'Executive Diplomacy: Multilateralism, Unilateralism and Managing American Power' *International Affairs* **79** (1) pp. 37–51.

Schulte, G. (1997) 'Former Yugoslavia and the New NATO' *Survival* **39** (1) pp. 19–42.

Schulte, G. (1998) 'SFOR Continued' *NATO Review* **2** pp. 27–30.

Sedelmeier, U. and Wallace, H. (2000) 'Eastern Enlargement: Strategy or Second Thoughts?' in *Policymaking in the European Union*, Wallace, H. and Wallace, W. (eds), Oxford: Oxford University Press.

Sestanovich, S. (1997) 'The Collapsing Partnership: Why the United States has no Russia Policy' in *Eagle Adrift: American Foreign Policy at the End of the Century*, Lieber, R.J. (ed.), New York: Longman.

Shambaugh, D. (1994) 'Growing Strong: China's Challenge to Asian Security' *Survival* **36** (2) pp. 43–59.

Shambaugh, D. (2003) 'China and the Korean Peninsular: Playing for the Long Term' *Washington Quarterly* **26** (2) pp. 43–56.

Shlaim, A. (1983) *The United States and the Berlin Blockade, 1948–1949: A Study in Crisis Decision-making*, London: University of California Press.

Sinn, H.W. and Werding, M. (2001) 'Immigration Following EU Eastern Enlargement' *CESIFO Forum* **2** (2) pp. 40–7.

Sjursen, H. (1999) 'Enlargement and the Common Foreign and Security Policy: Transforming the EU's External Identity?' in *Back to Europe: Central and Eastern Europe and the European Union*, Henderson, K. (ed.), London: UCL Press.

Sloan, S.R. (1995) 'US Perspectives on NATO's Future' *International Affairs* **71** (2) pp. 217–32.

Sloan, S.R. (1995) 'NATO and the United States' in *NATO in the Post-Cold War Era*, Papacosma, S.V. and Heiss, M.A. (eds), New York: St Martin's Press.

Slocock, B. (1999) ' "Whatever Happened to the Environment?": Environmental Issues in the Eastern Enlargement of the European Union' in *Back to Europe: Central and Eastern Europe and the European Union*, Henderson, K. (ed.), London: UCL Press.

Smith, C.J. (1996) 'Conflict in the Balkans and the Possibility of a European Union Common Foreign and Security Policy' *International Relations* **13** (2) pp. 1–21.

Smith, H. (1995) *European Union Foreign Policy and Central America*, London: Macmillan.

Smith, H. (2002) *European Union Foreign Policy: What It Is and What It Does*, London: Pluto Press.

Smith, K.E. (1998) 'The Use of Political Conditionality in the EU's Relations with Third Countries: How Effective?' *European Foreign Affairs Review* **3** pp. 253–74.

Smith, M. (1984) *Western Europe and the United States: The Uncertain Alliance*, London: Allen and Unwin.

Smoke, R. (ed.) (1996) *Perceptions of Security: Public Opinion and Expert Assessments in Europe's New Democracies*, Manchester: Manchester University Press.

Snyder, J. (1990) 'Averting Anarchy in the New Europe' *International Security* **14** (4) pp. 5–41.

Soetendorp, B. (1999) *Foreign Policy in the European Union*, London: Longman.

Solana, J. (2003) 'A Secure Europe in a Better World', SO138/03, 20 June 2003.

Solomon, G.B. (1998) *The NATO Enlargement Debate, 1990–97: Blessings of Liberty*, Westport, Conn.: Praeger.

Spence, A. and Spence, D. (1998) 'The Common Foreign and Security Policy from Maastricht to Amsterdam' in *Foreign and Security Policy in the European Union*, Eliassen, K.A. (ed.), London: Sage.

Sperling, J. (1999) 'Enlarging the EU and NATO' in *Europe in Change. Two Tiers or Two Speeds: The European Security Order and the Enlargement of the European Union and NATO*, Sperling, J. (ed.), Manchester: Manchester University Press.

Sperling, J. and Kirchner, E. (1997) *Recasting the European Order: Security Architectures and Economic Cooperation*, Manchester: Manchester University Press.

Spiro, P.J. (2000) 'The New Sovereigntists: American Exceptionalism and Its False Prophets' *Foreign Affairs* **79** (6) pp. 9–15.

Stent, A. (2002) 'American Views on Russian Security Policy and EU–Russian Relations', paper for the IISS/CEPS European Security Forum, 14 January 2002, http://www.eusec.org/stent.htm.

Stockholm International Peace Research Institute (2002) *SIPRI Yearbook 2002: Armaments, Disarmament and International Security*, New York: Oxford University Press.

Strange, S. (1971) *Sterling and British Policy: A Political Study of an International Currency in Decline*, London: Oxford University Press.

Swann, D. (1986) *The Economics of the Common Market*, 6th edn, London: Penguin.

Talbot, R.B. (1978) *The Chicken War*, Ames: Iowa State University.

Tarnoff, P. (1990) 'America's New Special Relationships' *Foreign Affairs* **69** (3) pp. 67–80.

Tarschys, D. (1995) 'The Council of Europe: The Challenge of Enlargement' *The World Today* **51** (4) pp. 62–4.

Taylor, T. (1984) *European Defence Cooperation*, Chatham House Papers 24, London: Routledge.

Thatcher, M. (1993) *The Downing Street Years*, London: Harper Collins.

Thurow, L. (1992) *Head to Head: The Coming Economic Battle Among Japan, Europe and America*, New York: Norrow.

Timmermann, H. (2000) 'European–Russian Partnership: What Future?' *European Foreign Affairs Review* **5** (2) pp. 165–74.

Tinbergen, J. (1965) *International Economic Integration*, 2nd rev. edn, Amsterdam: Elsevier.

Tompson, W. (2002) 'Begging Ends' *World Today* **58** (2) pp. 16–18.

Trenin, D. (2002) *The End of Eurasia: Russia on the Border Between Geopolitics and Globalization*, Moscow: Carnegie Endowment for International Peace.

Trenin, D. (Spring 2002) 'Silence of the Bear' *NATO Review*, http://www.nato.int/docu/review.htm.

Trenin, D. (2002) 'A Russia-within-Europe: Working Toward a New Security Arrangement', paper prepared for the IISS/CEPS European Security Forum, Brussels, 14 January 2002.

Ullman, R. (1983) 'Redefining Security' *International Organization* **8** pp. 129–53.

Ullman, R. (1990) 'Enlarging the Zone of Peace' *Foreign Policy* **80** pp. 102–20.

Ullman, R. (ed.) (1996) *The World and Yugoslavia's Wars*, New York: Council of Foreign Relations.

United Kingdom Foreign Affairs Committee, Second Report from the Foreign Affairs Committee (2002) *'British–US Relations', Response of the Secretary of State for Foreign and Commonwealth Affairs*, London: HMSO.

United Kingdom House of Lords Select Committee on the European Union (2003) 'A Fractured Partnership? Relations Between the European Union and the United States of America', House of Lords, Session 2002–03, 30th Report, 1 July 2003, HL Paper 134, London: HMSO.

United Nations Environment Programme, International Institute for Sustainable Development (2000) 'Structure of the World Trade Organization', *Environment and Trade: A Handbook*, http://www.iisd.org/trade/handbook/3_1.htm.

United States Department of Defense, *Joint Vision 2020*, http://www.dtic.mil/jointvision/jvpub2.htm.

Vandamme, L. (2001) 'Schengen and Integration of Schengen in the European Union With a View to Enlargement' *Collegium* 22 pp. 113–18.

Van Eekelen, W. (1992) 'WEU's Post-Maastricht Agenda' *NATO Review* **40** (2) pp. 13–17.

Van Ham, P. (1999) 'Europe's Precarious Centre: Franco-German Cooperation and the CFSP' *European Security* 8 (4) pp. 1–26.

Van Ham, P. (2000) 'Europe's Common Defense Policy: Implications for the Trans-Atlantic Alliance' *Security Dialogue* 31 (2) pp. 215–28.

Van Oudenaren, J. (1999) 'EU Enlargement: The Return to Europe' in *Europe Today: National Politics, European Integration, and European Security*, Tiersky, R. (ed.), Oxford: Rowman and Littlefield Publishers.

Vernet, D. (1999) 'Kluge Ausschöpfung begrenzter Souveränität: Die Europa-Politik der rot-grünen Koalition' *Internationale Politik* 54 p. 16.

Von Hippel, K. (2000) *Democracy by Force*, Cambridge: Cambridge University Press.

Waever, O. et al. (1993) *Identity, Migration, and the New Security Agenda in Europe*, London: Pinter.

Waites, B. (ed.) (1995) *Europe and the Wider World*, London: Routledge.

Walker, M. (2000) 'Variable Geography: America's Mental Maps of a Greater Europe' *International Affairs* 76 (3) pp. 459–74.

Wall, D. (2002) 'North Korea and China' *The World Today* 58 (12) pp. 21–2.

Walt, S.M. (1998/99) 'The Ties That Fray: Why America and Europe are Drifting Apart' *The National Interest* 54 pp. 3–11.

Waltz, K.N. (1993) 'The Emerging Structure of International Politics' *International Security* 18 (2) pp. 44–79.

Waltz, K.N. (2000) 'Structural Realism after the Cold War' *International Security* 25 (1) pp. 5–41.

Watt, D.C. (1984) *Succeeding John Bull: America in Britain's Place*, Cambridge: Cambridge University Press.

Webber, M. (2001) 'Third-Party Inclusion in European Security and Defence Policy: A Case Study of Russia' *European Foreign Affairs Review* 6 (4) pp. 407–26.

Wegs, J.R. and Ladrech, R. (1996) *Europe Since 1945: A Concise History*, 4th edn, New York: St Martin's Press.

Weidenfeld, W. (ed.) (2002) *Europa-Handbuch*, Bonn: Bundeszentrale für politische Bildung.

Weidenfeld, W. and Wessels, W. (eds) (2002) *Europa von A bis Z*, Bonn: Bundeszentrale für politische Bildung.

Weller, M. (2002) 'Undoing the Global Constitution: UN Security Council Action on the International Criminal Court' *International Affairs* 78 (4) pp. 705–9.

Wexler, I. (1983) *The Marshall Plan Revisited: The European Recovery Program in Economic Perspective*, Westport, Conn.: Greenwood.

White, A. (2001) *Understanding European Foreign Policy*, Basingstoke: Palgrave.

Whitman, R.G. (1999) 'CFSP After Enlargement' in *The Enlargement of the European Union: Issues and Strategies*, Price, V.C., Landau, A. and Whitman, R.G. (eds), London: Routledge.

Wiessala, G. (2002) *The European Union and Asia Countries*, London: Sheffield Academic Press.

Williams, N. (1996) 'Partnership for Peace: Permanent Fixture or Declining Asset?' *Survival* 38 (1) pp. 98–110.

Wohlforth, W. (1999) 'The Stability of a Unipolar World' *International Security* 24 pp. 5–41.

Wood, P.C. (1994) 'France and the Post-Cold War Order: The Case of Yugoslavia' *European Security* 3 (1) pp. 129–52.

Woods, R.B. (1990) *A Changing of the Guard: Anglo-American Relations 1941–46*, Chapel Hill: University of North Carolina Press.

Woodward, B. (2002) *Bush at War*, New York: Simon and Schuster.

Woodward, S. (1995) *Balkan Tragedy: Chaos and Dissolution after the Cold War*, Washington D.C.: Brookings Institute.

World Bank (July 2003) *World Development Indicators*, http://www.worldbank.org/data/databytopic.

World Trade Organisation (2001) *Trading into the Future*, 2nd rev. edn, www.wto.org/english/res_e/doload_e/tif.pdf.

World Trade Organisation (2002) 'International Trade Statistics 2002', http://www.wto.org/english/res_e/statis_e/its2002_e/chp_3_e.pdf.

World Trade Organisation (2003) 'Share of Goods and Commercial Services in the Total Trade of Selected Regions and Economies 2001', http://www.wto.org, July 2003.

Wörner, M. (1992) 'A Vigorous Alliance – A Motor for Peaceful Change in Europe' *NATO Review* 40 (6) pp. 1–8.

Wright, J. (1997) 'European Security – Post-Bosnia' *European Security* 6 (2) pp. 1–17.

Wróblewski, S. 'History of GATT and WTO', http://knfib.zr.univ.gda.pl/History%20of%20GATT%20and %20WTO.htm.

Wurm, C. (ed.) (1995) *Western Europe and Germany: The Beginnings of European Integration 1945–1960*, Oxford: Berg.

Yahunda, M. (1998) 'European and Asian Policies' in *Europe and the Asia Pacific*, Maull, H. Segal, G. and Wanandia, J. (eds), London: Routledge.

Yergin, D. (1977) *Shattered Peace: The Origins of the Cold War and the National Security State*, Boston: Houghton Mifflin.

Yost, D. (1990/91) 'France in the New Europe' *Foreign Affairs* 69 pp. 107–28.

Yost, D. (2000) 'The NATO Capabilities Gap and the European Union' *Survival* 42 pp. 97–128.

Young, J. (2000) *Britain and European Unity 1945–1999*, Basingstoke: Macmillan.

Young, O.R. (1972) 'The Actors in World Politics' in *The Analysis of International Politics*, Rosenau, J.N., East, M.A. and Davies, V. (eds), New York: Free Press.

Zakaria, F. (1997) 'The Rise of Illiberal Democracy' *Foreign Affairs* 6 (6) pp. 22–43.

Zelikow, P. (1992) 'The New Concert of Europe' *Survival* 34 (2) pp. 12–30.

Zimmermann, W. (1996) *Origins of a Catastrophe: Yugoslavia and its Destroyers – America's Last Ambassador Tells What Happened and Why*, New York: Times Books.

Zoellick, R. (1990) 'The New Europe in a New Age: Insular, Itinerant or International? Prospects for an Alliance of Values', US State Department Dispatch, 24 September 1990.

Newspaper articles, press releases and speeches

Albright, M. (1999) 'The Right Balance will Secure NATO's Future' *Financial Times*, 7 December 1999.

Alden, E. (2002) 'Europe Freezes Terrorist Assets Worth $35 Million' *Financial Times*, 8 April 2002.

Andrews, E.L. (2003) 'Strong Dollar, Weak Dollar: Anyone Have a Scorecard?' *New York Times*, http://www.globalpolicy.org/socecon/crisis/2003/0924strongweakdollar.htm.

Archdiocese of St Paul and Minneapolis, Office for Social Justice, 'The International Debt Crisis', http://www.osjsom.org/debt.htm.

Archytas, H. (2002) 'The Future of Globalization', http://lautbry.tripod.com/cpce/globalization/.

Aussenwirtschaft Österreich (2001) 'EDF – European Development Fund', http://www.wko.at/awo/services/drittstaaten/edf.htm.

Bailes, A.J.K. (1999) speech to St Anthony's College, 'Under a European Flag? From WEU to EU', 29 November 1999.

Baker, J. (1989) 'A New Europe, A New Atlanticism: Architecture for a New Era', Berlin Press Club, 12 December 1989, US Department of State, Current Polity, no. 1233.

Barnard, B. (June 1999) 'Euro, Dollar, Yen: What Role will Europe's Single Currency Play in World Markets?' *EUROPE Magazine* 387 p. 8, http://www.eurunion.org/magazine/9906/euro.htm.

Baroness Scotland of Asthal QC (2001) speech to the House of Lords, 2 May 2001, http://www.fco.gov.uk.

Black, I. (2003) 'Patten Warns US Over Aid for Iraq' *The Guardian*, 14 January 2003, http://www.guardian.co.uk/Iraq/Story.

Blair, A. (1999) 'Doctrine of International Community', speech in Chicago, 22 April 1999, http://www.fco.gov.uk/news.

Blair, A. (1999) speech at the Lord Mayor's Banquet, 22 November 1999, http://www.fco.gov.uk.

Bolton, J.R. (2001) remarks to the 5th Biological Weapons Convention RevCon Meeting, 19 November 2001, http://www.state.gov/t/us/rm/janjuly/6231.htm.

British Broadcasting Corporation News (1999) 'Cancer Scare Over US Beef', http://news.bbc.co.uk/1/hi/business/the_economy/334874.stm.

British Broadcasting Corporation News (2001) 'EU and US End Banana War', http://news.bbc.co.uk/1/hi/business/1271969.stm.

British Broadcasting Corporation News (2001) 'Nice Treaty', http://news.bbc.co.uk/2/hi/in_depth/europe/euro-glossary/1230330.stm.

British Broadcasting Corporation News (2003) 'EU to Hit Back in US Steel Row', 4 November 2003, http://newsvote.bbc.co.uk.

Brittan, L. (1998) 'Europe and the United States: New Challenges, New Opportunities', speech given to the Foreign Policy Association, New York, September 1998, http://www.eurunion.org/news/speeches/1998/1998index.htm.

Brown, G. (2002) 'The UK and the United States: Realising Churchill's Vision of Interdependence', speech made by the Chancellor of the Exchequer to the British American Business Inc, New York, 19 April 2002, http://www.britanusa.com.

Burghardt, G. (2001) 'Prospects for EU–US Trade Relations', paper held at Duke University http://www.eurunion.org/news/speeches/2001/010215gb.htm.

Cable News Network (2003) 'Bush Administration Lifts Steel Tariffs', http://www.cnn.com/2003/ALLPOLITICS/12/04/elec04.prez.bush.steel/.

Canada, Government of (2002) 'Autumn 1973 – The OPEC Oil Crisis: Forcing Up World Oil Prices', http://canadianeconomy.gc.ca/english/economy/1973opec.html.

CBSnews.com (2003) 'U.N. Lifts Sanctions On Libya', http://www.cbsnews.com/stories/2003/09/01/attack/main571001.shtml.

Clinton, W. (1993) first inaugural speech, 20 January 1993, http://www.australianpolitics.com/usa/clinton/speeches/inaug93.shtml.

Cornwell, R. (2002) 'Monterrey Aid Pledges Fail to Hit UN Target' *The Independent*, 22 March 2002.

Delegation of the European Commission in Japan (2002) 'EU–Japan Economic and Trade Relations', http://jpn.cec.eu.int/english/eu-relations/e3-03.htm.

Dempsey, J. (2003) 'Big Powers Get Behind EU Foreign Policy' *Financial Times*, 20 June 2003.

Du Boff, R. (2001) 'Rogue Nation', 19 December 2001, http://www.nonviolence.org.

ECDPM (2001) 'Cotonou Infokit: Innovations in the Cotonou Agreement', http://www.oneworld.org/ecdpm/en/cotonou/04_gb.htm.

Echaleco, H. (2003) 'Chile Ratifies Free Trade Agreement With the EU' *Pravda.Ru*, http://english.pravda.ru/main/2003/01/15/42069.html.

ECRE (2002) Observations on the Presidency Conclusions of the European Union Council Meeting, 21 and 22 June 2002, 27 June 2002, http://www.ecre.org/statements/seville.shtml.

Elliott, L. (1999) 'US Triumph in Banana War', http://www.guardian.co.uk/banana/Story/0,2763,206264,00.html.

European Commission (May 1991) 'Joint Declaration on Relations between the European Community and its Member States and Japan', http://europa.eu.int/comm/external_relations/japan/intro/joint_pol_decl.htm.

European Commission (1997) 'European Union to Join North Korea Nuclear Security Body', 22 May 1997, http://www.eurunion.org/news/press/1997-2/pr34-97.htm.

European Commission (1999) 'Presidency Conclusions Helsinki European Council 10 and 11 December 1999', http://europa.eu.int/rapid/start/cgi/guesten.ksh?p_action.gettxt=gt&doc=DOC/99/16|0|RAPID&lg=EN.

European Commission (2001) 'EU Commission Prohibits GE's Acquisition of Honeywell' *News Release* 52 (1), http://www.eurunion.org/news/press/2001/2001052.htm.

European Commission (2001) 'European Union Steps Up Fight Against Terrorism', 20 September 2001, http://www.eurounion.org/news/press/2001.

European Commission (2001) 'EU Trade with Main Partners 2000 (Mio euro)', http://europa.eu.int/comm/external_relations/peru/intro/perumainp.pdf.

European Commission (2001) 'The Cotonou Agreement' *Europe on the Move*, Luxembourg: Office for Official Publications of the European Communities, http://www.delsur.cec.eu.int/en/eu_and_acp_countries/cotonou/print.htm.

European Commission (2001) 'The Transatlantic Economic Partnership' *Economic Relations*, http://europa.eu.int/comm/external_relations/us/action_plan/3_trade_economy_release.htm.

European Commission (2002) 'Highlights of EU–US Cooperation, July 2001–June 2002', http://www.europa.eu.int/comm/external_relations/us/news/highlights.

European Commission (August 2002) 'Bilateral Trade Relations: ACP Countries (77)', http://europa.eu.int/comm/trade/bilateral/acp/index_en.htm.

European Commission (September–October 2002) 'The ACP–EU Council of Ministers Explained' *Courier ACP–EU* **194**, http://europa.eu.int/comm/development/body/publications/courier/courier194/en/en_018_ni.pdf.

European Commission (2003) 'European Commission Adopts Annual Programme for Kosovo', 25 April 2003, http://europa.eu.int/comm/external_relations/see/news.

European Commission (2003) 'EU–Russia Summit, St Petersburg, 31 May 2003', http://europa.eu.int/comm/external_relations/russia/sum05_03/js.htm.

European Commission (2003) 'EU Trade with Main Partners 2001 (Mio euro)', http://europa.eu.int/comm/external_relations/andean/doc/trade/eutrade03.pdf.

European Commission (2003) 'EU–US Bilateral Economic Relations' *European Union Factsheet*, http://europa.eu.int/comm/external_relations/us/sum06_03/eco.pdf.

European Commission (2003) 'North Korea: Commission Grants EUR 9.5 Million in Emergency Humanitarian Food Aid for Children', IP/03/20, 8 January 2003, http://europa.eu.int/comm/external_relations/north_korea/intro/ip03_20.htm.

European Commission (2003) 'Signature of MNEPR', 21 May 2003, IP/03/724, http://europa.eu.int/comm/external_relations/russia/intro/ip03_724.htm.

European Commission (January 2003) 'The EU–ASEAN Partnership' *The EU's Relations with ASEAN – Overview*, http://europa.eu.int/comm/external_relations/asean/intro/index.htm.

European Commission (February 2003) 'Overview' *The EU's Relations with Mexico*, http://europa.eu.int/comm/external_relations/mexico/intro/index.htm.

European Commission (March 2003) 'ASEAN Regional Forum (ARF)', http://europa.eu.int/comm/external_relations/asean/intro/arf.htm.

European Commission (April 2003) 'Overview' *The EU's Relations with Chile*, http://europa.eu.int/comm/external_relations/chile/intro/index.htm.

European Commission (May 2003) 'EU–Japan Economic and Trade Relations', http://europa.eu.int/comm/external_relations/japan/intro/eco_trade_relat.htm.

European Commission (May 2003) 'Mutual Recognition Agreement' *The EU's Relations with Japan*, http://europa.eu.int/comm/external_relations/japan/intro/mra.htm.

European Commission (June 2003) 'Overview' *The EU's Relations with Latin America*, http://europa.eu.int/comm/external_relations/la/index.htm#1a.

European Commission (September 2003) 'Overview' *The EU's Relations with the Andean Community*, http://europa.eu.int/comm/external_relations/andean/intro/index.htm.

European Commission (September 2003) 'Overview' *The EU's Relations with Mercosur*, http://europa.eu.int/comm/external_relations/mercosur/intro/index.htm

European Commission (September 2003) 'The EU's China Policy' *The EU's Relations with China – Overview*, http://europa.eu.int/comm/external_relations/china/intro/index.htm.

European Commission (October 2003) 'Overview' *The EU's Relations with Central America*, http://europa.eu.int/comm/external_relations/ca/index.htm.

European Commission (October 2003) 'The Asia–Europe Meeting (ASEM) – Overview', http://europa.eu.int/comm/external_relations/asem/intro/index.htm.

European Commission (October 2003) 'EU–ACPs: Opening of Trade Negotiations with West and Central Africa', http://europa.eu.int/rapid/start/cgi/guesten.ksh?p_action.gettxt=gt&doc=IP/03/1334|0|RAPID&lg=EN&display=.

European Commission (November 2003) 'EU–Mercosur: Trade Minister Agrees Roadmap for Final Phase of Free Trade Negotiations', http://www.europa.eu.int/comm/external_relations/mercosur/intro/ip03_1544.htm.

European Commission (2003) Statement by the General Affairs and External Relations Council, http://europa.eu.int/comm/external_relations/north_korea/intro/gac.htm#nk191102.

European Commission, 'Asia Relations', http://europa.eu.int/comm/external_relations/asia/rel/index.htm.

European Commission, 'Chronology of EU–Latin America and EU–Caribbean Relations' History of the EU–Latin America–Caribbean Relations, http://europa.eu.int/comm/world/lac/chrono_en.htm.

European Commission, Joint EU–US Action Plan, http://europa.eu.int/comm/external_relations/us/action_plan/index.htm.

European Commission, Medium-term Strategy for Development of Relations between the Russian Federation and the European Union (2000–10), 1999, unofficial translation, http://europa.eu.int/comm/external_relations/russia/russian_medium_term_strategy/.

European Commission, 'The EU and Andean Community', http://europa.eu.int/comm/world/lac/and_en.htm.

European Commission, 'The EU and Mercosur', http://europa.eu.int/comm/world/lac/merc.htm.

European Commission, 'The EU and the Organisation for Security and Co-operation in Europe (OSCE)', http://europa.eu.int/comm/external_relations/osce/.

European Commission, 'The EU's Actions in Support of the Stabilisation and Association Process', http://europa.eu.int/comm/external_relations/see/actions/sap. htm.

European Commission, 'The EU's Relation with Russia: EU–Russian Trade', http://www.europa.eu.int/comm/external_relations/Russia/intro/trade.htm.

European Commission, 'The EU's Relations with South Eastern Europe (Western Balkans)', http://europa.eu.int/comm/external_relations/see/index.htm.

Fuchs, R.A., 'Dancing Around the Steel' europaspiegel, http://www.fu-berlin.de/eurosi/english/steel_09_03.html.

Germany, Federal Republic of, Auswärtiges Amt (2001) 'UN Scale of Assessments (regular budget) in 2001' The Finances of the United Nations, http://www.auswaertiges-amt.de/www/en/aussenpolitik/vn/finanzen_html.

Golino, L.R. (2002) 'Time to Thank Europe for its Help on Terrorism' Global Beat Syndicate, 9 July 2002, http://www.atlanticcomunity.org/Golino%20July%202002%20art.

Gomez, B. (2003) 'Chile, Singapore Free Trade Pacts a Priority, Says Gen. Grassley' Washington File, http://usinfo.state.gov/regional/ar/trade/03012702.htm.

Gordon, M.R. (2000) 'Bush Would Stop U.S. Peacekeeping in Balkan Fights' New York Times, 21 October 2000.

Gow, D. (2002) 'Britain's Costs Rise as Germans Cut Plane Order' The Guardian, 5 November 2002.

Grupo de Río, 'Información Básica sobre el Mecanismo Permanente de Consulta y Concertación Política – Grupo de Río', http://www.rree.gob.pe/domino/nsf/GrupoRio.nsf/MarcoGeneralGR?OpenFrameSet.

Haass, R.N. (2002), 'US Engagement based on Cooperation, Consultation', 26 June 2002, http://www.useu.be/BackForth/june2602HaassEngagement.html.

Harding, G. (1999) 'Bid to Narrow Gap in Lomé talks' European Voice 5 (5) p. 10.

Harding, G. (1999) 'WTO Has Yet to Win Over ACP States' European Voice 5 (33) n.p.

Human Rights Watch (2001) 'Human Rights Implications of European Union Internal Security Proposals and Measures in the Aftermath of the 11 September Attacks in the United States', http://www.hrw.org/press/2001/11/eusecurity-memo.htm.

Human Rights Watch (2003) 'Asian Security Talks Risk Giving Green Light to Repression: Human Rights Abused in Name of Fighting Terrorism', 16 June 2003, http://www.hrw.org/press/2003/06/asean061603.htm.

Kohl, H. (1996) 'Security for a United Europe', speech given to 33rd Conference on Security, 3 February 1996.

Lamy, P. (2000) speech to the American Enterprise Institute, 18 December 2000, http://www.eurunion.org/news/speeches/2000/2000index.htm.

Lamy, P. (2002) 'Time to Give Teeth to Europe's Foreign Policy', speech by EU Trade Commissioner, 30 October 2002, European Policy Centre, http://www.theepc.net/en/default.asp?TYP=SEARCH&LV=279&see=y&PG=CE/EN/detail&AI=219&l=.

Lefebvre, A. (2003) 'US–Europe Tensions Grow as Washington Talks Down the Dollar' *World Socialist Web Site*, http://www.wsws.org/articles/2003/jun2003/doll-j04_prn.shtml.

Leonard, D. (2001) 'Schengen Poses Tough Hurdle For Candidates' *European Voice*, 20 September 2001.

Lugar, R.G. (1995) 'NATO Enlargement and US Public Opinion', speech at the Center for Strategic and International Studies Conference on 'NATO's Role in European Security', Washington D.C., 3 March 1995.

Mitchell, D.J. (2002) 'European Cult of Multilateralism', 7 November 2002, http://www.washtimes.com/commentary/20021107.

Nielson, P. (2003) 'Statement on Iraq to the European Parliament', 12 February 2003, http://www.europa.eu.int/rapid/start/cgi/guesten.

Norton-Taylor, R. (2002) 'The US Will Be Legislator, Judge and Executioner', *The Guardian*, 18 November 2002.

O'Sullivan, J. (2002) 'They Don't Get the U.S.' *National Review Online*, 2 July 2002, http://www.nationalreview.com.

Office of the US Trade Representative (2003) 'Free Trade Area of the Americas', http://www.ustr.gov/regions/whemisphere/ftaa.shtml.

Osinskaya, D. (2003) 'EU Does Not Want Russia Walking on Its "European" Lawn' *Rosbalt News*, 30 June 2003, http://www.rosbaltnews.com.

Patten, C. (2002) speech at the Plenary Session of the European Parliament, 4 September 2002.

Patten, C. (2002) 'EU–US: The Indispensable Partnership', 3 December 2002, http://europa.eu.int/comm/external_relations/news/patten/sp_wdr.

Patten, C. (2002) speech at the European Business Club Conference, 28 May 2002, http://www.europa.eu.int/external_relations/news/patten/sp02_235.htm.

Patten, C. (2002) 'Developing Europe's External Policy in an Age of Globalisation', speech at Central Party School, Beijing, 4 April 2002, http://www.europa.eu.int/comm/external_relations/news/patten/sp02_134.htm.

Patten, C. (2002) 'Declarations as Regards the EU–Russia Summit and the Situation in Chechnya', 12 November 2002, http://www.europa.eu.int/commission/external_relations/news/patten/IP02_1655.htm.

Patten, C. (2002) 'Jaw-Jaw, not War-War', 14 February 2002, http://news.ft.com/ft/gx.cgi/ftc?pagename=View&c=Article&cid=FT33CZ00PXC&live=true.

Pfaff, W. (1997) 'US Ambitions Outstrip Its Domestic Appetite' *International Herald Tribune*, 10 July 1997.

Pfaff, W. (2000) 'The US Campaign is Skirting Key Foreign Policy Issues' *International Herald Tribune*, 15 January 2000.

Prodi, R. (2000) statement on Korean Peninsular: North–South Summit, IP/00/625, 15 June 2000, http://europa.eu.int/comm/external_relations/south_korea/intro/ip_00_625.htm.

Rademaker (2003) 'The Commitment of the United States to Effective Multilateralism', statement to the Conference on Disarmament in Geneva, http://www.useu.be/BackForth/Feb1303RademakerMultilateralism.html.

Ries, C.P. (2001) remarks of US Principal Deputy Assistant Secretary of State for European and Eurasian Affairs to the Southern Center for International Studies annual seminar on Europe, 23 October 2001, http://www.usembassy.org.uk/europe.

Ries, C. (2002) 'The U.S.–EU Trade Relationship: Partners and Competitors', http://www.state.gov/p/eur/rls/rm/2002/15491pf.htm.

Robertson, Lord G. (2002) speech in London, 24 January 2002, http://www.nato.int/docu/speech/s020124a.htm.

Robinson, S. (2000) 'France Could Split NATO, Clinton Aide Warns' *Daily Telegraph*, 21 January 2000.

Rühe, V. (1995) 'Bundeswehr und Europäische Sicherheit', speech, 23 October 1995.

Rumsfeld, D. (2001) remarks by US Secretary of Defence at Munich Conference on European Security Policy, 3 February 2001, http://www.defenselink.mil/speeches/2001/s20010203-secdef.html.

Rumsfeld, D. (2002), remarks at National Defence University Washington D.C., 31 January 2002, http://www.defenselink.mil/speeches/2002/s20020131-secdef.html.

Schnabel, R. (2002) 'U.S.–EU Relations: Drift or Common Destiny?' http://www.state.gov/p/eur/rls/rm/2002/14755pf.htm.

Schröder, G. (1999) 'Germany's Foreign Policy Responsibilities in the World', speech at the German Society for Foreign Policy (DGAP) Berlin, 2 September 1999.

Settle, M. (2001) 'King of the Coalition: Blair – The Mission' *Sunday Herald*, 7 October 2001.

Solana, J. (2002), 'Europe's Place in the World: The Role of the High Representative', speech, Stockholm, 25 April 2002.

Solana, J. (2003) 'Mars and Venus Reconsidered: A New Era for Transatlantic Relations', Albert H. Gordon lecture at the Kennedy School of Government Harvard University, 7 April 2003, http://www.useu.be/TransAtlantic/030407SolanaHarvard.htm.

Steyn, M. (2001) 'Very Well, Then, Alone' *The Spectator*, 22 September 2001.

Steyn, M. (2002) 'Put Up or Shut Up: Europe Spends Zip on Defence and Sneers at America's "warmongering"' *The Spectator*, 5 October 2002.

Straw, J. (2001) speech at the Royal United Services Institute, 11 December 2001, http://www.fco.gov.uk.

Synovitz, R. (1999) 'Slovakia: Economic Reforms Necessary For EU Membership Talks', http://www.rferl.org/nca/features/1999/06/F.RU.990604115313.html.

Tisdall, S. (2001) 'Conflict Looms Over Rapid Reaction Force' *The Guardian*, 29 March 2001.

Tisdall, S. (2002) 'Bush Struggles with "Foreign Policy Stuff"' *The Guardian*, 26 April 2002.

Unattributed (2000) 'ACP–EU Ministerial Meeting' *European Voice* 6 (6) p. 30.

Unattributed (2000) 'EU–US Beef Dispute Update' *ICTSD Bridges Weekly Trade New Digest*, http://www.ictsd.org/html/weekly/story8.21-03-00.htm.

Unattributed (2000) 'The Third World Debt Crisis', http://www2.gol.com/users/bobkeim/money/debt.html.

Unattributed (2001) 'EU to Open Ties With North Korea', 14 May 2001, http://www.cbsnews.com/stories/2001/05/14/world.

Unattributed (2001) 'The European Union Adopts Comprehensive Anti-Terror Measures', 28 December 2001, http://www.ict.org.il/spotlight/det.cfm.

Unattributed (2001) 'EC–ACP Cotonou Waiver Finally Granted' *Bridges Weekly Trade News Digest* 5 (39), http://www.ictsd.org/weekly/01-11-15/story2.htm.

Unattributed (2002) *Bananadrama 1: The EU Banana Regime*, http://www.bananalink.org.uk/trade_war/trade_war_main1.htm.

Unattributed (2002) *Bananadrama 2: Challenges to the EU Banana Regime*, http://www.bananalink.org.uk/trade_war/trade_war_main2.htm#chal.

Unattributed (2002) 'The Steel Trap' *Wall Street Journal Europe*, 22 March 2002, p. 6.

Unattributed (2002) 'Tibet NGOs Slam Political Apathy by European Union on China at the UNCHR', 10 April 2002, http://www.tibet.com/NewsRoom/unchr-2.htm.

Unattributed (2002) 'Border Controls "Set to Remain" ' *European Voice*, 12 September 2002, http://www.knoweurope.net/cgi/quick/full_rec?action.

Unattributed (2003) EU Statement on DPRK, 11 February 2003, http://www.delkor.cec.eu.int/en/whatsnew/dprk.htm 2002.

Unattributed, 'Banana GATT Case (BANANA)', http://www.american.edu/TED/banana.htm.

Unattributed, 'Enlargement of the European Union', http://www.wikipedia.org/wiki/Enlargement_of_the_European_Union.

Unattributed, 'GATT Rounds', http://www.nadir.org/nadir/initiativ/agp/free/wto/rounds.htm.

Unattributed, 'The End of Communism', *The New World Order Files*, http://user.pa.net/~drivera/46commieend.htm.

Unattributed, 'The European Union and the World', www.delguy.cec.eu.int/en/eu_global_player/3.htm.

United Nations High Commissioner for Refugees, Statistics, http://www.unhcr.ch/cgi-bin/texis/vtx/statistics.

United States Mission to the European Union (1990) 'Declaration on US–EC Relations', htttp://www.useu.be/TransAtlantic/transdec.html.

United States Mission to the European Union (2001) 'Joint U.S.–EU Statement on Combating Terrorism', 20 September 2001, http://www.useu.be/Terrorism.

United States Mission to the European Union (2001) 'U.S. Welcomes New EU Measures to Fight Terrorism', 28 December 2001, http://www.useu.be/Terrorism.

United States Mission to the European Union (2002) 'Fact Sheet: NATO Collaboration Contributes to Global War on Terrorism', 24 October 2002, http://www.useu.be/Terrorism.

United States Mission to the European Union (2002) 'Fact Sheet: Six-month Overview of the War on Terrorism', 11 March 2002, http://www.useu.be/Terrorism.

United States Mission to the European Union (2002) 'Kananaskis Summit Document: The G8 Global Partnership Against the Spread of Weapons of Mass Destruction', 27 June 2002, http://www.useu.be/Categories/Defense/June2702WeaponsRussia.html.

United States Mission to the European Union (2002) 'Highlights of U.S.–EU Co-operation from July 2001–June 2002', 28 June 2002, http://www.useu.be/Terrorism.

United States Mission to the European Union (2002) 'Transatlantic Relations – The EU–US Partnership', http://www.useu.be/TransAtlantic/Index.html.

United States Mission to the European Union (2003) 'Commerce's Aldonas: Shoring up the U.S.–EU Trade, Economic Relationship', http://www.useu.be/Categories/Trade/Apr2803AldonasUSEURelationship.html.

United States Press Conference Secretary (2003) remarks by Colin L. Powell at the St Regis Hotel Beijing, China, 24 February 2003, http://www.uspolicy.be/Issues/NorthKorea/northkorea.htm.

United States State Department (2001) EU General Affairs Council Statement, 8 October 2001, http://www.usinfo.gov/topical/pol/terror/01101214.htm.

United States State Department (2002) 'Fact Sheet: NATO Coalition Contributes to Global War on Terrorism', 24 October 2002, http://www.useu.be/Terrorism/EUResponse/Oct2402NATOFactSheet.html.

Waugh, P. and Brown, C. (2002) 'Hawkish Blair Tries to Calm the Doubters' *The Independent*, 8 April 2002.

Wittrock, O., 'Das neue Dreieck' *europa-digital*, http://www.europa-digital.de/text/aktuell/dossier/euro/dreieck.shtml.

Whitney, C.R. (1999) 'NATO at 50: With Nations at Odds, Is it a Misalliance?' *New York Times*, 15 February 1999, p. 7.

World Economic Forum (2001) 'Euro Rising, Dollar Falling', http://www.weforum.org/site/knowledgenavigator.nsf/Content/Euro%20Rising,%20Dollar%20Falling_2001?open&country_id.

Wright, R. (2000) 'Prospects for EU–Russia Economic Relations', speech by Head of the European Commission Delegation to Russia at the RECEP conference, 20 December 2000.

Zoellick, R.B. (2001) 'Prepared Statement of Robert B. Zoellick U.S. Trade Representative before the Subcommittee on Trade, Committee on Ways & Means of the U.S. House of Representatives', p. 3, www.ustr.gov/speech-test/zoellick/zoellick_3.pdf.

Zwaniecki, A. (2002) 'US–EU Partnership Must Adjust to New Era', 3 December 2002, http://www.useu.be/Terrorism/EUResponse/Dec0302HaassDamUS.

Regularly consulted websites

http://www.atlanticcommunity.org
http://www.bits.de
http://www.britainusa.com
http://www.cbsnews.com
http://www.ecb.int
http://www.economist.com
http://www.efta.int
http://www.europa.eu.int
http://www.eurunion.org
http://www.eusec.org
http://www.fco.gov.uk
http://news.ft.com
http://www.globalsecurity.org
http://www.guardian.co.uk
http://www.hrw.org
http://www.imf.org
http://www.ita.doc.gov

http://www.knoweurope.net
http://www.nato.int
http://newsvote.bbc.co.uk
http://www.osce.org
http://www.state.gov
http://www.statewatch.org
http://www.theepc.net
http://www.un.org
http://www.unctad.org
http://www.usembassy.org.uk/europe
http://www.useu.be
http://www.usinfo.gov
http://www.ustr.gov
http://www.washtimes.com
http://www.worldbank.org
http://www.wto.org

Index